Designing the Landscape

An Introductory Guide for the Landscape Designer

Tony Bertauski

Trident Technical College

PEARSON

Prentice
Hall

Upper Saddle River, New Jersey
Columbus, Ohio

Library of Congress Cataloging-in-Publication Data

Bertauski, Tony.
   Designing the landscape : an introductory guide for the landscape designer / Tony Bertauski. — 2nd ed.
      p. cm.
   Includes index.
   ISBN 978-0-13-513510-5
1. Landscape design. I. Title.

SB472.45.B47 2008
712—dc22   2008021708

Editor-in-Chief: Vernon Anthony
Acquisitions Editor: Jill Jones-Renger
Editorial Assistant: Doug Greive
Project Manager: Alicia Ritchey
Operations Specialist: Laura Weaver
Interior Design: Diane Ernsberger
Cover Designer: Diane Ernsberger
Cover Art Photo: Tony Bertauski
Director, Image Resource Center: Melinda Patelli
Manager, Rights and Permissions: Zina Arabia
Manager, Cover Visual Research and Permissions: Karen Sanatar
Director of Marketing: David Gesell
Marketing Manager: Jimmy Stephens
Marketing Assistant: Les Roberts
Copyeditor: Sue Grutz

This book was set in Helvetica Light by S4Carlisle Publishers Services and was printed and bound by Bind-Rite Graphics.

Pearson Prentice Hall™ is a trademark of Pearson Education, Inc.
Pearson® is a registered trademark of Pearson plc
Prentice Hall® is a registered trademark of Pearson Education, Inc.

Pearson Education Ltd., London
Pearson Education Singapore Pte. Ltd.
Pearson Education Canada, Inc.
Pearson Education—Japan

Pearson Education Australia Pty. Limited
Pearson Education North Asia Ltd., Hong Kong
Pearson Educación de Mexico, S. A. de C.V.
Pearson Education Malaysia Pte. Ltd.

10 9 8 7 6 5 4 3 2
ISBN: 978-0-13-513510-5
ISBN: 0-13-513510-9

To an original design, unduplicated and immeasurable: *my family*

Contents

1 The Interview   1

Setting Up the Interview   1
Appear Professional   2
Neatly Dressed   3
Act Professional   3
What to Bring   3
What to Get from a Client   6
Upon Arrival   10
Discussion of the Design Work   11
Client Information   13
Design Fees and Contract   18
Make the Next Appointment   21
Inventory and Analysis   21
Other Considerations   21

2 The Base Map   23

Plan Drawing   23
Drafting Tools   23
Site Survey   31
Lot   32
Obtaining the Site Survey   39
Proofread the Site Survey   39
Measurements   40
What to Locate on Site   50
Creating the Base Map   51

3 Inventory and Analysis   62

Items Needed   62
Inventory and Analysis   62
Drawing the Analysis   97

4 Functional Principles   102

People Spaces   102
Outdoor Room Concept   104
Basic Functions   109
Front Yard   110
Side Yard   134
Backyard   139

5   The Concept Plan   151

Space   152
Analysis   152
Activities and Materials   152
Concepts   154
Alternate Concepts   163

6   Design Principles   167

Design Attributes   168
Balance   180
Connection   185
Interest   198
Flow   203
Mass Planting   210

7   Preliminary Design   218

Client Presentation   218
The Preliminary Design Process   219

8   Plants and Hardscapes   241

Plant Material and Selection   241
Hardscapes and Other Materials   261

9   The Master Plan   302

Drawing the Master Plan   303
Rough Sketching the Master Plan   306
Layout Ground Plane and Label   306
Symbols and Textures   306
Plant List   306
Print   309

10   The Presentation   314

What to Bring to the Presentation   314
What the Presentation Is NOT   315
What the Presentation IS   316
Starting the Presentation   318
Present in an Orderly Fashion   319
Visually Support Your Design   320
Concluding the Presentation   324

Appendices:

A   The Design Process   327

B   Software and Books   350

C   Estimating the Materials   355

D   Computer Graphics   373
        Software Products   373

E   Butterfly Gardening   383

F   Deer   387

G   Xeriscaping   393

H   Design Projects   395

I   Low-Voltage Lighting   408

Index   435

Preface

Why another landscape design book? There are numerous books on designing the landscape, many of which are very good at presenting the design process and design principles. Among all of these books, there is a great deal of variety regarding illustrations, depth of coverage, and cost. Although I have great admiration for some of these publications, they were not the most suitable books for our horticulture program.

Like many horticulture programs, especially at two-year colleges, students take one class in landscape design with the hope that they will gain an understanding and appreciation of the functionality and aesthetics of design, and to be able to read and understand plan drawings as well as to draw their own. Since students are limited to one semester to study landscape design, the typical textbook, although very informative and thorough, is difficult for students to digest because of the arrangement and/or overwhelming amount of information. As a result, the majority of students end up spending a lot of money on a text they hardly use except for looking through illustrations. Although many texts make great references for advanced learning, they may not be the most useful in an introductory landscape design class.

The intention of this text is to present an approach to landscape design starting with interviewing a client and ending with presenting the design in a format that is concise, readily illustrated to facilitate learning, and, most importantly, can be easily applied in the landscape design industry. This book focuses on residential design, although many of the concepts and steps can be applied to commercial projects as well. In early chapters it covers the roles of a designer and how to find work. Then begins a successive approach to the design process beginning with interviewing the client: how to present yourself, what to bring to the interview, and what questions should be answered. The chapters following Chapter 1, "The Interview," discuss how to take and record measurements (Chapter 2, "The Base Map") and what observations should be made to formulate a design plan (Chapter 3, "Inventory and Analysis") while on site. The book then proceeds with chapters that investigate the function, or usefulness, of the design (Chapter 4, "Functional Principles") and how to draw a concept plan (Chapter 5, "The Concept Plan"); a chapter on design principles (Chapter 6, "Design Principles") looks at creating a visually appealing plan and how to use design principles to draw a preliminary design (Chapter 7, "The Preliminary Design"); a chapter on plant selection and hardscape (Chapter 8) discusses the materials that will be used to formulate the master plan, the final design (Chapter 9, "The Master Plan"). The final chapter addresses how to present a design (Chapter 10, "The Presentation") to clients or in the classroom, which most design books do not cover. Presentation skills cover how to make an effective presentation, making the point that presentation is not reading the plant list but rather how the needs of the site analysis are addressed functionally and aesthetically, as well as why plants and hardscape material are selected and their role in the design. The appendices cover topics such as estimating materials, computer design, attracting and repelling wildlife, research resources, and low-voltage lighting.

My hope is that students will be able to use this text cover to cover over the course of a semester, making it easier to understand and effectively supplement their learning in class and provide them with the skills to be effective landscape designers.

Online Instructor's Resources

To access supplementary materials online, instructors need to request an instructor access code. Go to **www.pearsonhighered.com/irc**, where you can register for an instructor access code. Within 48 hours after registering, you will receive a confirming e-mail, including an instructor access code. Once you have received your code, go to the site and log on for full instructions on downloading the materials you wish to use.

Acknowledgments

There were many contributions made to this book—photos, interviews, support, and otherwise—that without such it would not have been possible. The people and companies below supplied photos (many from Web sites) or consultation that proved invaluable:

Anne Muecke and Horticopia (www.horticopia.com)

Bill Hoch at the University of Wisconsin (www.midwestlandscapeplants.org)

Chris Briand at Salisbury University (www.salisbury.edu/arboretum/)

Robert Kleinberg Landscaping in East Lansdowne, PA (www.kleinberg.com)

Big Sky Landscaping in Clackamas, OR (www.bigskylandscaping.com)

Thomas Riccardi and Visual Impact Software (www.visualimpactimaging.com)

Craig Smith and Blue Ribbon, LLC in Maryland (www.blueribbonllc.com)

Mary Ann Patterson at American Horticultural Society (www.ahs.org)

Thom Hood at Good Earth Landscaping in Charleston, SC (www.thegoodearthinc.com)

Gary Pribyl and King's Materials, Inc. in Cedar Rapids, IA (www.kingsmaterials.com)

Ron Spiller and JRW Decks in Seattle, WA (www.jrwdecks.com)

Jim Watson and Decks by JRW in Portland, OR (www.decksbyjrw.com)

Doug Hihn and Monet's Gardens in Mt. Pleasant, SC

Trish Emery at Confederate Rose Designs in Goose Creek, SC

Those who provided moral support, professional guidance, or just sound advice and friendship also made this book possible:

Ann Lovering for her home

Sandy Plance for her expertise with CAD

The Horticulture program at Trident Technical College, including Mack Fleming, Sharon Coke, Gray Spencer, and many others

Thanks to John Autrey for lending his expert advice to the lighting appendix. Also, thanks to Ken Griess of Texas Natural Concepts, LLC for permission to use their spectacular lighting pictures.

Prentice Hall for answering all my silly questions

The reviewers of this book:

John Kahre—Tulsa Community College

Lin Frye—Johnston Community College

Kathryn Johnson—Gateway Technical College

Gregory Davis—Kansas State University

And all those who have had a creative impact on my life, the list would be too long for this page.

Introduction

To many people, the landscape design industry is a very satisfying endeavor. It offers the opportunity to be creative, starting on paper with a concept and seeing it come to completion, watching it grow and change over the years, and also having the chance to help clients beautify their property and satisfy their expectations. Students in a horticulture program should be aware of what the job of landscape designer entails. It is not always sitting at a table in an air-conditioned office drawing plans for a contractor to install. Quite often, the landscape designer is part of a design/install company that offers design as a part of their services. Oftentimes, these large companies employ only one or two designers. With small landscape companies, the designer may be the installation contractor as well. Many of the freelance designers who avoid the dirty end of the job still find themselves involved in the installation part, even if only in a supervisory capacity.

Even though the number of job opportunities for the landscape designer is small in comparison to the rest of the horticulture industry, there are encouraging trends. The American Nursery and Landscape Association (www.anla.org) notes that the amount of money spent on landscape designs nearly doubled from 1997 to 2002, although the design spending in 2002 has still only 2 percent of the total landscape service expenditures.

The design job that works exclusively at the table is less often a landscape designer than it is the landscape architect. What's the difference between these positions?

Landscape architects are registered professionals, often referred to as an "L.A." They are required to complete 5 years of study at an accredited institution. They often work on larger, more complex projects that may be commercial or residential. It requires skill in layout and planning, in addition to a good understanding of construction as well as plants. This position often requires in-depth site analysis, plan drawing (drafting and computer), and installation supervision. Drawing skills may include everything from planting plans to full-colored perspective drawings for presentation.

Landscape designers, on the other hand, may be certified through a program of study. The length of study varies greatly between programs, from as little as a few classes in related subjects to a 4-year degree from an accredited institution. Designers are often considered more of a "plant person," working with landscape and nursery businesses and on residential and commercial projects. Depending on the position, the landscape designer is often responsible for the plan drawing, selling the design, and installation supervision. In many cases, the landscape designer serves more as a salesperson than he or she does as a designer.

There are many landscape designers who do freelance design. They often focus on designing for residents or homebuilders. In some cases, when the design is complete and accepted, depending on the designer and agreement, their obligations to the project are over. The client takes the design and finds someone to install it, or the client does the installation. In many cases, it behooves the client as well as the designer for the designer to be involved in the installation in a supervisory capacity. This bodes well for the client and designer to ensure that the design is installed according to their plans. Small changes to the layout and placement can have a large impact on the design. In this case, the landscape designer prepares a materials list and installation specifications that are passed on to a landscape contractor, or placed out for bids among several companies. Many freelance designers quickly establish relationships with companies they can trust.

People and Business Management

This book is not intended to address business management, however, it is a good idea to briefly mention a few important details pertaining to business. It is advisable to do more research and education in this area from other sources.

As with many facets of horticulture, it is often said that plant knowledge has only been part of the success of designing and managing plants. Just as important is dealing with people and managing the business. As much as the general public dislikes public speaking, it is one of the most important skills to learn. Designers will need to be able to clearly discuss and present ideas to clients. Oftentimes this means working interpersonally with a few people but also may expand to presenting work to a group of people, such as a board of directors. Taking a class in public speaking will help develop invaluable skills of communication.

Often, regardless of design talent, poor business management can eventually cause the company to fail. At the very least, take a small business management class to learn how to write a business plan, know what the liability issues are if the company is a sole proprietor business, and other legal issues. What should the designer consider before launching a landscape design company?

Business License

Check with the county, or counties, in which your company will be doing business. Each county will require a business license. The cost will vary with the county and the amount of business the company does.

Business Plan

Write a business plan that will identify the company's niche in the industry and determine if the company will be financially viable. Who are the clients? What are the company's services? What are the costs? What is the profit? If the company cannot make money it will eventually fail. Writing a business plan will set the company in a successful direction.

Financing

Once a business plan determines overhead, the company will need to invest in supplies and space. Designing may require a minimum investment of drafting supplies that can be used at home, or as much as computer hardware and software and surveying and installation equipment that will require storage. Once the investment amount is determined, a loan will need to be secured to finance the company. Besides discussing options with a banker, look into government programs that can provide funding and consultation at low interest rates or for free.

Accounting

Become familiar with accounting principles. Keeping receipts, automobile mileage, and home office hours are important components of tax deductions. Consider hiring a certified public accountant (CPA) to handle the company's finances. A CPA will help you balance books and prepare taxes.

Finding Work

Starting out in landscape design can be challenging and very time consuming until design and drawing skills develop and become more time-efficient. Be patient. Take whatever work you can get in the beginning for experience and portfolio. Be sure you charge a fair fee for your work. Do not do too many free designs. Sell your expertise and plan for word-of-mouth to spread for more work.

Starting Out

Regardless if you plan on working for a design firm or on your own, begin designing as soon as possible, even while you are taking design classes. Start designing landscapes for friends and parents. Not only will this help build confidence and experience, but it will also help develop a portfolio. Charge a fee, whatever you are comfortable with (although your parents should get a hefty discount). Getting a few designs in your portfolio will make you comfortable to seek work outside of family and friends.

College Contacts

Let the professor know you are interested in part-time design work since many people will call a local college to hire students. Approach the professor after class so that he or she knows you are serious about designing and not just taking the class for the degree.

Freelance Designer

Word-of-Mouth

To start a design business the word has to get out. Your best advertisement is your reputation that spreads word-of-mouth. Once the business becomes established over time, word-of-mouth often becomes the primary method of getting the next project. In a survey done by the Gallup poll (www.anla.org/industry/facts/consumerswant.htm), the number one quality people valued in landscape services was *good references and reputation*. This is the driving force of referrals; somebody in the neighborhood or a friend of the client sees the work and contacts your business. If the design is being installed, placing a sign to identify your company will help.

Start off by telling everyone you know: accountant, doctor, dentist, real estate agent, lawyer, and all of your friends. The more people who know about your endeavors, the more likely work will come your way. Just a simple, "I'm starting a landscape design business" will do. Pass along business cards and/or brochures. Often these acquaintances will talk to someone on this topic with your business in mind.

Advertising

Advertising in the Yellow Pages can be effective as well as expensive. The local daily newspaper is another source of advertising. Do not forget about advertising in small community newspapers that publish once or twice a week. These can be very inexpensive to advertise in and very effective.

Consider advertising on your vehicle with a magnetic sign or window sticker with phone number and services.

Plant Nurseries and Construction Companies

A business card or brochure can be posted at plant nurseries where people often request help for their landscape needs. Introduce yourself to the nursery manager. The more you do business with them, and the more good things they hear about you (word-of-mouth, again), the more business they'll pass your way. After all, the more you design, the more plants they sell to your clients.

Other options can also include contacting *construction companies* to inquire if they need designs for new subdivisions. Contact the *county municipality* to get the names of companies that are building in the area.

Landscape Design Company

Some people prefer to start designing with a company to "learn the ropes" before starting their own business as a freelance designer. These positions often vary on the number of designers kept on staff and the role of the designer. Some companies utilize designers as a salesperson to find prospective clients, other companies use designers only part-time in the office and the rest of the time in the field for installation.

Classified Ads

Positions can sometimes be found in the *classified ads* of the newspaper. There are also *job bulletins* specifically for the horticulture industry that list landscape design openings. A couple of very good Internet job bulletins for job searching are:

http://www.landscapejobs.com/

http://www.hortjobs.com/

http://www.horticulturaljobs.com/

http://www.ihirelandscaping.com/

http://www.florapersonnel.com/

http://www.bloominggoodjobs.com/

http://www.constructiondeal.com/

http://www.servicemagic.com/

http://www.earthwormjobs.com

http://www.lawnandlandscape.com/classifieds

Landscape Contractors

Graduating students would benefit from sending out resumes to landscape companies. Call the company as a follow-up to see if they received the resume and schedule a time to come by and present your portfolio.

Trade Shows

Get involved in local horticulture associations and attend trade shows. Most associations sponsor a statewide trade show where vendors from the horticulture industry display their products and services. Many times there are job boards where companies will post openings. This is also a great opportunity to network with the industry. Bring copies of resumes and/or business cards. There's nothing like meeting potential employers face-to-face to make a lasting impression.

A good Web site containing links to state and regional organizations: http:bluestem. hort.purdue.edu/plant/nursery_landscape_org.html

1 The Interview

Objectives

- Learn how to conduct an interview
- Learn how to appear professional
- Know what to bring to an interview
- Know what information to get from the client
- Understand about contract and design fees

The **interview** is the initial meeting with the prospective client for whom design services will be provided. This is a meeting not only for the client to interview the designer, but for the designer to interview the client as well. The designer may choose not to work with a client who can be difficult to work with or unreasonable in what they want for what they are willing to pay.

The interview takes place whether the designer is working for a landscape company or as a freelance designer. In some cases there is no interview, such as working for a building contractor before a home is occupied.

The interview may have been the result of a **referral** from a previous client or answering an advertisement. There are a few general guidelines for setting up and proceeding with the interview.

Setting Up the Interview

Screen the Client

Before agreeing to meet every person who inquires about design services, **screen** the client by asking a few questions to ensure they understand the scope of services and fees. This could save a lot of time with a person who only wants a few recommendations on plants along the foundation. Usually referrals are good clients because they are familiar with work done for previous clients.

If the prospective client wants to schedule an interview, ask them to do a little homework before the appointment. First, have them consider landscapes they like whether they come up with locations or pictures from magazines. The client should also understand what a site survey is and how they can locate it. Next, have them think about how much money they want to spend on the installation.

Meet at the Residence

Plan for the interview to take place at the residence. This way observations can be made while on-site. It also helps the clients show and explain the areas of concern.

Meet All the Clients

If working for a couple, it is preferable to schedule the interview while both people are present, whenever possible. In many cases this will be difficult because one of them is working. Meeting in the evening or on weekends can make this more feasible. Not having one of them there can create communication problems. The designer can avoid callbacks that change design requests, or worse, cancellation of the entire project because the spouse doesn't agree with the fee.

The One-Hour Interview

One hour is often sufficient to meet the clients, gather site information, and come to an agreement on services. Depending on the project and scope of services, as much as a couple of hours may be required. Much of the time will be spent gathering information about the clients. What services do they want? What are their personalities? What plants do they like? Do they have kids or a dog?

Free Interview or Consultation Fee?

Many designers do not charge for the initial meeting because screening the calls determines how serious the client is about contracting the company's services. Some designers charge a consultation fee, such as $100, in lieu of a free interview. This would include a little more than just an interview, such as helping the client with design ideas around the yard in a very general sense. The consultation fee is often rolled into the design fee if the client chooses to contract the company for a design. If the client decides not to hire the designer then the time is not wasted.

Appear Professional

Be presentable at your initial meeting to convey a sense of confidence and quality (Fig 1–1). Some people place a great deal of importance on appearance and how it relates to work. Make a good first impression.

(a)

(b)

Figure 1–1 **Meeting the Client**
(a) Dress professionally. (b) The initial meeting should take place at the residence with both husband and wife. The designer spends about an hour in the interview presenting the portfolio and assessing the clients' needs and wants.

Neatly Dressed

Most clients will feel confident in a designer who is clean and tidy instead of one who comes out of the field sloppy and unkempt. Although you are competent, don't let an untucked shirt change the client's perception.

Clean Hands, Hair, and Clothes

Although this may seem silly, this is an industry that moves soil. It is easy to forget dirt under fingernails and grass stains on the knees because the designer was helping with an installation before the interview. Carry hand soap and towels in the car so that you can clean up before any meeting and smell fresh. As the designer, your professional appearance should be clean.

Act Professional

Professionalism is the practice of maintaining integrity and timeliness. Follow some very simple steps to convey your commitment and trustworthiness. Clients are giving the designer money and they want to be taken seriously.

- Be on time
  - Better yet, be 5 minutes early.
  - If you're going to be late, calling the clients is a professional courtesy.
- Follow through on commitments
  - Preliminary designs or estimates should be finished and delivered when promised. If you are running behind schedule, call or e-mail the client.
- Don't make excuses
  - Sometimes things go wrong that are not within your control. Focus on correcting them rather than blaming others.

Contact Information

Program the client's phone number into your cell phone. You won't forget it. Also, consider doing as much work with e-mail as possible. This keeps a written record of the commitments, albeit nonbinding and informal. Make a folder of each client on your e-mail and store all communication. It often takes less time to work through e-mail than it does via phone.

What to Bring

There are several items to include on every site visit to get necessary information and be efficient with time. Find a way to bundle these items into an easy-to-carry package (Fig. 1–2).

Clipboard or Notebook

Take notes during the first visit. A clipboard will allow you to walk around the property while securely carrying several documents and scratch paper.

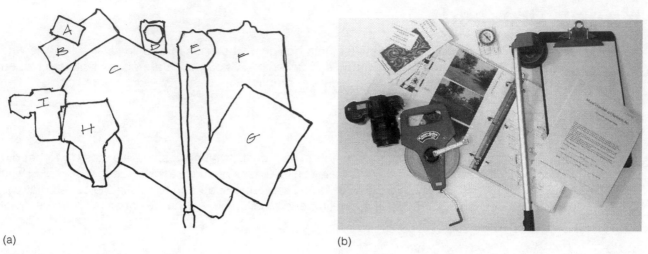

(a)

(b)

***Figure 1–2* Interview Tools**
Several items that should come along on the interview: (a) business card, (b) brochure, (c) portfolio, (d) compass, (e) measuring wheel, (f) clipboard, (g) contract, (h) tape measure, and (i) camera.

***Figure 1–3* Compass**
A compass is necessary to verify
magnetic north.

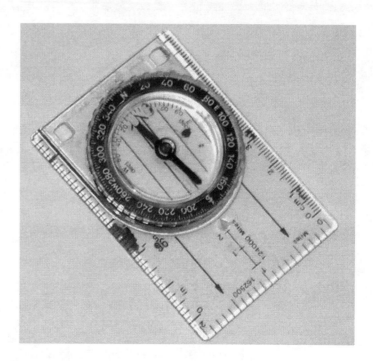

Measuring Wheel or 200′ Tape Measure

Even with a site survey provided by the client, several measurements may be necessary. A measuring wheel is easier to handle for one person than a measuring tape. However, a tape measure will be required to make some measurements on rough terrain or around objects in the way.

Compass

Use the **compass** to find magnetic north (Fig. 1–3). This is especially helpful when a site survey is not readily available.

Camera (Digital or Film)

Photos, taken by either a film or digital **camera,** are helpful to refer back to when at the design table, as well as to store in a portfolio as before and after photos.

Contract

Some designers like to have a simple contract to be signed by the end of the first meeting. Others prefer to send a proposal and contract after the initial interview.

Portfolio

Present clients with previous design projects via a **portfolio** (Fig. 1–4). Also have a couple of addresses of previous projects that have been installed that clients can drive by to see. This can also be a time to discuss the cost of various projects to gauge how their budget compares.

Laptop Computer

A **laptop computer** can be used to present a digital portfolio (Fig. 1–5). Software can be used to demonstrate various effects, such as lighting (see Chapter 10).

PowerPoint Presentation

Learn how to make a digital presentation of your previous projects. Include copies of your drawings and before/after pictures. The PowerPoint presentation can be loaded onto a Web site or burned onto an inexpensive CD and given to the client. Bring along a laptop and present it to the client to generate ideas and answer questions.

***Figure 1–4* Portfolio**
This is a concise portfolio assembled in a three-ring binder that contains pictures, sketches, and reduced plan drawings. It is helpful to show clients past design work. *(Photo courtesy of Big Sky Landscaping, Inc., Clackamas, OR.)*

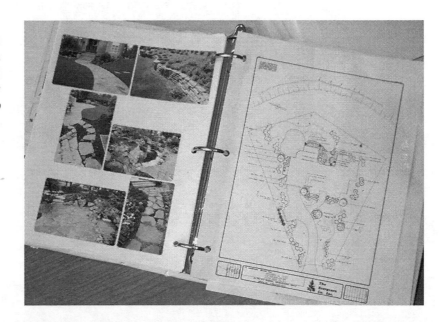

Figure 1-5 **Laptop Computer**
For those designers who will utilize design software or present a portfolio digitally, the laptop computer can easily show the client ideas and past projects.

Business Card and Brochure

Make sure clients get a **business card** (Fig. 1–6). A good idea is to give the client three business cards: one for each spouse and another to give to a friend. This is an excellent opportunity to have referrals passed along to other people by word of mouth. **Brochures** are even better. They can provide several photos of work and present design philosophy and achievements. Business cards and brochures can be easily designed and printed on a home computer.

Make Your Own Business Cards and Brochures

Business cards are inexpensive. Just go to a retail copier, such as Office Max, Staples, or Kinkos, and they'll print 500 for a minimal fee. Or you can get them at online Web sites for even less. The problem, sometimes, is you have to buy them in bulk. When information changes, such as a phone or fax, you throw them away and buy another box. Print your own business cards to save money and keep them up to date. Purchase business card templates on heavy card stock.

Free Templates

The Microsoft Web site has free templates. This is a great resource for contracts, stationery, invoices, and whatever else a business needs to be self-sufficient. Go to http://office.microsoft.com/templates to find business card designs and brochure templates to be downloaded. Type in your own information and print as needed.

What to Get from a Client

Trust

The client should feel comfortable with the designer. The client should feel confident that the designer's skills and decisions will meet their needs.

green jeans
creative landscape design and installation

marge puckhaber.owner
phone.843.559.1710
greenjns2@aol.com

PHONE 884-6114
FAX 884-6178

The Good Earth, Inc.
CREATIVE LANDSCAPING

THOM HOOD
VICE PRESIDENT

1495 HARBORGATE BLVD.
MT. PLEASANT, SC 29464

The Good Earth, Inc.
1495 Harborgate Blvd.
Mt. Pleasant, South Carolina 29464

Petal
Sepal
Blade
Stem
Bulb
Root

Monet's Gardens
in Charleston

Figure 1–6 **Business Cards and Brochures**
There are several ways to leave company information. A business card is the easiest, although tri-fold brochures are good to include photos of projects and description of services and accomplishments.

Tip Box
Other Good Ideas

Door hanger. Develop a small sign to hang on the client's front door in case they have not arrived for the appointment. It tells the client that you were there.

Compact disc. With CD burners being affordable, create a CD of business goals and services along with a digital portfolio containing before and after designs. This will provide clients with a database of plant and landscape images that they can get ideas. This may be the Web site burned on to a CD (Fig. 1–7).

Figure 1–7 Compact Disc
Burning a CD of your company's services along with a digital portfolio can be an inexpensive way to advertise.

Web site. Have a **Web site** created that has similar information as the CD. The Web address can appear on your business card, brochure, and other items. It is easy to pass around and allows prospective clients to look at design work on their own time (Fig. 1–8). Do a Google search (http://www.google.com) for "landscape design companies" or go to the following links to see examples:

http://www.zenjapaneselandscape.com   http://www.bigskylandscaping.com

ttp://zitolandesign.com   http://www.jrwdecks.com

Figure 1–8 Web Site
With most people connected to the Internet, having an inexpensive Web site that displays a portfolio and services is a convenient way to advertise. Having the Web site address on the business card can draw easy traffic. *(Photo courtesy of Courtney Smith.)*

Catalogs. Some larger firms keep in touch with clients by publishing a catalog with news and tips about the clients' landscapes (Fig. 1–9).

THE GOOD EARTH LANDSCAPE COMPANY
The Good News

QUARTERLY NEWSLETTER   SUMMER 2001

SUMMER CALENDAR

June

Plant Iris – Bearded types can be transplanted while in bloom. Actually, that is the best time to buy because you can see the color. You can also divide and replant existing clumps after they bloom.

Seeds – It's not too late to plant annuals. And if your needs are large or your budget small, consider sowing seeds directly into prepared garden beds. Zinnias and Sunflowers respond well.

Flowers – Annual and perennial beds, as well as roses, can use a boost, especially where the soil is sandy or the season has been rainy. Apply slow-release fertilizer for maximum benefit with minimum effort.

Vines – Train the new growth of clematis, yellow jessamine, and other twining vines to guide them onto the trellis. The new canes of climbing roses usually need some help too. Use loose, dark green twist ties to hold the new growth in place.

July

Pumpkins – If you're going to grow your own jack-o'-lantern, it's time to plant. Choose a sunny spot with plenty of room for the vine. Plant three seeds on a small mound of enriched soil.

Photographs – Take pictures of your garden several times during the growing season. This will help you remember what plants to consider when it comes time to start your garden for next year.

Annuals – Deadhead your annuals to promote continued blooming.

August

Collecting – It's time to gather grasses, pods and flowers for dried wreaths and arrangements. Wreaths are easier to make while the plant material is fresh; let it dry after it is attached.

Compost – This is a good time to begin a compost pile. Although you can get very scientific about it, all you really need is an inconspicuous corner where you can take spent plants, fallen leaves, and vegetable trimmings from the kitchen. Turn the pile occasionally, and you have good soil amendments by spring.

Pecans – During drought, water your pecan tree to prevent the nuts from dropping prematurely. Place a soaker hose beneath the outer edge of the canopy and allow it to run until the soil is thoroughly soaked.

ATTA BOY AWARDS

JANUARY:
Shane Johnson,
Bobby Potter
FEBRUARY:
Don Beck,
Sean McDuffie
MARCH:
Dale Fox,
Justin Clark

THINKING OF MOVING YOUR INDOOR PLANTS OUTSIDE FOR THE SUMMER?

The process of gradually acclimating indoor-grown plants to outdoor conditions like direct sunlight, cold soil, strong winds, and pelting rain is called *hardening off.* About two (2) weeks before your area's last frost date, reduce water, giving your seedlings just enough to prevent wilting, and keep a fan on them at low speed, to toughen stems. After a week, place the plants outside for a few hours in a spot sheltered from sun and wind. Check their soil regularly for moisture taking care not to let it get too dry. Increase exposure incrementally, then plant out.

Figure 1–9 **Company Catalog**
Some companies follow up with clients by sending quarterly catalogs that offer maintenance advice and company updates. *(Photo courtesy of Good Earth, Inc., Charleston, SC.)*

Commitment

Get a firm commitment. Some designers like to use a simple **contract** to establish the terms of agreement. It is legally binding, but more than that it instills a sense of commitment to the project.

Site Survey

A survey of the property will save time (covered in the next chapter). If a site survey cannot be obtained, be sure to include additional time in the project for the collection of necessary measurements.

Photos

Take plenty of photos to avoid having to go back and check on details. Photos are great reminders of details that may have been overlooked or forgotten, like the color of the house or the position of a shed.

Schedule the Next Meeting

If an agreement and commitment have been reached during the interview, then schedule the next meeting to present the preliminary plan. This depends on the designer's schedule and the size of the project, but a good time frame for many residential projects is about 7 to 10 days.

Tip Box
Follow-Up Call

A good professional courtesy is to call the clients a few days after the initial interview and ask if there is anything they may want to add.

Upon Arrival

Arrive Early

Always be on time, and if possible 5 to 10 minutes early. Showing up late never gives a good first impression. Being punctual gives the impression of trustworthiness. In fact, a good practice is to call in the morning or at least 30 minutes ahead of time to confirm the appointment. Arriving early creates an opportunity to drive around the neighborhood and assess the landscape styles and cost. This will impact the design for the prospective client.

If being late is unavoidable, call as soon as possible to inform the clients of the situation and when they can expect you to arrive.

Small Talk

Allow several minutes of small talk with the clients. Talk to the kids if they are there and reach down to pet the dog. This will set a relaxed tone for the rest of the interview and will allow you to get familiar with your clients' personalities.

Discussion of the Design Work

Quiet Setting

Find a quiet place to sit down—the kitchen, living room, or even outside on the deck (Fig. 1–10) or any place that minimizes distractions like the television. Don't be shy to request a quiet, comfortable setting if you notice one. If the clients want to walk around and discuss the project, that's great. But there should also be time set aside to sit down and discuss services and compensation.

Design Philosophy

Once the clients have had several minutes to discuss what they want, take a few minutes to talk about your design philosophy. This can include showing a portfolio and discussing low-maintenance designs, flowing lines, or easy maintenance.

Some design suggestions could include:

- Use of native plants

- Proper spacing to minimize maintenance

- Utilize amendments to maximize growth and minimize pests

- Use of evergreens to keep interest through the entire year

They should also be aware of the cost of the services. It wouldn't be prudent to spend an hour to interview only to find the clients shocked to hear what it will cost them. If they understand the price range of the design services and are agreeable to it, then the interview can proceed. However, if screened properly the clients will be familiar with the fees and services.

Once an understanding is reached on services and fees, begin discussing the project in detail.

Figure 1–10 **Sitting at a Table** When discussing the design, find a place to sit with clients that is free of distractions where notes can be taken and ideas discussed.

Opening the Discussion

Allow the clients to express what they want. Open the discussion by asking an open-ended question:

"How can I help you?" or *"What can I do for you?"*

This will give the clients an opportunity to discuss why they contacted the designer—if it's just to give them some ideas of what to do with the front yard or to create a design concept for the entire property. If calls are screened carefully, the designer should already be familiar with what they want and they should know how you do business. Regardless of how much the designer knows, the clients will feel more involved in the design if they're allowed to express their desires.

Listen to the Client

Although the designer records observations and an analysis of the surroundings, the most important source of information is what the clients want. While they are talking, have a clipboard or note cards and take notes vigorously. Writing everything down achieves the following:

- It will be a reminder of things later at the design table.
- It communicates to the clients that the designer is actively listening. Everything they say is jotted down and helps instill confidence that the designer is taking the project seriously.
- It can help remind clients of the discussion if there is a dispute later on in the project about what was discussed.

Give clients plenty of time to discuss what they want to do. Spend time listening and acknowledging their comments and wishes. If some things sound unreasonable or out of reach, then propose a suggestion and possible solution, otherwise just listen and take notes. Don't force your opinion over what they want.

What Does the Client Want?

Oftentimes it becomes the job of the designer to help the clients know what they want. In some cases they may be requesting something that is in complete opposition to their living style. This would be the case with clients who have a formal living style and are requesting wildflower beds, or clients who want a specific plant that is wrong for the site or location. This requires some insightful, gentle discussion to determine what the client is really asking. Instead of wildflowers, do they really just want a lot of color? Instead of that particular plant, do they simply like the tropical characteristics?

Project Cost

Design fees may have been discussed, but how much do they want to spend on the installation of the design? This will affect the extent of the design and bring the feasibility of their wishes into focus. If they want a large flagstone patio but only wish to spend a couple hundred dollars on it, then they should be aware of what it would cost to build it. Most clients will have a preset range of money in mind to spend on landscaping.

Here are some points to educate clients that landscaping is a good investment:

- Landscaping can add about 10 percent to a home's value (Gallup Organization).
- The cost of landscaping can be recovered by 100 percent to 200 percent (Clemson University).
- Landscaping can reduce energy costs by as much as 50 percent (American Public Power Association).
- More facts can be found on the American Nursery and Landscape Association Web site, http://www.anla.org/industry/facts/valueof.htm.

Tip Box

Budget Examples

Have pictures of previous projects and what they cost. This gives a client an idea what, say, $5000 will buy them.

Some designers estimate that landscaping should cost about 10 percent of the value of the residence. For example, if a residence is valued at $100,000, then $10,000 should be earmarked for landscaping. Another rough estimate is to calculate $2 per square foot of the property. Both of these approaches would include all hardscaping as well as plants. In most cases either one of these estimates is much higher than the cost of most projects. The majority of clients want to spend about half as much as either one of these estimates.

Tip Box

Phasing-In

One solution to ease the sticker shock is to discuss **phasing-in** the design. Approach the design to be installed over the next three to five years. Do the front yard the first year, the deck the second year, backyard beds the third, and finish the side yards the fourth year. This makes the project reachable.

Client Information

This discussion may take place at any time during the interview, not necessarily in the order it's laid out. In most cases these discussions will take place throughout the interview.

The following are some questions to ask the client and to record. These are certainly not the extent of the interview questions. In fact, many of these will often lead to other questions and conversations that will further define what the client wants.

Family

How many family members?

Ages?

Occupations?

Are there any allergies to consider, such as bees or specific plants?

Are there any pets to consider?

Dogs are often the most destructive on plant material. If they do have a dog, do they want to develop a dog run? If not, consider avoiding plants susceptible to being trampled, such as annuals and perennials.

Design Goals

Always give the clients the opportunity to address their design goals. This most likely will have already been addressed when the discussion was opened with "How can I help you?" However, during the course of the interview other concerns may arise.

Lifestyle

Asking them questions about how they use their residence, or intend to use it, will help define the project needs as well as lead the client to other ideas. The following are sample questions.

What kind of things do you do in the:

Front yard?

Side yard?

Backyard?

For instance, do you have outdoor hobbies or storage needs? Where do you spend time relaxing, entertaining, and recreating?

Hobbies

Do you have any outdoor hobbies, such as gardening?

How about the children? Is there a need to develop an area for them to play?

Entertaining

Do you spend time entertaining guests?

Large crowds? Small? Informal? Formal?

Is there a need for a deck or patio?

If there is an existing one, is it large enough?

Do you need to develop an area for outdoor cooking and eating?

Views

Are there views you would like to keep?

Are there views you would like to block?

Are there any unpleasant items to be screened, such as a utility box, air-conditioning unit, nearby traffic.

What about views from inside the house?

Is there any need for privacy from the neighbors?

Client Preferences

Find out what their preferences are concerning plants, hardscapes, and other features.

Do you prefer informal, natural areas, or layouts that are more formal?

This may be apparent by observing their living habits, the way their house is kept, and their taste in décor.

What level of maintenance would you care to have?

In the vast majority of cases, clients will stress low maintenance. They don't want to have to deal with it, or at least they want to spend less money to have someone else to maintain it. Rarely will the designer hear someone request a "high-maintenance landscape." However, if a client would like to develop a rose garden make sure they are aware of the maintenance requirements.

What are your favorites plants?

There may be specific plants or just general characteristics.

"I love lilacs."

"Anything that has fragrance."

"I like tropical-type plants (palms)."

What are your least favorite plants?

Find out if there are plants they are allergic to or just don't care for.

"Can't stand those mulberry trees. The birds eat the fruit and then leave it all over everything."

"Don't use any of those yucca plants."

"Don't use anything I have to spend a lot of time pruning."

Tip Box
Landscape Design Examples

Ask if there's a yard they've seen that they really like. If it's convenient, stop by to get an idea of what they like. Ask the client what it is they like about it.

Ask about other parts of a design they may be interested in looking at, such as water features, low-voltage lighting, and irrigation.

Questionnaire

Prepare a handout that they can fill out ahead of the interview (if possible), leave it with them, or go over it with them during the interview (Fig. 1–11).

LANDSCAPE DESIGN QUESTIONNAIRE

NAME: ______________________________

ADDRESS: ______________________________

CITY, STATE, ZIP CODE: ______________________________

PHONE: ______________________________

FAMILY

Name and age of family members

Are there any allergies? YES OR NO

Type of outdoor pets (please specify):

Time of day and season family most active in landscape: ______________________________

Is there a need for handicap access? YES OR NO

BUDGET

Will this design be installed by homeowner or contractor? YES OR NO

Approximate budget allowed for the design and installation: $______________________________

Or is it dependent upon consultation? YES OR NO

Would you consider implementing design over a few years to spread out cost? YES OR NO

SOIL/DRAINAGE

Are there problems with standing water in the landscape? YES OR NO

Is soil extremely heavy (clay) or sandy?

Are there steep slopes on the property? YES OR NO

VIEWS

Which rooms in the house offer the most common views to the outside?

Are there any views that need to be created, such as from an entertainment area? YES OR NO

Are there any unpleasant areas to be screened from view (utility box, traffic, A/C unit)?

Does there need to be more privacy in any areas?

Figure 1–11 **Questionnaire**

A questionnaire can be provided to the clients prior to the interview or downloaded from the Web site.

MICROCLIMATES

Answer any below that are applicable.

Where are there areas of full shade or full sun:_____

Where is there a need for more shade:_____

Where is there a need for noise reduction:_____

Where are there areas that need overhead protection:_____

Where are there areas too windy:_____

Where are there problems with snow or ice:_____

PLANT SELECTION

Answer any below that are applicable.

Name your favorite plants:_____

Any plants or materials you dislike:_____

Name your favorite colors:_____

Would you like to include: FRAGRANCE, ANNUAL FLOWERS, OR NATIVE PLANTS

CIRCULATION

Does the driveway need to be expanded? YES OR NO

Does the front walk need to be improved? YES OR NO

Is there circulation to other parts of the yard that needs to be accessible or improved? YES OR NO

ENTERTAINMENT

What is the average number of people you entertain:_____

Would you like to build or expand a deck or patio? YES OR NO

SERVICE

Is there a need for storage space (boat, trailer)? YES OR NO

Are garbage cans:

       ☐ Accessible YES OR NO

       ☐ Unsightly YES OR NO

       ☐ Need to be relocated YES OR NO

Is there a need for: FIREWOOD STORAGE, COMPOSTING, VEGETABLE GARDEN, SHED

(continues)

Figure 1–11 Questionnaire—continued
A questionnaire can be provided to the clients prior to the interview or downloaded from the Web site.

ACTIVITY

Please check any of the following to include in design:

☐ Kid's playground

☐ Cooking and eating

☐ Privacy area

☐ Firepit

☐ Recreation (horseshoes, volleyball)

MISCELLANEOUS CONSIDERATIONS

Please check any of the following you would be interested in including in landscape design:

☐ Water feature

☐ Low-voltage lighting

☐ Sculpture

☐ Butterfly garden

☐ Fence

☐ Energy efficiency

ADDITIONAL COMMENTS

Are there any other areas or problems you would like to address that are not mentioned on this questionnaire?

Figure 1-11 Questionnaire—continued
A questionnaire can be provided to the clients prior to the interview or downloaded from the Web site.

Design Fees and Contract

Some designers prefer to talk about their design fees at the beginning of the interview to get it out of the way. It is a good idea for the clients to have some idea of fees to avoid having to complete an hour-long visit and then not agree with the fees.

Design Fees

There is a great variance in what designers charge, most of which depends on experience. Designer **fees** range anywhere from $20 to $100 per hour. Some designers do not charge per hour but by the project. For example, a typical residential design ranges from $100 to $500. However, it's not out of the question for experienced landscape designers and landscape architects to charge $1000 or more for a residential design and much more for commercial projects.

Designers who work for a design/installation firm will often, as an incentive to get the contract for installation and maintenance, take the price of the design out of the cost of installation.

As a beginning designer, be comfortable with your fees. Charging less may help you get started and develop a portfolio as well as confidence. But don't sell yourself short; remember you are providing your expertise of plants and design. It can be pleasantly surprising to find out just how little most people know about plants.

The amount of time spent on a residential design project varies greatly between designers and the projects. Many designers expect to spend about 5 to 10 hours on an average project. They can expect to spend a various amount of time on the following phases of the design process:

Measurements, inventory, and analysis – 1 to 2 hours

Preliminary design(s) and digital imagery – 2 to 4 hours

Presenting preliminary design(s) – 1 hour

Master plan – 2 to 3 hours

Contract

Once the interview is complete, estimate the amount of time it would take to complete the project and propose a design fee (Fig. 1–12). Some designers prefer to prepare a formal **proposal** and contract and send it to the clients a few days after the interview. Some prefer a verbal proposal and simple contract to be signed before they leave the interview. And there are others who simply work on the "gentleman's handshake," no legally binding document. However, it is a good idea to have a simple contract signed by the clients. In addition to the legal ramifications, it provides a sense of commitment between the designer and the client.

Payment Schedule

A **payment schedule** is arranged in the contract so that part of the compensation is due before the project is complete. This can prevent a client from dropping the project after it has been started or nearly completed, with no payment. Some designers ask for a retainer fee, or money when the contract is signed to retain the designer's services. A **retainer fee** may be half of the design fee at the signing of the contract and the remainder due upon completion; or one-third at signing, one-third at the preliminary, and the remaining one-third at the master.

Another typical payment schedule is as follows:

Retainer fee upon signing the contract – 20 percent

Presentation of preliminary design(s) – 60 percent

Master plan – 20 percent

Pelican designs

Landscape design solutions

Proposal for Design Services
_____Residence

Scope of Work. Outlined below are the proposed tasks to be accomplished.

1. On-site measurement and development of the base map.
2. Analysis of existing on-site and immediate off-site conditions.
3. Development of a minimum of two Preliminary Diagrams.
4. Further refinement of one of the Preliminary Diagrams into a Master Plan.

Drawings. To be submitted according to the schedule outlined below.

1. Development of base map, site inventory, site analysis, and Concept Plans.
2. Two Preliminary Designs showing the location of all proposed site elements and existing site features that are to remain such as walks, driveway, fences, and plantings. These plans will be presented at your home for refinement and final approval.
3. One Master Plan showing the specific names of plant materials, other materials and patterns developed from the approved Preliminary Design, blackline, 24 x 36, for client retention.

NOTE: Scope of work does not include detailed construction or work drawings for any site structure, or actual construction and installation of the design. It is the client/installer's responsibility to determine the exact location of any buried utility services before digging.

Fee Payment Schedule
I will prepare and execute the above noted drawings and design services for the sum of
$_____, payment as follows:

       $_____ submitted with signed contract.
       $_____ paid upon completion and presentation of the Preliminary Design.
       $_____ paid upon completion and presentation of the Master Plan.

Contract Acceptance
Your signature below indicates your acceptance of the terms.

(Client)_____ Date_____

(Client)_____

Figure 1–12 Contract
A simple contract is a legally binding document that lays out a payment schedule and can be brought to the interview and signed upon completion of the interview or sent to the clients after the interview along with a proposal.

Make the Next Appointment

Once the fees and contract are completed, set the next appointment to present the preliminary design(s). This could be about seven to ten days after the interview, or dependant on mutual schedules. A designer should also consider asking the client for permission to return to the property, even if the client is not at home, to make observations or measurements.

Inventory and Analysis

After the interview, measurements and observations can be made for the inventory and analysis (discussed in the next chapter) or make a return visit.

Other Considerations

Some other things you might do following the initial interview:

Follow-Up Call

Two or three days after the interview, call the client(s) to touch base with them and see if there is anything they thought of since your visit.

Thank-You Card

Send a card thanking them for the opportunity to discuss their design needs. This is another way to keep in touch between the interview and the next visit. It appears professional and may help you to find your next client.

For a closer examination of the interview process, see Appendix A, "The Design Process," for the Grant Residence Interview.

Summary

The interview is an opportunity for the landscape designer to present services and fees to a prospective client in addition to learning their needs and goals. This generally takes an hour to complete. The designer should appear and conduct himself or herself professionally by dressing appropriately, arriving on time, and being organized. The designer may present a portfolio of past work to familiarize the clients with the designer's design philosophy and competence. If the services and fees are agreeable, then the clients should be given ample opportunity to discuss their wants and needs from the landscape while the designer takes notes. The designer may ask questions or a questionnaire may be made available for the clients to fill out so that the designer may accurately incorporate the needs of the family and their lifestyle into the design. When the discussion is completed, the interview is concluded with a signed contract and payment schedule or a commitment from the designer to send a proposal in a few days.

Key Terms

Brochures: include several photos of design work, philosophy, and achievements

Business card: 2″ × 3.5″ card with business name, phone number, and other information

Camera: used to take photos on-site, film or digital

Catalogs: news and tips about their landscapes sent to clients following their projects

Compact disc: contains business goals and services along with a digital portfolio

Compass: used to find magnetic north

Contract: legally binding document that the client signs and agrees to the services and fees outlined

Door hanger: small sign you can hang on a client's front door in case they are not present for appointment

Fees: designers charge anywhere from $20 to $100 per hour, or $150 to $500 a project

Interview: the initial meeting with the prospective client for whom you will provide the service of landscape design

Laptop computer: used to present a digital portfolio of past projects

Payment schedule: outlines when and how much of the fees will be paid to the designer

Phasing-in: installing the project over the next three to five years to spread out the cost

Portfolio: a collection of previous design projects to show to prospective clients

Proposal: a written document that outlines the services and fees of the designer

Referral: a previous client who has recommended your services to a potential client

Retainer fee: payment to reserve the designer's services

Screening: asking a potential client questions so that they understand your services and fees to avoid wasting time

Web site: contains business goals and services along with a digital portfolio; the Web address can appear on your business card, brochure, and other items

2 The Base Map

Objectives

- Understand the terminology relating to a plat, or site survey
- Know the drafting tools used to draw a base map
- Understand how to interpret plat information
- Learn how to take site measurements
- Be able to draw a base map to scale

The next step after the analysis is to draw an accurate base map. To do so, there are a few definitions you should be aware of in order to understand a site survey and base map, as well as the techniques in taking measurements.

Plan Drawing

A **plan drawing** is a two-dimensional drawing of an area that appears like a bird's-eye view looking from directly overhead, sometimes referred to as a "**plan view drawing**" (Fig. 2–1). It will be the plan, or map, on which the design will be illustrated.

Drafting Tools

Before discussing the components of a base map, it is important to be familiar with some of the tools and materials required to draw a plan.

Paper

Tracing paper, sometimes called **trash paper, onionskin,** or **bumwad,** is a thin translucent paper used to sketch ideas (Fig. 2–2). It is a *low-quality paper* that will be useful for sketching ideas such as the concept plan.

Vellum paper, or **rag vellum,** is a higher quality paper that is translucent and can be placed over previous drawings to trace. It is typically used for the final plan of lead drawings. **Mylar** is a high-quality paper that is actually drafting **film.** It can be used for the final plan but is often used when drawing with ink because ink can be easily erased from mylar. **Grid paper** has non-photo blue lines that will not show on a copy. The paper can be vellum or standard bond. The size of the grid squares can be 1/8″ or other to match the scale so that each block is equivalent to 1 foot.

> ### *Tip Box*
> ### No Guidelines Needed
>
> Grid paper saves time with guidelines to draw straight lines and letter. And many grids are equivalent to using a 10-scale (1″ = 10′); one box is equal to 1 foot, reducing the need to use the engineer scale as much (Fig. 2–3).

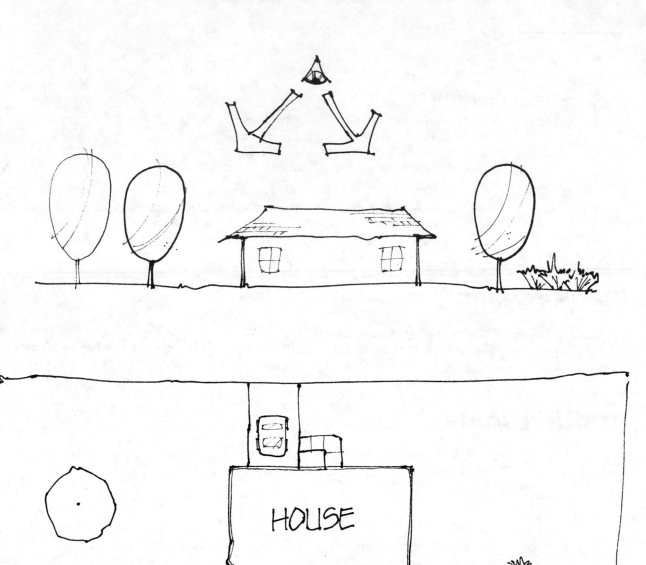

Figure 2–1 **Plan Drawing**
A plan drawing is a bird's-eye view looking directly from the site.

***Figure 2–2* Paper**
Tracing paper (bottom) is used to sketch ideas, while vellum and mylar are commonly used for the final drawing because of higher quality and longevity.

***Figure 2–3* Grid Paper**
Non-photo gridlines that do not show up on a copy reduce the need to draw guidelines.

The dimensions of the paper are dependant on the project. A **full sheet** is 24″ × 36″, which is typical for many projects (Fig. 2–4). This allows the designer to work in a comfortable scale that shows detail reasonably well. However, as the project permits, smaller sheets can be used. Typical sizes are:

Full sheet: 24″ × 36″

Half sheet: 18″ × 24″

Quarter sheet: 12″ × 18″

Lead

Lead is a good medium for beginners because it can be easily erased. It comes in degrees of hardness and softness (Fig. 2–5). **H** is used to designate hard lead that will draw thin, lighter lines. A number will come before H to give the degree of hardness. The higher the number, the harder the lead. 4H is used for guidelines and 2H is often

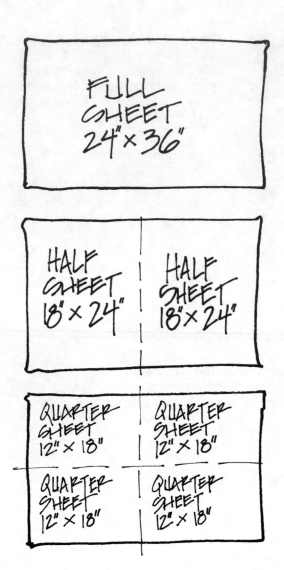

Figure 2–4 Paper Dimensions
A full sheet is common for many projects, but smaller projects may be on a half or quarter sheet.

FULL SHEET 24" × 36"

HALF SHEET 18" × 24"   HALF SHEET 18" × 24"

QUARTER SHEET 12" × 18"   QUARTER SHEET 12" × 18"

QUARTER SHEET 12" × 18"   QUARTER SHEET 12" × 18"

PENCIL 4H   INK 0.1 mm

PENCIL 2H   INK 0.3 mm

PENCIL H   INK 0.5 mm

PENCIL 2B   INK 0.7 mm

Figure 2–5 Lead and Ink
H leads (left) are harder leads that draw lighter lines; the higher the number the harder the lead. B leads are softer leads that draw thicker, darker lines; the higher the number the softer the lead. Various widths of ink tips (right) are used to get variations in line width. Tip widths are measured in millimeters.

used to draw details and sometimes used for lettering. H (without a number) is often used for general drawing.

B designates softer lead that draws thicker, darker lines. The higher the number, the softer the lead. HB is sometimes used for general drawing. Occasionally 2B is used, but it should be used with caution because it smudges easily.

Drawing pencils are wooden pencils without an eraser at the end, inexpensive, and easy to handle. **Lead-holders** operate like a mechanical pencil but hold larger sticks of lead. **Mechanical pencils** hold various thicknesses of lead (from 0.5 mm to 0.9 mm), which does not need to be sharpened (Fig. 2–6).

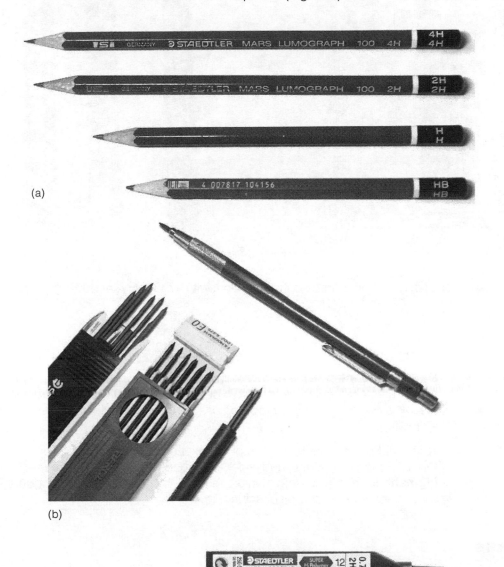

(a)

(b)

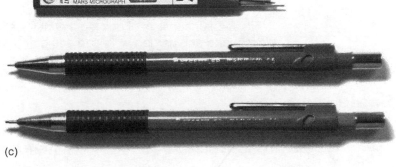

Figure 2–6 **Lead**
Often used by beginning designers because it erases easily. (a) Drawing pencils, (b) lead-holders, and (c) mechanical pencils.

(c)

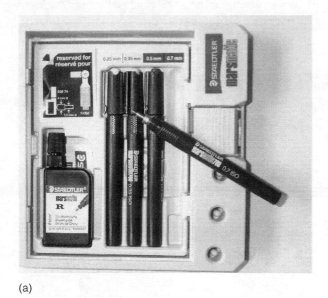

(a)

(b)

Figure 2–7 Ink
Ink provides a higher quality line but can be difficult to work with. (a) Technical pens. (b) Pigment liners.

Ink

Markers and **ink** provide excellent line quality. The contrast of black lines on white paper creates a very clean and legible document. Ink will not erase from vellum. *Be sure the ink is dry before moving tools across the vellum.* Otherwise, it will smudge and ruin a drawing.

Technical pens have tips made of metal and an ink reservoir. Sets will have very narrow tips, such as 0.2 mm, and wider tips around 1.0 mm. They are relatively expensive. **Pigment liners** are fiber-tip markers that also have a variety of line widths. They are relatively inexpensive and disposable (Fig. 2–7).

Compass

A **compass** is used to draw large circles or strike arcs for base map preparation (Fig. 2–8). It consists of one leg that has a sharp point that sticks into the middle of the circle and another leg with lead at the end. When the compass is spun around on the point, the lead draws the circle.

Scale

A **scale** is a ruler that has units to represent feet in the plan drawing (Fig. 2–9). It is used to draw the plan accurately. There are two types of scales: architect and engi-

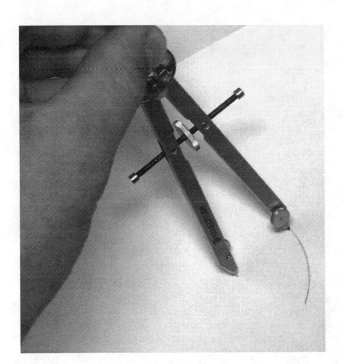

***Figure 2–8* Compass**
Used to draw circles or strike arcs in site plan preparation.

neer. An **architect scale** is based on units of an inch. For instance, the plan may be drawn so that every 1/4″ is equal to 1′. Many designs are drawn with an 1/8″ scale (every 1/8″ equals 1′), although it will depend on the scope of the project and size of the paper.

An architect scale can be confusing to use at first since it utilizes unit measurements running in both directions. The nice thing about working with increments of an inch is that a ruler can be used in case an architect scale is not available.

Tip Box

Landscape designers and architects commonly use the architect scale.

An **engineer scale** is based on *unit increments IN an inch*. The 10-scale has 10 evenly spaced increments per inch, the 20-scale has 20 increments per inch, and so on. So, if using the 10-scale, where every inch has 10 increments, the scale would be 1″ = 10′.

Tip Box

Surveyors commonly use the engineer scale. Therefore, any site survey obtained from clients or a city surveyor will most likely be drawn to an engineer scale.

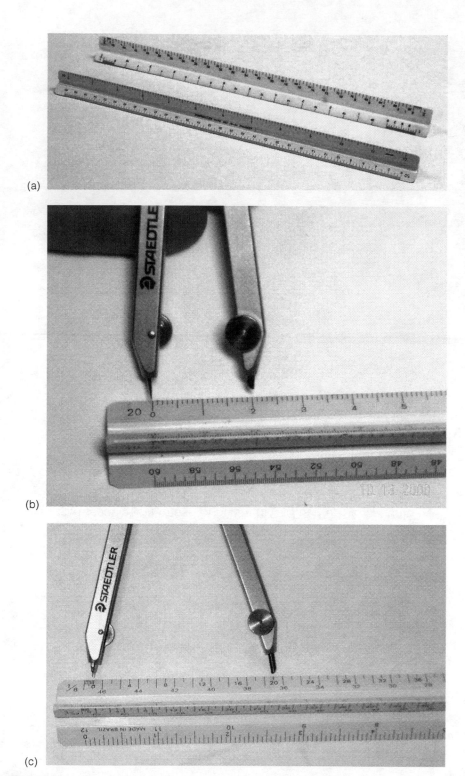

Figure 2–9 Scale

(a) The architect scale (above) and engineer scale (below) are often used to draw accurate plans. (b) The engineer scale is a measure of units in an inch, such as the 20-scale that has 20 units in an inch, which would be used as 1″ = 20′, or each individual unit is equal to 1 foot. The above compass is adjusted to 20 feet. (c) The architect scale is a measure of units of an inch, such as every 1/8″ = 1′. The above compass is adjusted to 20 feet.

Site Survey

The **site survey** contains the resident's lot with additional info. This is ideally the document you should obtain from the clients from which you will easily be able to design the plan drawing (Fig. 2–10). This survey is done by a registered land surveyor and shows the property lines and their length and bearings, the house located on the lot, and sometimes other objects like fences, driveway, sidewalks, and decks/patios. The site survey is commonly referred to as a **plat, mortgage plat,** or **closing survey.** This book will refer to this document as a site survey. Information in the survey is as follows: lot, bearings and distance of property lines, footprint, right-of-way, and easement. Setbacks and covenants may not be on the survey but are important to understand as well.

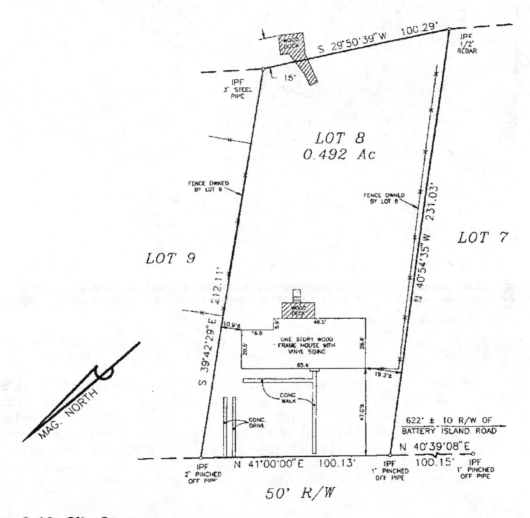

Figure 2–10 **Site Survey**

A site survey is a surveyor's map of the property, referred to as a plat, including the footprint of the house and other permanent objects such as driveway, deck, etc. It is usually obtained by the residents upon the closing of the house. It is important that the designer has a copy to draw an accurate plan to scale. (This survey has been altered to conceal the identity of resident and surveyor.)

Figure 2–11 Lot
A lot is a map of the resident's property. This plan includes all the
lots in the subdivision.

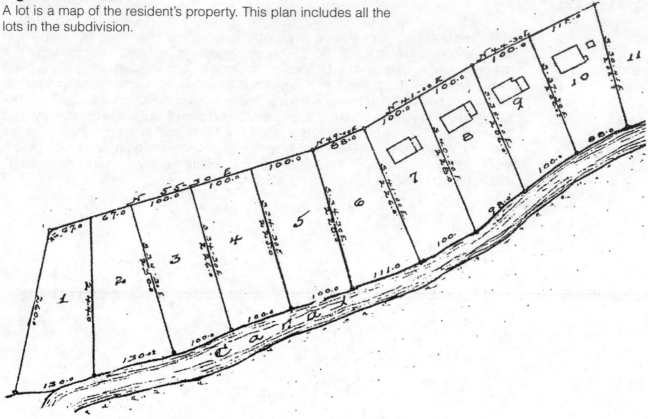

Lot

Lot refers to the residential property. It shows the **property lines,** which define the property boundaries (Fig. 2–11). Some residents may have a copy of the subdivision that
shows the layout of lots.

Property Stakes

Property stakes locate the beginning and end of a property line (Fig. 2–12). Stakes
are generally a metal bar (usually a 1/2″ diameter rebar) buried vertically in the ground.
The top of the stake is about 6 inches from the surface. Property corners may be identified by other permanent objects, such as a manhole cover, and would be indicated
on the survey. You can locate the general vicinity of the stake by sighting along a fence
line and 10′ in from the curb (assuming the right-of-way is 50′; see section on right-of-
way later in the chapter). Use a shovel to cut through the ground at an angle to hit the
stake.

Bearings and Length of Property Lines

The property lines show the **bearings**, which provide the orientation and the distance,
or length (Fig. 2–13). For instance, look at the property line on the left in Figure 2–10 between LOT 8 and LOT 9. The bearing is:

S 39° 42′ 29″ E 212.11′

Figure 2-12 **Property Stakes**
Property corners are established with property stakes, or other permanent objects such as a manhole cover. Property stakes are metal rods that are vertically located about 6 inches below the surface.

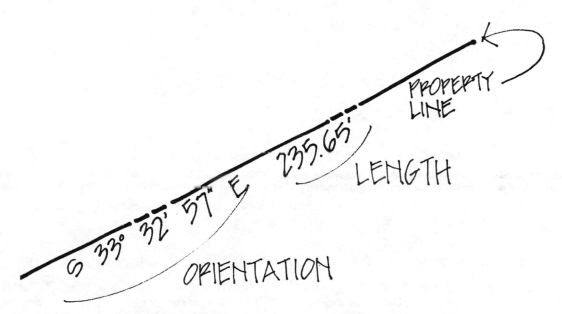

Figure 2-13 **Bearings and Length**
Information on the property lines of a site plan provides the orientation of the property line (as it relates to north, south, east, west) and length.

Bearings: The aforementioned property line is pointing in a direction that is 39 degrees, 42 minutes, and 29 seconds EAST of a SOUTHERN direction. (Although you are familiar with degrees, surveyors use minutes and seconds as smaller increments to more precisely measure angles.) In other words, if you draw a property line running directly NORTH-SOUTH, turn the property line as if it is stuck on a peg like a spinner exactly 39 degrees, 42 minutes, and 29 seconds in an EASTERLY direction (Fig. 2–14).

***Figure 2-14* Bearing Orientation**
The orientation can be related to how many degrees from the
north or south direction.

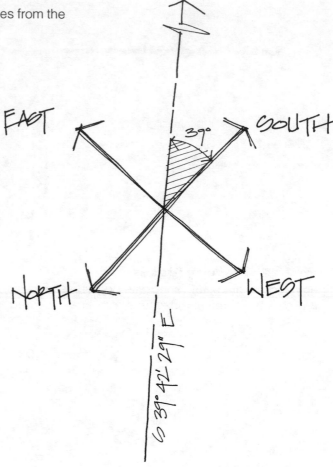

Length: The length of the property line is also indicated. In this case the property
line is 212.11 feet long.

Let's continue around the property lines in a clockwise direction.

   S 29° 50′ 39″ W 100.29′

Orientation: 29 degrees, 50 minutes, 39 seconds WEST (left) of SOUTH

Again, if the property line was mounted on a peg pointing in a NORTH-SOUTH
direction, turn it toward a WESTERLY direction exactly 29 degrees, 50 minutes,
39 seconds.

Length: 100.29′

   N 40° 54′ 35″ E 231.03′

Orientation: 40 degrees, 54 minutes, 35 seconds EAST (right) of NORTH

In this case, with the property line pointing in a NORTH-SOUTH direction, turn it
toward the EAST of NORTH exactly 40 degrees, 54 minutes, 35 seconds.

Length: 231.03′

   N 41° 00′ 00″ E 100.13′

Orientation: 41 degrees, 00 minutes, 00 seconds EAST (right) of NORTH

Finally, turn the property line exactly 41 degrees toward the EAST of NORTH.

Length: 100.13′

Footprint

The **footprint,** or the **floorplan,** of the house will be located within the lot. The footprint may or may not include the dimensions of the outer walls. In some cases a floorplan is included separately with the survey and indicates the wall dimensions and the location of windows and doors (Fig. 2–15).

Right-of-Way

The **Right-of-Way** (R/W) is a strip of land that is publicly owned, which includes the street and ground up to the front property line of the lot (Fig. 2–16). The width of the R/W varies, but it is often about 50 feet. Visualize the R/W by drawing an imaginary line down the middle of the street. This would be the middle of the R/W. Thus, the R/W would extend 25 feet in each direction of the line, a total of 50 feet wide.

If there is a public sidewalk running parallel with the street, the front property line is normally located just before the sidewalk. The sidewalk would be located in the R/W. In neighborhoods with no public sidewalks, the R/W may not even be noticeable. It would be approximately 10 feet, depending on R/W width, of turf that runs from the curb and appears like the front yard.

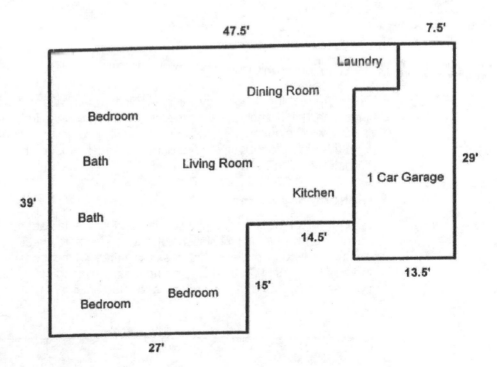

Figure 2–15 **Footprint**
An example of a house floorplan.

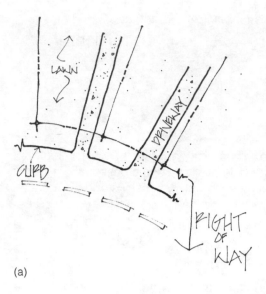

(a)

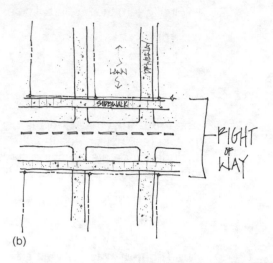

(b)

***Figure 2–16* Right-of-Way**
(a) The Right-of-Way (R/W) is the strip of land where the road and sidewalk are located. (b) The property line is usually located right at the edge of the sidewalk. (c) Where there is no sidewalk, the R/W is part of the front yard, usually 10 feet from the curb. Notice where the fence is located on the neighboring corner lot.

(c)

Be aware that the site survey will not indicate the R/W and curb, but only the property lines of the lot. Do not make the mistake of identifying the front property line as the curb. If a sidewalk is not present, the curb is usually another 10 feet or so, depending on R/W from the front property line. If you draw the design using the front property line as the curb, the design will be misrepresented.

Right-of-Way Access

Be aware that the city or county street department has access to the R/W and can excavate it for repairs or installations. It is a good idea to check with the local government before planting or making changes in this area. In most cases, they will ask that nothing be planted in it. At the least, do not plant anything of significant size or construct a permanent structure that cannot be relocated easily.

Tip Box

Include the Right-of-Way in the plan drawing. The site survey only shows the property line, while the front yard may actually extend another 10' to the curb.

Easement

An **easement** is a strip of land on the property that others have access to. This is primarily the case with utility companies that locate or install cable or drainage (Fig. 2–17).

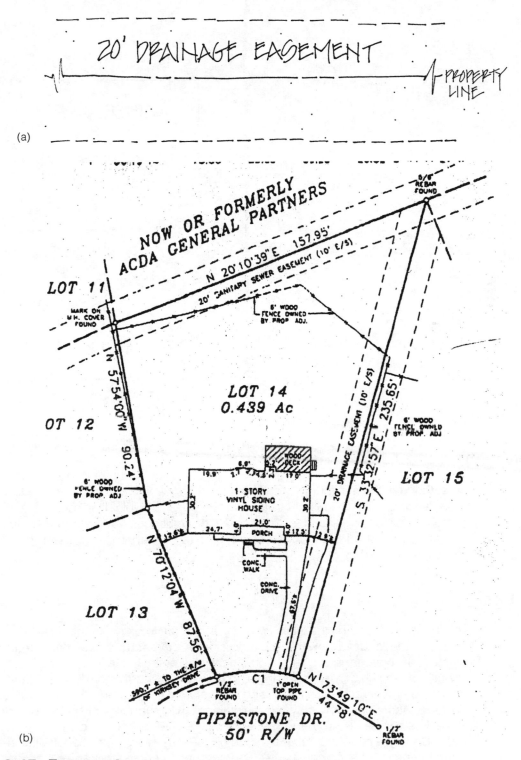

Figure 2–17 Easement

(a) An easement is an area along the property line that other authorities have legal access to, usually utility companies. Do not construct permanent objects in an easement, although fences are typically permitted.
(b) An easement is located on this site survey along the back and right property lines.

***Figure 2–18* Setback**
A setback is the distance from the front, side, and back property lines where construction can take place. The house must be located within the setback.

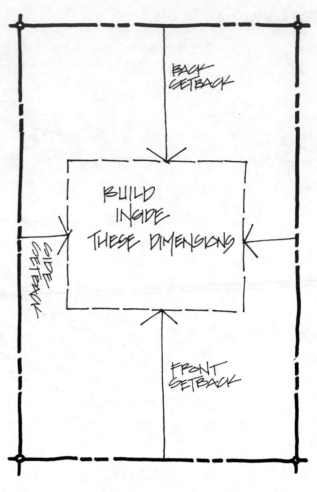

Setback

A **setback** is the minimum distance from a property line that any permanent construction can take place although this information does not typically appear on a site survey. Setbacks are included in the set of building ordinances that keep houses a specified distance from the front (front setback), side (side setback), and back property lines (back setback) (Fig. 2–18).

Covenants

Although not found on the site survey, it is important to be aware of restrictions that may apply to the landscape within a subdivision. A **covenant,** sometimes referred to as a **restrictive covenant,** is a legal agreement created by the land developer that a homeowner enters into when purchasing a house within a subdivision. These agreements are meant to preserve the quality of living and value of the property. Such restrictions could include plants and how they are maintained, minimum cost of house, color of house (even the shingles), and parking spaces (no cars in the front yard). This could keep the pink flamingos out of the neighborhood (Fig. 2–19). Most states require the seller to inform the buyer of such covenants. It is important to be aware if any covenants apply to the site and what they are. The owners should be aware of these; if they are not then contact the builder of the house.

Figure 2-19 Covenant
Covenants may restrict landscaping, such as the use of pink flamingos or certain plants and colors.

Obtaining the Site Survey

Most residents are given a copy of the site survey upon closing of the house which is often required by the lender to verify the property, which is why this document is commonly referred to as a mortgage plat. Make every effort to obtain a copy of this document; otherwise, it will take additional time and effort for you to draw an accurate plan to design. If the client cannot locate a copy, the county surveyor will most likely have a copy on file.

Tip Box

Locating the Site Survey

Look at the following locations to find the site survey:

    Closing papers

    County surveyor

    Architect of the house

    General contractor who built the house

    Mortgage company

Proofread the Site Survey

Take a few measurements to make sure that the site survey is accurate and up to date. This could save hours of wasted time and embarrassment. Additions or renovations since the last survey could change the accuracy of the site survey.

Measurements

Measurements of the property will be needed to locate objects and lay out the ground plan of the site. It's important to be accurate since the site survey will not always include all the objects or areas on site.

To take measurements, the following items will be needed:

- Clipboard

- Measuring wheel: This is the most convenient way to take measurements, but it may not work if the terrain is extremely rough or objects are in the way (Fig. 2–20).

- Measuring tape: 100′ or 200′ long (Fig. 2–21)

- Screwdriver: To hold the tape in place

Figure 2–20 **Measuring Wheel**
(a) A measuring wheel is a quick and easy way to get distance measurements. (b) A counter records the distance as the wheel turns.

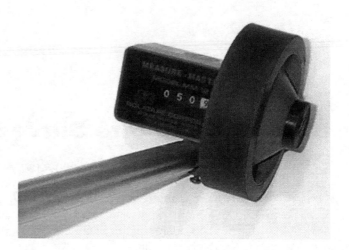

(a)

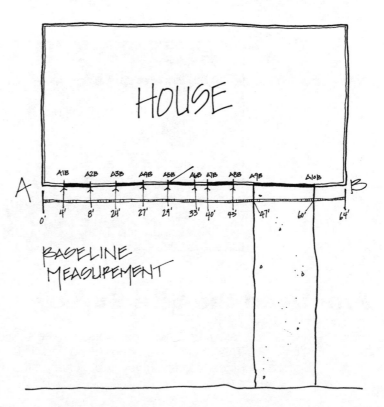

(b)

***Figure 2–21* Tape Measure**
(a) A measuring tape can be used to get measurements, ideally a 200-foot tape. (b) Measurements might
be in feet and inches or feet and decimals of a foot. Be
sure you know which unit is used. (c) Hold tape tight for
accurate measurement.

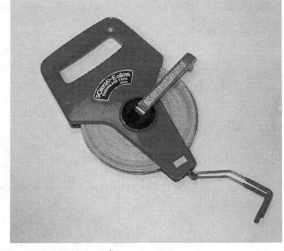

(a)

(b)

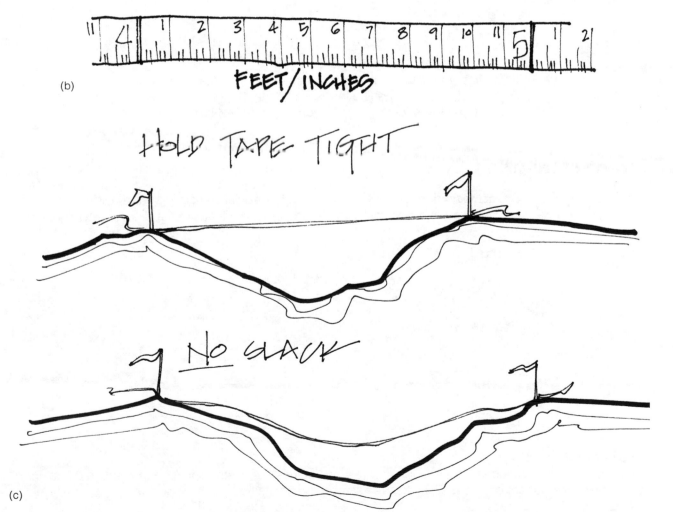

(c)

Units of Measurement

Know what units your equipment is measuring. Tape measures and measuring wheels will measure in feet/inches or decimals of a foot. Most field measurements do not need to be this accurate, but be familiar with the difference. Some feel that recording measurements in decimals is easier than inches because it uses one unit of measurement, feet, instead of two units, feet and inches, although this is primarily preference.

> ### *Tip Box*
> 22' 4" is not the same as 22.4'; 0.4' is equivalent to 4.8".

Converting the units is very simple. Since there are 12 inches in 1 foot, converting utilizes a factor of 12.

Converting Inches to Decimals

Divide inches by 12

$4'' \div 12 = .33'$

Converting Decimals to Inches

Multiply decimal by 12

$0.4 \times 12 = 4.8''$

Pacing

If you find yourself without a measuring tape or wheel, train your pace to equal 3 feet (Fig. 2–22). For most people this is a stride that is a little longer than their normal pace. Practice **pacing** a few times to get an accurate feel for a 3-foot step. Measure off a 30-foot course and practice a pace that will complete it in ten 3-foot steps.

Direct Measuring

Direct measuring is simply measuring from one point to another. If you are using a tape measurement, pull the tape tight. Any slack in the tape will skew the measurement (Fig. 2–21a).

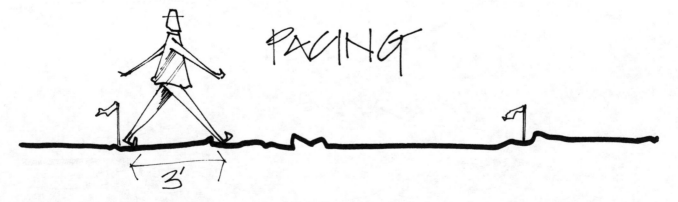

Figure 2–22 Pacing
Pacing is a quick technique to get a rough estimate of distance. Each step should approximate 3 feet. Practice pacing on a 30-foot course until it takes ten steps to complete it.

Baseline Measurement

Baseline measurement is the quickest way to obtain several measurements along one line (Fig. 2–23). It reduces the need to move the tape and minimizes compounding errors.

Obtaining Measurements Using a Baseline

To obtain measurements using a baseline, start at one end of the line and pull the measuring tape tight to the end of the line. At each point along the line, locate and record the measurement on the tape. Laying down the tape measure once can avoid re-staking the tape measure and compounding errors from one measurement to the next. If using a measuring wheel, start at zero and stop at each point to record the measurement, although it can be difficult to hold the wheel and write at the same time. Do not re-zero the wheel. Continue to the next point and record. Repeat until the end of the line is reached.

A good example would be locating the windows and door along the front of the house. Stake the tape measure on one corner of the house and pull it tight to the other corner. Starting at zero, locate the first edge of the first window and record the measurement on the tape. Next, record the measurement of the second edge of the window. Continue along the tape measure until you mark everything to the opposite corner. If using a measuring wheel, start at zero and stop at the first edge to record the measurement and continue on without re-zeroing the wheel.

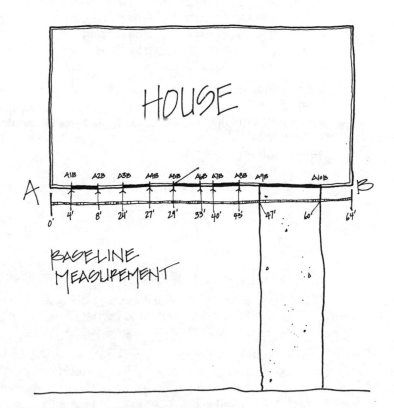

***Figure 2–23* Baseline Measuring**
Baseline measuring is taking measurements along a straight line starting at zero and recording each measurement without starting over at zero. It is more efficient and reduces errors from compounding when starting over at each point.

Recording Baseline Measurements

To keep measurements orderly, record them as follows.

The beginning and end of the line can be labeled with letters.

Zero mark: A   **End mark:** B

If more than one baseline measurement is taken on site, the letters can continue with C, D, etc.

The measurements between line A–B are numbered in order (1, 2, 3 . . .) as follows:

A1B = 4'   A6B = 33'

A2B = 8'   A7B = 40'

A3B = 24'   A8B = 43'

A4B = 27'   A9B = 47'

A5B = 29'   A10B = 60'

AB = 64' (Referring to the entire line)

Triangulation

Triangulation is a very useful way of locating objects on the property. **Triangulation** is the application of locating an unknown point from two known points (Fig. 2–24). In most cases there will be a house on the property that has two known points that can be used. Any other permanent structure such as a fence, curb, or storage shed can be used as a known point (Fig. 2–25).

Let's use the corners of a house as point A and point B (the same two points used in the previous example for baseline measurement). In the front yard there is a tree, we'll call point T. (If more than one tree is to be located, then label each tree T1, T2, T3, etc.) Point T can be located in its exact location in relation to the house from corners A and B.

1. Direct measure the distance from each known point to the unknown point.

    AT = 32'

    BT = 43'

    Point T (tree) can now be located from the footprint of the house.

2. Using a compass, adjust the legs to equal 43' in the scale of the base map. Stick the compass point into corner B and strike an arc with the lead across the approximate area where point T will be located.

3. Next, adjust the compass to equal 32' in the same scale. Stick the point into corner A and strike an arc with the lead so that it *crosses the first arc*. Where the intersection of the two arcs occurs is the exact location of point T in relation to points A and B (the corners of the house).

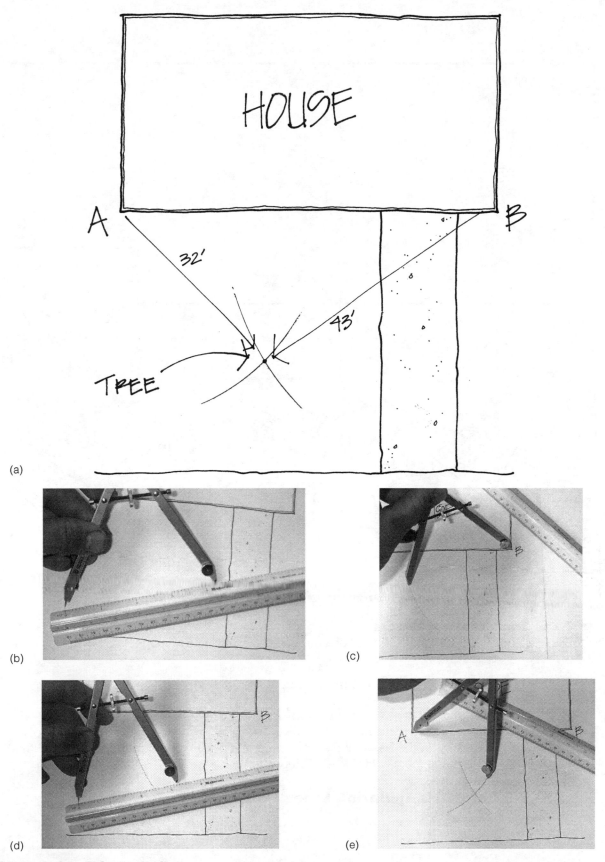

(a)

(b)

(c)

(d)

(e)

Figure 2-24 Triangulation

(a) Triangulation is locating an unknown point from two known points. An example would be locating a tree from two corners of a house. Label the corners A and B and measure the distance to the tree from each corner. (b) A compass is adjusted to scale to equal 43 feet and (c) an arc is struck from point B. (d) The compass is adjusted to equal 32 feet and (e) an arc is struck from point A, and where those two arcs cross is the location of the tree.

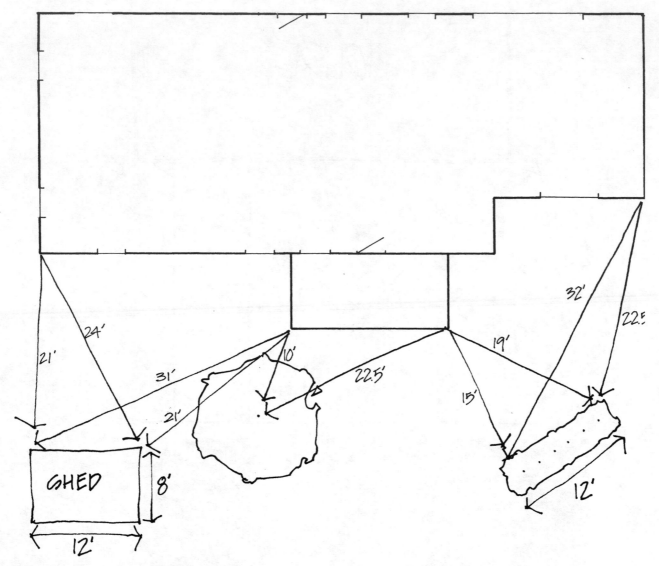

Figure 2–25 Triangulating Objects
In addition to trees being located, the corners of objects, such as a shed and a hedge, can be located to orient.

Triangulating a Curve

Triangulation can also be used to draw the curve of a curb or bed (Fig. 2–26). By randomly locating several points along the curve and triangulating them, the points can be drawn on the base map and then connected. Of course, the more points that are located, the more accurately the curve can be drawn.

Long Triangulation Lines

Students may run into the problem of triangulation lines that exceed the span of their compass. Without larger equipment, the arcs cannot be accurately marked with a standard compass.

Beam Compass or Extender Bar   A beam compass and extender bar have much wider spans that can be used to strike long arcs (Fig. 2–27). A **beam compass** is a long rod that has a point and a lead that can be slid up and down to adjust the length of the radius. An **extender bar** can be inserted into the end of the compass to increase the radius.

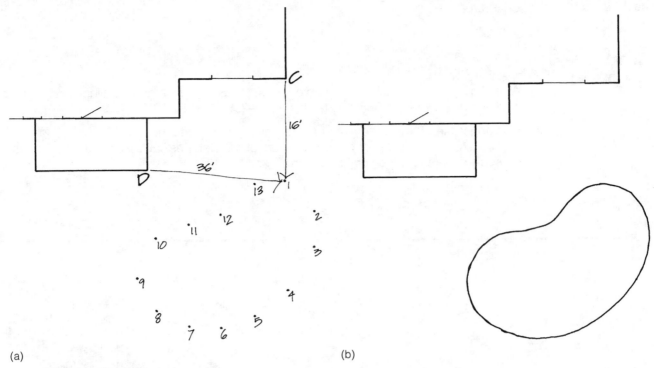

(a)

(b)

Figure 2–26 Triangulating a Curve

(a) A curve can be located by triangulating random points and then (b) connecting the dots. Of course, the more points triangulated, the more accurate the curve.

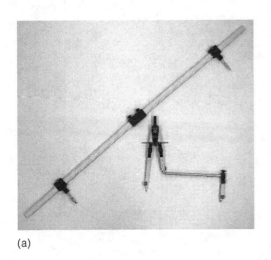

(a)

(b)

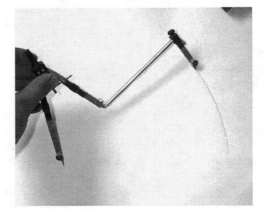

(c)

Figure 2–27 Beam Compass and Extender Bar

(a) For triangulating lines that exceed the capacity of the standard compass a beam compass (left) or extender bar attachment (right) can be used. (b) Beam compass. (c) Extender bar.

Grid

A **grid** can be useful to locate an object or accurately draw a ground plane area, such as the curving shape of existing beds (Fig. 2–28).

Use an existing form to measure parallel lines at measured intervals. The existing form can be a house, building, or curb. The length of parallel lines can be used to mark points along the curve and then connect them.

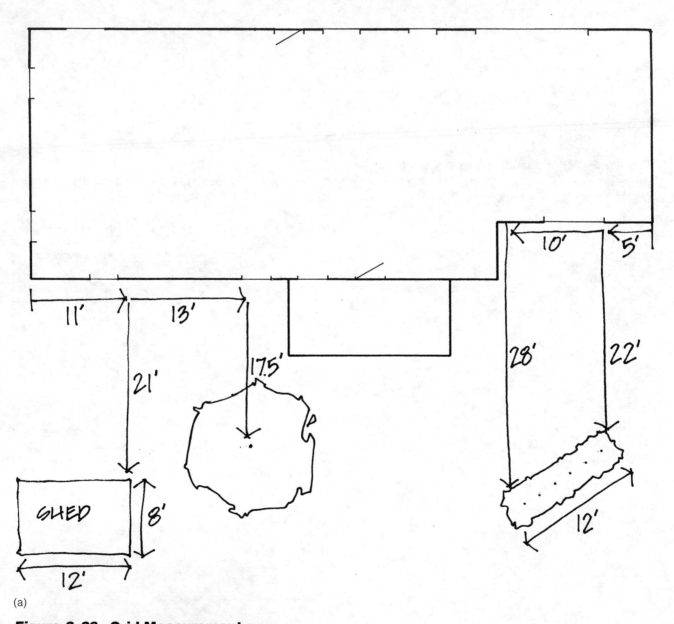

(a)

***Figure 2–28* Grid Measurement**
Another approach to locating objects is grid measurement. (a) Measure perpendicular from a permanent object, such as house or curb, to an unknown object.

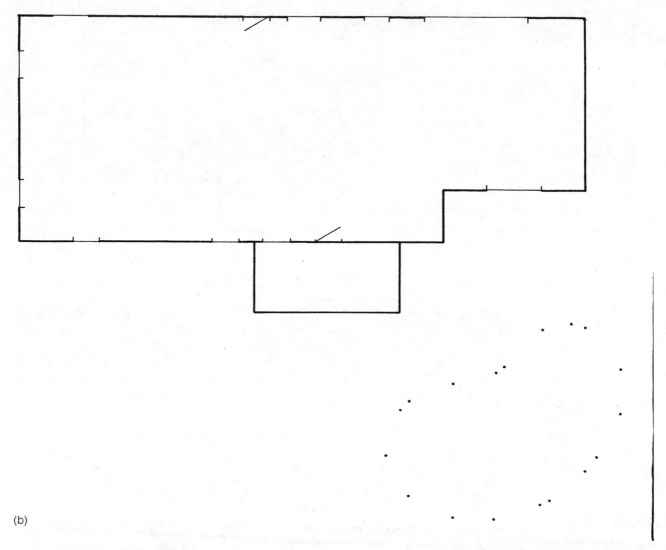

(b)

Figure 2-28 Grid Measurement—continued
Another approach to locating objects is grid measurement. (b) Locating a curve can be done by locating random points on the curve.

(Continues)

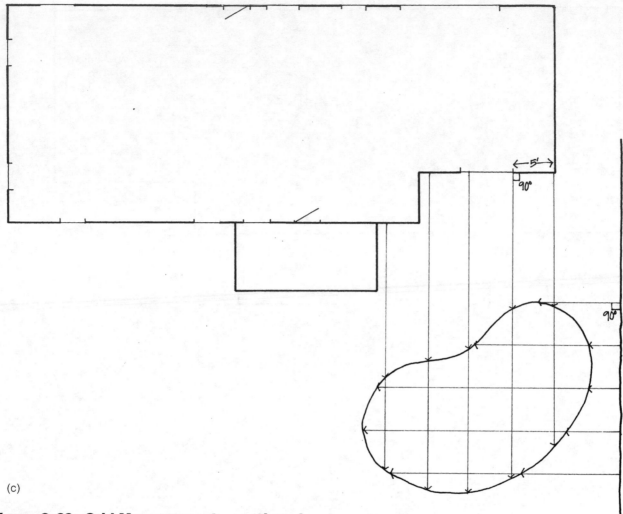

(c)

Figure 2–28 Grid Measurement—continued
Another approach to locating objects is grid measurement. (c) Connecting the dots.

What to Locate on Site

Items to be located on site:

Existing trees, shrubs, and other objects Method: Triangulation, grid

Dimensions of additions, such as decks or storage sheds Method: Direct measurement for dimensions; triangulating corners of additions that stand separate from house

Windows and doors on house Method: Baseline measurement

Sidewalks, driveway, beds, or other permanent fixtures Method: Triangulation, grid, and direct measurement

Property stakes from house (to locate the footprint on the lot) Method: Triangulation

Creating the Base Map

With all the measurements and site survey, the **base map** can be drawn in a scale that will be appropriate for the plan drawing. The base map is a plan drawing that includes all pertinent objects and areas on the property that will impact the design not found on the site survey. Some refer to this plan as a **site plan.**

The site survey acquired from the client will most likely be on an 8.5″ × 11″ sheet of paper, or similar size. Typically, this scale will not be large enough to design because the details would be difficult to read.

Instead, increase the scale of the plan drawing. In most cases, a scale of 1/8″ = 1′ or larger will be appropriate. If using an engineer scale, 1″ = 10′ or less will be appropriate. A 24″ × 36″ sheet of tracing paper will serve as the initial drawing for the base map, which can be transferred to vellum later, although smaller sizes of paper can be used depending on the detail of the project and the size of the property.

> ### Tip Box
>
> Draw the base map in a scale large enough so that detail is adequate to read. Most commonly used scales are 1/8″ = 1′ (architect) and 1″ = 10′ (engineer).

Printing Site Survey

One of the easiest ways to get the base map drawn to a larger scale is to have a blueprinter increase the size of the site survey (Fig. 2–29).

Every time the site survey is *doubled,* the scale is *reduced by half.* For instance, if the original scale is 1″ = 40′, then doubling it (200 percent) will make the scale 1″ = 20′. Having that survey doubled again (200 percent) would make the scale 1″ = 10′. (If the original survey were increased 400 percent, it would get the same result, Fig. 2–30.)

> ### Tip Box
>
> Every time the site survey is doubled in size, the working scale will be reduced by half.

Scanning Site Survey

A very simple approach to increase the size of the site survey is to use a standard flatbed scanner. This can be done with a home office scanner, however, you will be limited to the size of the original site survey. Most residential surveys are on a standard 8.5″ × 11″ sheet of paper or slightly larger, but commercial surveys may be too large. Scan the survey at 100 dpi (dots per inch) resolution.

Figure 2–29 Enlarging the Site Survey

Having a printer enlarge the site survey (original size in the lower middle of the enlarged) is an easy way to enlarge the base map to scale. Every time the survey is doubled, the scale is reduced by half.

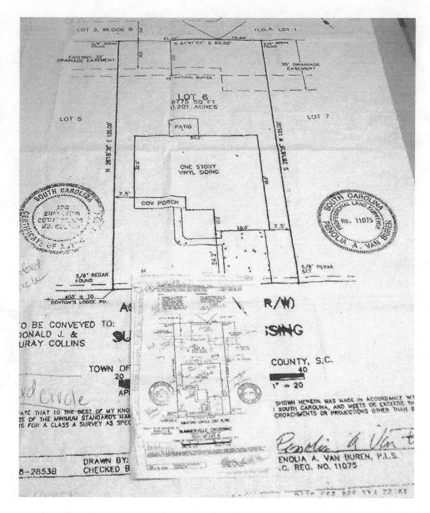

Figure 2–30 Enlarging Scale

Existing Scale	Convert to 1/8″ scale	Convert to 1/4″ scale	Convert to 10-scale	Convert to 20-scale
10-scale	1.25×	2.5×		
20-scale	2.5×	5×	2×	
30-scale	3.75×	7.5×	3×	1.5×
40-scale	5×	10×	4×	2×
50-scale	6.25×	12.5×	5×	2.5×
60-scale	7.5×	15×	6×	3×

Surveys are drawn in an engineering scale. Shortcuts to enlarging original scale (for left column) to the 1/8″, 1/4″, 10-scale, or 20-scale.

Once the survey is scanned as a digital image, it can be enlarged digitally and printed, even on a home office printer. Any graphics program can be used, but for Windows users, use the Paint program (it comes with Windows) and follow these directions:

Open the Paint program (Start Menu/Programs/Accessories/Paint)

Open scanned survey (File/Open)

Go to Image and select Stretch/Skew command

Enlarge the survey desired size (see Fig. 2–30)

If the original survey is a 30-scale (1″ = 30′), increase vertical and horizontal 300% to change the scale to a 10-scale (1″ = 10′)

Go to Page Setup (File/Page Setup) and verify, in lower right corner, it is set at: *Adjust to: 100% normal size*

Go to Print (File/Print)

The enlarged survey will print on several pages that can be lined up and taped together like a puzzle (Fig. 2–31). Verify the desired scale is correct by checking a known distance. Place tracing paper over the survey and draw the enlarged survey.

Correcting Scale

In some cases, the survey scale is incorrect. This is often the result of the survey being reduced or increased at a copy machine when it is faxed or used for storage. A few calculations can correct the scale.

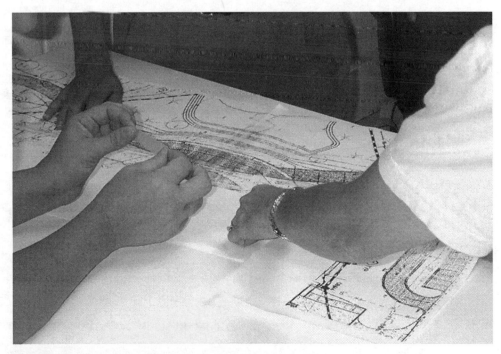

Figure 2–31 Scanning Survey
Students are taping together an enlarged site survey after it was scanned and printed on an office printer.

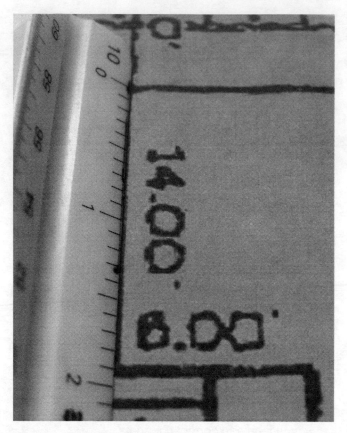

***Figure 2–32* Correcting Scale**
The line should be 14′ on the 10-scale but measures 19′ because the plan size has
been enlarged.

Identify a known measurement on the survey. For instance, find a line on the house
and note the correct length. In the example, the line should be 14′ long. Using an engineer or architect scale, find a scale that is closest to 14′ when placed on the line.
In the example, an engineer scale (10-scale) is used. The line measures 19′ instead
of 14′ (Fig. 2–32). Now calculate the amount to increase or decrease the size of the
survey so the 14′ line will equal 14′ on the 10-scale.

EXAMPLE   *Divide the correct length of the line by the measurement on the scale*

In our example, divide 14 by 19 = 0.74 or 74%

This means the current size of the survey is reduced 74 percent in order to be
corrected. By opening the scanned image of the survey, reduce by 74 percent and
print.

Another example would be if the survey is smaller than the correct scale. In this case,
the line that should be 14′ is now measuring 9′ on a 10-scale (Fig. 2–33).

14 divided by 9 = 1.6 or 160%

The current size of the scanned survey should be increased 160 percent to correct
the scale.

Once the scale is correct, see the previous section (scanning site survey) to create a
workable scale.

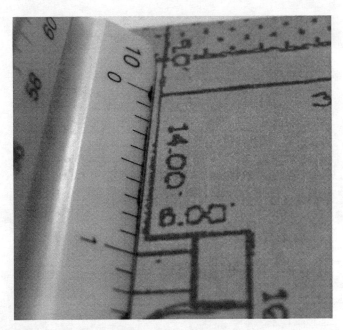

***Figure 2–33* Correcting Scale**
The line should be 14′ on a 10-scale but measures 9′ because the plan size has been
reduced.

Tip Box

Digital Camera Instead of a Scanner

If a scanner is not available, a digital camera can be used to change the
scale. By taking a photo of the survey and downloading the image, the scale
can be corrected.

Drawing the Base Map

If a printer is not available to increase the size of the site survey, it can be drawn to a
larger scale (Fig. 2–34).

Property Lines

Start by drawing the property lines. Use tracing paper to allow for notes and mistakes.
It can be transferred to vellum later.

It is important to draw the corners at the correct angle because not all property corners
are going to be 90 degrees. A simple approach to drawing the property lines is to slide
the original site survey underneath the tracing paper and line up the corners. Once the
angle of the line has been started, the entire length of the line can be drawn to scale.
Continue this until all the property lines have been completed (Fig. 2–35).

Footprint

On a separate piece of tracing paper, draw the footprint of the house. Include the location of the windows and doors.

In most cases, the corners of the footprint are square. Therefore, the 90-degree corner
of a triangle can be used to draw them.

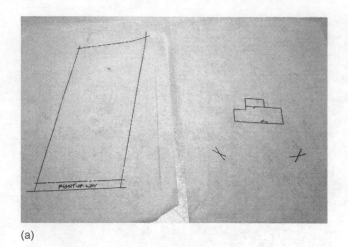

(a)

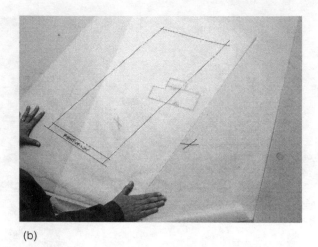

(b)

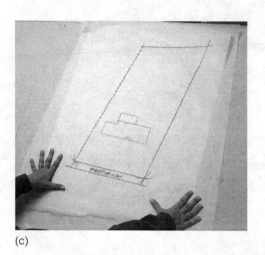

(c)

(d)

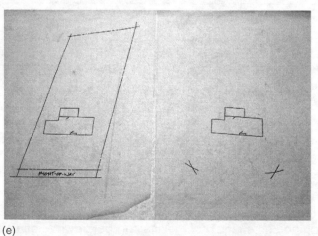

(e)

Figure 2–34 **Drawing the Base Map**

(a) If the base map has to be drawn to a larger scale, start by drawing the property lines on one piece of paper (left) and the footprint (right) on another piece. The footprint should have the property stakes triangulated on it. (b) Slide the footprint and property stakes underneath the property lines. (c) Then, line up the property stakes (below) with the property corners (above) to orient the footprint on the property. (d) Transfer the footprint onto the above sheet with the property lines (e) to finish.

Figure 2–35 **Drawing Property Lines**

Many properties will not have square corners. A quick way to duplicate the angle is to slide the site survey underneath the paper and start the line. Then it can be drawn to desired length.

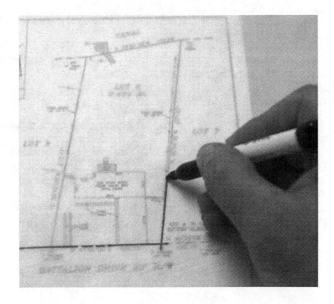

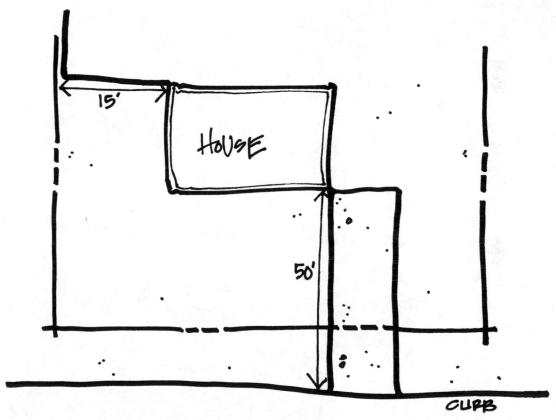

Figure 2–36 **Locating Points to Center Footprint**

If property stakes cannot be located, measure to other permanent points to center the footprint. Examples include where the driveway meets the curb or to a fence (usually located close to the property line).

Property Stakes

On the footprint, locate the property stakes that were triangulated from the house. If you cannot locate the property stakes, then triangulate to another permanent point, such as where the driveway meets the street (Fig. 2–36).

Locate the Footprint on the Lot

With the sheet of property lines laying flat on the table, slide the sheet with the footprint underneath. Rotate the footprint until the property stakes on the footprint are located directly under the corners of the property lines. This will orient the footprint within the property lines. Trace the footprint on the sheet with the property lines.

Add Other Objects and Areas

Any other objects or areas that were located on site can now be located on the base map (Fig. 2–37). This might include triangulating existing trees, the grid location of existing beds and driveway, or noting the location of windows and doors.

This completes the base map with property lines and footprint. This can now be slid underneath higher quality paper, such as vellum, to trace and begin designing.

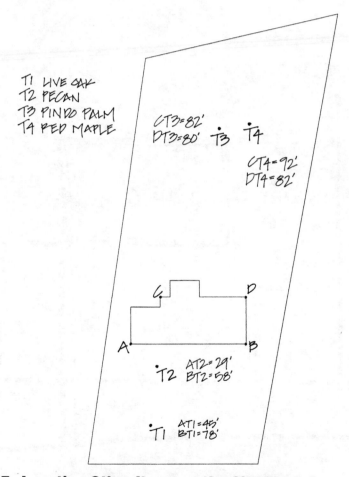

Figure 2–37 **Locating Other Items on the Site Plan**
After the base map is drawn, locate other objects that will remain or have an impact on the design.

Tip Box

Some designers, after transferring the base map to vellum, will add the border and title block (see Chapter 7) and make multiple copies on vellum for the preliminary design, master plan, or other plans. This is referred to as a **base sheet** (Fig. 2–38). This way the base map does not need to be redrawn multiple times.

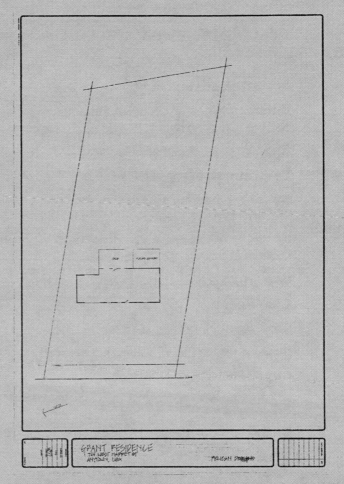

Figure 2–38 Base Sheet
Make multiple copies of base map with border and title block so base map doesn't have to be redrawn.

Summary

A plan drawing is a two-dimensional drawing of an area that appears like a bird's-eye view looking from directly overhead. It will be the map on which the design is illustrated. A lot is a plan drawing that includes the property lines, while a base map includes more information such as the location of the footprint, driveway, fences, deck, and other objects. Most clients will have a copy of a site survey of their property, which was included in the closing papers when the house was purchased. Site measurements will have to be taken to locate existing objects not included on the site survey. A tape measure or measure wheel can be used to take direct or baseline measurements, while triangulation or grid measurements can be used to locate objects on the base map. A site survey can be increased in size by a printer and kept to scale; each time it is doubled in size the scale is reduced by half. The base map can also be drawn to scale by selecting a working scale and drawing the property lines on one page and the footprint with property stakes on a separate page that can be slid under the property lines, lining up the property stakes with property corners to properly center the footprint.

Key Terms

Architect scale: based on units of an inch

B lead: designates softer lead that draws thicker, darker lines; the higher the number, the softer the lead

Base map: a plan that includes all objects on site pertinent to the design

Base sheet: the base map with border and title block added to make multiple copies

Baseline measurement: obtains several measurements along one line; it reduces the need to move the tape and minimizes compounding errors

Beam compass: a long rod that has a point and a lead that can be slid up and down to adjust the length of the radius

Bearings: indicate the orientation of property lines

Bumwad: see tracing paper

Closing survey: see site survey

Compass: used to draw large circles or strike arcs for site plan preparation

Covenant: a legal agreement created by the land developer that a homeowner enters into when purchasing a house within a subdivision; sometimes referred to as a restrictive covenant

Direct measurement: measuring from one point to another

Drawing pencils: wooden pencils without an eraser at the end; inexpensive and easy to handle

Easement: strip of land on the property that others have access to

Engineer scale: based on unit increments in an inch

Extender bar: inserted into the end of the compass to increase the radius

Film: see Mylar

Floorplan: see footprint

Footprint: layout of the house plan

Full sheet: 24″ × 36″ dimensions; typical for most projects

Grid: use an existing form to measure parallel lines at measured intervals to locate points

Grid paper: has non-photo gridlines that do not show up on a copy

H lead: designates hard lead that will draw thin, lighter lines; the higher the number, the harder the lead

Half sheet: 18″ × 24″ dimensions

Ink: provides excellent line quality

Lead: good medium for beginners because it can be easily erased

Lead-holder: operates like a mechanical pencil but holds larger sticks of lead

Lot: refers to a plan drawing of the property that includes property lines and bearings

Markers: used to draw with ink

Mechanical pencil: holds various thicknesses of lead (from 0.5 mm to 0.9 mm), which does not need to be sharpened

Mortgage plat: see site survey

Mylar: high-quality paper that is actually drafting film used for the final plan; often used when drawing with ink

Onionskin: see tracing paper

Pacing: an estimation technique for measuring distance; each step is approximately equal to 3 feet

Pigment liners: fiber-tip markers that have a variety of line widths; relatively inexpensive and disposable

Plan drawing: two-dimensional drawing that appears like a bird's-eye view looking from directly overhead

Plan view drawing: see plan drawing

Plat: refers to a site survey of the resident's property

Property lines: define the site boundaries

Property stakes: locate the beginning and end of a property line

Quarter sheet: 12″ × 18″ dimensions

Rag vellum: see vellum paper

Restrictive covenant: see covenant

Right-of-Way: strip of land that is publicly owned, which includes the street and ground up to the front property line of the lot

Scale: ruler that has units to represent feet in the plan drawing

Setback: the minimum distance from a property line that any permanent construction can take place

Site plan: sometimes used to refer to base map

Site survey: surveyor's map of the property

Technical pen: has a tip made of metal and an ink reservoir; relatively expensive

Tracing paper: thin translucent, low-quality paper used to sketch ideas

Trash paper: see tracing paper

Triangulation: an unknown point that is located from two known points; a useful way of locating objects on the property

Vellum paper: high-quality, translucent paper used for the final plan

3 Inventory and Analysis

Objectives

- Know the process of collecting and analyzing inventory
- Understand the role of analysis in the landscape design
- Learn the importance of circulation, views, and site conditions

Information about the site needs to be gathered and evaluated. This is the process of **inventory** and **analysis,** which some refer to as **needs assessment.** The interview revealed the clients' needs and wants and the next step for the designer is to study the site; assess the strengths and weaknesses; and while considering the clients' needs and wishes, develop a plan of action (Fig. 3–1).

Taking inventory of the site involves recording what already exists on-site. This is similar to the storeowner who takes inventory of what is sitting on the shelves. There is no direction or possible solutions taken at this point, just collecting and recording information.

From the inventory, the analysis will develop. The inventory will be evaluated to determine what changes or actions need to be made. The analysis uncovers the problems and the potentials. The inventory is evaluated for areas that are problems and need to be corrected, as well as potentials that can be utilized in the design. This, as mentioned, will be the basis for a plan of action to develop a functional, aesthetic landscape design.

> ### *Tip Box*
>
> *Inventory* is fact.
>
> *Analysis* is evaluation and action.

Items Needed

- Site survey
- Clipboard

Use the site survey to take notes (Fig. 3–2). It's often much easier to take inventory on the map than with written notes. Taking data in the backyard can be quickly noted on that part of the map as opposed to the front yard. If a site survey is not available at the time of the inventory, then rough sketch the site. Although it's not to scale, the notes will make sense.

Inventory and Analysis

The following are areas and situations to make note of for inventory and analysis.

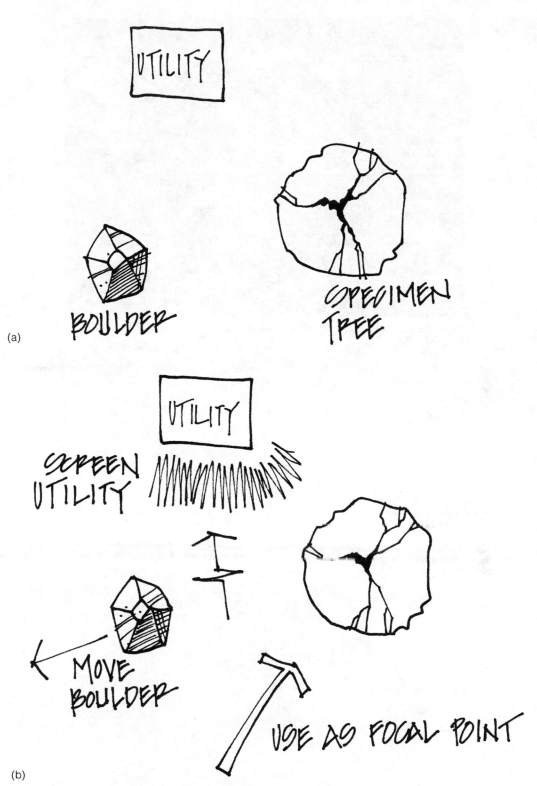

Figure 3–1 Inventory and Analysis
(a) Inventory is recording what is present on site, or observing problem areas such as poor views. (b) Analysis is taking action in response to the inventory.

(a)

(b)

Figure 3–2 **Observations**
(a) Using a clipboard, take the inventory and notes concerning the analysis while on-site. (b) Using the site survey makes it easier to take notes.

(a)

(b)

Figure 3–3 **Window Height**
(a) Make observations of window height to avoid plants that will block views; (b) use plants that are low growing.

House

Color of the House and Materials

This may have a large impact on the color of paving material, such as repeating the bricks used in the foundation as a border along the flagstone entry walk.

Locate Doors and Windows

- Doors will impact circulation patterns
- Windows will have an effect on the plant size. Avoid placing large shrubs in front of windows which will screen the view as well as create a security hazard (Fig. 3–3). Measuring from the ground to the bottom of the window will facilitate plant selection.

Identify Rooms (Fig. 3–4)

- Bathrooms and bedrooms will be more private with views through windows.
- Kitchen and living room will utilize views to outdoors.

Circulation

Parking

Assess whether there is enough room to accommodate the clients' parking needs (Fig. 3–5).

Primary Paths

Identify the major routes of foot traffic, such as the entry walk (Fig. 3–6). Note how guests would comfortably approach the house from the road.

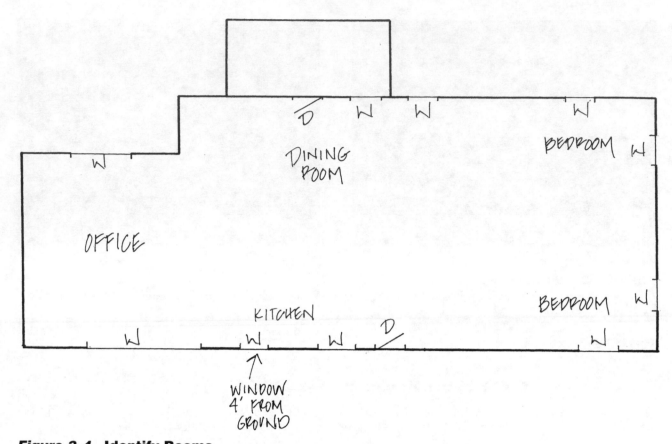

Figure 3-4 Identify Rooms

Make note of rooms on the floor plan that will impact views and circulation.

Figure 3-5 Parking

Observe if parking space meets needs.

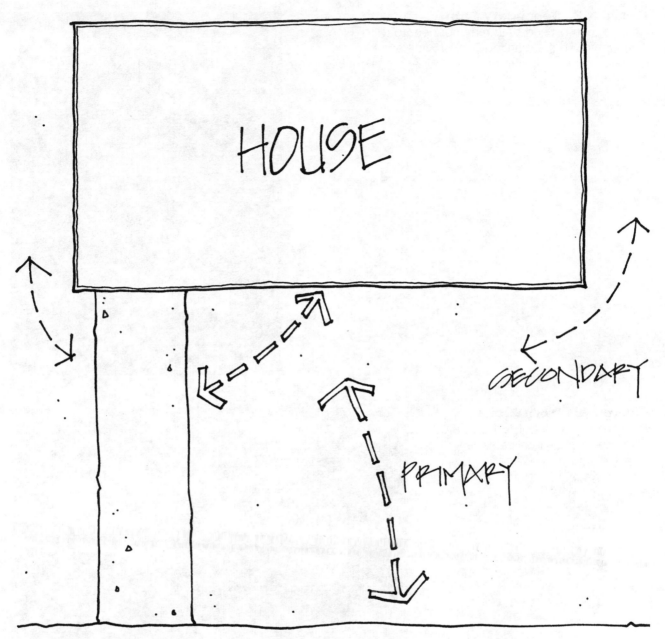

Figure 3–6 **Circulation**
Observe path of circulation, or foot traffic. Make note of paths that are primary, frequently traveled (large arrows) and secondary, infrequently used (small arrows).

Secondary Paths

Identify areas of infrequent foot traffic, such as around the side of the house or to the back door (Fig. 3–7).

Pavement

Note whether the pavement for vehicular and pedestrian traffic is sufficient for the purpose. Areas of worn grass may indicate a need for a harder, more permanent surface (Fig. 3–8).

***Figure 3-7* Secondary Path**
An infrequently used path may not need paving. Flagstones through the planting bed provide an open area for residents to walk out the front door and straight into the front yard.

***Figure 3-8* Worn Areas**
Take note of areas of turf that are worn down from foot traffic which may indicate a need for a harder, more permanent surface.

Utilities (Fig. 3-9)

Septic Tanks

A **septic tank** is a private sewage treatment plant for an individual residence, often found in rural areas where houses are far enough apart that a public sewer system would be too expensive (Fig. 3-10). If the clients have a septic tank, then note the location. Large trees can rapidly plug a septic tank with roots and prevent it from draining, especially trees that love water like willows!

Figure 3-9 Utilities

Note the location of utilities and other objects that may need to be screened from view or carefully avoided.

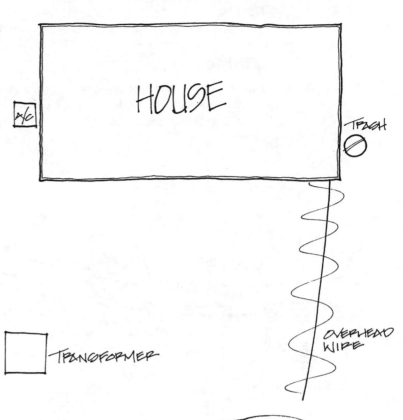

Figure 3-10 Septic Tank

Avoid planting trees near a septic tank, which would clog it with roots.

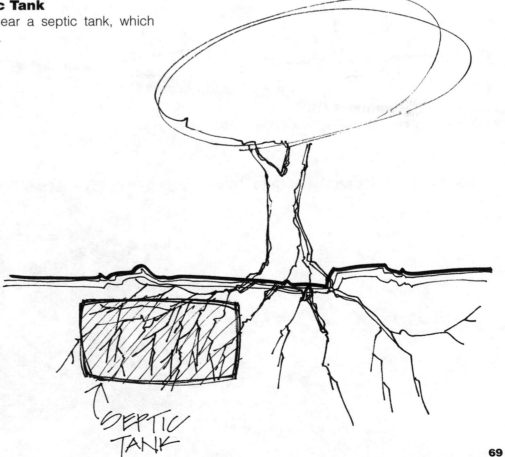

Overhead Lines

Note the location and approximate height of **overhead lines,** or power lines, that run to the house or along the road to avoid planting large trees under them (Fig. 3–11).

Utilities

Air-conditioning units are often noisy and unsightly (Fig. 3–12). Note their location to visually screen and allow space for ventilation. Other utilities include electrical boxes, pumps, gas meters, or cable boxes.

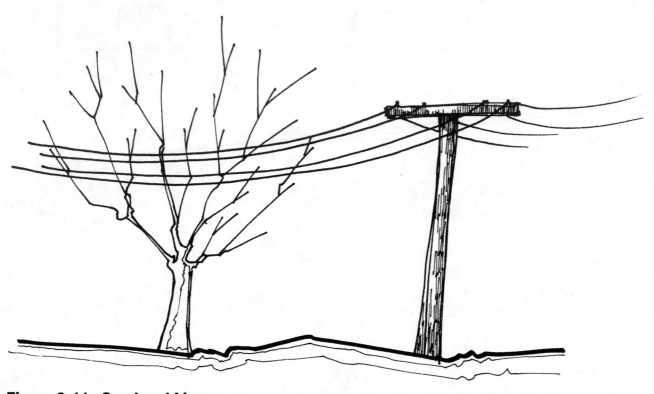

Figure 3–11   Overhead Lines
Avoid planting trees that will grow into overhead power lines.

Figure 3–12   Air Conditioner and Other Utilities
The A/C unit can often be a noisy, visual problem in the side or backyard.

Trash Cans

Trash cans are also unsightly but need to have adequate access from the house and to the curb for pickup (Fig. 3–13). Note where trash cans are stored and the path used to access and move them.

Storage Areas

Like trash cans, **storage areas** can be unsightly but accessible. Locate areas used to store materials or equipment, whether it's a shed or out in the open (Fig. 3–14).

Figure 3–13 **Trash Cans**
Ideally, trash cans are not pleasing to see but they need to be accessible. This home-owner built a fence panel to hide the trash from the street.

Figure 3–14 **Storage**
Storage area is important; it is often a place where equipment is stored and locked. It should be accessible but not become a visual problem.

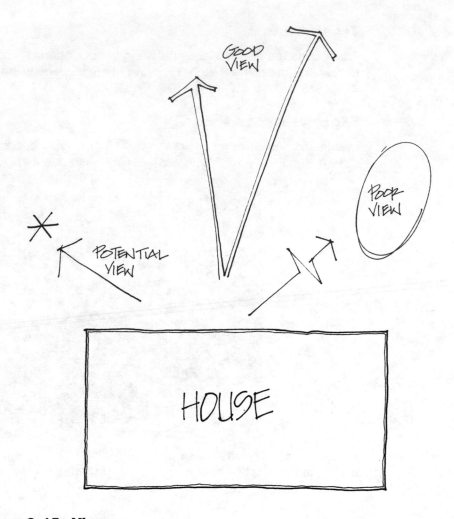

Figure 3–15 Views
Three important types of views should be studied: poor views that will need to be blocked, good views that need to be maintained, and potential views that are locations where a good view should be created.

Views (Fig. 3–15)

Poor Views

Note distasteful views. They could include

- Objects, such as utility boxes and air conditioners (Fig. 3–16)

- Lack of privacy from neighbors

- Unsightly areas of the yard, such as storage

(a)

(b)

Figure 3–16 **Poor View**

Utilities are items that are often eyesores. (a) Transformer. (b) Screening unpleasant utilities may not be advisable when they need to be seen. There are too many shrubs around this fire hydrant in an attempt to soften the view.

Good Views

Note attractive views that already exist (Fig. 3–17) such as a:

- Golf course
- Lake
- Wooded area

(a)

(b)

Figure 3–17   Good View
(a) Water is often a preferable view that needs to be preserved from the house or entertainment area. (b) The view of the mountain range can raise the value of the residence
considerably.

Potential Views

Note areas that would utilize and appreciate an interesting view (Fig. 3–18) such as:

- Entertainment area
- Views from inside the house

> ### *Tip Box*
> ### Views from Inside the House
>
> Take the time to go inside the house and look through all the windows to see
> the views from inside. Time spent in the family room and dining room may
> utilize the views more than the bedrooms and bathrooms.

(a)

(b)

***Figure 3–18* Potential View**
(a) Views from inside the house or from the entertainment area (deck below window) (b) should be enhanced with landscaping.

Exposure

Verify magnetic north with a compass (Fig. 3–19). North, south, east, and west exposures have different impacts on the environmental conditions, how these areas can be used, and plant selection.

Light and Temperature

In the Northern Hemisphere, the sun always shines from the south (Fig. 3–20). This will have an effect on sunlight intensity, temperature, and moisture/humidity around the house and site.

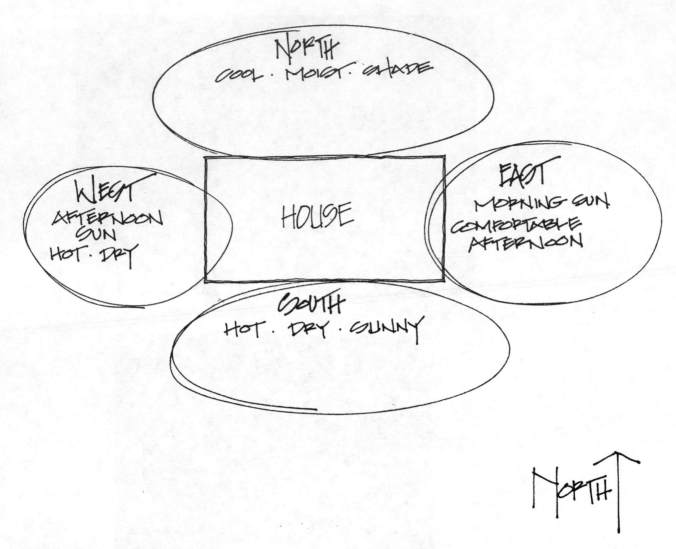

Figure 3–19 Exposure
Make note of magnetic north, which will impact the temperature, moisture, and prevailing wind around the house.

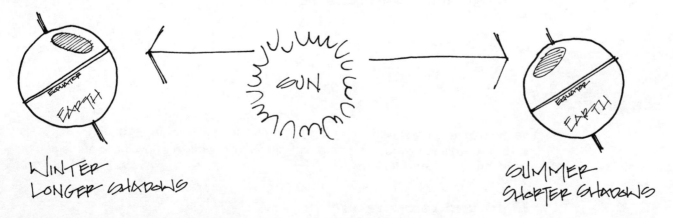

Figure 3–20 Northern Hemisphere
In the Northern Hemisphere, sunlight enters the atmosphere from the south.

Northern exposure receives full shade most of the day. It stays cooler and remains the dampest. This is why in an open, temperate forest moss only grows on the north side of a tree (Fig. 3–21).

Southern exposure receives full sun and gets hotter than the northern exposure. This is why snow melts off the south side of a hill before the north side (Fig. 3–22a).

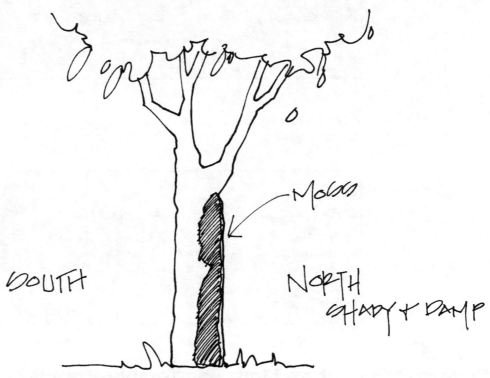

Figure 3–21   Northern Exposure
Since sunlight enters from the south, the north side of objects, such as a house or trees, is shaded throughout most of the day. This is why moss grows on the north side of a tree, where it is more shady and moist

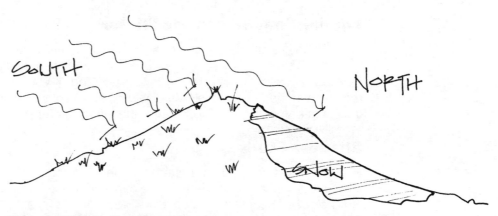

Figure 3–22a   Southern Exposure
Since sunlight enters from the south, the south side of objects or areas warms quicker because sunlight is more intense. This is why snow melts first on the south side of a hill.

Eastern exposure receives full sun in the morning when temperatures are cool and shade in the afternoon when temperatures are hot. These areas stay cooler and damper than the western exposure.

Tip Box

Take Advantage of the Eastern Exposure

Locate an entertainment area for optimal comfort, or locate plants that need protection from high temperatures.

Western exposure gets morning shade and the hot afternoon sun. It tends to be warmer and drier.

Tip Box

Screening the Southwest Exposure

It is more environmentally responsible to screen the house from the **southwest exposure.** This will help keep the house cooler by keeping the hot afternoon sun off of it. By using deciduous trees to screen, the leaves will fall in the autumn and allow the southwest exposure to warm the house in the winter months (Fig. 3–22b).

Seasonal Impact on Light and Temperature (Fig. 3–23)

Shorter Shadows in the Summer

In the summer the orientation of the earth makes a shorter, more direct path for the rays of the sun. This makes the sun appear higher in the sky and also results in warmer temperatures than winter. Therefore, in the summertime the shadows are shorter.

Longer Shadows in the Winter

Winter is the result of a longer path for the sun's rays to reach the earth and therefore there are longer shadows. As a result, it is important to note the time of the year that you make observations of where shadows are falling. If you are on-site during the winter months and plan to select shade plants in an area of shade, it may be in full sun come the summer months, which will cause the plants to burn.

Shadow Study

Shadows add interesting patterns to the ground plane, shifting and changing throughout the day (Fig. 3–24). This can add interest to a rather dull area, such as large slabs of concrete or a bare wall. Ideal locations are entry walks and entertainment areas.

Pay attention to how shadows fall on the ground from existing trees and other objects and note where shadows would add interesting detail in highly visible areas.

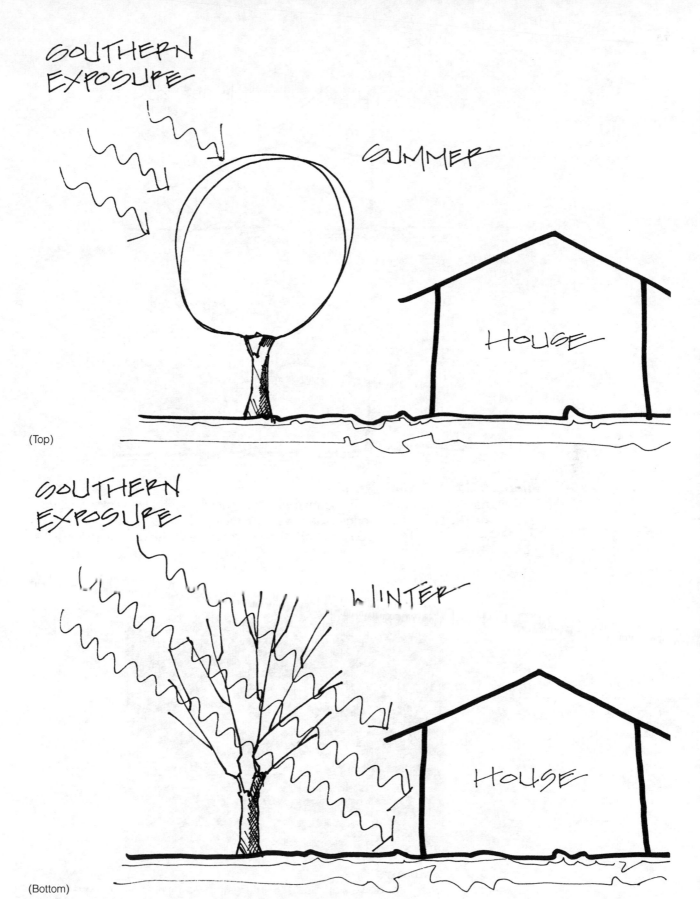

(Top)

(Bottom)

Figure 3–22b Screening Southwest Exposure
Using deciduous trees to screen the southwest exposure (Top) blocks the summer sun to cool and (Bottom) allows the winter sun to warm.

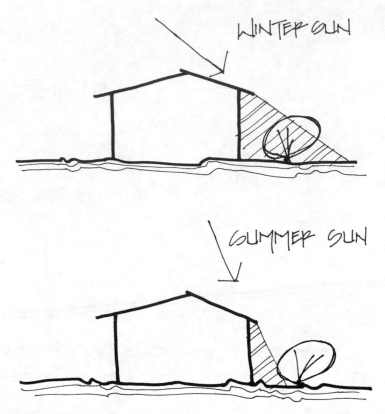

Figure 3–23 Seasonal Sun

Beware that the angle of the sun changes with the season. During the winter, the sun is lower in the sky and creates longer shadows while the opposite is true during the summer. Make note that observations of shady areas during the winter may be in full sun in the summer.

Figure 3–24 Shadows

Pay attention to where shadows would add an interesting visual element to a wall or the ground plane, such as this entry walk.

Wind

Where wind is a factor, windbreaks are necessary. Breezy conditions are comfortable in the summer, but can be unsavory in cool weather. However, it can make entertaining and eating difficult, blowing anything lightweight across the yard, such as paper plates and napkins.

The **prevailing wind** comes from the west (Fig. 3–25a). Colder prevailing winds come from the northwest during winter months and warmer winds during the summer come from the southwest (Fig. 3–25b).

Windbreaks can be developed with dense plantings, fences, or berms. Wind will hit the windbreak and be diverted up and over the desired area, creating a calm pocket of air. Some sources report that a windbreak can slow wind speed distance as much as 30 times the height of the windbreak. This means a 10′ tall windbreak of dense trees can slow wind as far as 300′, although most of the protection will come near the windbreak.

Dense plants and many wooden fences will allow some wind to filter through to prevent the dead space that can become humid and stale in hot weather, moving the air slightly enough to make it comfortable.

Blocking the wind also adds an insulating effect on the house that can conserve energy by lowering the windchill effect on the home. Be sure to keep space between the windbreak and the house. Hedges that grow up against the house hold moisture and can cause rot.

Tip Box

Blocking the Winter Wind

Screen the NW wind to reduce the impact of the cold winter wind on the house.

Allowing the Summer Breeze

During the summer months, consider screens that will allow the prevailing wind to cool areas outdoors, such as playgrounds or entertainment areas.

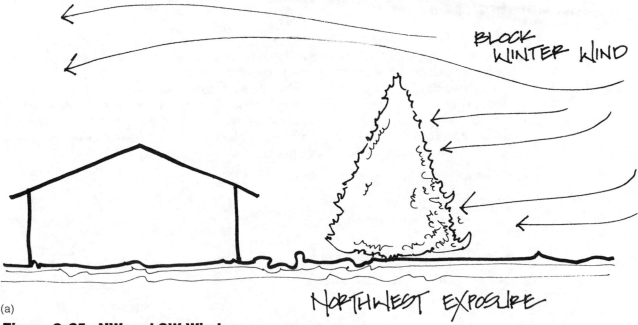

(a)

Figure 3–25 NW and SW Wind
(a) Screen the prevailing winter wind from the northwest to make the house more energy efficient.

(continues)

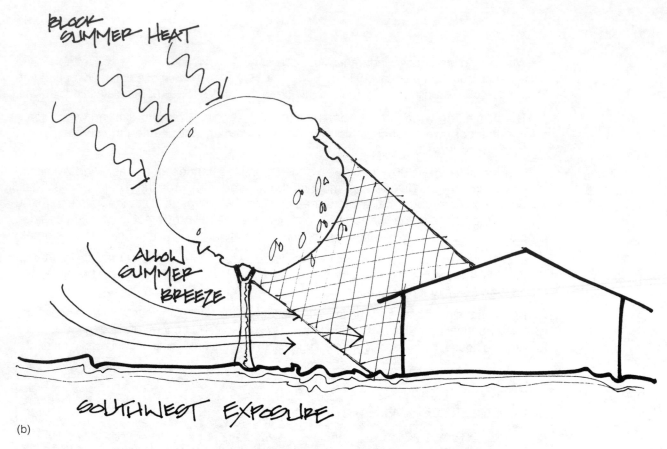

BLOCK SUMMER HEAT

ALLOW SUMMER BREEZE

SOUTHWEST EXPOSURE

(b)

Figure 3–25   NW and SW Wind—continued
(b) During the summer allow the prevailing wind from the southwest to cool the summer heat.

Existing Landscapes

There will be variation from project to project on how many existing plants will remain (Fig. 3–26). Some clients may request that all existing plants be relocated or removed for a new design, while others will want to expand on what is already present. Existing plants may provide important roles already, such as screens, while some may be potential specimen plants or focal points (Fig. 3–27). In many cases, large trees will remain because of their value or because local laws prohibit their removal. Some designs will locate all existing plants and indicate whether the plant is to be removed, relocated, or remain so the contractor knows what to do with it (Fig. 3–28).

For all existing plants, note the following:

- Identification

- Location

- Height and spread of canopy

  o For large trees, note the diameter of the trunk

- Condition

  o Note apparent damage or disease

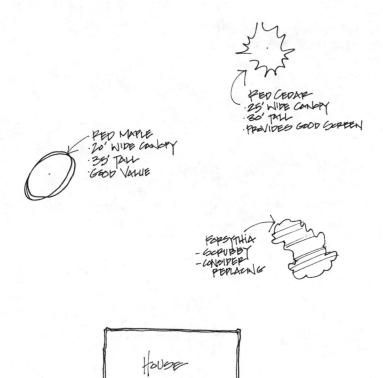

RED CEDAR
- 25' WIDE CANOPY
- 30' TALL
- PROVIDES GOOD SCREEN

RED MAPLE
- 20' WIDE CANOPY
- 35' TALL
- GOOD VALUE

FORSYTHIA
- SCRUBBY
- CONSIDER REPLACING

HOUSE

Figure 3–26   Existing Plants
Note existing plants, their condition, size, location, and whether they need to be removed or included in the design.

Figure 3–27   Existing Plant Value
From the back porch, the live oak in the neighbor's yard is an exceptional specimen that should be preserved for view.

Figure 3–28 **Remove, Relocate, or Remain**
Existing plants are often located on a plan and noted
whether they are to be removed, relocated, or remain so
the contractor knows what to do with them.

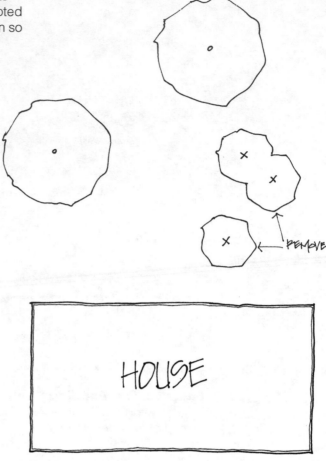

Soil

Collect a soil sample to determine texture, structure, pH, and other nutritional status
(Fig. 3–29). Collect a small handful of soil 6 inches deep from several spots on the residence using a **soil probe,** a t-handle instrument with a hollow core. This is used to pull
a soil sample at the correct depth (Fig. 3–30). Remove any debris and place in a plastic bag or jar. Submit a sample for a **soil test.** Most extension agencies of state univer-
sities provide a soil test for a nominal fee.

Texture

The **soil texture** is the proportion of sand, silt, and clay (Fig. 3–31). This will have an impact on plant material and the extent of renovation. For instance, palms grow well in
sandy soil but not in clay.

Sandy Soil   **Sand** is the largest soil particle of the three. It is a solid particle of silica
that resists compaction. Sandy soil contains 70 percent sand. It drains well, but is susceptible to drying out too quickly and has low fertility.

Clay Soil   **Clay** is the smallest soil particle and is very porous and plastic in nature.
It compacts easier than sand. Clay soil contains at least 40 percent clay. It holds nutrients and water very well but tends to remain too moist and often has low aeration.

Clay may be a problem when the building contractor has removed the topsoil and left
a clayey subsoil. Check the soil near the foundation of the house as well as out in the
yard to determine if clay has been left from construction.

(a)

Test	Results	SOIL TEST RATINGS					Calculated Cation Exchange Capacity
		Very Low	Low	Medium	Optimum	Very High	
Soil pH	5.8						14.5
Buffer pH	7.69						meq/100g
Phosphorus (P)	216 ppm						Calculated Cation Saturation
Potassium (K)	59 ppm						
Calcium (Ca)	2071 ppm						%K 1.0
Magnesium (Mg)	161 ppm						%Ca 71.4
Sulphur (S)	47 ppm						%Mg 9.3
Boron (B)	1.9 ppm						%H 17.1
Copper (Cu)	3.8 ppm						%Na 0.9
Iron (Fe)	150 ppm						
Manganese (Mn)	21 ppm						K : Mg Ratio
Zinc (Zn)	25.9 ppm						0.11
Sodium (Na)	31 ppm						
Soluble Salts	0.13 mmho/cm						
Organic Matter	3.0 % ENR 122						
NO3-N							

(b)

Figure 3–29 Soil Test

(a) Collecting a soil sample 6 inches deep from several places can assess the soil texture and structure (b) as well as submitting for a soil test to analyze the nutritional status and pH.

Figure 3–30 Soil Probe

A t-handle instrument that is used to pull soil samples 6 inches deep.

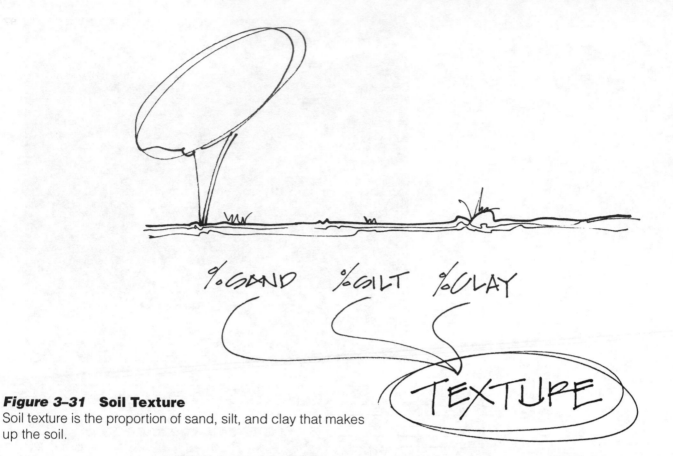

Figure 3–31 Soil Texture
Soil texture is the proportion of sand, silt, and clay that makes up the soil.

Tip Box

Texture Analysis

Ribbon test. Roll a handful of moist soil and squeeze between your thumb and fingers in your palm (Fig. 3–32). Roughly classify the soil texture based on the length of the ribbon formed:

> **No ribbon:** at least 50 percent sand
>
> **Less than 2 inches:** roughly 25 percent clay
>
> **Between 2 and 3 1/2 inches:** roughly 40 percent clay
>
> **Greater than 3 1/2 inches:** 50 percent clay

**Figure 3–32
Ribbon Test**
Squeeze a handful of moist soil in the palm of your hand and measure the length of ribbon that can be formed without breaking to roughly determine soil texture.

> *Tip Box*
>
> ## Jar Test (Fig. 3–33)
>
> 1. Fill a quart jar half full with soil, then add enough water to bring the jar 3/4 full.
>
> 2. Shake vigorously until all the soil breaks apart and suspends in the water.
>
> 3. When set down on the table, the sand will settle out within minutes, the silt will settle over the next few hours, and the clay will require 24 hours to settle.
>
> 4. After a day, there will be three distinct layers: sand on the bottom, silt in the middle, and clay on the top. Measure the height of each layer in millimeters and divide each layer by the total height of the whole soil sample to get the percentage of each layer.
>
> 5. Use a texture triangle to classify the soil texture.

Silt Soil   **Silt** is a particle that is in between sand and clay in size and porosity. It is not as dry and infertile as sand, and it drains better than clay.

Loamy Soil   The ideal soil is referred to as **loam,** which is an intermediate mixture of sand, silt, and clay.

Take a look at the soil in several areas around the property several inches deep. Be sure to check around the foundation as well as out in the yard. Special planting instructions will need to be specified for the contractor if soil texture problems exist.

Depending on the soil, the plant selection will have to be adapted to such texture as determined on-site if the soil is not amended.

Amending Soil   Sandy soil can be amended with 2 to 3 inches of organic matter, such as compost or hardwood mulch, tilled into the soil. This is often limited to planting beds with flowers, shrubs, and trees since it can be expensive. Clay soils can be amended or even replaced at considerable cost.

Structure

Structure is the arrangement of the soil particles (Fig. 3–34). Ideally, the structure of the soil should provide enough pore space to be well aerated with oxygen and to drain well. The condition of most concern regarding structure is compaction. With compaction, structure lacks adequate pore space, reducing aeration and drainage that will directly impact the health of the roots.

Look for causes of compaction, whether it was due to an earlier construction or ongoing traffic. Areas of high foot or vehicular traffic will be susceptible to compaction, and if plants are to be placed near these areas, then they should be adapted to limited rooting space. These areas may be more suited to hardscapes to tolerate the traffic. If the causes of compaction are no longer present, consider recommending cultivation or aeration to prepare the soil.

(a)

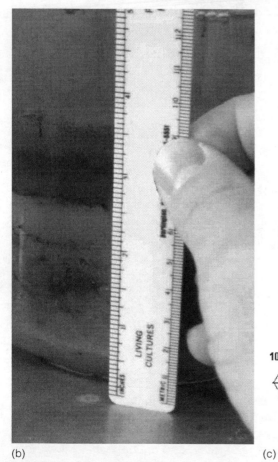

(b)

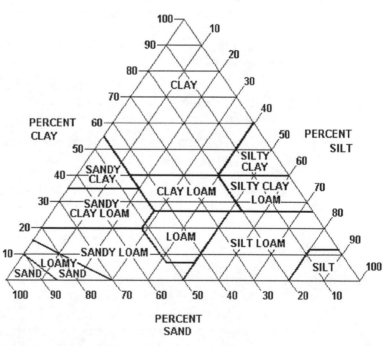

(c)

Figure 3–33 **Jar Test**

Fill a quart jar half full with soil and 3/4 to the top with water and shake vigorously; (a) after 24 hours, soil will settle out into distinct layers: sand on bottom, silt in middle, and clay on top; (b) measure each layer in millimeters and divide each layer by the total height of the whole soil sample to get the percentage of each layer; (c) the texture chart can be used to classify the soil texture by connecting the lines of the particle sizes. If the sample has 50% sand, 10% clay, and 40% silt, connecting the lines and the points classifies the sample as a loam soil.

88

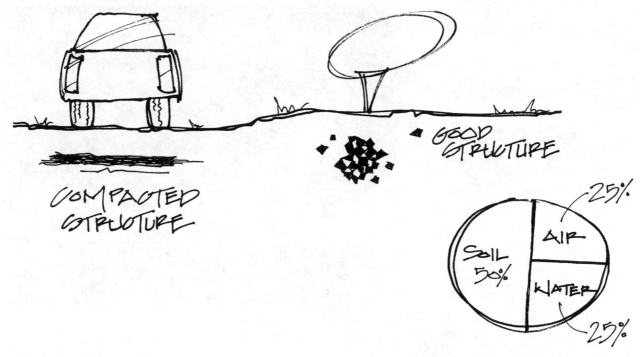

Figure 3–34 Soil Structure
Soil structure is how soil particles are arranged to make up the pore space where water and air are stored for healthy roots. Soils tilled with compost have good soil structure. Compacted soils have poor structure that lacks pore space.

Figure 3–35 Soil pH
The pH of soil is a measure of the acidity and has a large impact on nutrient availability.

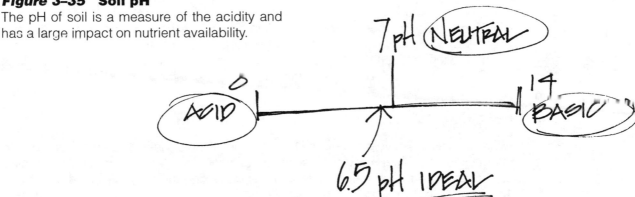

pH

The **pH** of the soil affects the ability of the plants to uptake nutrients, primarily micronutrients (Fig. 3–35). It is measured on a scale from 0 to 14. A pH of 7 is **neutral**; pH lower than 7 is **acidic** and higher than 7 is **basic,** or referred to as **alkaline.** A pH of 6.5 is considered to be ideal for most plants.

Changing Soil pH If one of these conditions is present on-site, the pH can sometimes be corrected if it's not too extreme. The pH can be easily raised with an application of **lime.** To lower pH, elemental **sulfur** can be used, although with less success because soil has a high buffering capacity against lowering pH. How much of either lime or sulfur will be needed is told on a soil test.

Figure 3–36   pH Meter
An inexpensive pH meter can be used to assess the soil pH.

If correcting the soil is not feasible, then select plants that are adapted to those conditions. One example is **acid-loving plants** such as azaleas, begonias, gardenias, and hydrangeas.

pH Meter   An inexpensive **pH meter** can be used without having to get a soil test (Fig. 3–36). Mix a cup of soil with a cup of water and stir until the soil is completely suspended. Allow it to sit for a day and then dip the pH meter into the water. This is not as accurate as a soil test, but it is accurate enough to uncover pH problems.

Fertility

A soil analysis will reveal any nutrient deficiencies that will need to be amended before installation. Phosphorus and potassium are major nutrients that are immobile in the soil and are best corrected before installation by cultivating the nutrients in the upper 6 to 12 inches of the soil.

Landform

In some parts of the country, landform is very integral to the design. **Mounds** can provide privacy. Make a note where the landscape naturally rises. This may be ideal to create a semiprivate "outdoor room" that is visually separate from the rest of the yard and/or public.

Berms are mounded ornamental beds, sometimes fairly small. Berms have good drainage but also add the element of changes in elevation. If the topography is relatively flat, make note where berms would be desirable. Pay attention to how a berm would affect the surface drainage (water running across the surface of the ground) so it does not create drainage problems. For instance, creating a berm in front of the house may divert the runoff from the roof back to the house (Fig. 3–37).

Figure 3–37 Berm
(a) Consider where water will go when topography is changed so it doesn't create problems. (b) This is an example of a berm too close to the house. Water will drain back to the house and cause moisture problems.

Steep **slopes** may be susceptible to erosion (Fig. 3–38). Water runs down the slope too quickly and creates rivulets in the soil, eventually digging deeper. Planting along a slope may be sufficient, but more severe slopes may require retaining walls, or terracing, to reduce the steep runoff.

Low areas and gullies can be drainage problems. Pay attention where water may settle. If you are visiting the site during the dry season, ask the client if they've noticed water draining slowly. Drainage may need to be installed.

Altering Topography

Pay attention to recommended changes to the existing topography. The client may have a drainage issue and the designer may solve it by filling the area with soil and eliminating low spots (Fig. 3–39). However, this may simply divert water to the neighbor's property, which could create problems.

Figure 3–38 Steep Slopes

(a) Steep slopes can erode and create maintenance problems. (b) Low growing ground cover is a possible solution. (c) Although more expensive, terracing is another option.

(a)

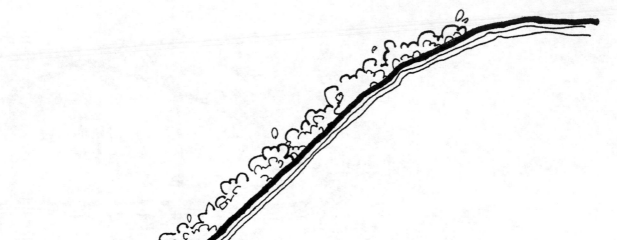

(b)

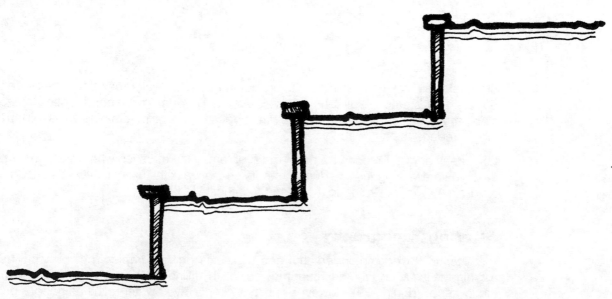

(c)

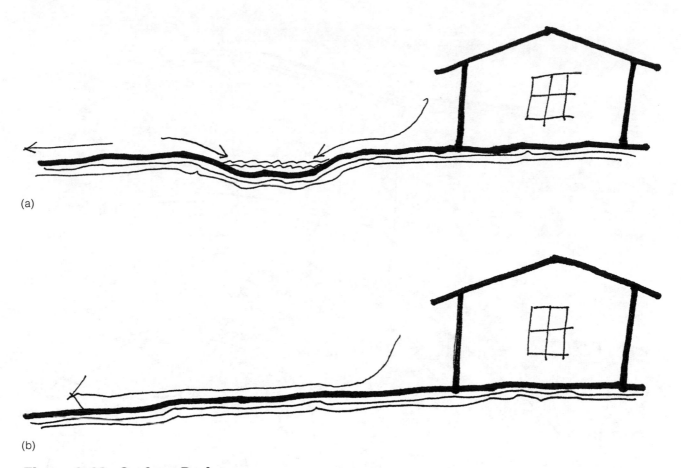

(a)

(b)

Figure 3–39 **Surface Drainage**
(a) Low areas can create drainage problems. (b) Regrading the topography can direct water away. Just be sure the surface drainage doesn't go into a neighbor's yard and create problems.

Topographic, or Contour, Map

Commercial designers should be familiar with **topographic maps** that may be bound with the site survey. **Contour lines** illustrate points of elevation above mean sea level. Anywhere along that contour line is the same elevation (Fig. 3–40). The closer contour lines are drawn, the steeper the slope. The farther contour lines are apart, the flatter the ground. Changes in topography will be illustrated with contour lines.

Drainage

Note any areas where water is standing (Fig. 3–41). If you're on-site during a dry period, ask the clients if there are any areas where water stands after it rains. This can especially be a problem in the path of circulation, making it difficult to walk without getting muddy or wet.

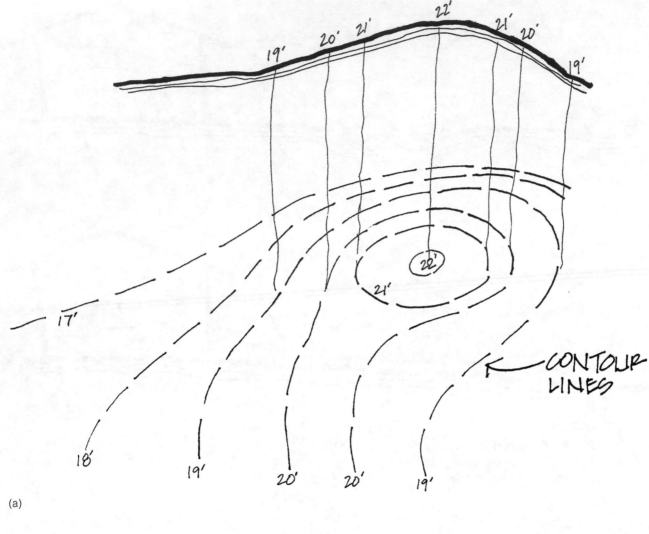

(a)

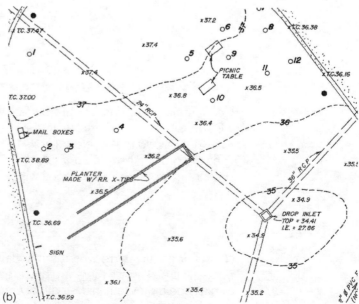

(b)

Figure 3–40 Topography

(a) Contour lines indicate points of elevation above the mean sea level. Anywhere along a contour line, such as 19', would be the same elevation. (b) On this topographic map, note the contour lines (dashed lines). The lower elevations all lead to the drain (drop inlet). Also, note the spot elevations in-between the contour lines marked with an X, giving an exact elevation at that point.

Figure 3–41 Wet Areas
(a) Make note of areas that are holding water. If the weather is dry, ask the residents if they notice areas that hold water. (b) This patio would flood until drainage was installed.

Foundation

Look at the grade around the foundation of the house. It is imperative that water drains on the surface away from the house, especially when it is built on a basement or crawl space. Water that drains under the house can cause mildew and rot.

Surface Drainage

Make note of the topography and any obvious signs of low spots that hold water due to improper grading (Fig. 3–42).

Downspouts and Gutters

Note the location of **downspouts** from gutters. These should extend away from the house to avoid foundation problems. Also, these areas will be the wettest and could have a negative impact on some plants (Fig. 3–43).

***Figure 3–42* Drainage**
Water should drain readily away from the foundation of the house. Any changes to the landscape should not affect this.

***Figure 3–43* Downspout Location**
Make note of downspouts from gutters that will need to be re-routed or select plants that cannot tolerate wet conditions.

Pets, Hobbies, or Other Notables

During the interview, make note of events, objects, or animals that could influence the design. Outdoor hobbies or recreational activities may require changes to the topography. Pets, in particular dogs, will need to be accounted for (Fig. 3–44). Pets can destroy plants, dig holes, or wear paths through planting beds. This may be an issue to work on with the client, as far as pets that run free or stay in a kennel. At the very least, the design should include sturdy plants that aren't harmful to the pets (thorns or poisonous). Avoid things like delicate annuals and perennials that don't stand a chance.

Figure 3–44 **Dogs and Other Considerations**
Dogs can destroy a garden. Note pets or hobbies that may require special consideration for plant selection and design.

Drawing the Analysis

An effective approach to developing the analysis is done with graphics and short descriptions (Fig. 3–45). From the analysis, other phases of the design process will be
built. If the analysis is graphically drawn on the base map, then the next phase of the
plan drawing can be done right over the top of it.

It is important to keep in mind the analytical approach. Every statement and graphic
should express doing something and not the situation (which is the inventory), regardless of how vague the action may be. This will include statements or terms such as

- Needs to be . . .
- Create . . .
- Allow for . . .
- Develop . . .
- Improve . . .

Not every point on the inventory will have an analytical statement. Some inventory will
be good information that is not a particular strength or weakness. For instance, if the inventory of the soil is "good loamy soil," then this would not necessarily require an analytical assessment. It's good soil.

Develop the analysis with bold graphics and brief statements on the base map (Fig.
3–46). These graphics are not only valuable for the designer's thought process; they will
also be referred back to in the next phase of the design. Some designers graphically
develop the analysis so it can be presented along with the preliminary or master plan
to support the design.

For a closer look at Inventory and Analysis, see Appendix A, "The Design Process," for
the Grant Residence Inventory and Analysis.

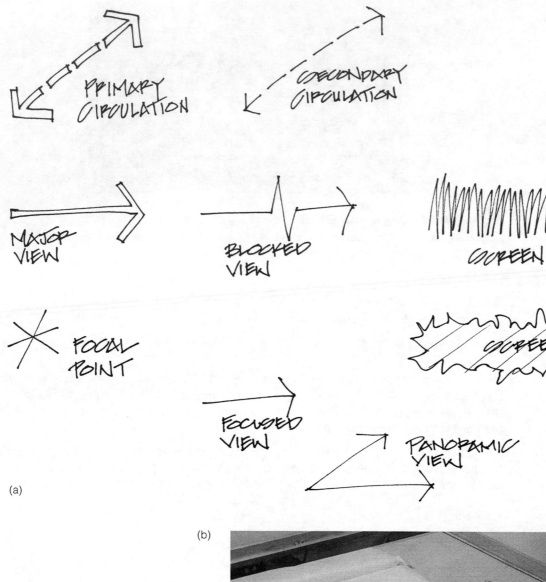

PRIMARY CIRCULATION

SECONDARY CIRCULATION

MAJOR VIEW

BLOCKED VIEW

SCREEN

FOCAL POINT

SCREEN

FOCUSED VIEW

PANORAMIC VIEW

(a)

(b)

Figure 3–45 Analysis Graphics
(a) Some simple ways to graphically illustrate the analysis. (b) Analysis is sketched on tracing paper with soft lead.

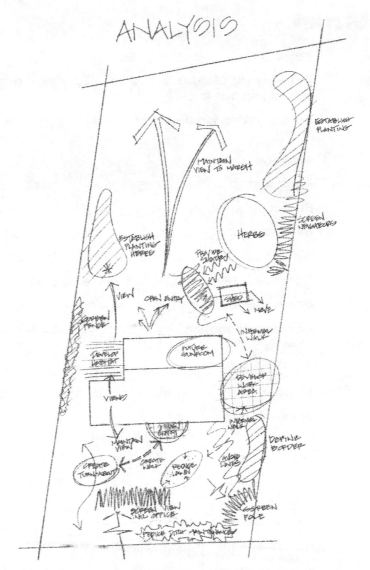

Figure 3–46 Graphical Analysis of Grant Residence
This is a graphical analysis of the Grant residence.

Summary

The inventory and analysis follow the interview and, by using the information from the interview, the designer develops a "needs assessment," or a plan of action to guide the design. This is critical to the functional, or useful, aspect of the design. The inventory is observing the site conditions and elements, and the analysis takes the inventory to determine the problems and potentials that will make up the plan of action. Areas that are analyzed include the house, circulation, views, utilities, exposure, soil, landform, wind, and drainage. The analysis can be illustrated graphically with short verbal descriptions that can be used in the next phase of the design process. The graphical analysis can also be used during the presentation to the client to support the design.

Key Terms

Acid: pH lower than 7

Acid-loving plants: tolerate low soil pH; examples include azaleas, begonias, gardenias, and hydrangeas

Air-conditioning units: often noisy and unsightly and need screening and ventilation

Alkaline: pH higher than 7

Analysis: based on the inventory, determines the problems and the potentials

Basic: see alkaline

Berms: mounded ornamental beds, sometimes fairly small

Clay: the smallest soil particle, which is very porous and plastic in nature

Contour lines: illustrate points of elevation above mean sea level

Downspouts: extensions from gutters

Eastern exposure: receives morning sun when it's cooler and afternoon shade when it's hotter

Good views: areas or objects that already exist and can be accentuated in the design

Inventory: observing and recording what already exists on-site

Jar test: determining soil texture by mixing a soil sample in a jar with water, which separates soil into three distinct layers of sand, silt, and clay

Lime: used to raise soil pH

Loamy soil: ideal soil is referred to as loam, an intermediate mixture of sand, silt, and clay

Mounds: elevated ground that can provide privacy

Needs assessment: another term for "inventory and analysis"

Neutral: pH of 7

Northern exposure: receives full shade most of the day

Overhead lines: avoid planting tall trees under power lines

pH: affects the ability of plants to uptake nutrients

pH meter: used to obtain pH of soil

Poor views: unsightly areas or objects that need to be removed or screened

Potential views: areas that would utilize and appreciate an interesting view

Prevailing wind: comes from the west; colder prevailing winds come from the northwest during winter months and warmer winds during the summer come from the southwest

Ribbon test: quick test to roughly determine the soil texture by squeezing soil in the palm of the hand

Sand: the largest soil particle of the three

Septic tank: a private sewage treatment plant for an individual residence

Silt: particle that is in between sand and clay in size and porosity, not as dry and in-fertile as sand and drains better than clay

Slopes: inclined ground that may be susceptible to erosion

Soil probe: t-handle instrument with a hollow core used to obtain a soil sample

Soil test: analysis of soil that reveals pH and nutritional status

Soil texture: the proportion of sand, silt, and clay

Southern exposure: receives full sun and gets hotter than the northern exposure

Storage areas: can be unsightly areas but need to be accessible

Structure: the arrangement of the soil particles

Sulfur: used to lower pH

Surface drainage: study of water draining across the top of the ground

Southwest exposure: often screened to provide shade for relief from the hottest part of the day

Topographic maps: see contour lines

Trash cans: unsightly but need to have adequate access from the house and to the curb for pickup

Western exposure: gets morning shade and the hot afternoon sun; tends to be hotter and drier

4 Functional Principles

Objectives

- Know the basic functions of the landscape
- Understand the functional aspects of the front, side, and backyard
- Learn how to incorporate functionality into landscape design

People Spaces

The landscape should be more than just window-dressing for the house. The fundamental purpose of residential design should be to make the landscape functional. To achieve an order of usable space, an understanding of the **functional** aspects of a residence is important.

How People Use Their Landscape

Every client has different taste. A design has to address how the client will use the landscape. Indoor-oriented people may like views from inside the house and spend little time outdoors (Fig. 4–1). Outdoor people want space to work on a vegetable garden or harvest herbs and entertain large parties on a deck (Fig. 4–2). Each design must be unique to the client. And each design must function as such.

(a)

(b)

Figure 4–1 **Indoor View**
Some clients are indoor people, only interested in how their yard looks. Improving the feel of a primary path (front door to driveway) takes advantage of common views. (a) Before; (b) after.

***Figure 4–2* Outdoor Living**
Outdoor-oriented people prefer to develop functional rooms outside. This cozy sitting area is a comfortable retreat in the backyard.

Extension of Indoor Living Space

The landscape should support the activities of the residents. It could be compared with the floor plan of the home, which supports various activities such as cooking in the kitchen, sleeping in the bedroom, eating in the dining room, etc. In this way, the property is organized to improve the quality and comfort of outdoor living. Outdoor activities include, but are not limited to, cooking, eating, recreating, entertaining, work/hobbies, and relaxation (Fig. 4–3).

***Figure 4–3* Living Space**
Just as the kitchen is the place for cooking and eating indoors, the same spaces can be created outdoors.

Outdoor Room Concept

Designers organize the landscape into outdoor rooms. These rooms are much like the rooms in the house, composed of floors, walls, and ceilings (Fig. 4–4). Outdoor rooms, however, utilize much different materials to define space.

Floors

Floors are the **ground plane** of the landscape. They can be made from turf, hardscapes, mulch, or ground cover (Fig. 4–5).

Turf

Turf typically makes up the majority of the ground plane (Fig. 4–6a). The lawn is one of the most functional components of the landscape, easily maintained by mowing. It is soft and ideal for recreation. It is also highly valued to the environment. In arid parts of the country, however, very little turf is used in order to conserve water.

Some people love grass. They love to mow it, manicure it, and rake it. Others despise grass and consider it a nuisance. Tastes vary. But besides mowing once a week, grass is often easier to maintain than large planting beds. Grass is also very beneficial to the environment. Turf's photosynthetic capacity absorbs carbon dioxide from the atmosphere. Turf transpires water and cools the ground. It also has a fibrous root system that effectively filters dust and pollutants.

Hardscapes

Concrete, pavers, flagstone, and decks are examples of hardscapes. While most homes have concrete driveways and sidewalks, their impermeability can cause drainage problems. In highly developed areas, commercial developers build retention ponds to catch runoff from large parking lots. In some parts of the country, there is a tax on the amount of impermeable surface to help develop proper storm sewers.

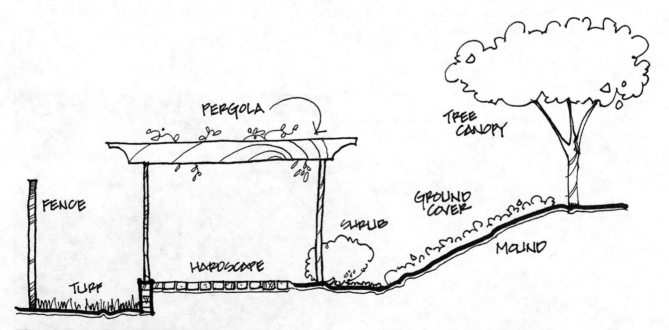

Figure 4–4 Outdoor Rooms
Outdoor rooms are created with floors (turf, hardscapes, mulch, ground cover), walls (fence, shrub, tree, mound), and ceilings (pergola and vine, tree canopy).

Figure 4–5 **Outdoor Floor**
The outdoor floor is any material on the ground plane, such as a deck or turf.

(a)

(b)

Figure 4–6 **Turf and Ground Cover**
(a) Turf makes up a large portion of the landscape. (b) However, in areas where shade becomes a problem, ground cover can be used.

Permeable hardscapes include dry-laid pavers on a bed of sand or compacted gravel paths. This allows water to percolate between the sand-filled cracks rather than run off.

Mulch

Mulch is shredded hardwoods or chipped bark, to name a few. It is an excellent material to cover the soil in planting beds around trees and shrubs. It moderates soil temperature and moisture fluctuations. Even though it reduces weeds as opposed to bare soil, it's still susceptible to weed invasion. Mulched areas can be high maintenance in the first three to five years. Once plants fill the bed, mulching needs lessen.

***Figure 4–7* Weed Barrier**
A layer of weed fabric suppresses weed growth under mulched beds.

Weed barrier is a synthetic, breathable fabric that prevents weeds from emerging through mulch (Fig. 4–7). This is effective for several years, but eventually weeds will germinate on top of the fabric. By the time weeds germinate on top of the weed barrier, shrubs and ground cover should fill the plant bed and smother the weeds.

Ground Cover

Ground cover, such as ivy, will cover a planting bed quickly (Fig. 4–6b). It eliminates the need for mulch and often outcompetes weeds. Ground cover is an excellent choice where turf is not needed (or can't grow, such as under a shade tree) and low maintenance is desired.

Walls

Walls create separation, screening, and a sense of enclosure (Fig. 4–8). **Screening** comes in varying degrees. **Total screens** can be an 8-foot-tall brick wall that no one can see past. **Partial screens** give a sense of separation and block views to some de-

(a)

(b)

***Figure 4–8* Outdoor Walls**
The upper deck (a) is visually separated from the lower deck (b) by the vine growing on the railing next to the steps.

***Figure 4–9* Enclosure**
The upper deck is partially enclosed with the vine-covered pergola and railings.

gree. Loose shrubs or lattice fence panels are examples. **Implied screens** create a conse of separation without obscuring views. A low-growing bed of shrubs creates separation, but doesn't block the view.

Tip Box
The Comfort of Enclosure

Enclosure is important to convey a sense of comfort from the elements, in particular wind and sun. Enclosure often feels more comfortable compared to sitting in a wide-open space (Fig. 4–9).

Fence

Nowadays, most backyards are enclosed with a 6-foot-tall privacy fence (Fig. 4–10). Backyards are where most people seek privacy. In some parts of the country, brick walls are more common. Picket fences and chain-link fences are used more for enclosing an area for safety and security, such as confining a dog, but they offer no privacy.

Lattice

Much like fences, the crisscross construction of lattice panels is a unique pattern that creates partial screen. It is often used as a structure for climbing vines.

Figure 4–10 **Fencing**
Fences are a common means of outdoor walls. Plants can soften the long, monotonous run of wood panels.

Shrubs

Shrubs are effective walls that offer softer texture and more interesting colors than most fences. However, they take time to grow and some clients don't want to wait years for a shrub screen to develop.

Mounds

Changes in elevations can be effectively used to create separation. Berms and mounds can be low and imply screening or higher for a complete screen. They can be combined with a retaining wall to add interest and functionality to holding soil.

Ceilings

Ceilings are the overhead enclosure of the outdoor room. As mentioned in the wall section, ceilings lend a comfortable atmosphere. They can be complete ceilings, such as an awning, that protect from rain and sun or partial ceilings, such as a tree canopy, to protect from sun and somewhat from rain.

Roof

Porches, gazebos, and sheds have a ceiling with a shingled roof that sheds water. These constructions are acceptable in certain areas and are the most expensive. They are the most protective ceiling in the outdoor room.

Tree Canopy

Trees planted near a sidewalk or entertainment area provide a comfortable overhead ceiling (Fig. 4–11). The photosynthesizing leaves can cool the area underneath more than shade from a roof.

Tree canopies also allow some sunlight to penetrate to the ground and create interesting shadow patterns. The leaves move in the breeze, adding elements of motion and sound. They vary in texture and color and feel more natural.

However, newly planted trees take time to develop. And trees drop leaves and fruit and can become messy. Trees can make pools high maintenance, clogging the filter with leaves and seeds. Soft, pulpy fruits can make a mess on sidewalks and decks and even attract insects like bees and wasps.

Figure 4–11 **Tree Canopy**
The tree canopies provide a ceiling for the entry walk.

Figure 4–12 **Pergola**
The pergola provides a structure for jasmine vines. The vines provide protection from the sun and the flower fragrance is potent during the spring.

Pergolas

Pergolas are inexpensive ceilings (compared to a shingled roof) (Fig. 4–12). They are an open construction of boards that can be covered with lattice for additional protection. They add shadows to the ground and some protection from the sun. Mostly, they lend a sense of enclosure with minimal protection from the elements.

Most often, pergolas are used as support for vines. Over time, vines fill in and protection from the elements, such as the sun, can be quite good, having the same benefits as the tree canopy.

Basic Functions

The residential property can be divided into three general-use areas: public, private, and utility (Fig. 4–13). **Public areas** of the residence are within view and open to the public. This area would serve to present an appealing appearance to the neighborhood, facilitate a safe, interesting approach onto the property, and occasionally entertain guests. The public area is typically regarded as the front yard and occasionally the side yard (depending on the lot).

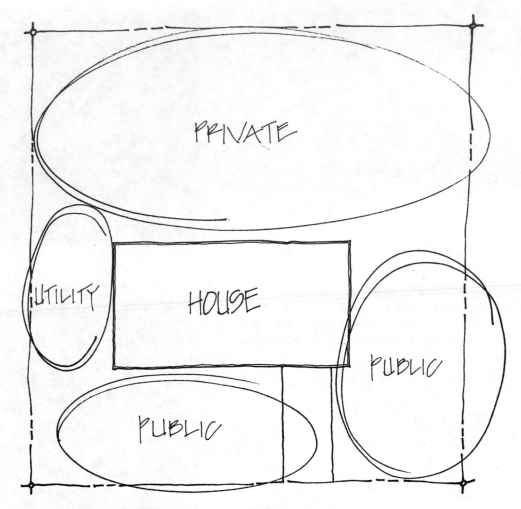

***Figure 4–13* Functional Aspects of Residence**
The residence is usually divided into public, private, and utility areas. The front yard is public, the backyard is private, while the side yard may be public or private depending on the property. Utility areas are typically in the side and/or backyard.

Private areas are screened from the public view and used to entertain guests, for recreation and hobbies, or for the family to relax. This is typically in the backyard and occasionally the side yard (like the public area, it depends on the lot).

The **utility areas,** sometimes referred to as the **service areas,** are sections of the residence typically kept out of sight. They function as areas for storage, gardening, trash, compost, or other items that are functional but often unsightly, noisy, or odorous.

This chapter will look at the primary functions of the landscape in three areas: front yard, side yard, and backyard.

Front Yard

The front yard is considered the public area, although there are exceptions where the front yard can be more private and enclosed. Many designers look at the front yard as having one purpose: getting people from the street to the front door. Although this is a major function of the front yard, let's look at other major components of the front, their function, and how they can be addressed in the design.

> ### *Tip Box*
> Many designers believe the main purpose of the front yard is to get people to the front door.

Curb Appeal

Curb appeal is how the front of the house looks from the road, either driving by or walking. Curb appeal is what most people want from a design, whether it's to increase the value of their property, to take pride in their landscape, or to "keep up with the Joneses" (Fig. 4–14).

Traditional landscaping primarily dealt with foundation planting (Fig. 4–15). This usually consisted of an evergreen hedge across the front of the house to hide the foundation. This hedge was often sheared into a box or other geometric forms.

The hedge was often punctuated with a large evergreen shrub planted at each corner and sometimes at both sides of the front door. Corner plantings were done to blend the sharp corners of the house with the ground and surroundings. Although the traditional landscaping was better than a barren landscape, it was often an unchanging green wall that lacked interest.

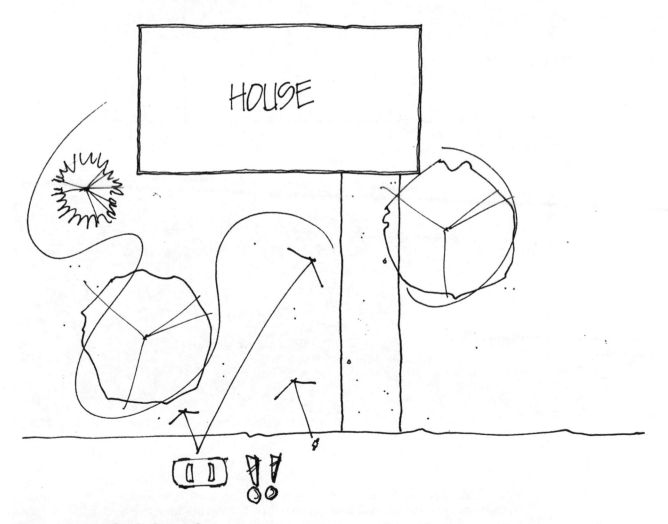

Figure 4–14 Curb Appeal
One thing that most residents are interested in is improving the curb appeal of their front yard.

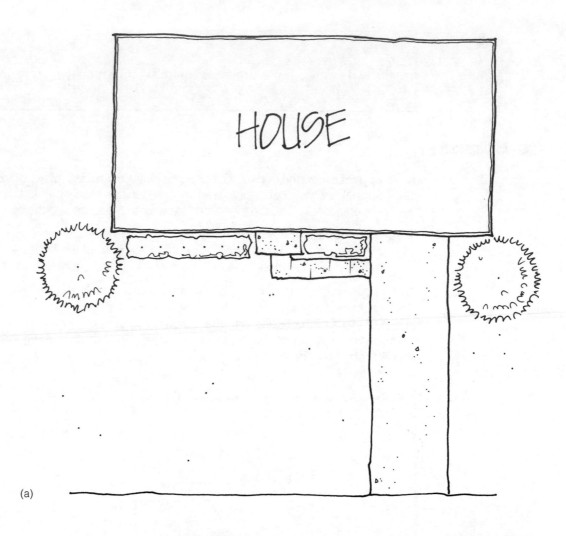

(a)

(b)

***Figure 4–15* Traditional Land-scaping**

(a) Traditional landscaping consists of green hedges that are sheared into boxes and have corners punctuated with taller shrubs. (b) Lacks color and interest.

Ideally, the landscape should generate visual interest from the curb. It should contain an element of uniqueness, balance, and color. If done skillfully, the landscape will continually draw interest as it changes throughout the year with various flower colors, fall color, and winter characteristics.

Framing the House

A common approach to creating curb appeal is using the landscape as a frame for the house (Fig. 4–16a). This is often done by planting large trees or shrubs on both sides of the house to focus an observer's attention within its boundaries.

Draw Attention to the Front Door

Framing the house helps to draw attention to the front door as well as the approach. Some designers use a **funneling effect,** planting larger items on the outside and placing progressively smaller plants closer to the door so that attention is naturally drawn to the door (Fig. 4–16b).

Figure 4–16a **Framing**
To create curb appeal, the landscape should act as a frame for the house.

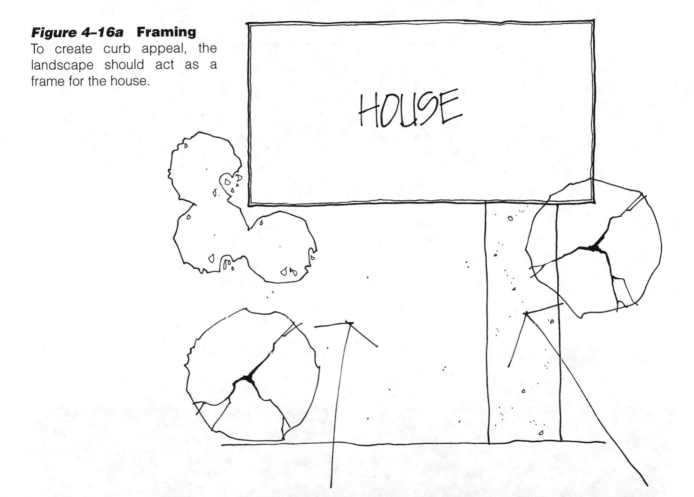

Figure 4–16b **Funneling Effect**
Designers sometimes funnel the attention of a visitor to the front door by planting larger items on the outside and placing progressively smaller plants closer to the door.

It is also important to avoid hiding the entrance or causing confusion on how to get there (Fig. 4–17). A person should be able to identify the front door and how to get there. If the entrance is visually screened, it blocks the view from the street, not to mention the views from the inside of the house.

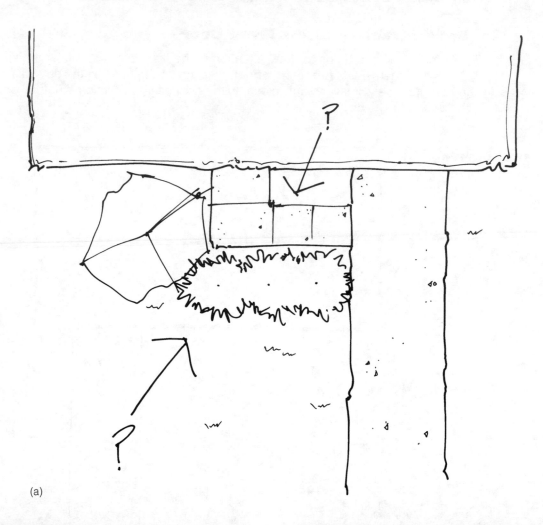

(a)

(b)

(c)

Figure 4–17 **Hidden Door**
(a) Avoid tall plantings that screen the front door. (b) The front door is easy to find. (c) Where is the front door now? (digitally enhanced)

Blend the House with Its Surroundings

Houses have corners and angles in stark contrast to the natural landscape of trees, shrubs, and turf (Fig. 4–18). This is evident in new subdivisions where there are few large plants helping to balance the houses and integrate them with their surroundings. To some people, these neighborhoods feel too harsh.

Landscaping helps tie the house to the ground and blend it into the surroundings. Plants help to balance the structures with the landscape and *soften* the sharp corners of the house.

Defined Borders

Some front yards focus most of the landscaping directly in front of the house and don't come out much farther than a few feet (Fig. 4–19). This leaves ill-defined space that blends front yards of the entire neighborhood together, separated only by the driveways (Fig. 4–20). This can create a sense of disconnection between the front of the house and the rest of the lawn, in addition to lacking distinction from the neighbors.

Even a simple extension of the foundation bed can be effective in defining the front yard (Fig. 4–21). This also helps integrate the front lawn with the foundation planting. The bed doesn't have to come all the way to the curb, but simply pulling out into the yard several feet can imply some separation. The beds may include trees and shrubs, or simply ground cover to imply separation.

(a)

(b)

Figure 4–18 **Blending of House with Environment**
(a) The house appears out of place with its surroundings. (b) Landscaping helps integrate the home with its surroundings by softening corners and edges. *(Photos courtesy of Visual Impact Imaging.)*

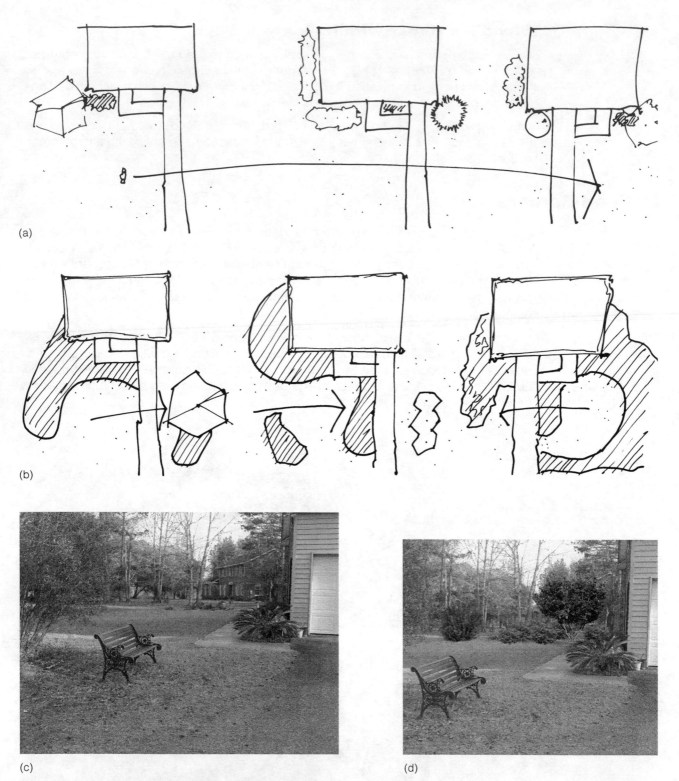

(a)

(b)

(c)

(d)

Figure 4–19 Front Yard Definition
(a) Neighborhoods typically lack defining borders between front yards. (b) Landscape beds and plantings can help define the front yard and draw attention to the house. (c) This entry walk focuses on the neighbor's house. (d) Defining the side yard keeps the focus on the clients' yard (photo digitally enhanced).

(a)

(b)

Figure 4–20 **Defining Borders**
(a) From the front yard there is little definition or interest except for driveways for several houses. (b) Beds and plantings help define the area and add visual interest. (digitally enhanced)

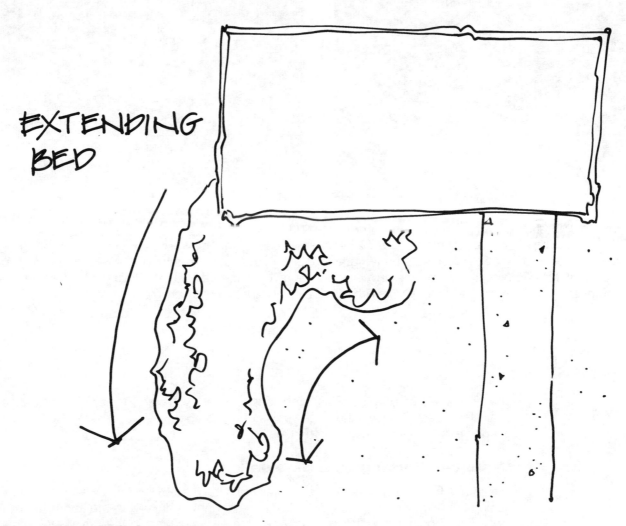

EXTENDING BED

Figure 4–21 **Defining Borders**
A simple extension of the landscape bed with low plantings can visually help define the front yard.

(a)

(b)

(c)

Figure 4–22 Driveway
(a) The driveway is a visually dominant feature because it is so large. The warm, tan color and aggregate texture creates a more appealing feature than gray concrete. (b) Assess whether there is enough room to park all cars. (c) Widening the end of the driveway can be an inexpensive solution. Paving is expensive but very appealing. *(Photo (c) courtesy of Blue Ribbon LLC, Maryland. www.blueribbonllc.com)*

Driveway

The driveway's primary purpose is obviously to park vehicles. Review the residence analysis to determine whether it serves its purpose adequately. Consider if there is a need to expand the parking area (Fig. 4–22).

Driveway Serving as a Sidewalk

Oftentimes the driveway serves as the walk from the road to the entry walk that continues up to the front door (Fig. 4–23). Most one-car garage driveways are about 10 to 12 feet wide to accommodate one car. When the car is parked in the driveway it often leaves little room for approaching guests to walk on the concrete. What often results is people walking around the car and in the grass.

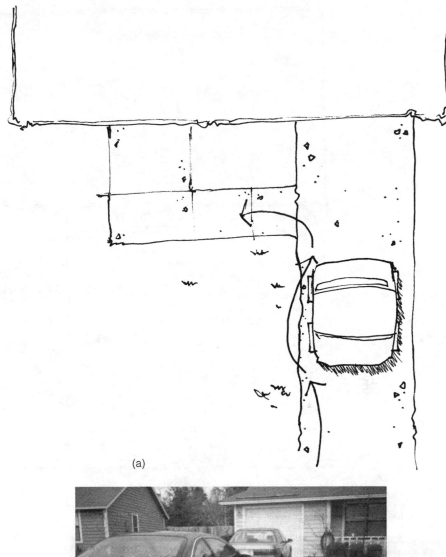

(a)

(b)

***Figure 4–23* Driveway Approach**
(a) The driveway often serves as the approach to the entry walk and front door.
(b) This can often be obstructed by a parked car, which does not allow room for
foot traffic.

Consider widening the driveway for a walking lane (Fig. 4–24). Using a paving material
other than concrete helps to visually separate it from the driveway. This extension will
accommodate the approach as well as provide a landing area for getting in and out of
the car.

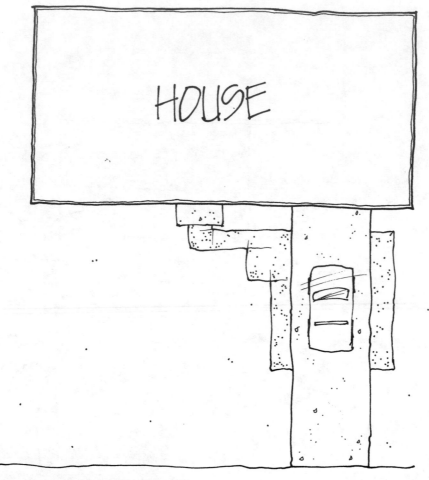

(a)

(b)

(c)

Figure 4–24 **Approach Walk**
A simple widening of the driveway with a material other than that used for the driveway can help facilitate foot traffic to the entry walk around parked vehicles.

(d)   (e)

Figure 4–24   Approach Walk—continued

Avoid Screening Driveway View

Avoid planting on the corners of the driveway where it meets the road, which will hinder the driver's view when backing out (Fig. 4–25).

Roundabout

Seldom considered, roundabout driveways make it convenient for residents to drive in and out of the driveway (Fig. 4–26). This is especially true when backing out onto a busy road or a road with an obstructed view. Driving forward, rather than backing out, is often easier and safer to do. The roundabout is very functional, but it will often consume much of the front yard with hardscapes. Offset the large amount of driveway by using more interesting material other than concrete.

Entry Walk

The **entry walk** provides access from the road or from the driveway to the front door. It has the following functions:

• Provides a safe approach

• Guides people through the landscape

• Influences their views

Common Shortcomings of Entry Walk

Many entry walks are poorly done (Fig. 4–27). They are often the result of the building contractor pouring an inexpensive slab of concrete.

Poor Route   Many entry walks have two 90-degree turns from the driveway to the front door (Fig. 4–28). This results in an awkward approach and shortcuts across the corner. The reason for this shape is because it is the easiest and quickest way for a contractor to pour the sidewalk.

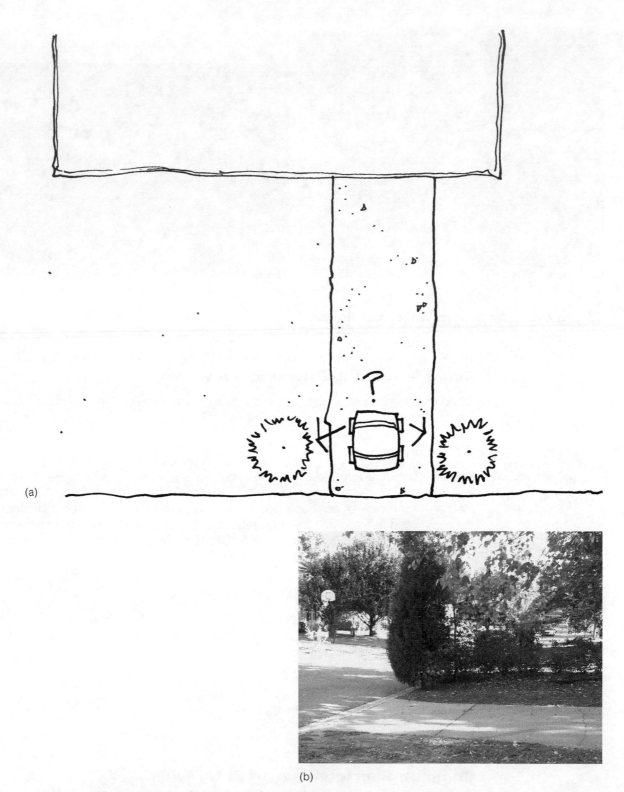

(a)

(b)

Figure 4–25 Screen Driveway
(a) Avoid screening the view of a car backing out of the driveway. (b) An obstructed view from a driveway can be hazardous.

Figure 4–26 Driveway Alternatives
Roundabouts are convenient and safe, removing the need to back onto a busy road, but they require a lot of space.

Figure 4–27 Poor Entry Walk
This entry walk is a square corner that does not facilitate approaching foot traffic. It is too narrow to allow more than one person to approach, and shrubs (recently cut) were allowed to cover half the sidewalk, leaving about only 1 1/2 feet open.

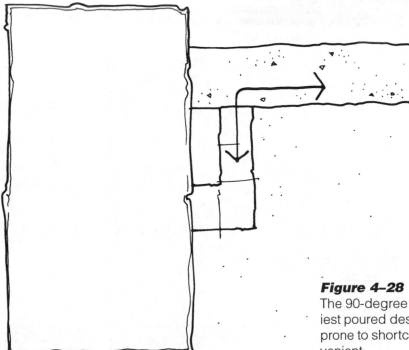

Figure 4–28 Poor Route
The 90-degree turn is common because it is the easiest poured design for the building contractor, but it is prone to shortcuts at the corner because it is not convenient.

Narrow Approach The width of most sidewalks is 3 feet, which is wide enough to accommodate one person comfortably (Fig. 4–29). If two or more people approach the house they will have to line up single file or walk in the grass.

Overgrown Walk Shrubs planted too close to the walk eventually grow over it leaving even less room (Fig. 4–30).

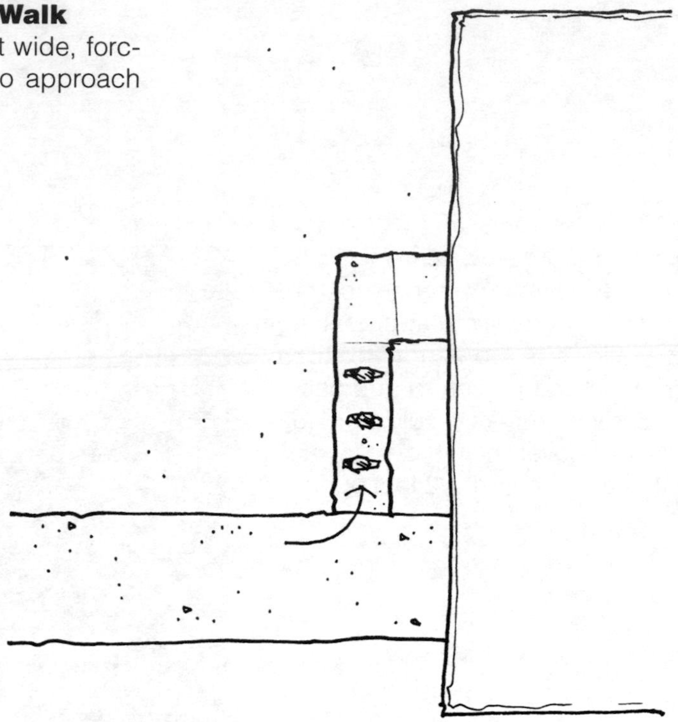

Figure 4–29 Narrow Walk
Most walks are only 3 feet wide, forcing two or more people to approach single file.

Figure 4–30 Overgrown Walk
Close plantings or wrong plant selection eat up more of the already small entry walk, making it nearly irrelevant.

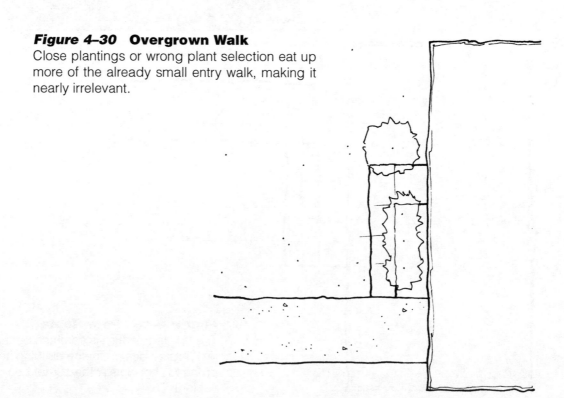

Effective Entry Walks

If the designer has the opportunity to design and build the entry walk, the designer can ensure a comfortable, safe, and interesting path with the following approaches (Fig. 4–31).

(a)

(b)

(c)

(d)

***Figure 4–31* Effective Entry Walk**
(a) This entry offers a wide opening and proper route to the front door, as well as unique material, to make the approach safe and interesting. (b) This entry has been expanded with flagstone from the original concrete sidewalk. (c) Steps, materials, width, and landscaping make this entry walk effective. *(Photo courtesy of Decks by JRW Portland, Oregon.* www.decksbyjrw.com*)* (d) A wide, sweeping entry is simple but effective visually and functionally. *(Photo courtesy of Big Sky Landscaping, Inc., Clackamas, OR.)*

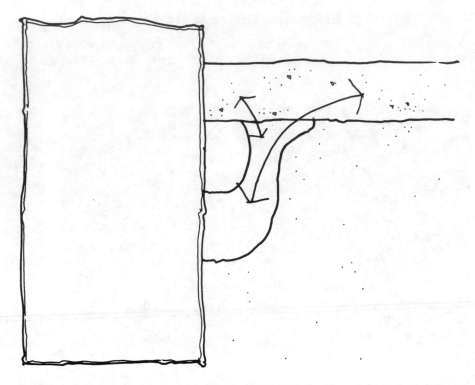

***Figure 4–32* Good Route**
The entry walk should be a convenient route that aids most commonly traveled paths.

Facilitate Circulation   Study the most common walking routes and lay out the walk accordingly (Fig. 4–32). If the majority of traffic comes up the driveway, then allow for someone to enter the walk smoothly. People feel more comfortable rounding corners rather than turning at an abrupt 90-degree turn. However, the walk does not necessarily need to be a straight line between two points. That can be mundane. Instead, a few slight bends in the walk are more interesting.

Also consider if access to other parts of the front besides the front door needs to be addressed. This may include a common path to one side of the house, or both sides. Also allow for access to the lawn from the front door (Fig. 4–33). This may just be allowing for space to walk through a bed with stepping stones and not necessarily a concrete path.

Wide Approach   Create a wide entrance to the entry walk that acts like a funnel to approaching traffic (Fig. 4–34). Once past the opening, the narrowest portion of the walk should be a minimum of 4 feet (Fig. 4–35).

Create Multiple Views   Take advantage of turns along the entry walk to develop different views and to create an interesting, varied approach (Fig. 4–36).

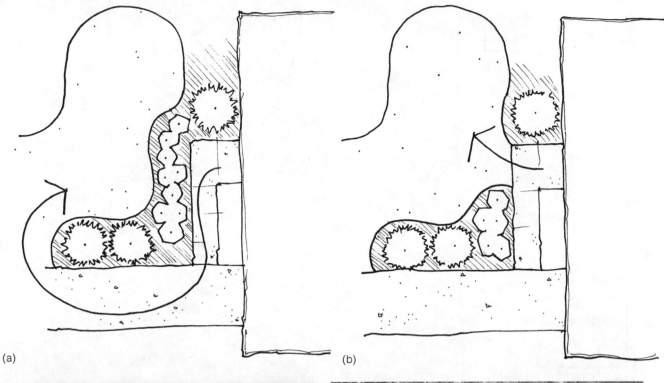

(a)

(b)

(c)

(d)

Figure 4–33 Secondary Access

(a) Avoid blocking access to other parts of the yard, such as isolating the entry walk from the front. (b) Leaving a simple opening or path is often sufficient. (c) The door is isolated from the yard unless cutting through the plants or walking up the driveway. (d) The small addition to the entry walk allows access through the planting bed into the front yard. (e) The railing on the porch was removed to create a side access, transforming the dead space on the front porch to secondary access.

(e)

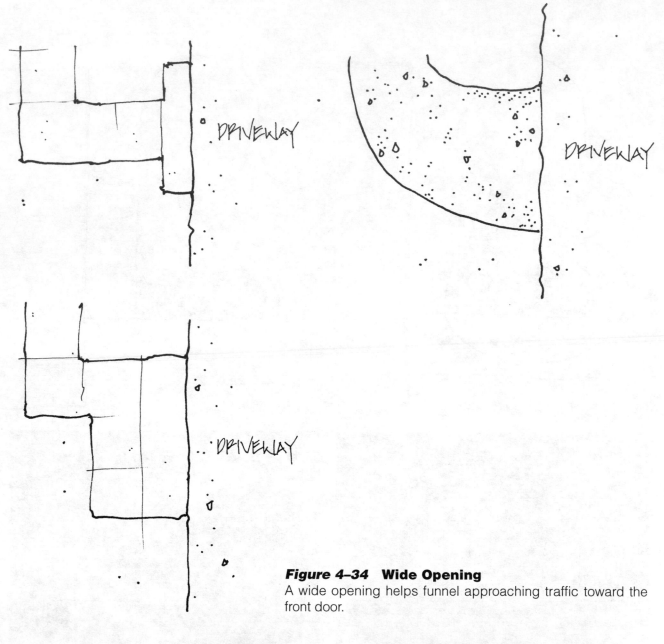

Figure 4–34 Wide Opening
A wide opening helps funnel approaching traffic toward the front door.

(a)

(b)

Figure 4–35 Entry Walk Width
Entry walks 4′ wide create a comfortable approach. (a) This entry walk suffers the typical 3′ width and overgrown shrubs. (b) The new design is wider and uninhibited.

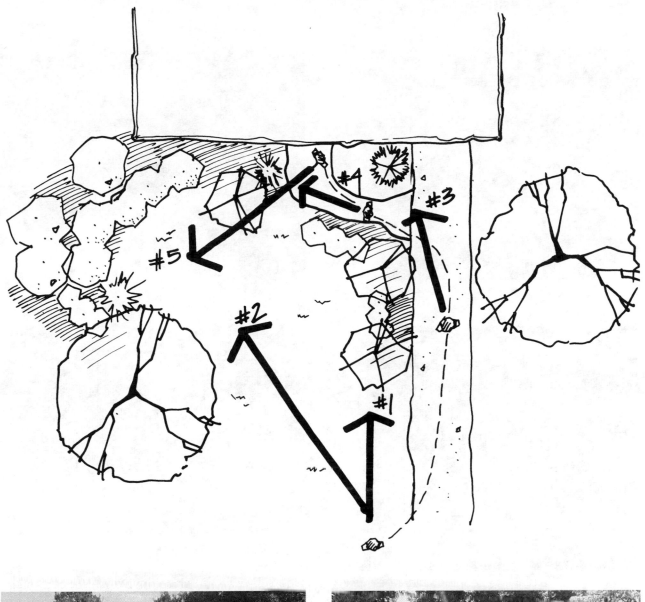

(a)

(b)

Figure 4–36 **Multiple Approaching Views**

Consider the various views as one approaches the front door. (a) The beginning approach views the front of the bed; (b) then overlooks the yard toward the corner planting;

(continues)

Figure 4–36 **Multiple Approaching Views—continued**
(c) then sees the planting near the entry opening; (d) then the entry walk #4 (close-up) planting at entry steps and (e) finally overlooks the yard again near the steps toward the planting near the curb.

Direct from Road   The sidewalk from the front door to the road is not as common as it once was (Fig. 4–37). After all, using the driveway as the approach saves money. However, when appropriate (or desired by clients), this may be a consideration. Use this opportunity to make an interesting, yet not out of the way, approach.

Greeting Area

The greeting area refers to the area, such as a porch, where guests stand at the front door.

Size

The greeting area should be large enough so that at least two or three people can comfortably stand near the front door (Fig. 4–38). **Stoops** are usually small concrete pads that hold only a few people. If there is a door that opens out, the guests will have to step off the stoop to allow the door to open.

(a)

(b)

Figure 4–37   Entry Walk from Road

(a) This entry walk to the road has rarely been used. (b) After removal, simple step-stones lead the home-owner to the mailbox.

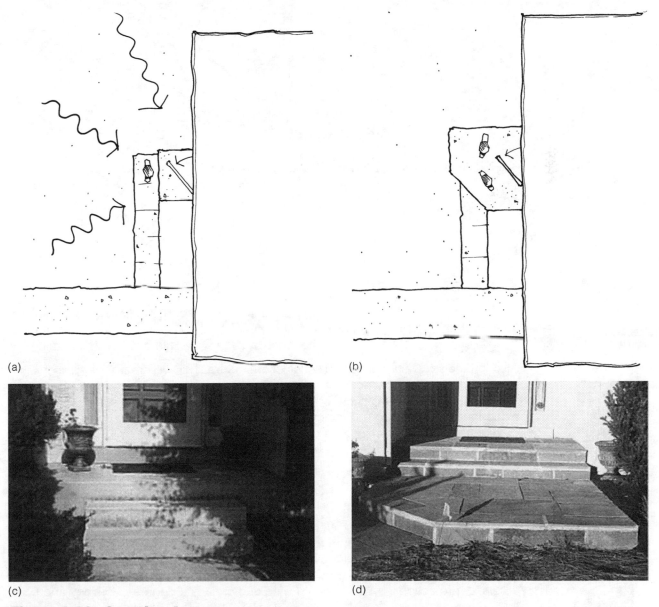

(a)

(b)

(c)

(d)

Figure 4–38   Greeting Area

(a) The greeting area, which is a stoop or porch, is often too small and exposed to the elements. (b) This stoop is large enough so that visitors can remain while the front door opens. (c) This stoop is too small to allow guests to be greeted at the front porch, but (d) is expanded with a warm material to be more welcoming. *(Photos courtesy of Robert J. Kleinberg Landscaping, East Lansdowne, PA.* www.kleinberg.com*)*

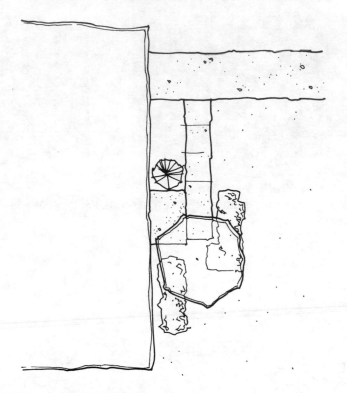

***Figure 4–39* Enclosing the Greeting Area**
Enclosure of the greeting area adds an element of comfort and semiprivacy without screening the front door.

Protection

The greeting area should have some protection from the elements (Fig. 4–39). Overhead protection helps get guests out of the rain. A porch does that easily with the extension of a roof. Stoops, on the other hand, may provide little overhead protection.

Also, protection should provide a sense of **enclosure.** This will create a feeling of semiprivacy when at the front door. Front doors that have a stoop completely exposed to the street make guests feel uncomfortable, like they are standing on a stage. By planting along the sides and perhaps the overhead of a tree canopy will make guests feel more comfortable as well as more protected from the elements like wind, rain, and sun. However, do not make the mistake of screening the front door so that the door is not visible from the road.

Sitting Area

Although entertaining guests often takes place in the privacy of the backyard, some people like a sitting area in the front yard. This may be the front porch or a separate paved space (Fig. 4–40). This provides a nice greeting area for brief, semiprivate visits as well as neighborhood activities. Planning for some enclosure with trees and shrubs allows for protection from the sun and wind and creates a degree of privacy and comfort.

(a)

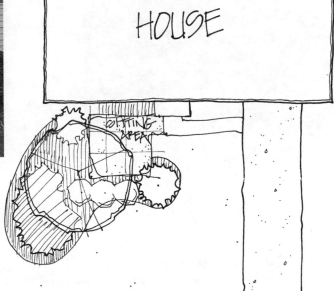

(b)

(c)

(d)

Figure 4–40 **Entertaining at the Greeting Area**
(a) The front porch or (b) other area can serve as an area to entertain guests. (c) Partial enclosure of front porch creates a comfortable atmosphere. (d) Greeting area is expanded to casually host guests. *(Photo (a) courtesy of King's Material, Inc. Cedar Rapids, IA.* www.kingsmaterial.com*; Photo (d) courtesy of Blue Ribbon LLC, Maryland.* www.blueribbonllc.com*)*

Figure 4–41   Greeting Interest
Items of interest, such as a (a) fountain or (b) formal pond, add appeal to the front door.

Interest

Provide elements of interest near the greeting area (Fig. 4–41). Not only is this a high-traffic area, it helps draw interest to the front door.

Side Yard

There's a great deal of variation in the side yard, depending on the size and shape of the lot as well as the orientation of the house. Side yards are generally narrow and shady, primarily used to get people from the front to the backyard (Fig. 4–42). They are often used as the utility area.

Tip Box

The side yards of a typical residence have little more function than to connect the front yard with the backyard.

Circulation

Because the main purpose of a side yard is often to **circulate** traffic to the backyard, creating a path that guides people is useful (Fig. 4–43). Allow for space to comfortably get to the backyard, and consider if there needs to be enough room to get equipment, like a riding mower, through the area. Although a concrete or a paved path would be ideal, many clients may not want to spend money on a secondary path where turf would function just as well.

Figure 4–42 Side Yard

Most side yards are narrow, shady spaces that simply connect the front to the backyard, as well as store utility items such as garbage.

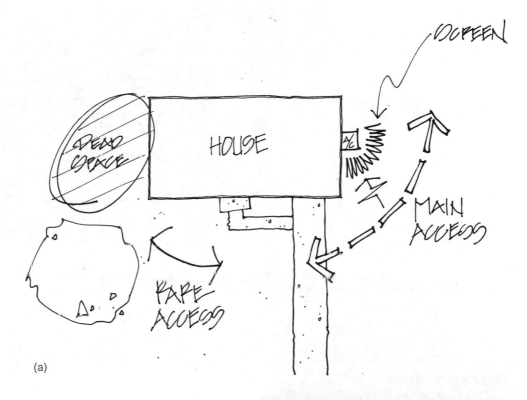

(a)

(b)

Figure 4–43 Circulation

(a) Circulation patterns throughout the residence should facilitate foot traffic. (b) This side yard gets the homeowner to the backyard. The small trees provide a ceiling and make the walk more comfortable.

(a)

(b)

Figure 4–44 Storage
(a) Locate areas of storage in less visible areas. (b) Storage areas screened with plants.

Storage Area

In some cases the side yard is considered dead space and used for **storage** (Fig. 4–44). Many residents will park a seldom-used camper or boat there, as well as other items such as firewood, garbage cans, or construction material.

Screening

Consider the unslightly items that are along the side (Fig. 4–45). If an air-conditioning unit is there, consider screening it with a low lattice fence or small shrubs (Fig. 4–46). However, be careful not to smother the unit, preventing airflow and operation.

If garbage cans are stored there, then create a screen that would hide them but still leave adequate access to them.

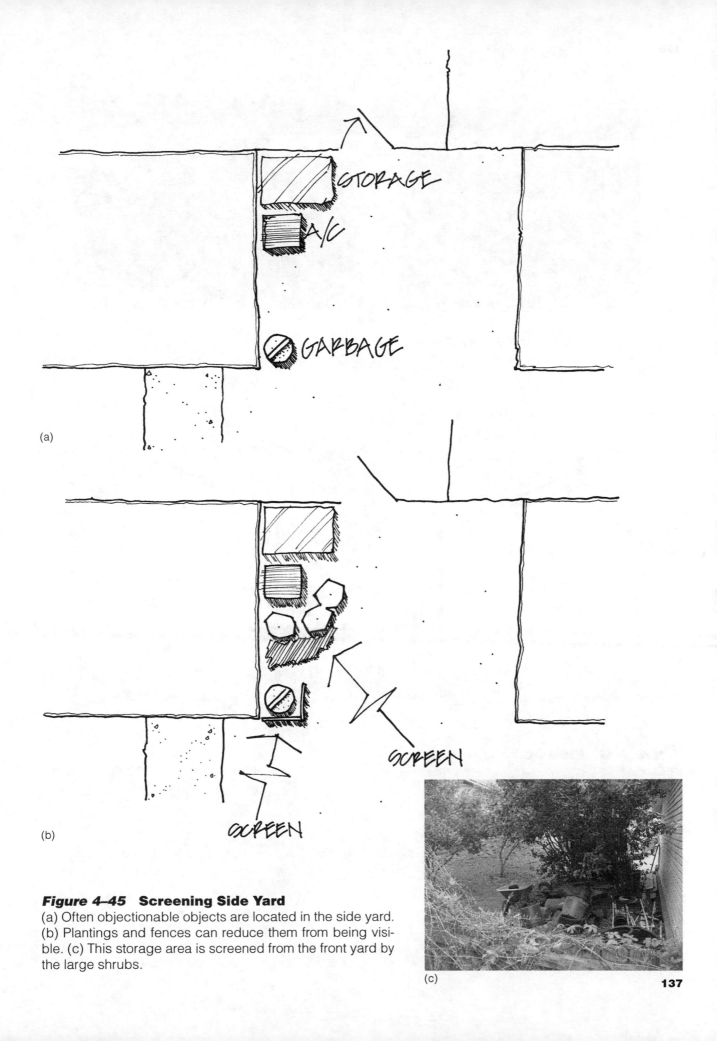

(a)

(b)

(c)

Figure 4–45 Screening Side Yard
(a) Often objectionable objects are located in the side yard.
(b) Plantings and fences can reduce them from being visible. (c) This storage area is screened from the front yard by the large shrubs.

(a)   (b)

Figure 4–46   Screening the Air-Conditioning Unit
(a) These A/C units located in the side yard are screened from (b) the front yard with a small lattice fence panel.

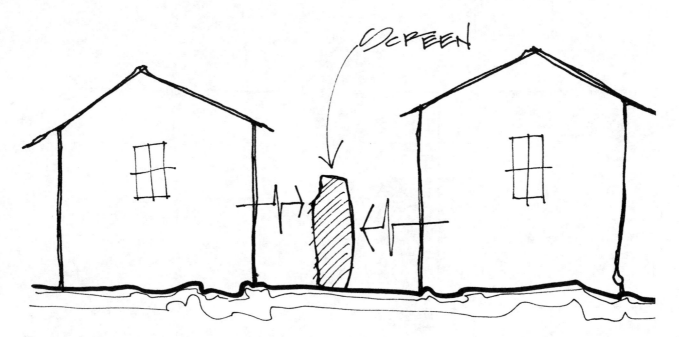

Figure 4–47   View from the Neighbor
Because side yards are narrow, views may need to be screened so that the neighbor is not looking directly into the client's home.

Look at whether views from the neighbor's house need to be screened from seeing into the client's house (Fig. 4–47).

Curb Appeal

Some side yards can be large and in view of the public (Fig. 4–48). In this case, the side yard would be part of the curb appeal that the front yard addresses.

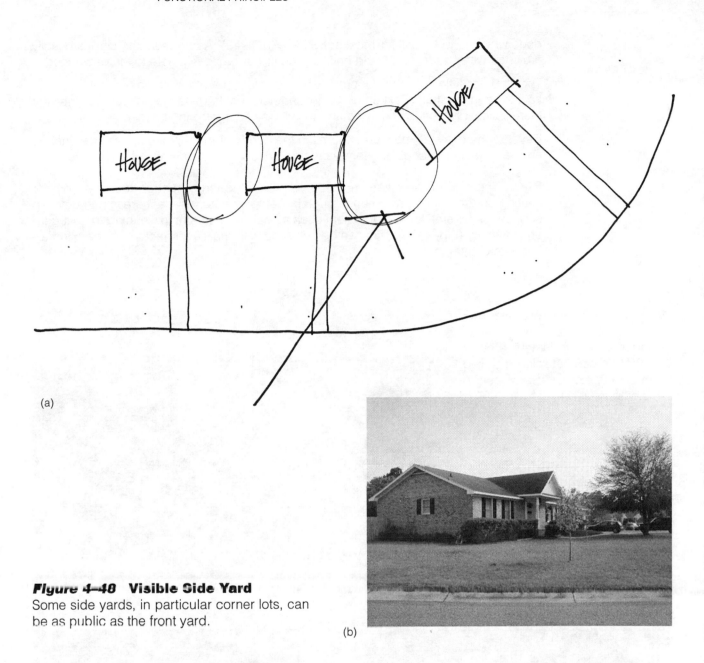

Figure 4-48 Visible Side Yard
Some side yards, in particular corner lots, can
be as public as the front yard.

(a)

(b)

Backyard

The backyard is generally the private area. It's primarily used for entertaining guests, eating, relaxing, recreation, and hobbies.

Developing the Backyard

Entertainment

An **entertainment area** may just be a simple place that two people can go to relax and look out over the backyard, or as complex as an area for parties and various functions. Typically, the entertainment area is a 10′ × 10′ concrete slab that comes off the back door, which is too small for most activities (Fig. 4–49). As a result, the slab is usually crowded with chairs, table, and grill, leaving little room to circulate to the back door.

The slab has little enclosure or protection from the elements. With no overhead protection, the sun creates an extremely bright and hot area. With nothing planted on the side there is little protection from wind and the views of neighboring houses.

Develop the entertainment area to match the needs of the residents. This may just be an area to accommodate the family or large enough to host parties of 20 people.

Size The size of the entertainment area should be large enough to allow room for seating and room for circulation through it. Complex entertainment areas can develop subspaces for smaller entertainment such as eating, sunbathing, reading, or just general intimacy (Fig. 4–50). This can be achieved with multilevel decks or separating areas with plantings.

Figure 4–49 **Entertainment Slab**
A common entertainment area is the 10′ × 10′ concrete slab, installed by the contractor, which is open to the elements and too small.

(a)

(b)

Figure 4–50 **Entertainment Size**
The size of the entertainment area should correspond to the client needs. (a) Simple, single-level decks are suitable for small gatherings while (b) large, multilevel decks can host larger crowds. *(Photo (a) courtesy of JRW Decks in Seattle.* www.jrwdecks.com*)*

(a)

(b)

(c)

***Figure 4–51* Patio Material**
(a and b) Pavers, (c) flagstone, or concrete are common patio materials.
(Photo (a) courtesy of Robert J. Kleinberg Landscaping, East Lansdowne, PA, www.kleinberg.com*; Photo (b) courtesy of King's Material, Inc., Cedar Rapids, IA.* www.kingsmaterial.com*)*

Materials Entertainment areas are often developed with a hardscape material to provide a solid footing as well as to separate them from the lawn. The most common types of materials used to develop entertainment areas are wood decks and patios. Patios can be constructed with pavers, flagstone, or concrete (Fig. 4–51).

Enclosure Entertainment areas are generally for intimate to semi-intimate gatherings (Fig. 4–52). Creating a sense of enclosure provides a comfortable setting for gathering. This can be any degree of enclosure, ranging from complete screening to implied enclosure.

Overhead: Develop an overhead plane with the canopy of a tree or the wooden structure of an arbor intertwined with vines (Fig. 4–53).

Sides: Trees and shrubs can be used to create any degree of enclosure (Fig. 4–54). Dense shrubs that are 6 feet tall have a high degree of enclosure, where lower shrubs have more of an implied enclosure. The lower the shrub, the more the separation is implied. In fact, a simple bed of ground cover can be a nice separation that creates no visual separation.

Cooking Many people like an area for grilling (Fig. 4–55). Consider whether this will be integrated into the sitting area or set as a separate BBQ pit. This area should have adequate proximity to the back door of the house to facilitate trips back and forth to the kitchen.

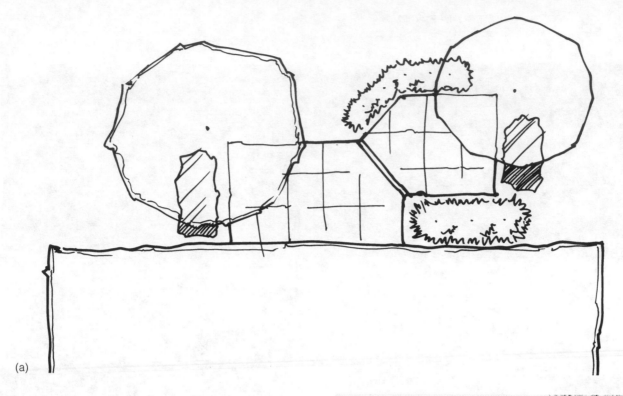

(a)

Figure 4–52 Entertainment Enclosure
(a) Partially enclosing the entertainment area overhead and along the sides adds to the comfort level and provides shade, protection, and privacy. (b) A large deck that has little protection from the sun and wind and provides no privacy from neighbors.

(b)

(a)

(b)

Figure 4–53 Overhead Enclosure
(a) This arbor provides a sense of overhead enclosure and comfort and provides a structure for fragrant vines to cover. (b) The canopy of the trees provides the overhead enclosure over this breakfast nook.

142

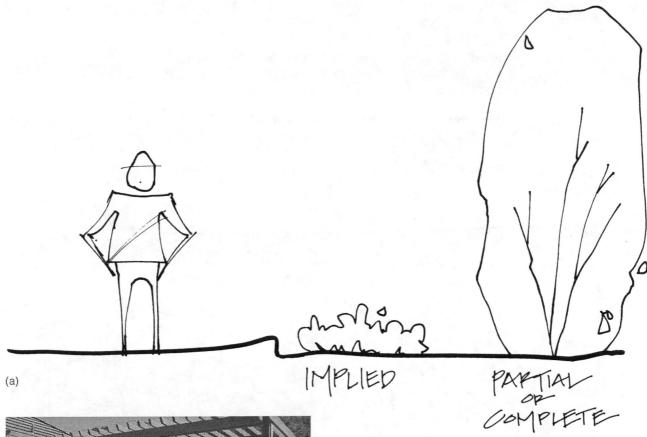

(a)

IMPLIED

PARTIAL
OR
COMPLETE

(b)

Figure 4–54 Side Enclosure

(a) Shrubs provide more enclosure from other areas, while ground cover implies separation without screening. (b) Lattice walls enclose the hot tub for semi privacy, allowing light and wind to pass through. *(Photo courtesy of Decks by JRW Portland, Oregon. www.decksbyjrw.com)*

(a)

(b)

Figure 4–55 Cooking Area

An area designated for outdoor cooking should be close enough to the house to make convenient trips to the kitchen. *(Photo (b) courtesy of Decks by JRW Portland, Oregon. www.decksbyjrw.com)*

Eating   Will there be a permanent outdoor area developed for eating outside or will this be integrated into the entertainment area? Eating areas ideally should have some protection from the wind and sun, even rain if possible.

Views and Other Elements of Interest   It is important to include elements of interest, in particular, views from the entertainment area to improve the comfort and appeal. Oftentimes there is little to break up the monotonous rhythm of the fence that runs the entire length of the backyard (Fig. 4–56). This creates very few interesting views

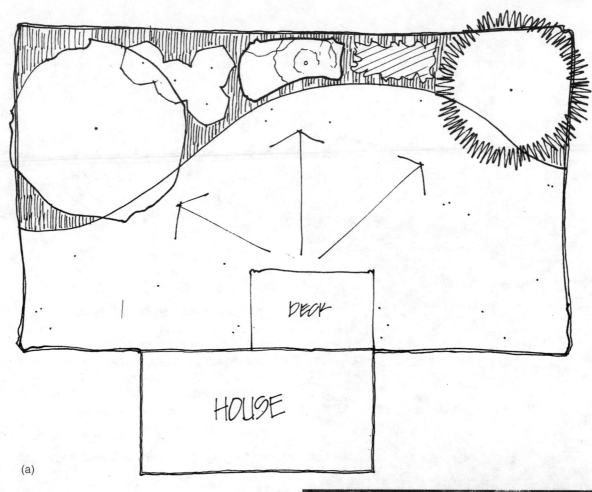

(a)

(b)

Figure 4–56 Entertainment Views
(a) Plantings can break up the long, monotonous run of privacy fence and provide interesting views. (b) From this deck, landscaping would help create an interesting view while entertaining.

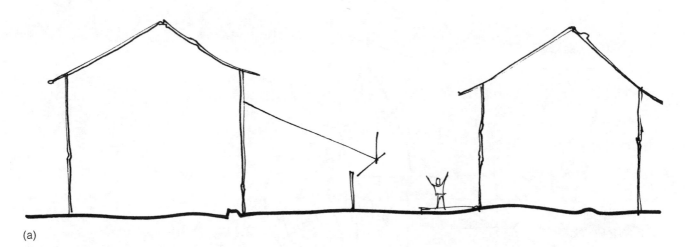

(a)

(b)

(c)

Figure 4–57 **Screening Views into the Backyard**
(a) A common problem is screening views that come over a 6′ privacy fence from neighboring two-story houses. (b) This backyard has little privacy, however (c) trees could enclose and screen the views from the tall neighboring homes.

looking out into the backyard. Also, make note of views that are unsightly and that need to be blocked. Pay attention to views from neighbors coming into the backyard (Fig. 4–57). Neighboring two-story houses look right down into the privacy of the backyard.

Other elements of interest include sound and fragrance. Water features add the dimension of a splashing sound and, sometimes, fish (Fig. 4–58). There are many plants that can add delightful fragrance when blooming.

Recreation

The other major activity in the backyard is recreation (Fig. 4–59). This can take many forms, depending on the needs of the residents.

Open Area A considerable amount of open area is needed for outdoor games, especially if there are children. It should be a continuous stretch of turf. However, the amount of open area is based on the client's wants.

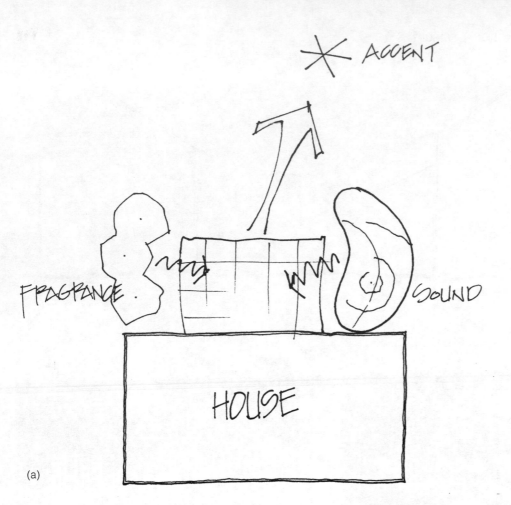

***Figure 4–58* Entertainment Interest**
(a) Accent plantings, fragrance, and sound offer interesting elements to the entertainment area. (b) A small pond provides trickling water and goldfish.

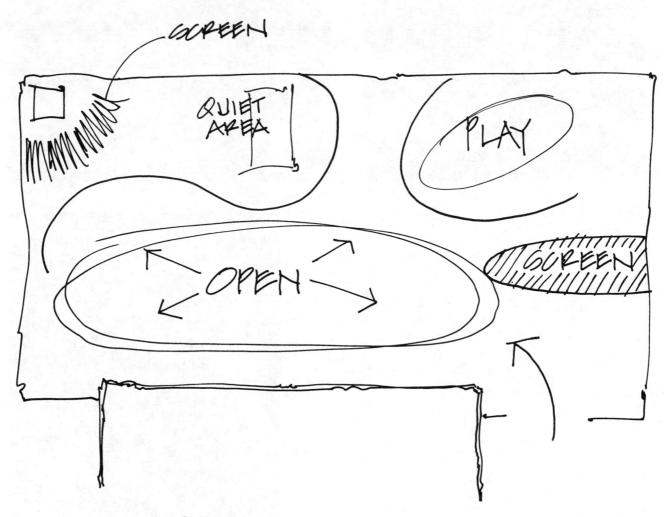

***Figure 4–59* Backyard Activities**
Several activities besides entertainment should be considered: open area for recreation, play area for children, quiet area, and screening views.

Playground   If the residents have small children, it may be important to develop an area for a playground, which could include a swing set and sandbox (Fig. 4–60). Be sure that this area is in good view from inside the house as well as out since parents will want to keep an occasional eye on small children.

Hobbies   There are many **hobbies** that can be addressed with the landscape. Gardening is one of the most common outdoor hobbies (Fig. 4–61). This may include flowers as well as vegetables. Although the resident may have many ideas to develop this area, there are a few things to consider:

Water source: If this is a vegetable garden, will there be adequate availability to water? It would be inconvenient to drag the hose across the yard.

Exposure: Is it shade or full sun? Vegetables require a lot of sun to grow successfully. Water gardens require at least 8 hours of sun for many aquatic plants to bloom.

(a)

(b)

(c)

Figure 4–60 Playground
The playground for children should be in view of the house (a) or entertainment area (b) so that the playground (in back) can be easily monitored. (c) A treehouse is not only a playground, but an interest element in the backyard. *(Photo (b) courtesy of Blue Ribbon LLC, Maryland.* www.blueribbonllc.com*)*

Figure 4–61 Garden
Gardening, a popular hobby, should be in full sun with easy access to water. This garden is placed in an area out of view from the house and entertainment area.

Summary

The landscape should be more than a pretty picture; it should be useful as well. Outdoor rooms are created with floors, walls, and ceilings, using materials such as turf, fences, and canopies, to develop people spaces that are functional. The basic areas of the landscape are public (in view of neighbors and passersby), private (entertainment, recreation), and utility (storage, garbage cans, air conditioner). These basic areas are found throughout the landscape, but typically the public area is the front yard and the private and utility areas are in the back. The side yard varies depending on the lot and can be public, private, or utility.

The front yard is primarily developed to facilitate a safe and interesting approach for guests to the front door, in addition to improving curb appeal. The front door should be easy to find from the street, and the entry walk should comfortably facilitate walking. The driveway, in addition to having adequate space for parking cars, often serves as the approach walk from the street to the entry walk. There should be enough room to comfortably walk with cars parked. The front porch should be large enough and sufficiently protected to greet a few guests at the front door; it sometimes serves as a semiprivate entertainment area.

The side yard is typically narrow and shady, primarily used to connect the front yard to the backyard. Oftentimes it is used as a storage area and should sufficiently screen unsightly items.

The backyard is often the site for recreation, entertainment, or hobbies that include playground, gardening, swimming, cooking, and eating. Areas should be developed to support the resident's activities, for children, pets, adults, or parties. Comfortable areas to sit and interesting views improve quality of life in the backyard. It is often a private area that is screened from the surrounding area.

Key Terms

Circulation: paths commonly used to walk through the landscape

Curb appeal: how the front of the house looks from the road

Enclosure: plantings or construction that provides a sense of protection and privacy

Entertainment area: place where people can go to relax or host parties and other various functions

Entry walk: provides access from the road or from the driveway to the front door

Floors: can be made from turf, hardscapes, mulch, or ground cover

Functional: landscape supports the activities of the residents

Funneling effect: planting larger items on the outside and placing progressively smaller plants closer to the door to draw attention to the front door

Ground plane: see floors

Hobbies: outdoor activities; gardening is common

Implied screens: create a sense of separation without obscuring views

Partial screens: give a sense of separation and block views to some degree

Private area: an area screened from the public view and used to entertain guests, recreation and for hobbies, or for the family to relax; often the backyard and occasionally the side yard

Public areas: within view and open to the public; often the front yard and occasionally the side yard

Screening: comes in varying degrees

Service area: see utility area

Stoops: small concrete pads that hold only a few people

Storage: areas to keep belongings and materials such as camper or boat, firewood, garbage cans, or lumber

Total screens: can be an 8-foot-tall brick wall that no one can see past

Traditional landscaping: primarily dealt with foundation planting that consisted of an evergreen hedge across the front of the house

Utility area: an area for storage, gardening, trash, compost, or other items that are functional but often unsightly or odorous; kept out of sight

Walls: create separation, screening, and a sense of enclosure

Weed barrier: a synthetic, breathable fabric that prevents weeds from emerging through mulch

5 The Concept Plan

Objectives

- Understand the components and function of the concept plan in the design process
- Learn the materials and techniques to draw the concept plan
- Know the concept plan graphics

The functional aspects of the landscape design in the previous chapter come together to form the **concept plan,** sometimes referred to as a **functional diagram** or **bubble diagram.** The concept plan is an organization of the ground plane to create functionality in the design. Looking at the base map, the concept plan organizes the space of the ground plane into lawn, planting beds, concrete, work area, and so forth. It is important to start with a good concept upon which to build the details of the design. Thus, the concept plan acts as the bones, or blueprint, on which the design is built. If the framework of the design is ill conceived, then the design is doomed from the start.

> ### Tip Box
>
> If the framework of the design is ill conceived, then the design is doomed from the start.

This phase of the design will involve loose sketching of ideas and concepts (Fig. 5–1). Materials include tracing paper, soft lead (HB or 2B), and the site analysis. These sketches are an exercise for the purpose of organizing thoughts and generating design ideas at the fundamental level. In some cases, a designer may draw the concept plan for presentation to support the analysis and solutions of the final plan.

Figure 5–1 Sketching Concept Plan
A loose approach to developing the concept plan.

Analysis ——➤ *Concept Plan*

As the design process unfolds in later chapters it becomes apparent that each step becomes more detailed. The concept plan, fundamental in nature, is very general. It utilizes amorphous **bubbles** drawn on the plan to designate areas. It is important that the concept plan stays general and not become bogged down in any detail of plant material or hardscape.

Be loose. Make mistakes. And uncover new, fresh approaches to the design!

Space

The concept plan uses bubbles to fill the entire space of the site. A bubble accounts for all the space. This avoids leaving any area up to speculation (Fig. 5–2).

Analysis

It is imperative that the concept plan addresses the analysis. The concept plan is built right over the top of the analysis. In fact, some designers tape a sheet of tracing paper over the top of the analysis to draw the concept plan (Fig. 5–3). Good organization should always address strong and weak points of the analysis (Fig. 5–4).

Activities and Materials

Using bubbles, the base map will begin to be divided into various activities, effects, and/or general materials (Fig. 5–5). The following is a basic list of areas, not all-inclusive, that can be used in any combination. Of course, the selection and arrangement of bubbles in a concept plan will depend on the needs of the client.

Beds: This can be as general as "planting areas" or "mulched beds" or can be as specific as "low shrubs, screen, large deciduous trees."

Lawn: An important component of most designs because it is inexpensive and supports many activities.

Hardscape: This refers to any hard surface such as a driveway, sidewalk, patio, or deck.

Screen: Areas that will block unpleasant sites from view or wind/sun exposure.

Focal points: Suggested development of an accent for view.

Activities: Designating areas for various activities. These include, but are not limited to

Garden

Work

Eating

Relaxation

Play

Entertainment

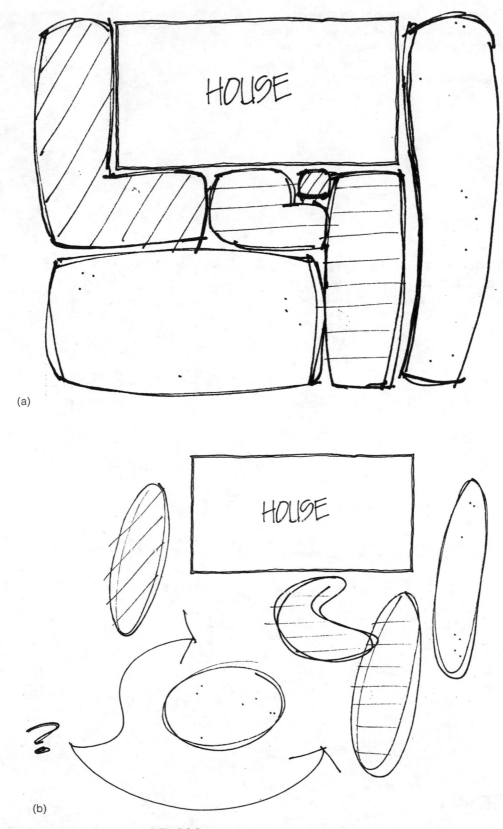

Figure 5–2 Concept Plan and Bubbles

(a) All areas are designated with bubbles to organize the ground plane. (b) Smaller bubbles leave too much open space that is undefined.

***Figure 5–3* Concept Drawing**
In order to address the analysis, some designers prefer to lay the concept drawing over the analysis, while some simply refer back to the analysis lying to the side.

***Figure 5–4* Concept and Analysis**
(a) The concept plan will address the analysis; (b) if not, the concept plan and, ultimately, the design will be much less functional.

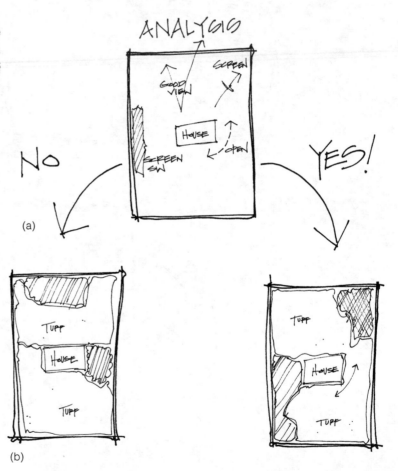

Concepts

What is being defined in the concept plan by these bubbles? Besides establishing materials and activities in these bubbles, size, location, circulation, views, and exposure are also considered in their development and placement.

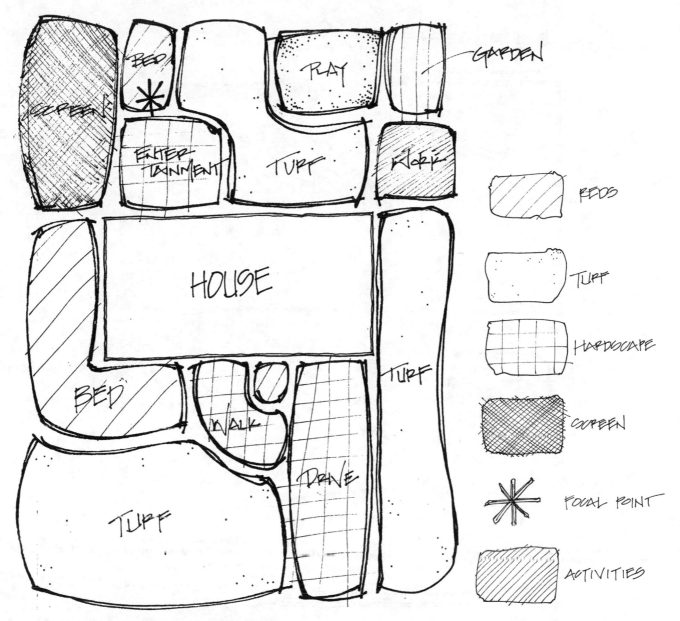

Figure 5–5 **Activities and Materials**
Each bubble represents a different function, or concept, on the plan.

Size

The bubbles in the concept are generally rough sketches but should approximate the size of each designated area. The size of the area is often dictated by the client's needs.

Entertainment

How large of an entertainment area is needed (Fig. 5–6)? If the client will host large parties, then the area may need to be as large as several hundred square feet. However, if the entertainment consists of an area where the family can sit and relax, then it may only be a couple of hundred square feet.

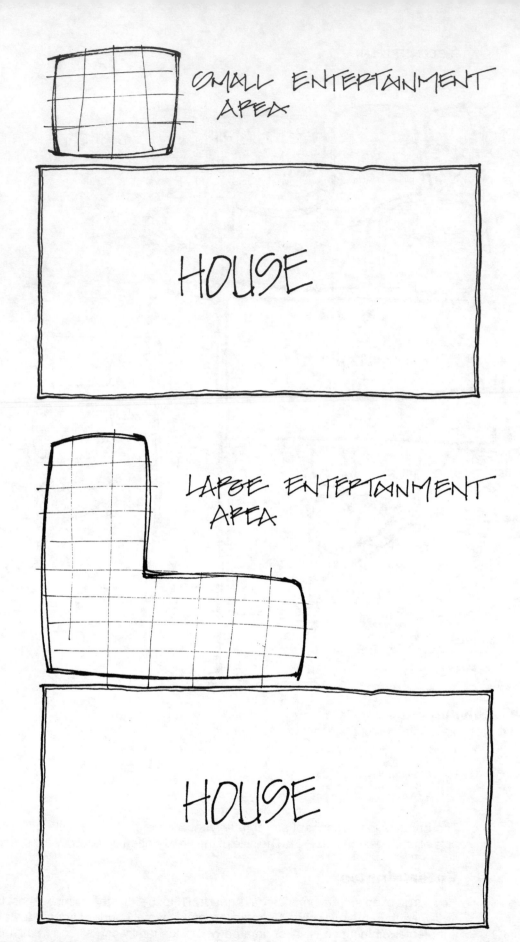

SMALL ENTERTAINMENT AREA

HOUSE

LARGE ENTERTAINMENT AREA

HOUSE

Figure 5–6 Entertainment Size
The size of the bubble is defined by the function of the entertainment area.

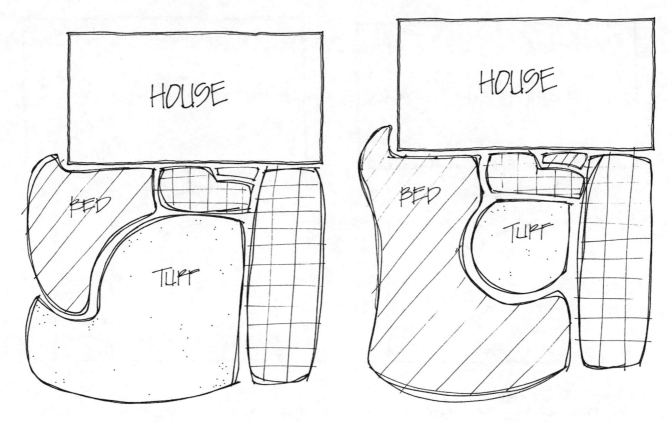

Figure 5–7 **Lawn Size**
The size of the lawn and bed bubbles is relevant to level of mowing, as well as the activities that would require turf (recreation) or beds (plantings).

Lawn and Beds

How much lawn will be required? Is there a need for play and recreation areas? Some residents like to have a good size lawn to maintain while others like bed space for trees, shrubs, and flowers (Fig. 5–7).

What kind of maintenance do the clients want? Lawns need to be mowed weekly during the summer. Planting beds need to be mulched, weeded, and occasionally pruned. However, the maintenance demands of planting beds, although higher during the first few years of establishment, eventually decrease if planting beds are designed properly for trees, shrubs, and ground cover to grow and smother most weeds and reduce mulching needs.

Entry Walk and Other Paths

The width of primary sidewalks, which is generally the entry walk going to the front door, should be no less than 4 feet wide (Fig. 5–8). Secondary walks where traffic is much lighter can be as narrow as 2 to 3 feet.

Location

The size of the bubbles allows for adequate space, but the bubbles also need to be located appropriately on the site.

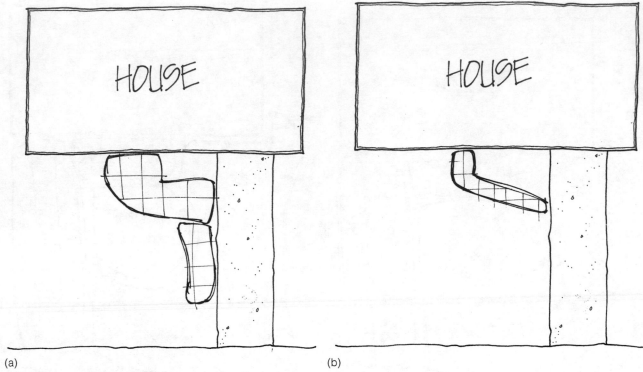

(a)   (b)

Figure 5–8   **Entry Size**
The size of the bubble should be roughly equal to the dimensions of the entry walk. (a) Represents a wide, welcome walk, while (b) represents a narrow walk.

Access

Make sure there is adequate access for each activity, as it requires.

- Gardening should be accessible to a water source (Fig. 5–9).
- Cooking should have close accessibility to the house kitchen.
- Work areas should be conveniently located near the garage or shed or at least a power source.

Visibility

- Playgrounds should be in a visible location so parents can watch children easily (Fig. 5–10).
- Storage areas should be accessible, but not so that they are a visual problem.

Circulation

The concept plan should address the circulation patterns observed in the analysis. Good circulation throughout the property makes a comfortable setting that is easy to navigate as well as facilitates safety (Fig. 5–11).

Primary Circulation

This pertains to major paths. The most common, and most important in many cases, is the front walk which facilitates pedestrians from the street or the driveway to the front door. These paths should be wide enough to allow two people to walk side by side. At a minimum they should be 4 feet wide.

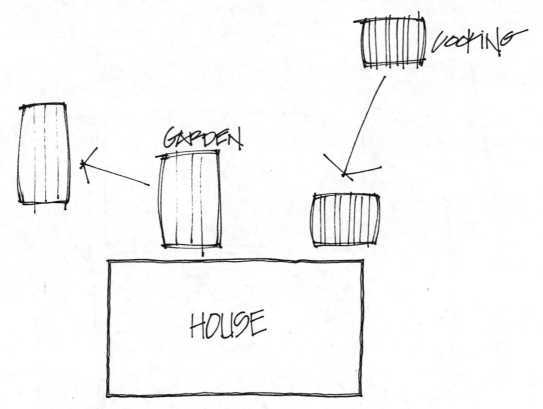

Figure 5–9   Access
The concept plan should locate activities and areas appropriately. Cooking should be closer to the house while the garden is often away from the house in full sun and accessible to water.

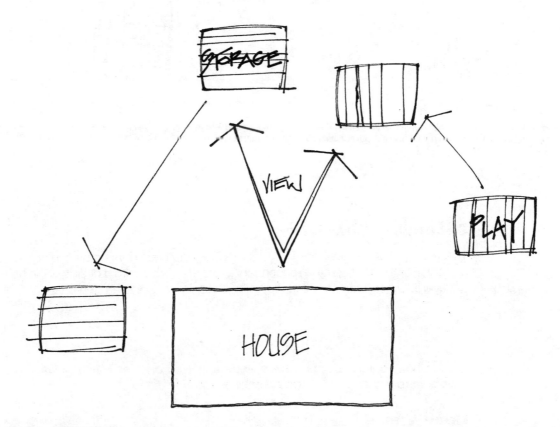

Figure 5–10   Visibility
Locate areas for appropriate exposure. Playgrounds should be within view of the house while storage areas are away from view.

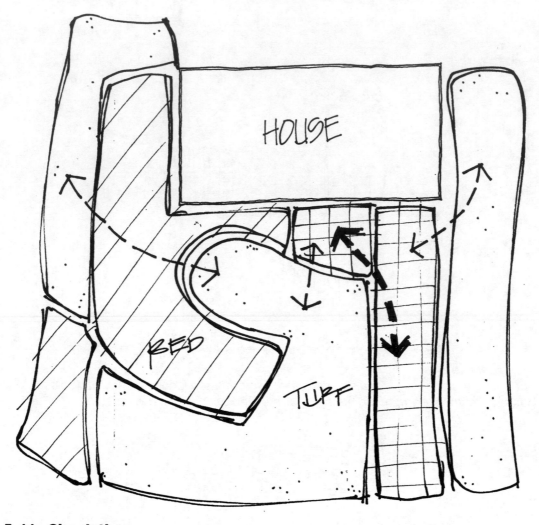

Figure 5–11 Circulation
Study the circulation patterns and layout bubbles in order to facilitate flow. Large arrows indicate primary circulation while smaller arrows indicate secondary circulation.

Secondary Circulation

These are paths that are infrequently taken. They are usually taken by one or two people at any given time. Most common secondary paths are from the front or side of the house to the backyard. Other paths may include traffic around work areas and entertainment areas.

View

Concept plans address the various views analyzed on-site. These views may be existing views (good and poor) and potential views (Fig. 5–12).

Good Views

There are good existing views that should be preserved. These are often addressed by keeping the view open or framing.

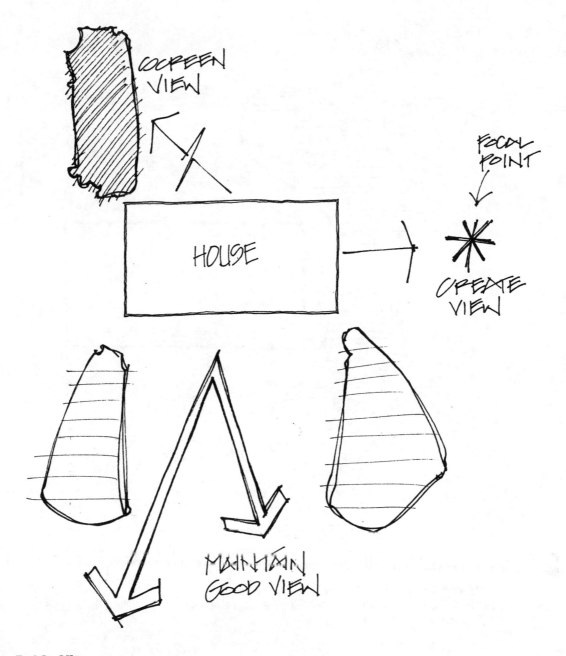

Figure 5–12 **Views**
The concept plan should address the views in analysis. The broken arrow indicates screening view, the star refers to a proposed focal point, and the large arrows indicate major views.

Poor Views

Plantings or fences screen poor views such as unsightly trash areas, storage, or traffic. These areas are noted on the concept plan to be blocked from common views, such as from an entertainment area or public area.

Potential Views

Some areas of viewing (entertainment or inside views) have very few interesting views. To increase the interest of these areas of viewing something can be created. This may be a focal point, such as a water feature or sculpture, or other themes, such as butterfly gardens.

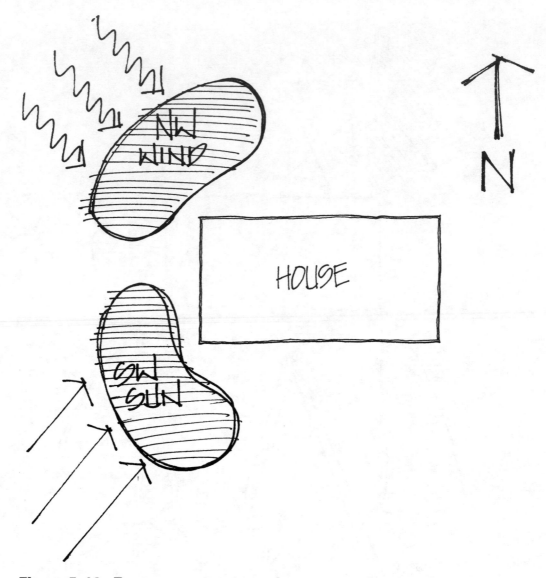

Figure 5–13 Exposure
The concept plan should screen the sun and wind according to analysis for energy efficiency.

Exposure

There will be areas on the site that need to be protected from the elements (Fig. 5–13).

Shade

Create shade for an entertainment area or to cool the southwest side of the house.

Wind

Provide a wind block to protect entertainment areas or the northwest side of the house when prevailing wind is a problem.

Enclosure

Create a sense of enclosure at entertainment areas or other gathering areas such as the front door, which makes them more comfortable.

Alternate Concepts

Most designers can "see" the design solution after being on site for a short while and talking to the client (Fig. 5–14). Through years of experience an intuition develops for a design approach. Most designers go with their first impression as the design solution. However, the concept plan can explore other solutions that are hardly considered because of the dominance of the first idea. By drawing out two or three concept plans, other fresh, exciting approaches are discovered and may be integrated with the original idea.

There is nothing wrong with the first impression, but it can become a blinder to other creative ideas. Another downside to the lack of exploration is hitting a rut, where all designs begin to look the same.

Some students are very attached to the first idea. So much so that they are very resistant to exploring anything else. I'm often approached by a student with the response, "I'll do another one, but I'll be using the first one." Or, between two concept plans, there are few differences. Maybe the lawn is a little bit smaller. Those students who finally relent and decide to go off and take an entirely different approach are often pleased with the results. They find they are excited with original, unique solutions never considered.

Summary

The concept plan, sometimes referred to as a bubble diagram or functional diagram, organizes the ground plane to create a framework on which the design will be built. It is fundamental that it addresses the analysis in order to be fully functional. Bubbles, which are somewhat amorphous, are used to designate areas of activity or material that will be refined in greater detail in later phases of the design process. These bubbles will fill the entire space of the plan to leave nothing undefined. The size and placement of the bubbles organize the ground plane depending on the intended function of the area, as well as visibility and desired access. A number of concept plans, each addressing the analysis, are quickly developed to work through new and different ideas in order to come up with a creative, functional solution to the analysis. Occasionally a designer may present the concept plan to the client to support the master plan.

Key Terms

Bubble diagram: see concept plan

Bubbles: outlines that define an area or activity

Concept plan: organization of ground plane to create a functional design

Functional diagram: see concept plan

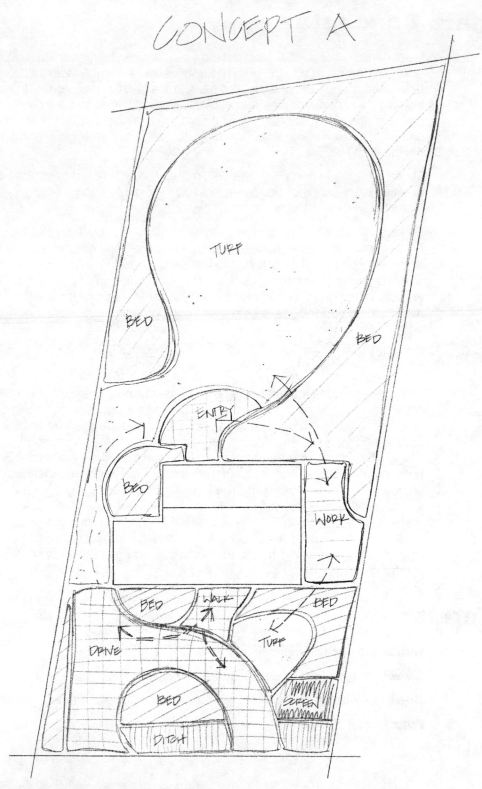

CONCEPT A

TURF

BED

BED

ENTRY

BED

WORK

BED

WALK

BED

DRIVE

TURF

BED

SCREEN

DITCH

Figure 5–14 Grant Concept Drawings

Three different concept plans that address the analysis of the Grant residence.

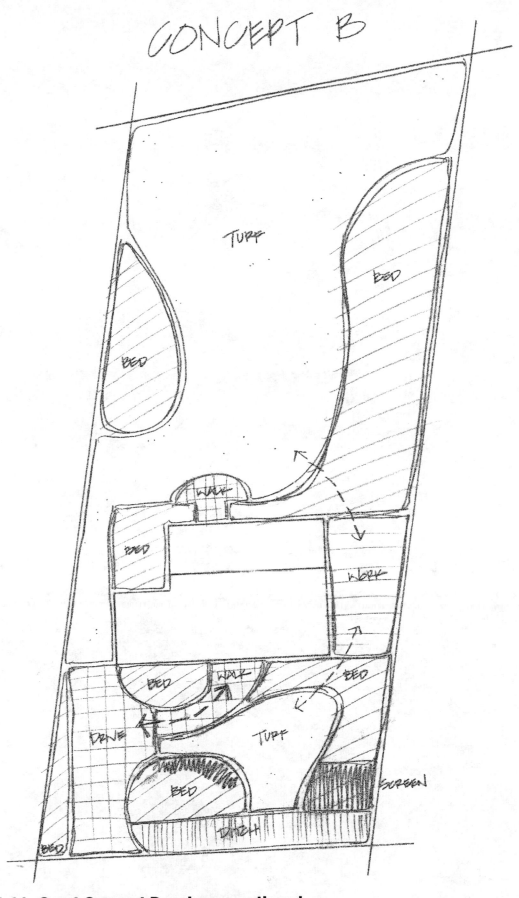

Figure 5–14 Grant Concept Drawings—continued

(continues)

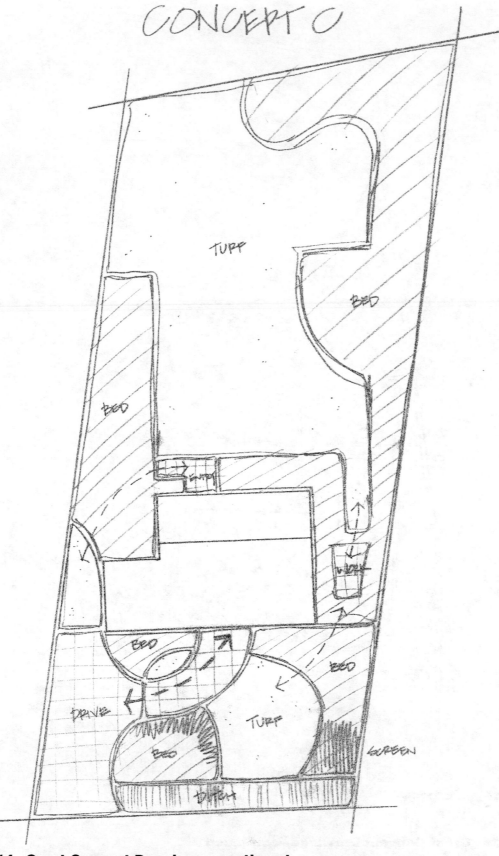

Figure 5–14 Grant Concept Drawings—continued

6 Design Principles

Objectives

- Become familiar with attributes of form, color, and texture and their use in design
- Understand approaches to balance in the landscape
- Be able to establish connection or unity in the design
- Know various means of creating visual interest in the design
- Be able to create a sense of flow or transition in the landscape
- Understand the application of mass planting

As the concept plan creates the useful or functional component of the landscape design, design principles create the aesthetic, or visual appeal. Design principles are useful not only to develop visual interest but also to create a sense of unity and order in the design concept. The goal should be to create a landscape that appears as a big picture where every component of the landscape belongs to the overall design. Compare it to a framed work of art (Fig. 6–1). There are interesting components within the work itself, with each individual part having a unique aspect. These differences within the frame make it interesting, keeping our attention moving throughout the work. But when you step back and look at it in its entirety, all the individual unique components belong to a theme.

The following design principles are proposed to help bring unity, order, and interest to your design.

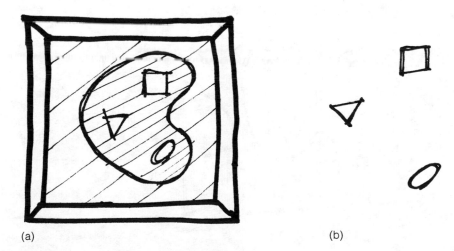

(a)   (b)

Figure 6–1   Cohesive Design
Like a framed work of art, the landscape design should be composed of individual components yet be connected as if part of (a) one composition rather than (b) random individual parts.

Design Attributes

Before discussing design principles, let us take a look at design **attributes,** in particular those that pertain to plants. Becoming familiar with these attributes will make it easier to understand design principles.

Form

Form is the outline of an object or plant, often thought of as the silhouette (Fig. 6–2). It is easiest to see it in an individual plant. Form can also be the total mass of plants when they are grouped together.

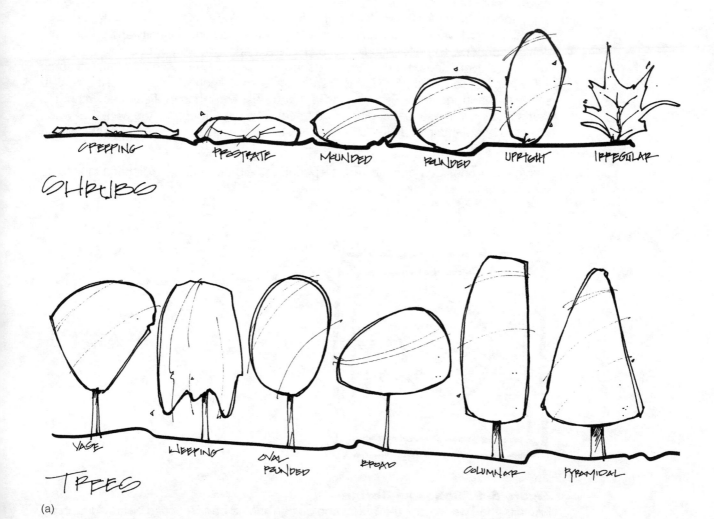

(a)

***Figure 6–2* Form**
(a) There are various forms in which plants can be categorized, from upright and columnar to broad and spreading.

(b)

Figure 6–2 Form—continued
(b) Plant forms can be very unique and, in this case, should be used carefully. Too much of a "loud" form that demands attention can be disruptive. (c) The vine growing up a white wall creates an interesting pattern or form. (d) This weeping form creates the effect of water falling into a dry creek. (e) The planting beds create a curving form of turf on the ground plane.

(c)

(d)

(e)

Form is manipulated when shrubs are tightly **sheared,** creating geometric forms out of the plants (Fig. 6–3). This may be the intention in formal gardens or in the practice of **topiary,** when a plant form is pruned into shapes of spirals or animals (Fig. 6–4). **Espalier** manipulates form by training a tree or shrub to grow flat against a wall or fence (Fig. 6–5). However, shearing is often abused and the natural form is lost.

There are a variety of natural plant forms to be aware of. It's important to be familiar with the various forms, so as not to have too much variety in the design.

Figure 6–3 **Shearing Form**
Pruning, in particular shearing, can dramatically change a plant form. Oftentimes it destroys the natural form.

Figure 6–4 **Topiary**
The technique of pruning plants into specific shapes, such as pom-poms, spirals, or animals. *(Photo courtesy of Visual Impac Imaging)*

Figure 6–5 **Espalier**
The technique of pruning plants to grow flat against a wall or fence.

Shrubs	**Trees**
• Creeping	• Vase-shaped/fastigate
• Prostrate	• Weeping
• Mounded	• Round
• Rounded	• Broad
• Upright	• Oval
• Irregular	• Columnar
	• Pyramidal

Color

Color in the landscape can be introduced from several parts of the plant. Most commonly color comes by way of flowers, but color is also useful from foliage, fruit, and branching. Color has an impact on human emotion. **Warm** colors (red, orange, yellow) create excitement while **cool** colors (blue, green, purple) have a calming effect.

Foliage

There are many shades of green that foliage can display: light green, silver green, blue green, and dark green (Fig. 6–6). Together a nice variety of green colors can create visual interest and contrast. Although foliage is commonly green there are selections that maintain foliage of other colors such as shades of red, purple, and yellow (Fig. 6–7). Burgundy, most popular with Japanese maples, is a common alternative and can be a nice change of pace among green foliage.

***Figure 6–6* Shades of Green**
A variety of green colors can create interest, from light green and blue green to dark green, as well as variegation.

***Figure 6–7* Foliage Color**
Colors other than green, such as the burgundy foliage of a Japanese maple, can add a nice change of pace. *(Photo courtesy of William A. Hoch.* http://www.midwestlandscapeplants.org)

Figure 6–8 **Variegation**
Variegated foliage is a popular selection because it is unique in color and pattern. It is often a good selection to create a focal accent because it attracts attention.

Figure 6–9 **Fall Color**
Not all plants have an appealing fall color like the brilliant red of these Firepower Nandina.

Variegation   Another consideration is **variegation,** which is the mottling or striping of foliage (and sometimes flowers) (Fig. 6–8). Variegation offers a unique display of foliage and can be used to create accent points among green foliage.

Fall Color   Some plants are well known for brilliant displays of fall color (Fig. 6–9). This may be bright colors of orange, yellow, red, or purple. These plants offer a great burst of color toward the end of the growing season when flowering colors are rare. Be aware that some plants have very little color in the fall, simply turning brown and falling to the ground.

Flowers

Flowers are often the most revered of many plants, whether it's for their color, shape, or fragrance. Some plants are highly prized for their flowering and as a result have numerous cultivars with a wide variety of flower characteristics. This is evident with roses, camellias, and azaleas. In contrast, other plants have flowers of insignificance, such as sycamores, maples, and conifers. Many people think the value of flowers lies mostly in the color (Fig. 6–10).

Length of Bloom   In many cases, color is provided by annual flowers that bloom all season long (Fig. 6–11). Perennial flowers, trees, and shrubs only flower for a portion of the season. However, the length of time varies greatly. Some may be a short bloom of a few days while other plants go on for several weeks.

Figure 6-10 **Flower Color**
Flower color is a very common means of introducing color into the landscape.

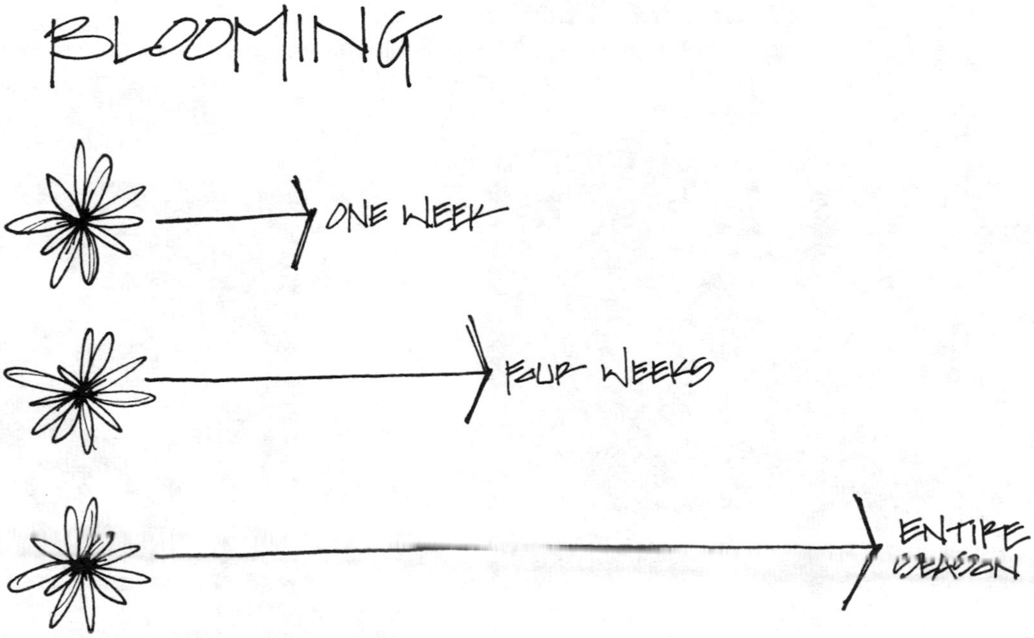

BLOOMING

ONE WEEK

FOUR WEEKS

ENTIRE SEASON

Figure 6-11 **Length of Bloom**
Be aware of how long a plant will bloom. Annuals bloom all season, while perennials range from a short week to several weeks of color.

Sequence   Another consideration when selecting flower color is timing (Fig. 6–12). Select plants so there is a **sequence** of flowering throughout the growing season. This creates a movement of change and interest throughout the entire season. Contrast this to a scenario where all plants in the design flower at the same time, creating an overwhelming blast of color and then after a few weeks appear green for the remainder of the season.

Spring flowering: Most plants flower during the spring. However, there is a lot of variation in spring flowering. Flowering can occur in early, mid-, or late spring.

Summer flowering: There are fewer plants that flower during the summer and even fewer in the fall. However, in southern parts of the country some plants will flower in the winter.

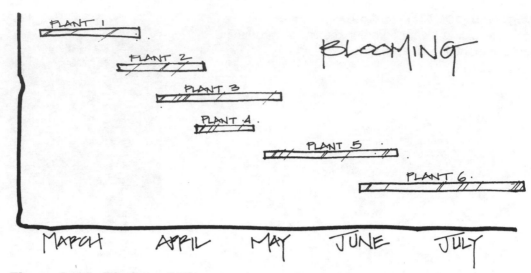

Figure 6–12   Timing of Bloom
Note when plants bloom, in particular perennials. Ideally, plants should provide a succession of blooms that provide a variety of color from early spring to late summer.

(a)

(b)

Figure 6–13   Fruit
Another way to introduce color into the landscape is fruit. It is often a great way to get color late in the growing season when few things are blooming. (a) Hollies are a popular shrub that gets bright red clusters of fruit, commonly used during the Christmas holiday. (b) Some fruit is valuable as a food source to attract birds, although beware of fruit sources that attract birds that make an enormous mess. (c) Pyracantha is valued for large clusters of bright red fruit.

(c)

Fruit

Some plants offer a great display of fruit that may even outdo the flowering. This may be in the form of color, shape, and edibility. Fruit can be used in conjunction with flowering as a sequence of color (Fig. 6–13). This is especially valuable when fewer plants are flowering late in the summer, but fruit is often starting to set and display.

Be aware of plants that offer very little fruit display. Hollies are a great example. Known for a heavy set of bright red fruit in the winter, some species of holly, valued for their glossy foliage, will not fruit. Some species of plants are **dioecious,** meaning that a plant is either male or female. For the female plant to set fruit, it requires a male plant, or **pollinator,** to be planted in the area. **Monoecious** species, those that have male and female flowers on the same plant, will fruit by self-pollination or pollination from nearby plants.

Branching

Some branches are brightly colored, creating a wonderful display in winter (Fig. 6–14). A perfect example is some of the multi-stem dogwood shrubs that have bright red or bright yellow twigs. Color can also be displayed on the trunk of trees, especially those that have exfoliating bark. Paper birches are prized for their bright white trunks, while many other trees exfoliate a cinnamon brown color (Fig. 6–15).

Figure 6–14 **Twig Color**
Colorful branches can introduce color in the winter.
(Photo courtesy of William A. Hoch. http://www.midwestlandscapeplants.org)

(a)   (b)

Figure 6–15 **Trunk Color**
Colorful trunks add color, especially exfoliating varieties. (a) Paper birch. (b) River birch.
(Photo (a) courtesy of William A. Hoch. http://www.midwestlandscapeplants.org)

Texture

The **texture** of a plant may refer to the foliage or branching and be classified as fine, medium, or coarse.

Foliage

Foliage often refers to the size of the leaves (Fig. 6–16). Large leaves are coarse and small leaves are fine in texture, although this may be relative to the surrounding plants. Oakleaf hydrangea is considered a coarse-textured plant when growing next to yaupon holly, but next to a fatsia, which has enormous leaves, it appears less coarse.

Branching

Large, blocky branching appears coarse in texture compared with thin, wispy branching (Fig. 6–17). Thus, a plant with fine-textured foliage may appear coarse once the leaves have dropped. A great example is the honeylocust, which has small leaves but knobby, coarse branches compared with the thin, flexible whips of the willow tree. The bark of the trunk can also have a coarse or fine texture.

(a)

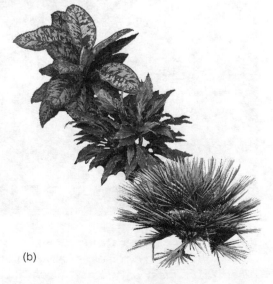

Figure 6–16 **Foliage Texture**
The size of the leaf is often the measure of a plant's texture. (a) The largest leaf (left) is coarse while the smallest leaf (right) is the finest texture. (b) The plant at the top is considered the coarsest. *(Photo (b) courtesy of Visual Impact Imaging)*

(b)

Figure 6–17 **Branch Texture**
Texture can also be a measure of the branching.
Large, gnarly branches (left) are coarse while the
thin, wispy branches (right) are fine textured.

Figure 6–18 **Texture Accents**
Coarse texture is more dominant than fine texture.
The large leaf herbaceous plant has a welcoming,
unique texture in the patio setting. It also has a
warm reddish color and contrasts nicely with the
fine-textured vine and bamboo behind it.

Coarse Texture   Coarse texture has a more dominant quality than fine texture and
can be used to accent an area (Fig. 6–18). It also tends to make a space feel smaller
and can be used to make wide-open spaces feel more enclosed (Fig. 6–19).

Fine Texture   Fine texture is often used in formal designs, such as tightly sheared
hedges. It is less dominant than coarse texture and often used as a unifying effect. Fine
texture also has a distant quality that creates a larger, more open feeling. This can be
used to open up, or "expand," small spaces such as a courtyard (Fig. 6–19).

COARSE
TEXTURE

(a)

FINE
TEXTURE

(b)

Figure 6–19 Texture and Space
(a) Coarse texture can make large spaces feel smaller and more intimate. Fine textures can make smaller spaces feel larger. (b) This perennial bed is loaded with large, coarse-textured plants so they can be easily seen from the house.

178

Maintenance Concerns

Homeowners appreciate easy-to-maintain designs. What may look outstanding on paper could be a nightmare to maintain. Ideally, a landscape design will mature with little maintenance and naturally fill space. Of course, some maintenance is inevitable, but avoid designs that exacerbate the problem (Fig. 6–20).

Overplanting

When plants are placed too close, the space becomes crowded. This is especially true near sidewalks and driveways. Unless the shrubs are pruned back on a regular basis, people will be driving into them or walking up against them. In some cases, homeowners give up and stop using the sidewalk altogether (Fig. 6–21).

Overplanting can occur for a couple of reasons. One is an attempt to get a finished look upon planting. Quality landscape design accounts for the mature size of plants so that it grows into the finished look over time.

Wrong Plant Choice

Planting the wrong plant can cause long-term problems. This is commonly in the form of placing plants that will become large in small spaces. For example, placing any shrub beneath a window will work just fine at planting since it's small at the time. However, in a few years the homeowners will be working to keep the shrub from engulfing the window if it matures to a large size. Plant small shrubs (at maturity) in small spaces.

Evergreen versus Deciduous

Evergreen plants hold their foliage all season long, often shedding old foliage in the spring as new foliage emerges. **Deciduous** plants drop their leaves in the fall and remain barren until new growth emerges in spring. **Semi-evergreen** plants hold some of their foliage, but not all. They are somewhere in between evergreen and deciduous. **Herbaceous perennials,** such as hostas and daylilies, die back to the ground and new growth emerges from the roots.

***Figure 6–20* Plant Maintenance**
Consider maintenance of design. This front sidewalk was intended to be a hedge, which requires frequent shearing. Neglect has rendered the sidewalk useless. Be sure to match the design to the client's wishes.

***Figure 6–21* Overplanting**
Shrubs are small at planting, but can quickly fill the space. Be sure to match the mature size to the space so shrubs don't overcrowd each other or grow into a sidewalk, as in the picture.

(a)

(b)

Figure 6–22 Evergreen versus Deciduous
Consider the balance of evergreen and deciduous plants in the design. This planting bed (a) contains seasonal color and interesting texture, but in the winter (b) it looks barren because all the plant material is deciduous and herbaceous.

It is important to balance evergreen and deciduous plants in the landscape. Too much evergreen can become monotonous. Too many deciduous plants in the landscape can look cold, dead, and barren in the winter (Fig. 6–22). Clients will have their own preference for evergreen versus deciduous.

Tip Box

Evergreen or Deciduous?

Evergreen provides visual stability. Deciduous lends change to the landscape. Use a mix of both for balance and interest.

Balance

Balance is a sense of equality. When an area has many items gathered on one side and only a few on the other an imbalance exists (Fig. 6–23). The same goes for a residence—when a house has several large trees on one side but only low-growing shrubs on the other side, it can appear unbalanced (Fig. 6–24).

Without balance, the design loses a sense of order. Approaching the house in the previous example, regardless of the plant selection and placement, something feels out of place, unbalanced . . . out of order.

There are two general forms of balance that are utilized in landscape design.

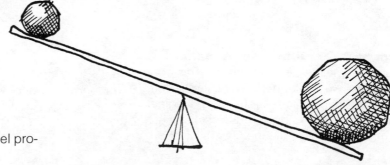

Figure 6–23 Imbalance
Like a balancing scale, a design must feel proportionately balanced to be cohesive.

(a)   (b)

***Figure 6–24* Landscape Balance**
(a) Too much of the landscape is located to the right along with the tallest part of the house, while (b) this landscape appears balanced. *(Photos courtesy of Visual Impact Imaging)*

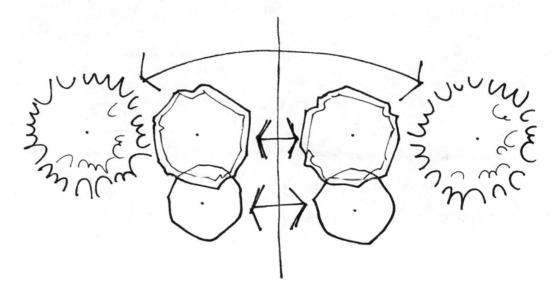

***Figure 6–25* Symmetrical Balance**
Symmetrical balance is a mirror image on both sides.

Symmetrical Balance

Symmetrical balance is a mirror image of both sides (Fig. 6–25). If a line were drawn down the middle, a symmetrical design would have the exact same placement and selection of plants and material on both sides (Fig. 6–26).

Think of a balancing scale and spherical weights (Fig. 6–27). If you placed a large weight on the right side, you would need to place a large weight of the same size and weight on the left to achieve symmetrical balance. If smaller weights were then placed on the right side, the same number of weights of the same size and weight would then be placed on the left side to achieve balance again.

Formal Character

Symmetrical balance is rather structured in how it is attained because of the exact repetition on both sides (Fig. 6–28). Because of this structured appearance, it has a formal nature. Symmetrical balance is normally seen in formal gardens where the hedges are tightly sheared.

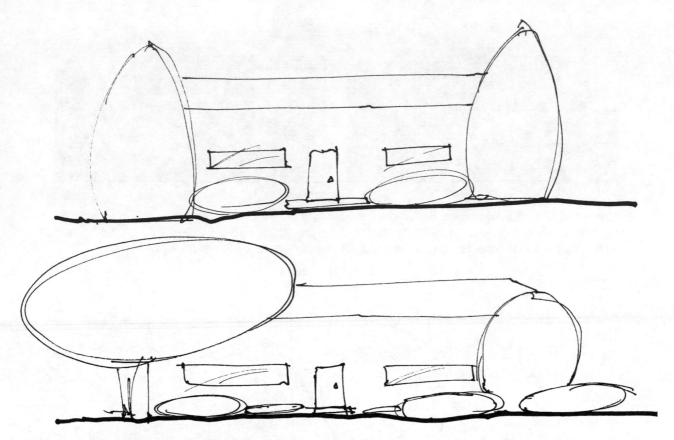

Figure 6–26   Symmetrical Placement
The same objects are placed on each side in the same location (top) to achieve symmetrical balance, while the bottom example uses a variety of objects to achieve asymmetrical balance.

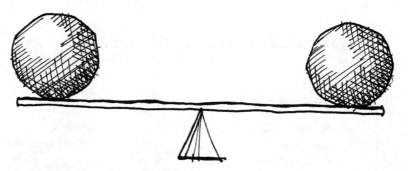

Figure 6–27   Symmetrical Scale
As an example, symmetrical balance is achieved on a scale using the same exact object on both sides.

Formulaic Balance

This is considered the easiest form of balance to achieve because it only has to be repeated on both sides (Fig. 6–29). Students new to design often find this to be a simple approach to achieving balance, although they should be aware that the overuse of symmetrical balance can begin to lack interest because it is too predictable.

Figure 6–28 Formal and Informal Balance
(a) Symmetrical balance (top) lends itself to formal design, while asymmetrical (bottom) is often used for a loose, natural balance. (b) Some botanical gardens utilize symmetrical balance to create formal design.

(a)

(b)

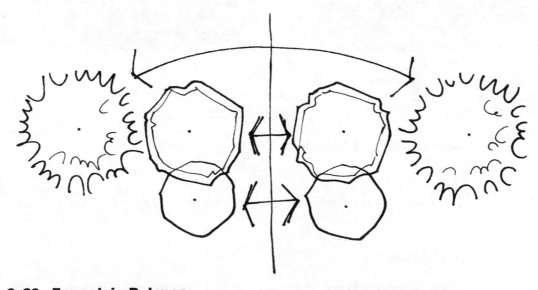

Figure 6–29 Formulaic Balance
Symmetrical balance is formulaic in the sense that objects are repeated on each side of an axis.

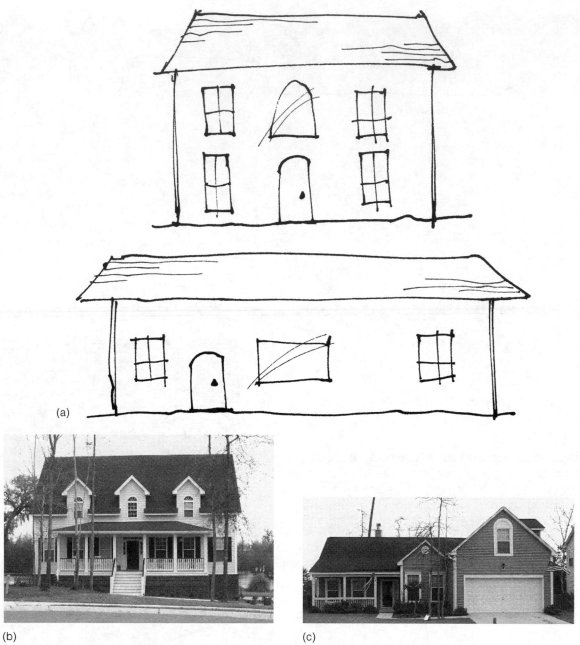

Figure 6–30 **Balanced Houses**
The house can impact the type of balance used in the landscape. (a) The top house is symmetrical while the bottom is asymmetrical. (b) Symmetrical house. (c) Asymmetrical house.

Symmetrical Houses

Some houses have symmetrical balance, front door in the middle of the house with the exact number and placement of windows on both sides (Fig. 6–30). If the house has this character, then it would be natural to repeat this style with a symmetrically balanced landscape as well.

Asymmetrical Balance

Asymmetrical balance is unstructured and more visually weighted than a calculated placement of material on both sides of an axis as in symmetrical balance. Some refer to it as a "gut feeling" of balance (Fig. 6–31).

With asymmetrical balance, if a large spherical weight were placed in the right side of a balancing scale, the left side would be balanced by adding something other than the exact same size and weight, such as several smaller weights that would equal the weight on the right side. Balance would be achieved without using the exact same material (Fig. 6–32).

Natural and Informal

Because of the unstructured nature of asymmetrical balance, it is more of an informal balance. It appeals to a loose, natural sense of balance.

Connection

A common element creates **connection** among the entire design, also referred to as **unity.** Without something that creates a visual recall of similar elements throughout the design, it can appear chaotic and lack a sense of unity. A couple of ways to create connection is by repetition and physically linking space.

Repetition

Repeating elements such as hardscapes or plants throughout a design is critical to creating unity (Fig. 6–33). Visual recall of seeing the same plants or a similar plant quality helps create connection.

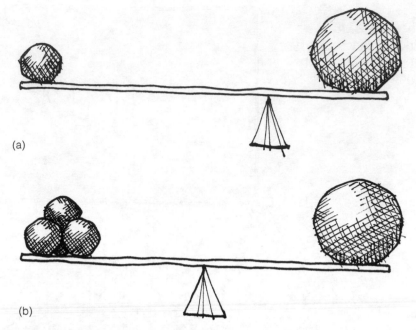

(a)

(b)

Figure 6–32 Asymmetrical Scale
(a) Asymmetrical balance is achieved by balancing a larger object with a smaller object and space, or (b) a collection of smaller objects to equal the weight of the larger object.

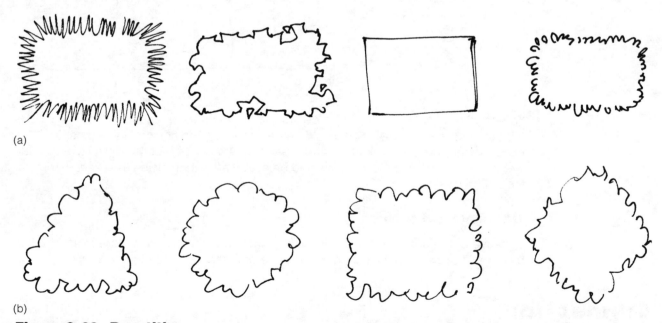

(a)

(b)

Figure 6–33 Repetition
(a) Repeating the rectangle connects the four objects that have various outlines. (b) Repeating the outline for different objects helps connect them.

Pay attention to qualities that you are using and repeat them throughout an area to connect space (Fig. 6–34). Beware of overzealously pursuing the unique qualities of too many different plants and hardscapes and losing the big picture (Fig. 6–35). Too many differences are disruptive.

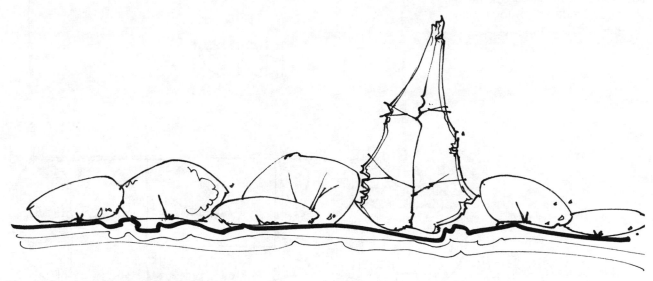

Figure 6–34 Repeating Objects
The left to right connection in this example comes from repeated plant material and only one different (taller) shrub for variety.

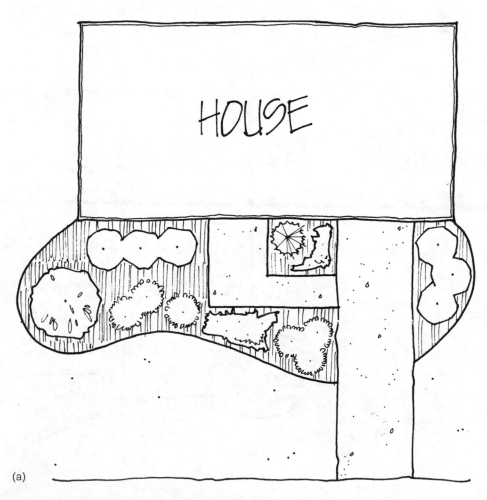

(a)

Figure 6–35 Repeating in the Plan
(a) Sufficient repetition of symbols.

(continues)

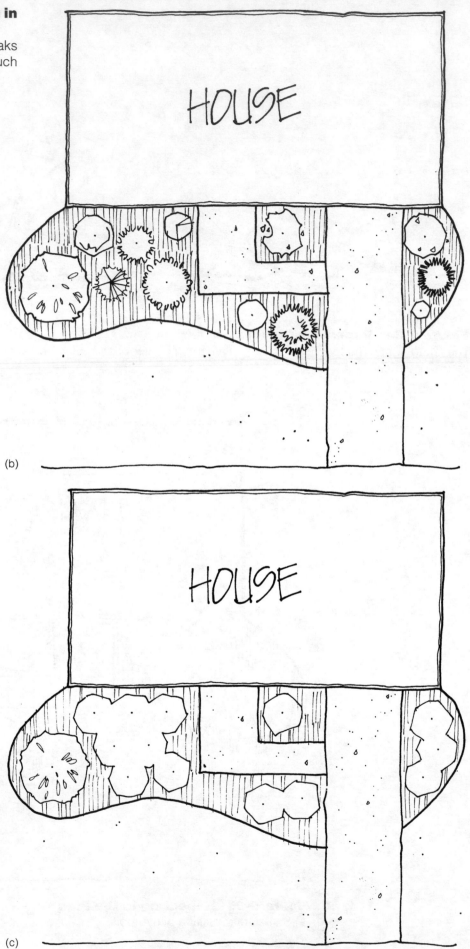

Figure 6–35 Repeating in the Plan—continued
(b) Too much variety breaks down connection. (c) Too much repetition is boring.

HOUSE

(b)

HOUSE

188 (c)

However, a word of caution to not be too repetitive or the design will become boring. There is nothing interesting about the same one or two plants used for the entire design.

Plant Repetition

Repeating the same plant throughout the design is the easiest approach to creating visual recall (Fig. 6–36). This is most effectively done with **foundation plants** (Fig. 6–37).

Figure 6–36 **Plant Repetition**
(a) Plants are sufficiently repeated in the plan to help connect or unify space. (b) The giant clumps of liriope are staggered along the entry walk to create visual continuity to the front door.

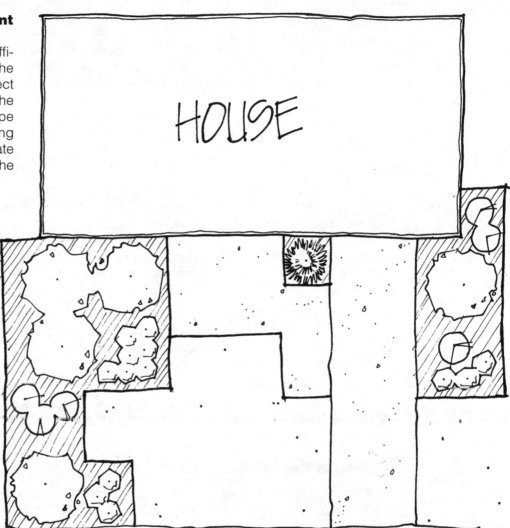

HOUSE

(a)

(b)

***Figure 6–37* Foundation Plants**
The plants on the right are low-profile without stand-alone qualities; typically repeated to help unify design. The plant on the left
would be more suitable as a specimen or an accent. *(Photo courtesy of Visual Impact Imaging)*

Foundation plants   The name **foundation plants** is a bit dated. The name origi-
nated from older homes, after World War II, when shrubs, typically sheared hedges,
were planted in front of the house to cover the brick foundation. Although still referred
to as foundation plants, some designers refer to them as **primary** or **filler plants** since
homes today don't have unpleasant brick foundations to hide.

Foundation plants are plants that have a nice, simple form but little outstanding qualities. They are valuable in the landscape because they balance the attention demanded
from specimen plants. Foundation plants bring unity to the design, or lay the foundation
(not necessarily plants used to cover the foundation of the house).

Foundation plants can be used in several different areas of the design because they
have a subtle appearance. Therefore, they provide a good visual recall throughout the
design by being seen in several places and helping connect the space between these
areas.

Material Repetition

The same principle of repetition can be applied to hardscapes (Fig. 6–38). Using the
same pavers or flagstone for walks and patio can create visual recall in different parts
of the residence.

Characteristic Repetition

Instead of repeating the same plant, plant characteristics can be repeated for a sense
of connection.

Texture: Similar textures of various plants can create a visual relationship (Fig. 6–39).

Color: Use color in various forms. For instance, red may appear in foliage, fall
color, fruit, and flowers of several plants in the landscape.

Form: Repeat similar forms, such as low mounding shrubs (Fig. 6–40).

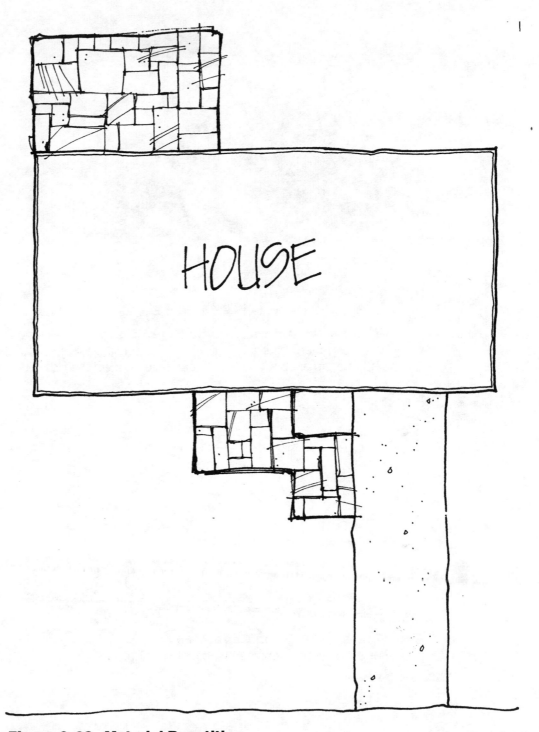

Figure 6–38 Material Repetition
Hardscape material is repeated in the plan to help connect the front and back portions of the design.

***Figure 6–39* Characteristic Repetition**
Repeating plant characteristics, such as similar leaf shape of the pittosporum shrub (left) and the akebia vine (right), can help connect the design.

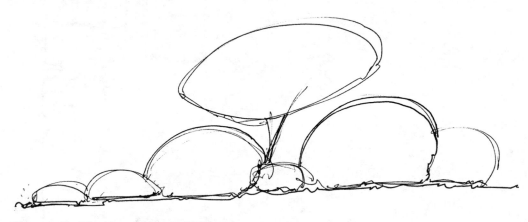

***Figure 6–40* Form Repetition**
Repeating plant forms can help unify design.

Linking Space

Another means of connecting space throughout the design is by physically linking plants with a common material or continuing ground lines.

Common Material

Seemingly random plants can be connected with a common material, such as a mulched planting bed, fence, or wall (Fig. 6–41). Enclosing plants in a bed of mulch or ground cover is one of the easiest ways to create connection in the landscape (Fig. 6–42). Even in existing random plantings, connection can be improved and appear to fit within the same design by pulling a bed around them.

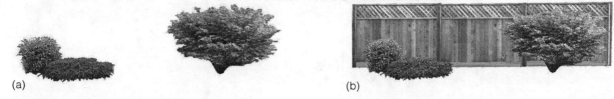

(a)   (b)

Figure 6–41 Linking Space
Connect space with a common material, (b) such as a fence, to link the two plantings. *(Photos courtesy of Visual Impact Imaging)*

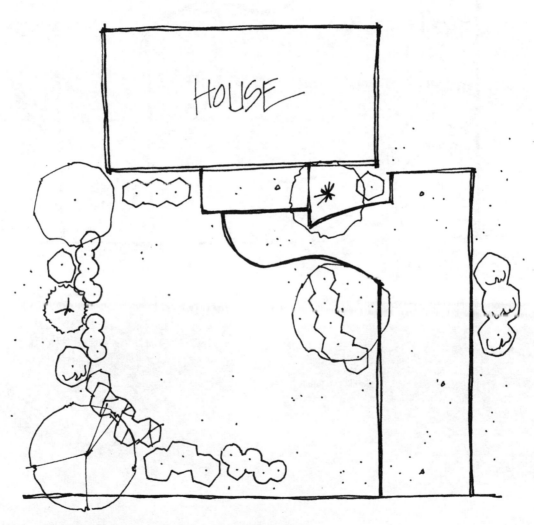

Figure 6–42 Linking Space with Common Material
(a) Without a mulched bed, plantings feel less connected.

(continues)

(a)

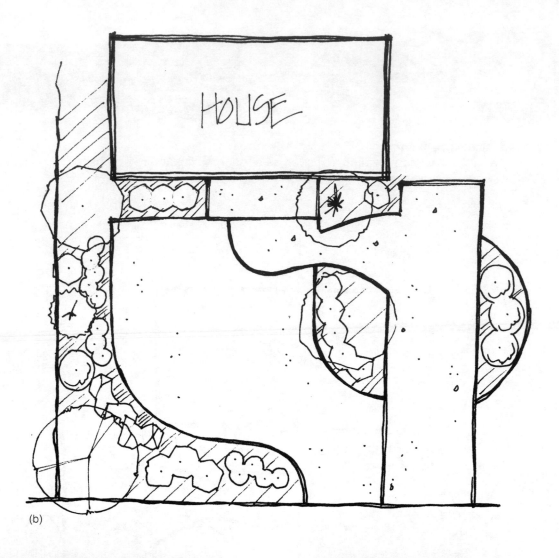

(b)

(c)

(d)

Figure 6–42 Linking Space with Common Material—continued
(b) A mulched bed can connect plantings. (c) These plants appear randomly planted in the corners and lack unity. (d) Simply placing a bed helps draw them together.

194

Ground Lines

Another means of linking space is continuing lines from beds, house, or other structures. One technique that some designers do with beds for a good sense of connection is to continue a bed line on the other side of a sidewalk or driveway (Fig. 6–43). This is a good way to connect across the broad expanse of concrete (Fig. 6–44). The same principle applies to continuing the ground lines from driveways, sidewalks, patios, and beds to improve flow and unity (Fig. 6–45).

Establish a bed line that continues from corners, doors, or windows of the house. This could also include the corners of other structures such as decks or patios. By continuing the lines from these structures the design integrates the residence, with the landscape creating a more effective and smoother connection with indoor and outdoor living.

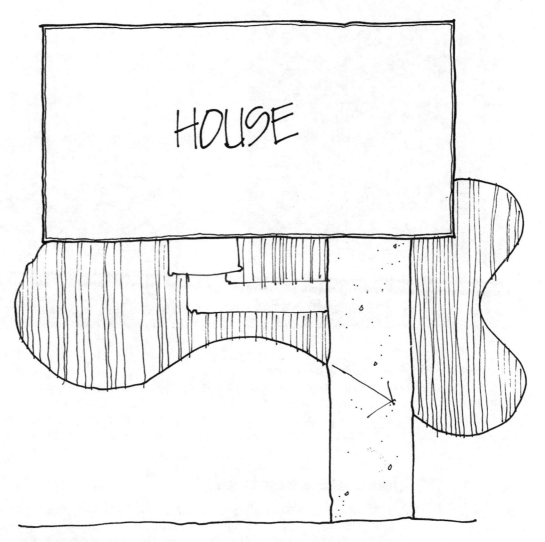

Figure 6–43 Ground Lines
By continuing a bed line across pavement, a sense of connection can be created.

(a)

(b)

(c)

(d)

***Figure 6–44* Continuing Bed Line**
(a) The nearest planting appears disconnected with the bed on the other side of the driveway, unless (b) the bed is changed to continue where the far bed left off to appear cohesive. (c) This small bed lines up with the planting bed on the other side of the driveway. (d) In this example, notice how the bedline continues in front of the annual bed even though the flagstone wall goes behind it.

Impossible Bed Lines

Tight curves and acute angles are difficult to maintain. Lawn mowers won't be able to cut the grass along the bed line without going into the planting bed and a weed eater will have to finish the job. In some cases, backing up and mowing in at different angles is time consuming (Fig. 6–46).

An attempt to make bed lines smoothly curving results in acute angles. These small areas are very difficult to maintain over time. Few things grow in these small spaces and they eventually erode, not to mention it's a visually weak connection.

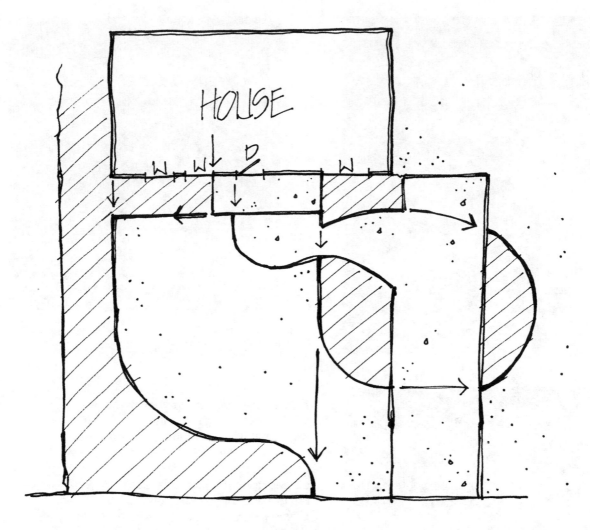

Figure 6–45 **Connect Ground Lines and Corners**
Continuing beds from corners of the house or other structures helps connect indoor and outdoor living. Unity is further improved by connecting ground lines from the driveway, sidewalks, patio, and beds.

Figure 6–46 **Maintenance Concerns**
Consider how much maintenance a design will require. This bedline had to be moved to allow space for the lawn mower between the tree and edging.

(a)

(b)

(c)

Figure 6–47 **Focalized Accents**

(a) An object or space that draws attention, such as a water feature, sculpture, or unique plant, is a focalized accent. (b) The infamous "gazing ball," not looked upon kindly by many designers, is an attempt at creating a focalized accent. (c) The waterfall, in addition to the sound, is a great focal point of motion for the entertainment area. *(Photo (a) courtesy of Chris Briand.* http://www.salisbury.edu/arboretum; *photo (c) courtesy of Big Sky Landscaping, Inc., Clackamas, OR.* www.bigskylandscaping.com)

Interest

The design has to have visual interest. For many residents, curb appeal (visual interest) is the most important aspect. The design needs to have qualities that make people admire the residence and even spark a desire to experience walking through the landscape. .To be successful it has to stir an element of curiosity.

Accent

Interest can be stirred by elements of **accent.** This can be achieved with a focalized accent or interesting effects such as contrasting textures.

Focalized Accents

Focalized accents are objects or plants that would directly attract an observer's attention. An example would be a sculpture, water feature, or specimen plant (Fig. 6–47).

Specimen plants refer to plants with some unique characteristics which can be planted alone as a focal accent (Fig. 6–48). Some of these characteristics may be continual, such as a unique form, or short-lived, such as when the plant flowers.

(a)

(b)

(c)

(d)

(e)

Figure 6–48 **Specimen Characteristics Form**
(a) This contorted tree creates an interesting form.
(b) The broad, coarse texture of the foliage can be used as
a bold specimen plant. (c) Bark: This mottled brown and
gray trunk is very appealing in the winter. (d) Flower: The
unique shape and/or color of the flowers can attract attention. (e) Foliage: This lacy burgundy foliage of the weeping
tree has a specimen quality. *(Photo (b) courtesy of Josh G.
Silliman.)*

199

Tip Box

Avoid "Overaccenting"

Be careful and don't become overzealous with accents (Fig. 6–49). Too many accents and the design becomes chaotic and loses a sense of unity. Every aspect of the design should not demand the same attention.

(a)

(b)

Figure 6–49 **Overaccenting**
(a) Too many specimens become too busy and void out the uniqueness of each plant. (b) The use of foundation plants helps to enhance the outstanding quality of a specimen plant.
(Photos courtesy of Visual Impact Imaging)

Characteristics of Specimen Plants

Form: Unusual forms such as weeping or contorted

Texture: Striking foliage, whether extremely fine or extremely coarse

Bark: Exfoliating bark that reveals interesting colors and texture

Flowering: Unique shapes or vivid color

Foliage: Interesting color or unique variegation

The attention and appeal of specimen plants is balanced, and enhanced, by surrounding foundation plants. Due to simple qualities, foundation plants help accentuate the unique qualities of specimen plants. The outstanding quality of the specimen stands out amid the foundation plants as opposed to an entire collection of specimen plants that can make the unique qualities less special.

Contrast

Contrast is the juxtaposition of two opposing qualities (Fig. 6–50). Contrast sparks a drastic change in the flow of surroundings and attracts attention. It can be created by one of the following:

Texture: Planting a fine-textured plant next to one of coarse texture. Texture can be measured as the size of the foliage or stems.

Form: A vertical form, such as yucca or ornamental grass, can be used to contrast with rounded or horizontal forms.

Color: Using plants with bright variegation near plants with green foliage.

(a)

(b)

(c)

Figure 6–50 **Contrasting Texture**
(a) Contrasting the fine texture of the vine with the coarse texture of ground cover draws attention. (b) Contrasting the vertical, sharp form of the grass with the rounded broadleaves is appealing. (c) Contrasting the bright-colored foliage with the surrounding green shrubs is attention-getting. *(Photos courtesy of Visual Impact Imaging)*

Curiosity

Curiosity can be used to pique the interest of an observer. When people are interested, they are stirred to investigate. Hiding, or screening, portions of the landscape or accenting narrow walks and corners can heighten curiosity.

Screening and Sound

Breaking up a large space with screens keeps one from experiencing the entire area and can lead one to investigate each space of the residence (Fig. 6–51). Take for instance a backyard. Using fences or shrubs keeps one experiencing a smaller outdoor room. By utilizing various forms or accents, one can be led from one outdoor room to the next by curiosity. A good example is the use of water (Fig. 6–52). The low trickling sound of a small fountain can draw one down a path to investigate what is around the corner.

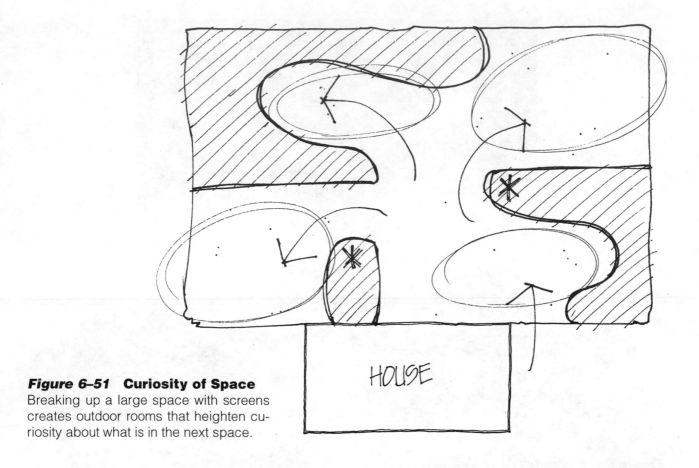

Figure 6–51 Curiosity of Space
Breaking up a large space with screens creates outdoor rooms that heighten curiosity about what is in the next space.

(a)

(b)

(c)

Figure 6–52 Curiosity of Sound
(a) The sound of trickling water can draw one's interest into other areas. (b) This fountain creates an echoing sound of water splashing at the end of a path. (c) This large water feature is a great addition to the entertainment area. *(Photo (c) only courtesy of Blue Ribbon LLC, Maryland.* www.blueribbonllc.com*)*

Tip Box

Fish are a great addition to ponds to add interest: living movement and brilliant color (Fig. 6–53).

Figure 6–53 **Goldfish and Koi**
Fish are a great addition to add interest:
living movement and brilliant color.

Narrow Walks and Corners

Traffic naturally flows through space that is long and narrow (Fig. 6–54). Corridors and sidewalks naturally pull people in that direction. To heighten this intuitiveness, curiosity can be stirred by placing a focalized accent at the end of the path, such as a water feature or sculpture. Something that grabs attention stirs one to wonder what else may be at the end of the path and around the corner.

The same can be applied at the corners to attract attention. Placing a focalized accent, such as a striking specimen, at a corner can stir curiosity about what's around it (Fig. 6–55).

Flow

Flow is the quality that carries the eye smoothly through the landscape. It is also referred to as **transition** or sequence. The flowing character may be formal or informal, but with both, one moves visually through the landscape with comfortable fluidity.

Line

A **line** can be seen where two materials meet or along the outline of a form. It can most easily be seen and created with the outline of planting beds. Bed lines stand out in the landscape because of the contrast created by green grass next to brown mulch. Good edging surrounding a bed should not be noticed, only the line created by the junction of materials.

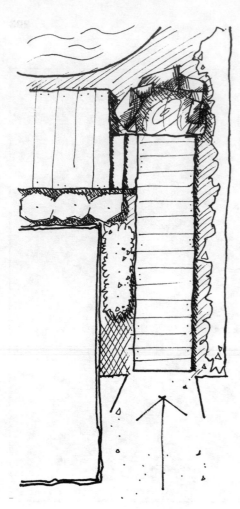

Figure 6–54 **Curiosity of Narrow Paths**
Placement of an accent, such as this water feature, at the end of a narrow space can entice observers down the path to see what's at the end.

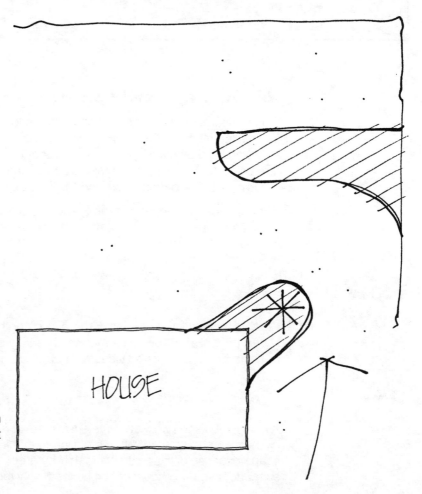

Figure 6–55 **Curiosity of Corners**
Placement of an accent on a corner can draw one's attention around to the next outdoor room.

HOUSE

Lines can be used to develop the character of the landscape in three ways:

Curving: Lines of the bed can create a nice flow through the landscape with broad sweeping arcs that gracefully move throughout the landscape (Fig. 6–56). Bed lines should flow in broad arcs and move easily from one arc to the next (Fig. 6–57). Curving lines are typically used to create an informal, loose character, often in conjunction with asymmetrical balance.

> ### *Tip Box*
> ### Sharp Bed Lines
>
> Although this is more related to maintenance, a sharp bed line is the most appealing. Steel edging has great value to beds not because it looks good, but because it creates a sharp, bending arc that holds this line with minimal maintenance.

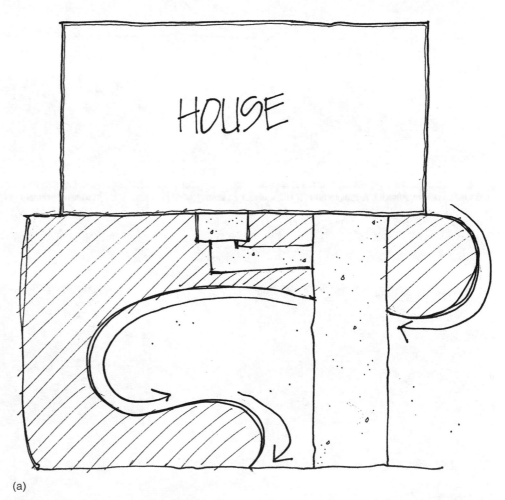

(a)

Figure 6–56 Curving Lines
(a) Wide sweeping bed lines create a natural moving flow.

(continues)

**Figure 6–56 Curving Lines—
continued**
(b) Oversealous curves get chaotic
and break up the flow.

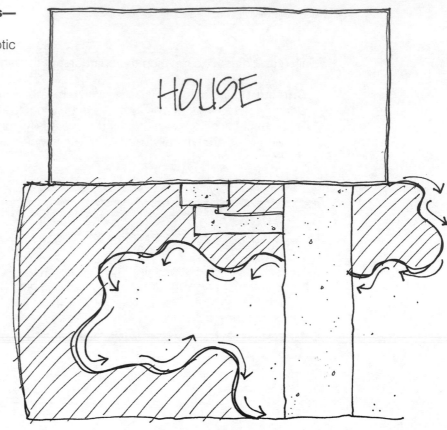

(b)

(a)

(b)

(c)

(d)

Figure 6–57 Curving Beds

(a) Example of a curving ground plane. (b) A wide sweeping bed line has a nice motion. (c) Steel edging helps maintain the broad arching bedline. (d) This curving bedline repeats the curving concrete line around the pool. *(Photo (a) courtesy of Visual Impact Imaging)*

Straight: Lines of the bed are straight and typically meet in 90-degree corners (Fig. 6–58). They are typically used to create a formal character, oftentimes in conjunction with symmetrical balance.

Arc and tangent: A unique approach that combines straight and curving lines, creating a structured layout with the flow of curves (Fig. 6–59).

Figure 6–58 Straight Lines
(a) Straight lines and square corners create a formal, structured flow. (b) Too many corners disturb the structure of the ground plane. (c) Example of straight-line beds. *(Photo (c) courtesy of Visual Impact Imaging)*

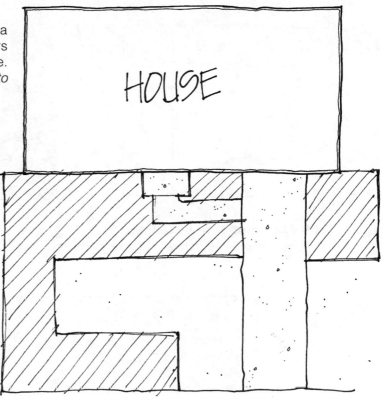

(a)

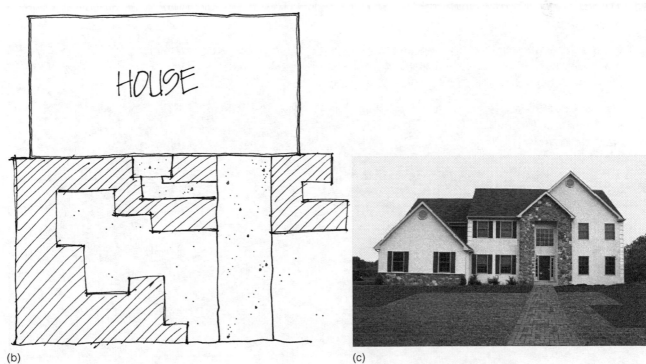

(b)

(c)

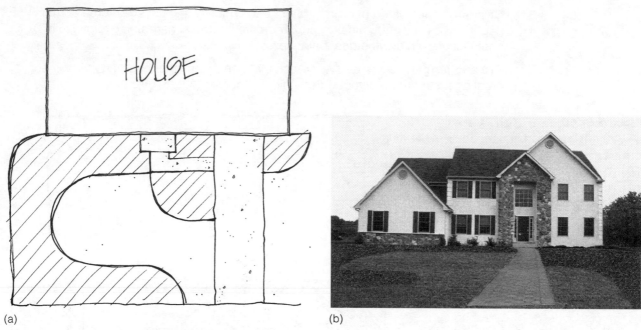

(a)   (b)

Figure 6–59 Arc and Tangent Lines
A unique combination of straight lines and curving arcs. *(Photo courtesy of Visual Impact Imaging)*

Tip Box

The overzealous use of line movement, in an attempt to create interest, can lead to a busy, chaotic feeling and disrupt the quality of flow (Figs. 6–56 and 6–58). The eye of the observer no longer moves smoothly through the landscape.

Tip Box

Berms are a good way to create a sense of flowing form. A berm is a change in the topography by mounding soil, often to create a planting bed. The changes in elevation add another dimension to the flowing interest of the ground lines (Fig. 6–60).

Figure 6–60 Berms
A change in the topography creates a flowing element in elevation.

Form

Lines that can lead the eye can also be created with the edges of walls, hedges, fences, and other construction (Fig. 6–61). Form is often used to develop a smooth transition from the ground plane to the house and surroundings (Fig. 6–62).

Figure 6–61 **Flowing Form**
Flow can be present in the form, such as the sweeping arcs on a fence.

(a)

(b)

Figure 6–62 **Transition**
Transition smoothly (a) between plants and (b) up from the ground plane for gradual flow.

Mass Planting

Trees, shrubs, and ground cover are often planted in groups referred to as **mass planting.** For one reason, large collections of a common material add a sense of balance. When allowed to grow together, several small shrubs can form one unique mass that can balance another large plant. Second, the small size of many shrubs and ground cover would have minimal impact if planted alone. Plants tend to lose connection throughout the design and the design begins to appear segmented with all the various plants growing as individuals. Third, with improved connection, mass planting can improve the flow of the design. As plants merge together, the eye travels through the landscape easier.

Spacing

Generally speaking, plants should be spaced so they begin to merge into each other at about 2/3 of their mature spread (Fig. 6–63). This creates a good mass without the negative effects of overcrowding (Fig. 6–64). If plants are spaced extremely close to mass together, they will begin to compete for water and nutrients and weaken the general health of each other. If they are overcrowded, they are less able to overcome drought and pests.

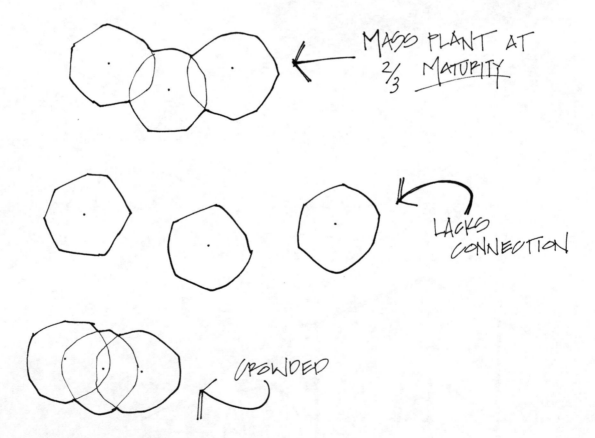

Figure 6–63 Mass Spacing
Mass plant with proper spacing to create a group of merging trees or shrubs; too close and the plants will compete with each other.

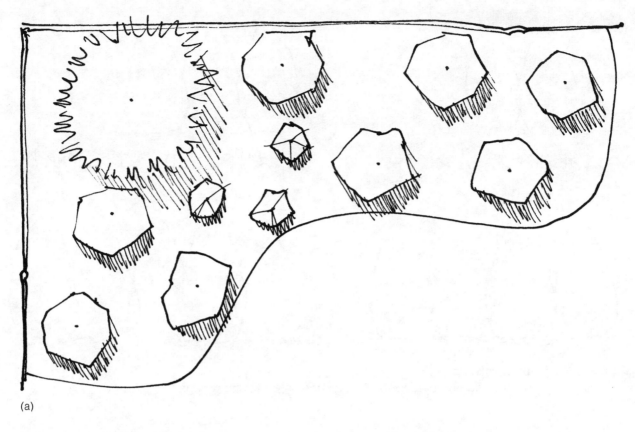

(a)

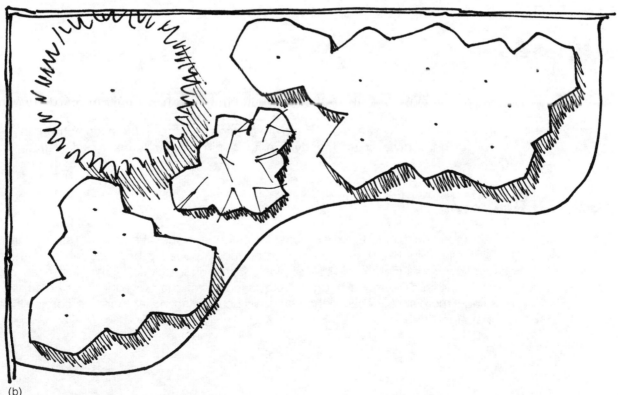

(b)

Figure 6–64 **Mass Spacing**

(a) The plants are evenly spaced and lack mass appeal. (b) Massing plants together creates better connection within the bed.

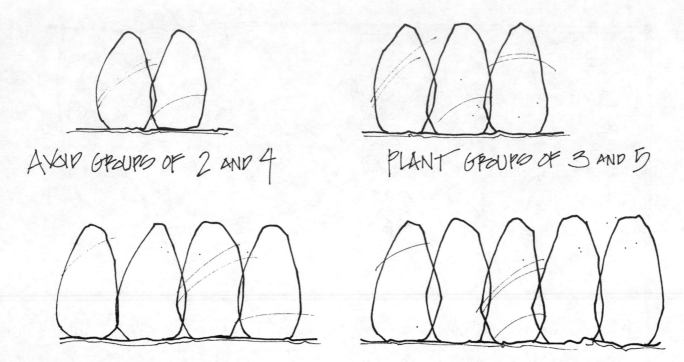

AVOID GROUPS OF 2 AND 4

PLANT GROUPS OF 3 AND 5

Figure 6–65   Odd Numbers
Mass plant with groups of odd numbers for better balance, in particular groups of three and five.

Odd Numbers

To improve the balance of massing and create a solid planting, groups of shrubs and trees should be planted in odd numbers (Fig. 6–65), in particular, groups of three and five. As the masses get larger the number of plants isn't easily discerned (Fig. 6–66). When two trees or shrubs are planted as a mass, the even number tends to be visually divided by the eye. A third plant establishes a solid grouping (Fig. 6–67).

Staggered Placement

When grouping plants together, consider staggering the placements rather than a straight line (Fig. 6–68). Staggering can be more appealing because the placement has a flow rather than a rigid row of plants, although there will be times to mass in a straight line, such as formal hedges. Staggering can also improve the massing appeal, making it more solid, because the plants will be growing closer together more so than in a straight line.

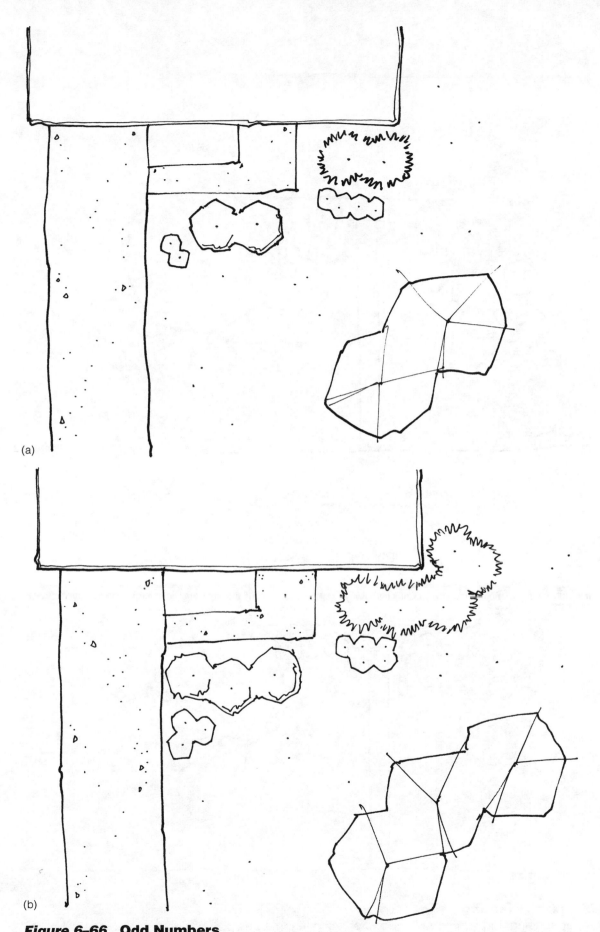

Figure 6–66 Odd Numbers

(a) Groups of two tend to visually divide in half. (b) Groups of three appear grounded and better balanced.

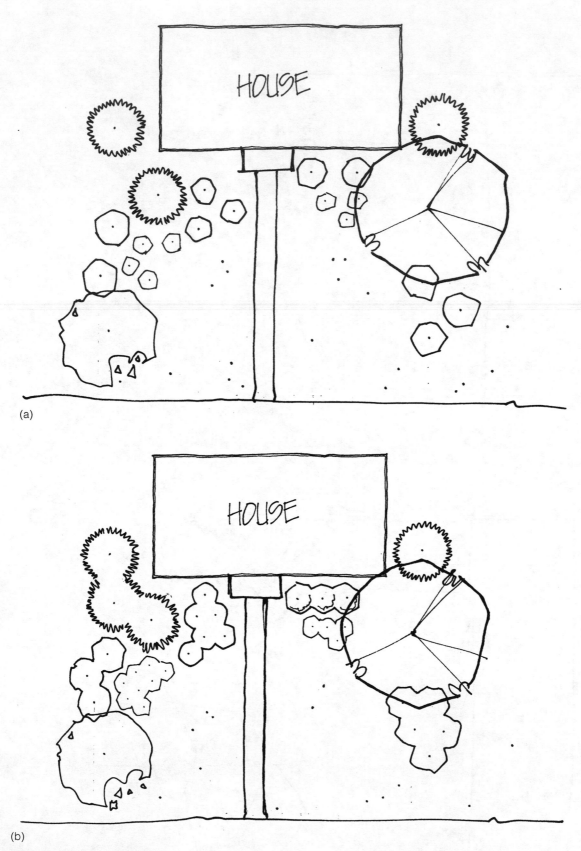

(a)

(b)

Figure 6–67 Mass Planting

(a) Lacks proper spacing and numbers. (b) Good spacing that merges plants together in numbers that appear better balanced.

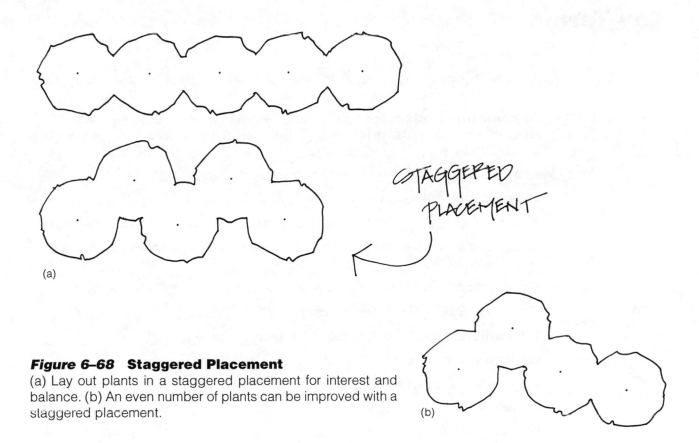

Figure 6–68 Staggered Placement
(a) Lay out plants in a staggered placement for interest and balance. (b) An even number of plants can be improved with a staggered placement.

Summary

As the concept plan creates the useful or functional component of the landscape design, design principles create the aesthetic or visual appeal. Form, texture, and color are attributes to plants and objects that are used to create an appealing landscape. Balance is important to create a sense of equality or order. Symmetrical balance is the formulaic approach of mirroring each side to achieve balance and is often associated with a formal characteristic. Asymmetrical is an informal balance that utilizes plants or objects of various sizes and types and is not a mirrored image of each side. Unity or connection helps to pull all the elements of the design into a big picture. Repeating plants or elements creates visual recall for a sense of connection. It can also be achieved by linking space with common materials, such as mulch or a fence, and continuing ground lines, such as the continuation of a planting bed on the other side of a driveway. Interest helps to create visual appeal. Focalized accents or interesting effects have striking qualities that grab attention. These are often enhanced with the balance of foundation plants, those that have few outstanding qualities, rather than a chaotic mass of specimens plants. Effective placement of accents, such as in corners or at the end of narrow paths, stirs curiosity and enhances the visual appeal. Flow is the smooth transition throughout the landscape, influenced by the line of the ground plane or outline of the form. Mass is the technique of plants placed close enough to merge together to create a large grouping of several smaller plants. It helps to unify and balance the design. Planting masses in odd numbers provides additional balance to the mass.

Key Terms

Accent: striking effect of quality that gets attention

Arc and tangent: unique approach that combines straight and curving lines, creating a structured layout with the flow of curves

Asymmetrical balance: unstructured balance relying more on a "gut feeling" rather than the calculated placement of material on both sides of an axis as in a symmetrical balance

Attributes: inherent characteristics or qualities

Balance: sense of equality

Berm: change in the topography by mounding soil; often used to create a planting bed

Color: elements in the design to attract attention or impact mood; flowers, foliage, branches, trunk, fruit

Connection: sense that all components of design are part of the big picture

Contrast: juxtaposition of two opposing qualities

Cool colors: have a calming effect; blue, green, purple

Curiosity: a quality or effect that piques the interest of an observer

Curved lines: sweeping bed lines in landscape; loose, informal quality

Deciduous: plants that drop their leaves in the fall; lends change to the landscape

Dioecious: plant is either male or female; requires a male plant, or pollinator, to be planted in the area for a female plant to set fruit

Espalier: manipulates form by training a tree or shrub to grow flat against a wall or fence

Evergreen: plants that hold their foliage all season long; provides visual stability

Filler plants: see primary plants

Flow: quality that carries the eye smoothly through the landscape; transition or sequence

Focalized accents: objects or plants that would directly attract an observer's attention

Form: the outline of an object or plant, often thought of as the silhouette

Foundation plants: simple plants that bring unity to design

Herbaceous perennials: plants that die back to the ground and new growth emerges from the roots

Line: can be seen where two materials meet or along the outline of a form

Massing: shrubs and ground cover are often planted in groups; also referred to as mass planting

Monoecious: plant has both male and female flowers; will fruit by self-pollination or from nearby plants

Pollinator: male plant of a dioecious species

Primary plants: basically foundation plants

Semi-evergreen: plants that hold some of their foliage, but not all; in between evergreen and deciduous

Sequence: see flow

Shear: tightly prune shrubs into geometric shapes

Specimen plants: have some unique plant characteristics that are visually appealing; form, texture, bark, flowering, or foliage

Straight lines: straight bed lines at 90° corners; more formal

Symmetrical balance: each side is a mirror image of the other

Texture: may refer to the foliage or branching and be classified as fine, medium, or coarse

Topiary: plant form pruned into shapes of spirals or animals

Transition: see flow

Unity: see connection

Variegation: the mottling or striping of foliage

Warm colors: create excitement; red, orange, yellow

7 Preliminary Design

Objectives

- Understand the role of preliminary design
- Learn how to construct a preliminary design
- Know how to draw a preliminary design

The preliminary design will take shape using the design principles outlined in the previous chapter. The design process, as mentioned earlier in this book, continues to proceed from general to specific with each phase. This is when the plan begins to resemble the landscape design. In this case, the preliminary design takes the bubble diagram of the concept plan and develops a plan with a defined ground plane and plant symbols. It is very important to follow the concept plan because it addresses the analysis and is fundamental to the functional aspect of the design.

Analysis → Concept Plan → Preliminary Design

Client Presentation

Some designers present the preliminary design to the client, whereas others will present the master plan. For the client, the preliminary will be the first look at the proposed design. Presenting the preliminary design has the advantage of getting feedback from the client and allows the designer to make any changes before establishing the specifics in the master plan.

Feedback

Feedback allows the clients to give their input on the design (Fig. 7–1). Having the opportunity to have an impact on the design makes the clients feel more involved in the project, which will increase their satisfaction with the final product. In many cases, the designer will create more than one preliminary design based on one or more concept plans from which the clients will choose or give feedback.

Having the feedback from the client during the preliminary design reduces the amount of time the designer would spend making changes after drawing the master plan.

Design Theft

Some designers may be concerned with design theft. This may happen when a client gets a master plan and decides not to accept. Afterward, a very similar design is installed. To reduce the chance of theft, some designers may leave an unlabeled copy of the preliminary design with the clients to look over on their own and to make changes. Don't hand over a completed master plan until the contract is completed in full.

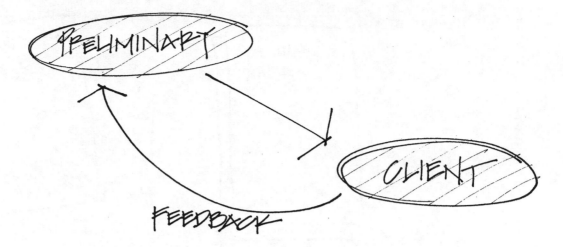

***Figure 7–1* Preliminary Feedback**
Some designers present the preliminary design to get feedback before proceeding with
the master plan.

Graphics

Since the preliminary is presented to the client, it should be illustrated with presentation
graphics (covered later in this chapter). This allows the client to read the plan easier
when symbols are representative of the plant characteristics and the ground plane texture represents the material.

The Preliminary Design Process

The following are steps to developing the preliminary design. Not all designers employ
all of the following steps, but they usually use some form of them during the design
process.

Utilizing the Concept Plan

The preliminary design builds on the concept plan (Fig. 7–2). Some designers like to
place the concept plan directly underneath a piece of tracing paper so that they can
draw the preliminary over the top of it. The concept plan can also be next to the preliminary for reference. Either way, the idea is the same—the preliminary design is refining
the bubbles of the concept plan into definitive lines and symbols.

Sketching the Preliminary Design

Start by drawing more than one preliminary design freehand with a soft lead on tracing
paper (Fig. 7–3). Be very loose and quick and do not worry about the detail. This allows
the designer to approach the organization of the ground plane and the balance of the
design efficiently, as well as try a couple of ideas for comparison before committing to
a definitive preliminary design.

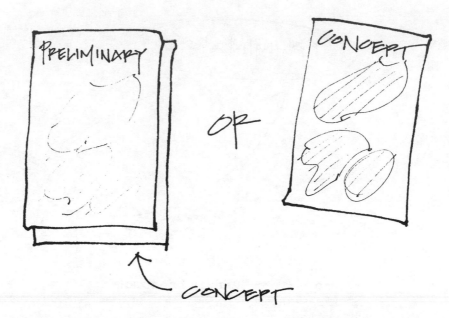

***Figure 7–2* Building a Preliminary Design from the Concept Plan**
The preliminary design should work from the concept plan. Some designers will place the concept plan under the preliminary to address the conceptual layout, while others will refer to it lying off to the side.

***Figure 7–3* Sketching the Preliminary**
Start by loosely sketching preliminary ideas with soft lead on tracing paper.

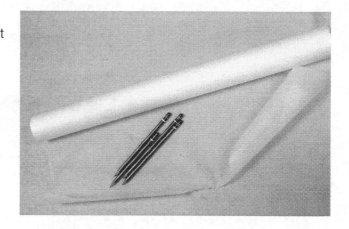

Starting with the Ground Plane

This doesn't have to be the next step, but many beginning students find that organizing the ground plane first makes it easier to start (Fig. 7–4). Once bed lines, lawn, and hardscapes are established, then symbols can be placed.

Sketching preliminary designs allows you to experiment with various bed lines such as curving or straight. Be consistent with the theme of the bed lines in the various areas of the residence. However, the bed line character doesn't necessarily have to be used over the entire property. The front yard may be straight, having more of a formal feeling, while the backyard can be free flowing and have a more relaxed and informal feeling.

***Figure 7–4* Sketching the Ground Plane**
Start by roughly sketching the ground plane: bed lines, walks, driveway, and so forth, according to the concept plan.

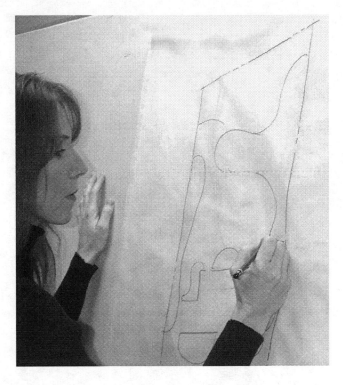

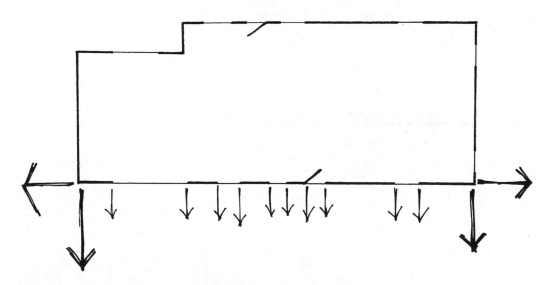

***Figure 7–5* Points of Extension**
Corners of the house, deck, or patio are major points of extension; windows and doors are minor points.

Connecting the Ground Plane   Work on integrating the ground plane by continuing lines from the house and the surroundings (as discussed in the "Connection" section of the previous chapter). Corners of the house, porch, deck, and patio are major points to extend into the landscape. Minor points of extension are things such as windows, doors, or change of materials (Fig. 7–5). When sketching the ground plane, experiment with lines that begin or end at these points (Fig. 7–6).

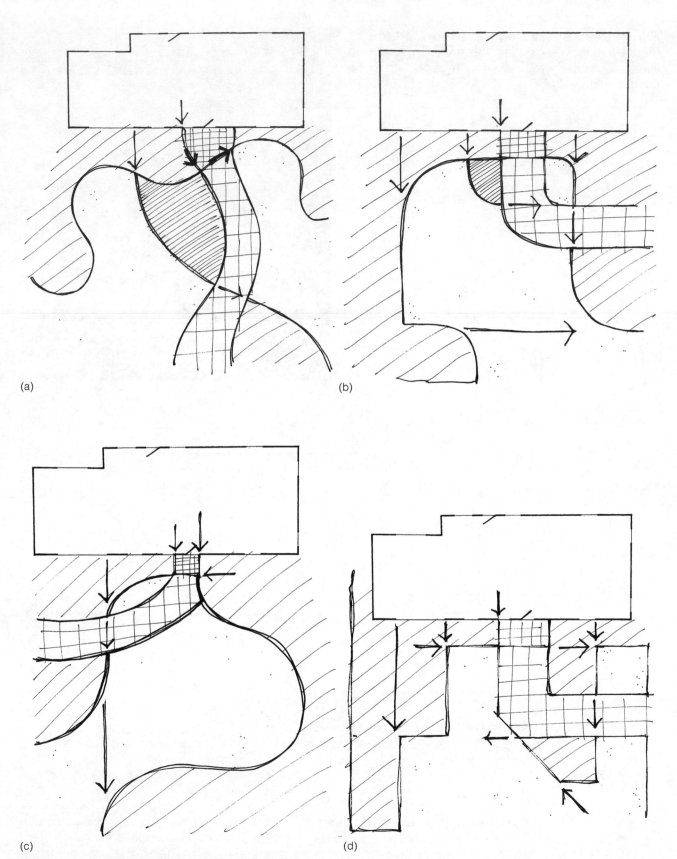

(a)

(b)

(c)

(d)

Figure 7–6 Integrating the Ground Plane
Various examples of integrating the ground plane with points of extension on the house: (a) curved theme,
(b) arc and tangent theme, (c) curved theme, and (d) straight-line theme.

222

Figure 7–7 Sketching Symbols

Follow the rough ground plane with quick circles to represent symbols of plants. This will later be refined to a more specific number and placement of material.

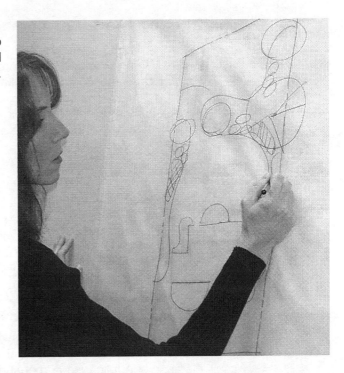

Tip Box

Instead of using symbols, some designers may use bubbles similar to the concept plan and label the bubbles with general plant descriptions (Fig. 7–8).

- Low, medium, tall shrubs
- Small, medium, tall trees
- Ground cover
- Deciduous or evergreen plants

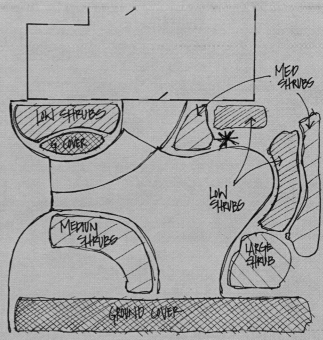

Figure 7–8
Sketching Bubbles
Some designers will continue using bubbles in the preliminary instead of symbols to define areas of plant types and sizes.

Placing the Plant Symbols

Once the ground plane is sketched, do quick symbol placements to get an idea of balance and flow (Fig. 7–7). These can just be quick and loose circles, both large and small. Do not be concerned with specific plants since plant names will not be addressed until the master plan. And do not spend too much time on the details of size, proportion, and exact placement since this is an exercise. These details will be developed in the next step.

Drafting the Preliminary Design

Now that you have some idea of direction for the preliminary design, it is time to draft an illustrative preliminary for the presentation. This draft should be accurate with size and placement of plant symbols, and the proportion and location of ground plane areas. It will be a much different approach than sketching, utilizing quality drawing techniques for a clear, legible plan drawing.

Drafting versus Computer-Aided Drawing (CAD)

Computer-aided drafting systems (or computer-aided drawing) are referred to as CAD. AutoCAD, originally released in 1982, is a software program that allows the user to draw lines, arcs, and circles. The advantage for designers using computer design is the ease of application and change. Symbols can be dropped onto the design with a click of a button, filling an area in a matter of minutes, and can be moved around just as easy. Labeling, coloring, and line drawing are just as quick and easy. Many pro-CAD users feel like computer design appears much more professional, while designers that draft by hand appeal to the artistry of line drawing. The disadvantage is the investment. Computer design can cost thousands of dollars in hardware and software, while drafting equipment can cost less than a hundred dollars. For this reason, many small freelance designers and especially beginning design students start by drafting. This chapter will look at drafting techniques (hand drawn) and computer drawing to compare the end results. However, for more in-depth information of computer drafting, refer to Appendix D for application techniques.

Drafting

The preliminary design should be drafted on vellum paper for quality lines and reproduction. Using lead pencils of various degrees of hardness is the easiest and most forgiving approach for beginning students. Ink creates excellent line quality but is much less forgiving. If ink is to be used, consider drafting on Mylar, which is a drafting film from which ink can be erased (Fig. 7–9).

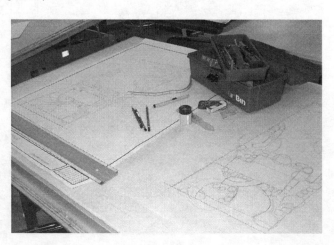

Figure 7–9   Drafting Tools
Tools used to draw a plan.

Figure 7–10 Border and Title Block

Border helps define the working area while the title block provides vital project information. (a) Drafted. (b) Pre-drawn.

(a)

The drawings and specifications detailed in this design are owned solely by The Evergreen Company of Hilton Head Island Inc. It is an original design. The plans may not be reproduced, published or used in any way without the written permission of The Evergreen Company of Hilton Head Island Inc.

A Landscape Design For:

p.o. box 817 bluffton, south carolina 29910
phone no. 1 (803) 681-2334

The Evergreen Co. Inc.

(b)

A **border** around the perimeter of the paper may be used to define the drawing area, although some designers prefer not to use one. There should be a **title block** included that contains the following information: client name and address, scale, north arrow, designer name, and date (Fig. 7–10).

The Ground Plane

Choose one, or a combination of a few, sketches to further develop into the preliminary design. The areas and symbols will be refined so that they are precisely drawn with sharp lines.

Ground Angles

Students tend to draw lines that meet at very acute angles, especially with curving lines. The idea is to allow for a smooth transition and to provide an easier approach to mowing the turf. However, acute angles can be difficult to maintain and often fail over time. It is often where concrete cracks or mulch and ground cover don't remain. As a general rule, the lines of the ground plane should meet close to square, or a 90-degree angle (Fig. 7–11).

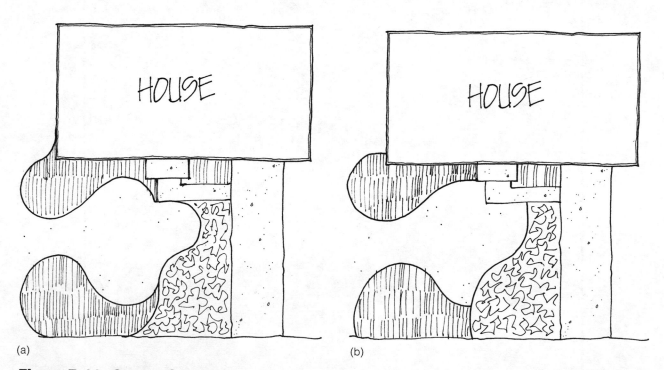

(a)   (b)

Figure 7–11 Square Corners
(a) Corners on the ground plane should not meet at an acute angle because it can be difficult to maintain and hardscapes can crack. (b) Instead, have the ground meet at angles closer to 90 degrees.

Figure 7-11 **Square Corners—continued**
(c) Where the turf meets the patio is a strong connection. *(Photo (c) courtesy of Big Sky Landscaping, Inc., Clackamas, OR.)*

(c)

Ground Labels and Textures

Use general labels in areas such as lawn, driveway, deck, patio, etc. (Fig. 7–12). This will help clarify the layout for the client. Textures help develop and aid the visual component (Fig. 7–13).

Turf   Areas of turf are typically designated by stipples. **Stippling** creates tonal value by placing dots close together. As dots are placed closer together, the value becomes darker.

Concrete and Exposed Aggregate   To symbolize concrete and exposed aggregate, use stipples of a coarser texture, using a combination of dots, circles, and triangles.

Ground Cover   Ground covers generally cover a large area. There are several textures that represent a loose foliage and can be drawn quickly.

Mulch   **Mulches** are used throughout beds to reduce weeds and moisture loss. Textures used for mulch are fairly nondescript, representing the coarse, dark qualities.

Stone and Bricks   Don't be concerned with patterns during the preliminary design. Specific patterns and construction will be established later in the master plan.

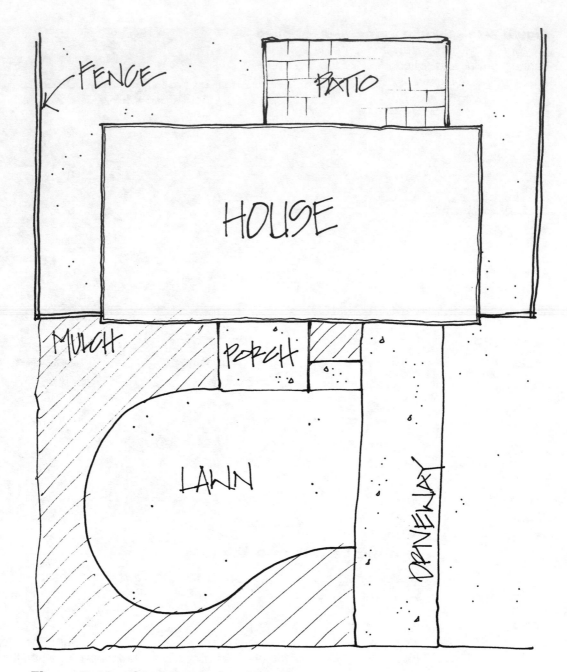

***Figure 7–12* Label the Ground Plane**
Place labels on the ground plane to avoid confusion.

There are many types and sizes of bricks and stones. **Stone** is often used in the form of flagstone, which is a sheet-like stone that comes in various colors and sizes. **Bricks** are smaller units when compared with stone. These also come in similar forms of **pavers**.

Wood   Decking is the most common feature utilizing wood.

Water   Water features are used as focal points because of their fluid movement, soothing sound, and naturalizing effects. They can easily be drawn with a rippling texture that reflects water movement.

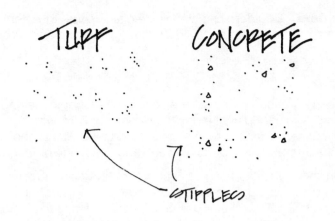

TURF

CONCRETE

STIPPLES

GROUNDCOVER

MULCH

WATER

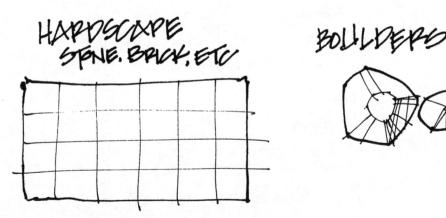

HARDSCAPE
STONE. BRICK, ETC

BOULDERS

Figure 7-13 Ground Plane Textures
Turf, concrete, groundcover, mulch, hardscape, water, and boulders.

Boulders   **Boulders** and stones are often used with water features and as a naturalizing effect. These are drawn with a variety of hatching and cross-hatching textures.

Plant Material

Once the ground plane has been established, begin placing the plant material. Again, in the preliminary plan the designer does not work with specific plants, rather general plant characteristics: size, placement, and type. Plants should be thought of in terms of trees, shrubs, ground cover, flowers, and specimen or foundation plants.

Beginning students often get hung up in the design process because they look at the empty base map and begin to place specific plants. What may result from this approach is losing sight of the overall design concept by being too focused on plants, or a creative block when becoming overwhelmed with all the options. It is all right to have plants in mind and rather difficult to not think of any plants, especially if the client has favorite plants to use. But the idea is not to get caught up in naming plants as they are placed. If there is an area to be screened, then place a large shrub and move on. The master plan may completely rearrange this area, so do not waste time on it at this point. Some designers may jot down a few plant names as they go, but, again, they are not trying to identify the symbols.

Symbols

The information that the symbols should convey include

• Size

• Placement of material

• Character (broadleaf, needle)

Size   The symbols should be drawn relative to scale to represent the diameter of a suitable plant. Use a circle template to place symbol outlines in the appropriate placement and at the correct diameter. Since specific plants are not being considered, the following is a general guideline for symbol diameters that can later be changed when specific plants are used (Fig. 7–14).

Trees

Large trees: 25'

Medium trees: 20'

Small trees: 15'

Shrubs

In the preliminary, shrubs may be represented by a mass outline and not necessarily show the individual shrubs.

Large shrubs: 10'

Medium shrubs: 5'

Small shrubs: 3'

Placement   The symbol helps locate the plant material. A center dot in the middle of the symbol represents the placement of the plant (Fig. 7–15). In the preliminary design, center dots may not be used since it is a generic design. However, the master plan will utilize center dots for all plant placements.

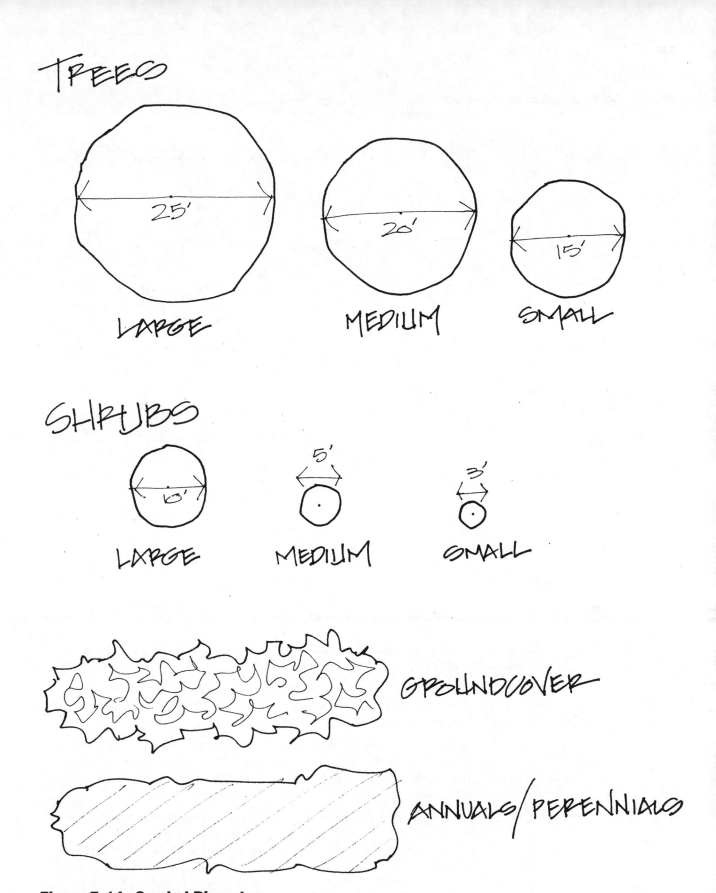

Figure 7–14 Symbol Diameter
The diameter of symbols should be generally related to large, medium, and small trees and shrubs. Other massing areas include ground cover and flowers, which can be represented by an outline.

Figure 7–15   Symbol Placement
Center dots, used to locate the proposed plant, can sometime be symbols other than a lot to signify a specific action.

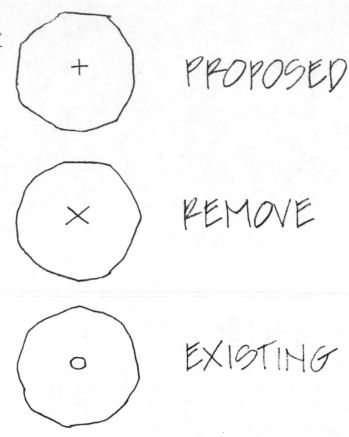

Character   Symbols are developed to help the client understand the plan as well as appear more presentable. Figure 7–16 presents examples of drawing symbols to more accurately depict general characteristics of plants.

> **Generic: Generic symbols** are used to represent any type of plant. They are typically foundation plants.

> **Broadleaf:** Any plant that has a flat, wide leaf is a **broadleaf.** These are typically deciduous plants, such as maples and oaks, but some evergreen plants also have a broadleaf as well, for example, hollies and magnolias.

> **Needle:** The **needle symbol** refers to any plant that has needle-like foliage, which are typically evergreens such as pines and spruce. There are some deciduous plants that have needle-like foliage, such as redwoods and cypress. It can also include barrier plants that have a prominent spiny nature.

> **Branched:** The **branched symbol** is typically used to represent deciduous plants since they lose their leaves, but can also be used for any plant with strong or unique branching habits. Branching symbols are often used for specimen plants that attract attention. These branching symbols tend to attract the most attention.

Grant Preliminary Design

Examples of completed preliminary design, both drafted and CAD, are illustrated in Figure 7–17.

Figure 7-16 Symbol Types

Symbols can represent types, or characteristics, of plant material. (a) Drafted symbols. (b) CAD symbols.

GENERIC

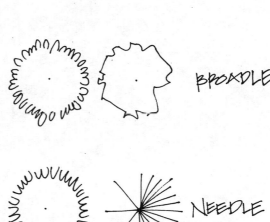

BROADLEAF

NEEDLE

BRANCHED

(a)

(b)

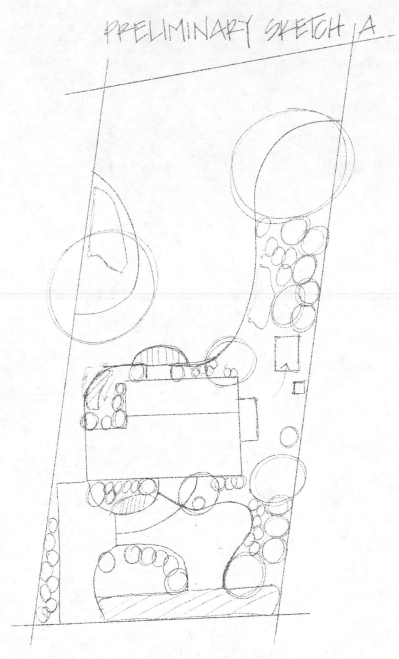

PRELIMINARY SKETCH A

***Figure 7–17* Preliminary Sketches and Designs**
Two preliminary plans, including a preliminary sketch for each one, based on concept plans presented in the previous chapter. Each preliminary set (A and B) includes sketch, drafted and a CAD drawing.

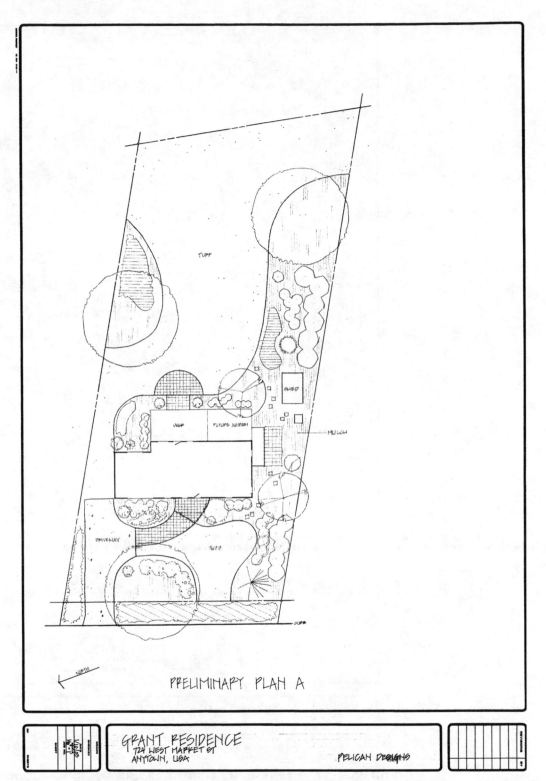

TURF

SHED

USDA   FUTURE SUNROOM   MULCH

DRIVEWAY   TURF

PRELIMINARY PLAN A

NORTH

GRANT RESIDENCE
724 WEST MARKET ST
ANYTOWN, USA   PELICAN DESIGNS

Figure 7–17   Preliminary Sketches and Designs—continued

(continues)

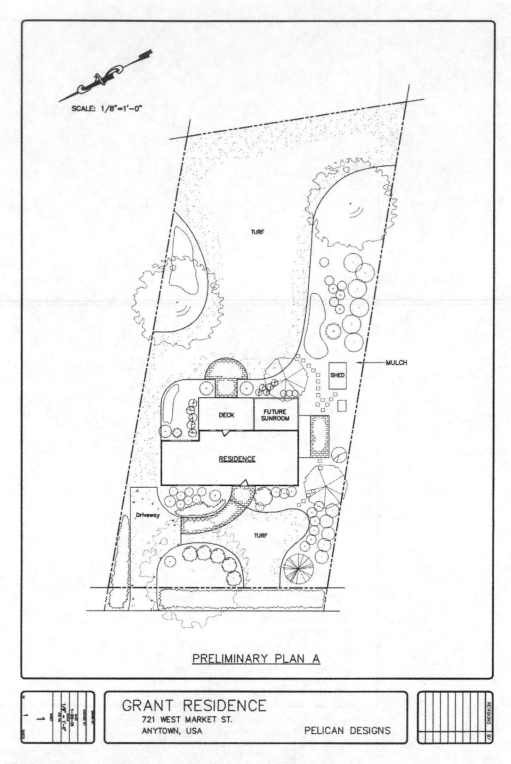

SCALE: 1/8"=1'-0"

TURF

MULCH

SHED

DECK | FUTURE SUNROOM

RESIDENCE

Driveway

TURF

PRELIMINARY PLAN A

GRANT RESIDENCE
721 WEST MARKET ST.
ANYTOWN, USA

PELICAN DESIGNS

REVISIONS BY

Figure 7–17 **Preliminary Sketches and Designs—continued**

236

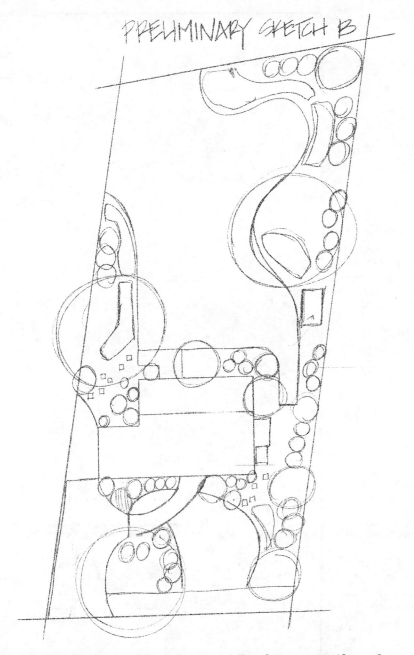

Figure 7-17 **Preliminary Sketches and Designs—continued**

(continues)

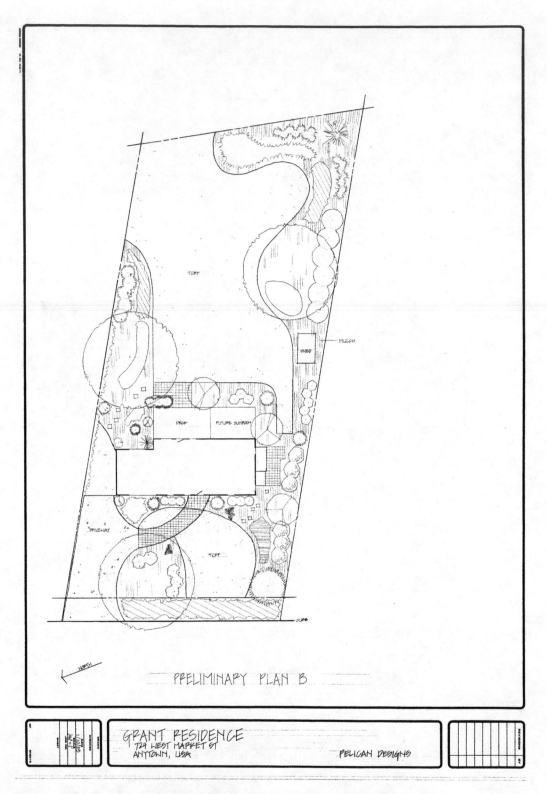

TURF

MULCH

SHED

DECK FUTURE SUNROOM

DRIVEWAY

TURF

NORTH

PRELIMINARY PLAN B

GRANT RESIDENCE
724 WEST MARKET ST
ANYTOWN, USA

PELICAN DESIGNS

Figure 7–17 Preliminary Sketches and Designs—continued

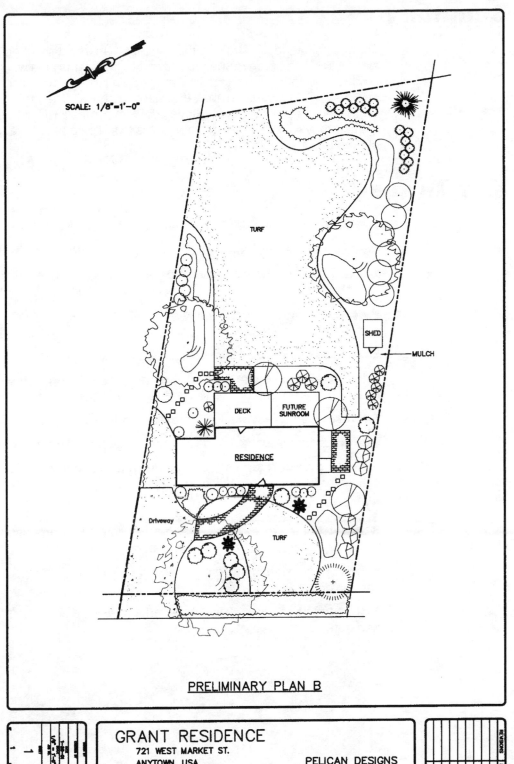

SCALE: 1/8"=1'-0"

TURF

SHED

MULCH

DECK

FUTURE SUNROOM

RESIDENCE

Driveway

TURF

PRELIMINARY PLAN B

GRANT RESIDENCE
721 WEST MARKET ST.
ANYTOWN, USA

PELICAN DESIGNS

REVISIONS BY

Figure 7-17 Preliminary Sketches and Designs—continued

Summary

The preliminary design refines the concept plan into distinct ground lines and symbols. It can be developed to present to the clients as a working design to get feedback before drawing the final master plan. Some designers will draw more than one preliminary design to allow the clients a choice. The preliminary plan will have ground lines and areas clearly labeled. Plant symbols will not be labeled with names; instead they will represent general plants to indicate plant size, placement, and characteristics.

Key Terms

Border: perimeter of the paper that may be used to define the drawing area

Boulders: used with water features and as a naturalizing effect

Branching symbol: represents deciduous plants since they lose their leaves, but can also be used for any plant with strong or unique branching habits

Brick: rectangular blocks typically 8" × 4" and a couple of inches thick, made of clay or concrete; used to pave

Broadleaf symbol: represents any plant that has a flat, wide leaf

Computer-aided drafting systems: software programs that allow the user to draw lines, arcs, and circles to create a landscape design

Generic symbols: used to represent any type of plant, typically foundation plants

Mulch: used throughout beds to reduce weeds and moisture loss

Needle symbol: represents any plant that has needle-like foliage, which are typically evergreens such as pines and spruce

Paver: see brick

Stippling: creates tonal value by placing dots close together; as dots are placed closer together, the value becomes darker

Stone: often used in the form of flagstone, which is a sheet-like stone that comes in various colors and sizes

Title block: contains client name and address, scale, north arrow, designer name, and date

8 Plants and Hardscapes

Objectives

- Learn the criteria affecting plant selection
- Understand general plant characteristics
- Become familiar with helpful resources in plant selection
- Be familiar with hardscape material uses and construction

The preliminary design has given shape to a balanced, functional plan. Now plants and hardscapes need to be considered because up to this point in the design process, specific materials have not been considered.

Plant Material and Selection

Many clients are interested in a landscape design to beautify their home with plants. Up to this point, the preliminary design has integrated the analysis of the residence with the client's wishes to come up with a functional plan that is interesting, balanced, and useful. There is a great variety of plant material available for the designer to use, many interesting forms, colors, sizes, scents, and so on. There are several factors that limit this selection if the design is going to be not only visually pleasing but also hardy and durable as well. The entire design process has led to an organized, visually appealing design, but if the plant selection is poor, the design will ultimately be a failure. Plants growing in the wrong location will not develop, and often eventually die. For instance, the placement of a shade plant in full sun will result in poor growth and eventually death, bringing into question the designer's reputation (Fig. 8–1).

Tip Box

The importance of proper plant selection cannot be overemphasized. Plants not adapted to growing conditions will fail, as will the design.

Figure 8–1 Plant Selection
This shade plant, Acuba, is sunburned (black margins) because of too much sun.

Plant Selection Books and Software

This section will cover much of the criteria that influence the decisions of plant selection. It does not cover specific plants. Refer to Appendix B for books and software for selection resources. There are many good books that list plants and categorize them in their best uses, such as flower color, sun exposure, fall color, and more. Color photos are helpful to make selections as well as discuss unfamiliar plants with clients.

In addition to books, there are several software programs that have selection capabilities based on given criteria (Fig. 8–2). This makes plant selection much easier for beginning students with limited plant experience. A user can select the hardiness zone of their area along with other conditions such as moisture, exposure, flower color and timing, form, size, fruit, thorns, and so on. The criteria can be set to filter out plants that

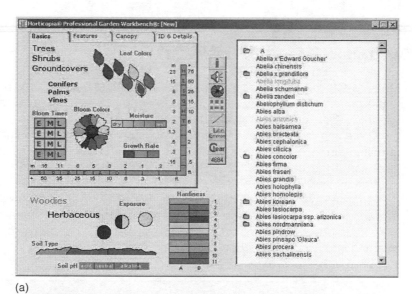

(a)

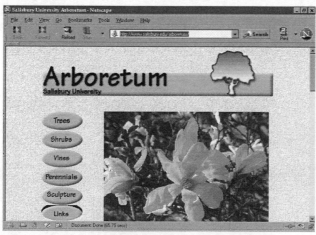

(b)

Figure 8–2 **Plant Software and Web Sites**

Plant selection can be aided by the use of books or, as shown, database software. (a) This is an example of *Horticopia* software. (b) Example of Web site *(http://www.Salisbury.edu/ arboretum)*. Some books will categorize uses of plants while software can suggest plants that fit selected criteria such as size, moisture, shade, hardiness, etc.

don't fit. For instance, set criteria to look for a shrub that is 3 feet tall and adapts to wet, shady conditions. The software database can then show a list of plants that meet these conditions in your selected hardiness zone.

Also make note of free Web sites that offer great databases of plant images and selection options that operate in a similar fashion to the software programs.

> ### *Tip Box*
>
> A good way to keep up to date with the latest and most popular books and software is through the American Nurseryman Publishing Company (*http://www.amerinursery.com*).

Availability

Obviously plant selection will vary depending on location. There are a few guidelines that will simplify selection and improve the likelihood of success.

Regional Plants

Start by limiting the plants to those that can be easily purchased in the area. Beginning students often overburden themselves by looking at an extensive plant materials book or lists from class of over 300 plants. Although there may be hundreds of excellent plants that can grow in the area, many of them will be difficult to find locally. There is nothing wrong with using unique plants, it is just difficult to attain them and can cause a problem for installation due to the time and cost of special ordering.

Local, Reputable Nurseries

Become familiar with regional plants and their availability and cost by compiling lists and catalogs from local reputable plant nurseries (Fig. 8–3). These plants will best adapt to the regional climate. The nursery should sell quality plant material that will be important to the development of the landscape design. Poor quality may be diseased, damaged, or stressed, which will reduce the chances of its establishment and survival.

Figure 8–3 Local Reputable Plant Nurseries
Collect and become familiar with local reputable plant nurseries and their inventory. It's a good indication of plants adapted to the region and makes availability easy.

Developing a Plant Palette

Consider creating a **plant palette** of the most adapted plants in your area. This can help limit the number of plants and simplify the selection process. It can also serve as a reference page whenever you are selecting plants for future projects. This list can be divided into various categories based on characteristics or cultural requirements as listed in this textbook. The list will continue to grow with experience.

Hardiness

The design will not be successful unless the plants thrive. Plants not adapted to the climate grow slowly, are susceptible to insects and disease, and simply look bad. Eventually they will not survive the cold winter or hot summer.

Hardiness zones are areas of average annual minimum temperature assigned throughout the United States that were established by the USDA (Fig. 8–4). The hardiness zone map was first published in 1960 and then updated in 1990. Plants are assigned a range of zones in which they will grow based on their cold hardiness, which is often the factor limiting where plants can grow year after year. Palms, for instance, can grow in the summer but cannot overwinter in northern climates. The United States is assigned zones 2 through 10. Each zone contains a range of 10 degrees, for instance areas within zone 2 have an average annual minimum temperature between −50 and −40, zone 3 is between −40 and −30, and so on. Plants are assigned a range of zones in which they are adapted to grow based on these minimums.

Be aware that heat hardiness has not been considered to the degree as cold hardiness, and that many factors affect plant adaptation such as moisture, soil conditions, and microclimates. Heat damage is much less apparent than cold damage because plants can survive for several years in a stunted, chlorotic condition before they fail. The American Horticultural Society (*http://www.ahs.org*) has produced a heat adaptability map that serves as a reference much like the cold hardiness map (Fig. 8–5). **Heat zones** are based on the average number of days over 86 degrees Fahrenheit, considered the threshold beyond which plants begin to suffer physiologically. For example, zone 1 is less than one day and zone 12 is over 210 days. It also assumes there are no other stresses, such as water deficiency, which can make plants more susceptible to heat damage.

Beginning students often find it difficult to select plants because they are new to the horticulture field. Researching what zones plants are assigned is important, but be aware that the extremes of adaptation can result in marginally healthy plants that do not look like the picture in the book. Beyond plant research, consult local nurseries or seasoned designers about the best plants to use in the area.

Also, be aware of the supplier. Just because a vendor is selling the plant doesn't mean it is adapted to the area. Some are guilty of selling plants marginally adapted at best (you might be surprised how little plant knowledge the manager possesses). It is advisable to buy from local reputable nurseries, especially those that buy from regional wholesale growers.

Cultural Requirements

Cultural requirements refer to growing conditions required for optimal growth. Two of the most important requirements are exposure and moisture.

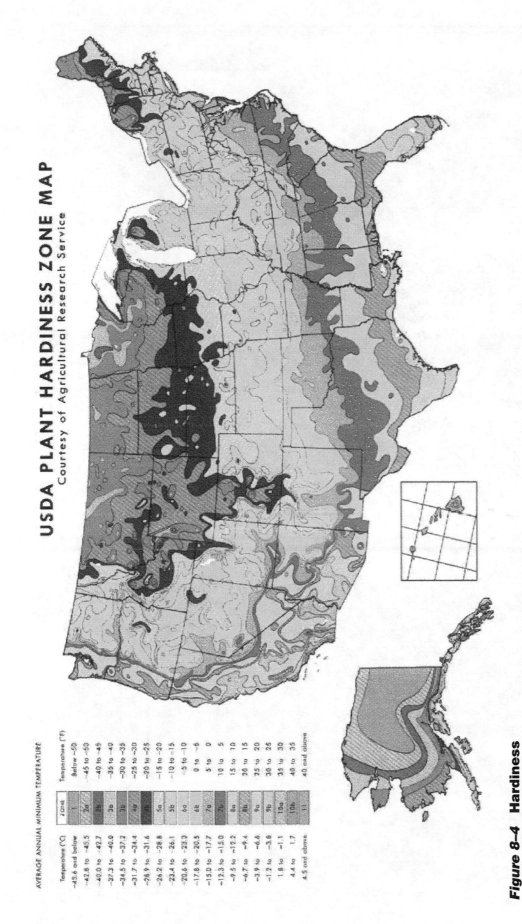

USDA PLANT HARDINESS ZONE MAP
Courtesy of Agricultural Research Service

AVERAGE ANNUAL MINIMUM TEMPERATURE

Temperature (°C)	Zone	Temperature (°F)
–45.6 and below	1	Below –50
–42.8 to –45.5	2a	–45 to –50
–40.0 to –42.7	2b	–40 to –45
–37.3 to –40.0	3a	–35 to –40
–34.5 to –37.2	3b	–30 to –35
–31.7 to –34.4	4a	–25 to –30
–28.9 to –31.6	4b	–20 to –25
–26.2 to –28.8	5a	–15 to –20
–23.4 to –26.1	5b	–10 to –15
–20.6 to –23.3	6a	–5 to –10
–17.8 to –20.5	6b	0 to –5
–15.0 to –17.7	7a	5 to 0
–12.3 to –15.0	7b	10 to 5
–9.5 to –12.2	8a	15 to 10
–6.7 to –9.4	8b	20 to 15
–3.9 to –6.6	9a	25 to 20
–1.2 to –3.8	9b	30 to 25
1.8 to –1.1	10a	35 to 30
4.4 to 1.7	10b	40 to 35
4.5 and above	11	40 and above

Figure 8–4 Hardiness

Plant temperature adaptation is based on cold hardiness, the annual average minimum temperature. Zones are assigned a hardiness zone number that is shown on the above map established by the USDA.

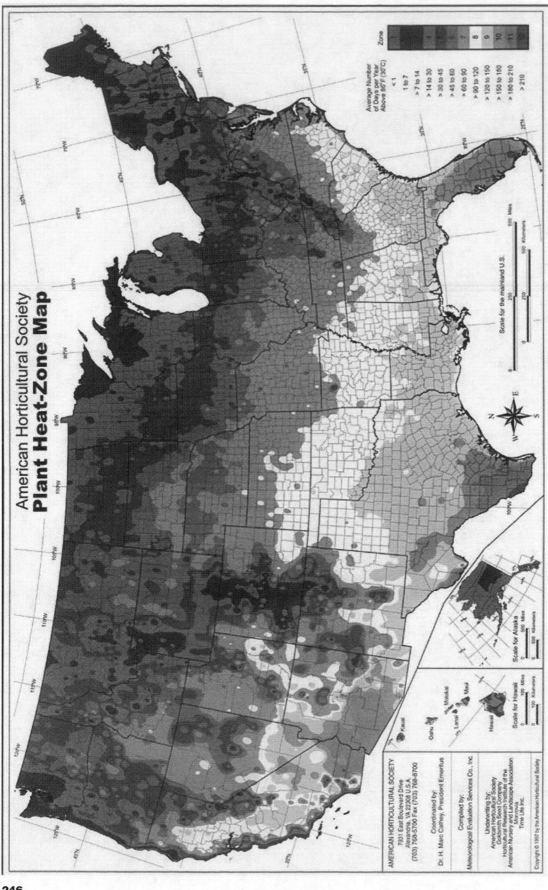

American Horticultural Society
Plant Heat-Zone Map

AMERICAN HORTICULTURAL SOCIETY
7931 East Boulevard Drive
Alexandria, VA 22308 U.S.A.
(703) 768-5700 Fax (703) 768-8700

Coordinated by:
Dr. H. Marc Cathey, President Emeritus

Compiled by:
Meteorological Evaluation Services Co. Inc.

Underwriting by:
American Horticultural Society
Goldsmith Seeds Company
Horticultural Research Institute of the
American Nursery and Landscape Association
Monrovia
Time Life Inc.

Copyright © 1997 by the American Horticultural Society

Zone	Average Number of Days per Year Above 86°F (30°C)
1	<1
2	1 to 7
3	>7 to 14
4	>14 to 30
5	>30 to 45
6	>45 to 60
7	>60 to 90
8	>90 to 120
9	>120 to 150
10	>150 to 180
11	>180 to 210
12	>210

Scale for the mainland U.S.

Scale for Alaska

Scale for Hawaii

Figure 8–5 **Heat Zone Map**

Plant temperature adaptation based on heat tolerance established by the American Horticultural Society. Zones are assigned similar to the cold hardiness map. *(Photo courtesy of the American Horticultural Society. www.ahs.org)*

Tip Box

Microclimate

Microclimates are areas or pockets that are warmer or cooler than predominate growing conditions in the area (Fig. 8–6). This may be due to urbanization, changes in topography, or surrounding trees. This is most noticeable in areas that are partially enclosed by walls. These areas are protected from cold, hard wind that can dry out plants and increase the chances of winter damage. Plants marginally adapted to the climate can survive these conditions much better in protected areas.

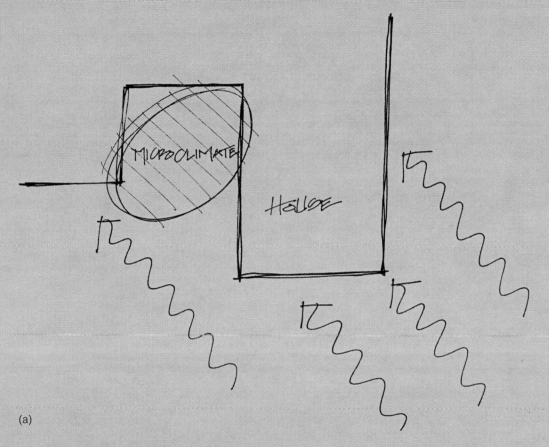

(a)

Figure 8–6 Microclimate

An area within a hardiness zone that is warmer or cooler due to protection or urbanization. (a) Often buildings protect a planting area from harsh winter wind and exposure to temperature extremes. (b) The dogwood tree is protected in the corner of the building and has grown about 20 feet, while dogwoods around the corner in full sun grew little and eventually failed.

(b)

Exposure

Exposure refers to the location of the plant with respect to light, wind, salt, city conditions, and durability (Fig. 8–7).

Light   There are sun-tolerant plants and shade-tolerant plants, as well as those adapted to a degree of both sun and shade. Shade plants in full sun will burn and sun plants in shade will grow poorly, if at all. Some plants have a broad range of sunlight adaptation that can grow in either full sun or full shade. Make note of plants that are adapted to both sun and shade because they are very versatile (Fig. 8–8).

Tip Box

Southwest Exposure Is the Hottest

What time of the day does the plant receive sun exposure? Late afternoon sun is the warmest. Some shade-tolerant plants can tolerate full sun in early morning because temperatures are relatively low.

Planting for Future Shade?   Be careful when planting for future shade. A newly planted large tree will not provide significant shade for several years. If shade-requiring plants are planted under the future large tree, they will be scorched in the full sun and fail before shade is there. One good way to address these areas is to select plants that tolerate full sun and shade.

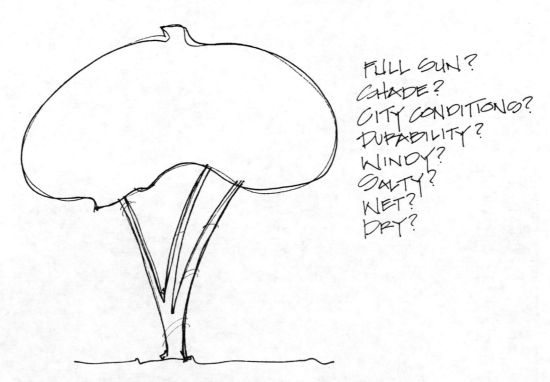

Figure 8–7   **Cultural Requirements**
There are several factors to consider when selecting a plant best adapted to the area.

(a)

(b)

Figure 8–8 **Shade**
(a) Turf is difficult to grow in full shade. (b) Consider shade-tolerant plants, such as ground cover, or just mulch.

Wind Windy areas can mechanically ruin some plants by physically damaging foliage and branches or rapidly drying the plant. Examples include coastal regions and the Midwest prairie.

City Conditions Some plants are not very tolerant of city conditions. Ozone and smog have a negative impact. This can greatly limit plant selection. Another impact of urban environments is paving and walls that can significantly raise the temperature (Fig. 8–9).

Figure 8–9 **Urban Impact**
Paving raises the temperature around plants. These plants are growing in tight wells in a hot area with a high level of pedestrian traffic.

Durability   Know which plants don't handle rough exposure, such as to pets and children. Delicate plants that have stems and leaves that break easily will not survive a big outdoor dog unless some protection is provided (Fig. 8–10).

Salt   Coastal regions have the limitation of exposure to saltwater, either to the roots or blown onto foliage. As a result, plants have to be salt-tolerant to survive (Fig. 8–11).

Figure 8–10 **Durability**
Plants may have to handle the rough conditions of pets or children. In this example, ornamental grass handles the surrounding playground well.

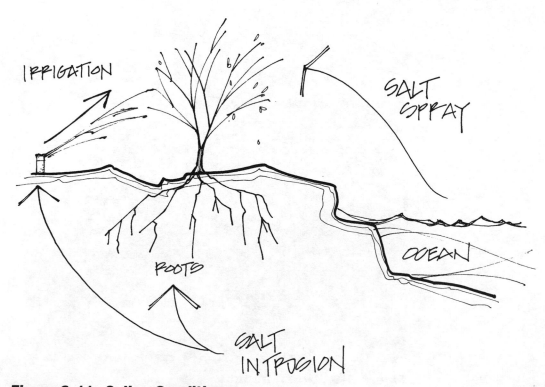

Figure 8–11 **Saline Conditions**
Plants must be salt-tolerant if the foliage is sprayed or the roots are exposed to saline water.

Moisture

Be familiar with predominately wet or dry conditions. Wet soil can cause root rot and lack of soil oxygen, while dry conditions can stunt growth and weaken tolerance and health. Choose plants adapted to either extreme.

Typically Wet Conditions

- Heavy soils
- High water table
- Areas near downspouts

Typically Dry Conditions

- Sandy soils
- Nonirrigated
- Arid climates

Soil

There are several facets of soil, which can be studied in Chapter 3, "Inventory and Analysis." The main components considered are: pH, structure, texture, and fertility (Fig. 8–12). Be sure if any soil conditions that are not correctable are noted before plant selection so that the plants selected are tolerant of such conditions. For instance, as mentioned in an earlier chapter, plants such as azaleas and rhododendrons are adaptable to acidic soils.

Wildlife

Plants can be used to attract or repel wildlife. Birds, butterflies, and even sometimes squirrels are appreciated by some people. (See Appendix E for suggestions on attracting birds and butterflies.)

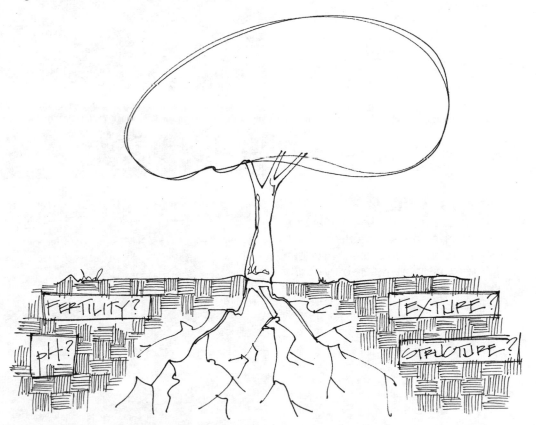

Figure 8–12 Soil Conditions
Consider soil factors when selecting plants, or whether the soil will need to be or can be altered to plants.

Birds

Hummingbirds are valued because of their unique flying habit. They are attracted to flowers to feed on nectar, in particular flowers that are red such as the orange-red flowers on the trumpet creeper vine, or red flowers on a bottlebrush shrub (Fig. 8–13). Other birds are attracted to fruit and seeds as a food source. Be aware that attracting birds to consume fruit can also create problems! Certain fruit, in particular mulberry, will cause birds to defecate in unwanted areas such as the driveway, automobiles, and entertainment areas.

Butterflies

Butterflies are a great addition to any landscape, especially along a pathway where they flutter up when people approach (Fig. 8–14). To attract butterflies, there are food sources to attract the larval (caterpillar) stage and food sources to attract the adult butterfly. The caterpillar will consume the foliage of food source plants so they should be planted to allow insect damage. Herbs are often a great source of food for caterpillars. Nectar is provided to the adult butterfly from flowers. There are numerous resources for creating a successful butterfly garden that will attract a great variety during the growing season.

Figure 8–13   Birds
Birds are attracted to fruit of some plants, while hummingbirds are attracted to flowers of others, such as this trumpet creeper vine. *(Photo courtesy of Chris Briand.* http://www.salisbury.edu/arboretum/*)*

Figure 8–14   Butterflies
Attract immature butterflies with larval food sources or adult butterflies with nectar sources. *(Photo courtesy of Chris Briand.* http://www.salisbury.edu/arboretum/*)*

Deer

Deer are the most notable wildlife that wreak havoc on a landscape by devouring flowers and foliage overnight, leaving behind nothing but bare ground or stems. The intensity of deer problems will depend on the deer population, drought conditions, and time of year. During dry summers, deer search harder for food that is limited in nonirrigated regions. Spring is the height of intense feeding because foliage is flush, succulent, and nutritious. Winter, when food is most difficult to find, may bring deer into the landscape to feed on woody stems.

Be aware if deer problems exist in the region of the design. If so, take precautions to select plants (or other methods) to resist deer. There are several good resources online for plants and methods, such as *http://www.mydeergarden.com*.

Plant Characteristics

Many plant characteristics were discussed in Chapter 6, "Design Principles," in reference to color and texture. This section will take a look at some other characteristics that will impact selection.

Thorns and Spines

Plants armed with sharp, pointed stems or leaves, such as a cactus, are sometimes referred to as barrier plants (Fig. 8–15). These are often used to repel people or animals, to direct traffic, or keep traffic out of sensitive areas.

Thorns are sharp, woody extensions that technically are a modified branch. **Spines** are sharp points that can grow on the margins or at the tips of foliage and are technically modified leaves.

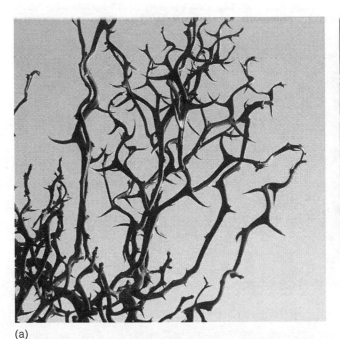

(a)

(b)

Figure 8–15 **Thorns and Spines**
Barrier plants have (a) thorns or (b) spines to repel people or animals.

Branching

Although branching is covered in Chapter 6, there are other considerations worth mentioning.

Exfoliating trunks and branches are valued assets to some plants (Fig. 8–16). These are especially noticeable when leaves have fallen from deciduous plants exposing a rich texture. Exfoliating trunks are noticeable anytime of the year, while the exfoliating branches are more valued after leaf drop.

One of the most unique plant characteristics is the **contorted,** or **corkscrew,** effect of branches that are twisted and curled (Fig. 8–17). These are highly coveted branches used in flower arrangements. This branching habit can make a great accent plant.

The **weeping** form has branches that are flimsy enough that there is little structural support (Fig. 8–18). As a result, these branches, which are typically newer growth, hang from the older limbs in a pendulous fashion. They move easily in the wind and lend a graceful form to the landscape.

(a)

(b)

***Figure 8–16* Exfoliation**
Exfoliating trunks and branches add rich texture to trees and shrubs. (a) Paperbark Maple. (b) Shagbark Hickory. *(Photo (a) courtesy of Chris Briand,* http://www.salisbury.edu/arboretum/; *photo (b) courtesy of William A. Hoch,* http://www.midwestlandscapeplants.org*)*

(c)

(d)

(e)

Figure 8–16 Exfoliation—continued
(c) Stewartia; (d) Chinese Elm; (e) Musclewood (no exfoliation but interesting texture); (f) Oakleaf hydrangea, exfoliating branches. *(Photo (f) courtesy of Chris Briand.* http://www.salisbury.edu/arboretum/; *photos (c), (d), and (e) courtesy of William A. Hoch.* http://www.midwestlandscapeplants.org*)*

(f)

Figure 8–17 Contorted Branches

The contorted branches of (a) Hardy Orange Flying Dragon, (b) Corkscrew Willow, and (c) Harry Lauders Walking Stick are unique specimens, especially in the winter. *(Photo (b) courtesy of William A. Hoch.* http://www.midwestlandscapeplants.org*)*

Figure 8–18 Weeping Branches

(a) Branches have less structural support than nonweeping varieties and hang gracefully from main limbs of the tree, such as these weeping pines and (b) weeping willow. *(Photo (b) courtesy of William A. Hoch.* http://www.midwestlandscapeplants.org*)*

Fragrance

The effect of fragrance adds another dimension to the landscape in addition to visual. Fragrance typically emanates from flowers and some, like gardenia, honeysuckle, and jasmine, can fill an entire yard (Fig. 8–19). Be aware that some plants have a good fragrance only when you stick your nose into the flower but have minimal effect on the surrounding area.

This is a wonderful dimension to add to an entertainment area or entrance where they would be most noticeable. Even planting these flowers near open windows can fill the house with fragrance.

Be aware that some plants may be malodorous. The Bradford Pear, for example, is valued for its white showy flowers in early spring but smells something like vomit, which can be overpowering at the entrance.

(a)

(b)

Figure 8–19   Fragrance
(a) The flowers of Tea Olive are visually insignificant but are highly valued for their potent fragrance. (b) Dwarf gardenia blooms in the summer next to the front door.

Figure 8–20 **Nuisance Fruit**
Some plants drop fruit that can be messy or malodorous. This ginkgo fruit is pulpy and when dropped on the ground can break open and reveal a rank odor. *(Photo courtesy of Chris Briand.* http://www.salisbury.edu/arboretum/*.)*

Nuisance Fruit

Be aware of plants that drop messy fruit (Fig. 8–20). This is a major concern in areas of traffic where the fruit would drop on sidewalks or parked cars. One example is ginkgo. The female tree produces a fleshy fruit that when broken open, smells awful!

Plant Size and Quality

The landscape designer will specify the size of plants to be installed and should be familiar with plant quality.

Size

The designer should understand the impact that plant size has on the cost of the design as well as how plants are sold (Fig. 8–21). This will have a great impact on the rate at which the design develops.

Larger Plants

- More expensive
- Fill in the intended design quicker

Smaller Plants

- Less expensive
- More time to fill the design

Inform the client that the design needs time to develop and grow into the plan that has been proposed. Some clients may expect the landscape to look like the plan drawing at the time of installation. Ideally, clients would like to install plants that fill the area immediately. But large plants are more expensive, take longer to establish, and are often not economically feasible. However, installing very small, inexpensive plants will look undersized and take too much time to fill.

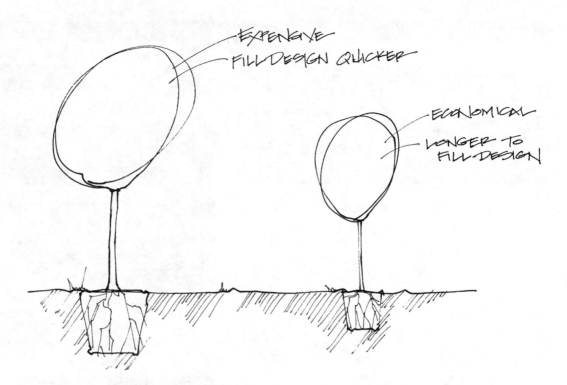

***Figure 8–21* Plant Size**
The designer will specify plant size and the client should be aware that the proposed design will take time to mature. Larger plants will fill the intended design quickly but will cost more to purchase.

Plant Production

Plants are grown at wholesale nurseries and sold to contractors or retail nurseries. Retail nurseries sell to contractors and the general public. Plants are produced and sold in plastic containers or balled-in-burlap.

Container Grown   **Container-grown** plants are grown in a plastic pot. They have the relative convenience of easy handling and planting anytime of the year (Fig. 8–22). The approximate volume of the plastic container is measured in gallons. For smaller containers, such as those used to sell annuals and perennial flowers or ground cover, inches may be used to describe the diameter of the container. Four-inch containers are a common size for annual flowers and some perennials.

> **One gallon:** Some perennials are sold in 1-gallon containers. One-gallon shrubs are also available but often considered too small for many applications because of the size and time required to fill the design.

> **Three and five gallon:** Three-gallon containers are commonly used for small to medium shrubs because they are economical and reasonable in size.

> **Ten, fifteen, thirty gallons and larger:** These sizes are used for shrubs and trees. Of course, the larger sizes are the most expensive.

Balled-in-Burlap   **Balled-in-burlap** are field-grown plants that are dug and wrapped in burlap to contain the rootball (Fig. 8–23). This type of production is often referred to as B and B. It is often specified for large trees and shrubs.

(b)

(c)

Figure 8–22 **Container-Grown Plants**
(a) Trees and shrubs are conveniently grown in black plastic containers. Sizes are measured in gallons: 1, 3, and 5 gallons are common examples, but larger sizes are used as well. (b) At a nursery, 1-gallon shrubs are grown on the right and 15-gallon trees on the left. (c) Annual and perennial flowers are typically sold in 4-inch containers.

The size of B and B plants can be specified by either

- Height from the ground to the top of the plant

  Example: Ten-foot *Acer rubrum,* Red Maple

- **Caliper,** which is the diameter of the tree trunk measured at 6 inches from the ground for trunks up to 4 inches in diameter and 12 inches from the ground for larger trees.

  Example: 1.5-inch caliper *Acer rubrum,* Red Maple

Bare Root   **Bare root** plants are generally small plants sold without soil around the roots. They are limited to planting during dormancy and are not often used by designers.

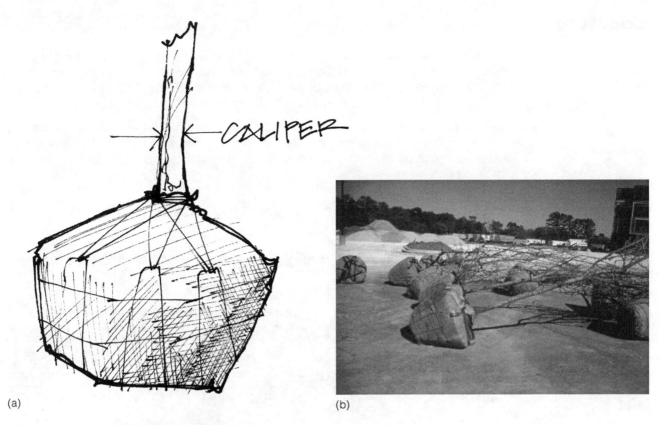

(a)   (b)

Figure 8–23 **Balled-in-Burlap**
A common method of plant production is the rootball wrapped in burlap. (a) The size is often dictated by caliper, the diameter of the trunk 6 inches from the rootball, although it can also be measured as the height of the plant. (b) Balled-in-burlap trees are ready to plant.

Tip Box

What Is the American Standard for Nursery Stock?

American Standard for Nursery Stock, sometimes referred to as the **ANSI Standards** or just the **Standard** for short, is from the American Association of Nurserymen (*http://www.anla.org*). The nursery industry recognizes this as the primary reference for the standardization of plant terminology. Many designers simply write in their specifications, "All plant material must conform to the American Standard for Nursery Stock."

Hardscapes and Other Materials

This section covers hardscapes, those components of the landscape other than plants, which are used to build walks, driveways, walls, decks, and so on. Other materials discussed include drainage, mulch, and lighting.

Although many times landscape designers are hired to design with plants after the general contractor has done much of the hardscaping, this chapter addresses hardscaping components so that the designer has some understanding of their uses and construction. In many cases, the designer will have little impact on designing the driveway, sidewalks, and patio. Landscape architects are more often hired rather than landscape designers at the initial planning phases and will have much more control of the hardscape portion of the landscape design.

Concrete

Concrete is one of the most inexpensive forms of paving. When installed properly it is very effective at supporting traffic safely without wear. Typically a minimum of 4-inch-thick concrete is used for the sidewalk, patio, and driveway. The driveway may be thicker and reinforced with steel rods to support the weight of automobiles.

Because the driveway is large, the expanse of concrete can be visually overwhelming (Fig. 8–24). The uninterrupted gray slab of concrete can also be a dull, uninteresting feature. To break up the monotonous expanse of concrete, there are different finishes to make an interesting surface (Fig. 8–25).

Figure 8–24 Driveways
Driveways are often very large, visually dominant features of the landscape.

(a)

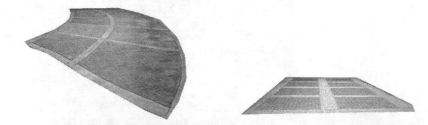

Figure 8–25 Unique Driveways
(a) Ways to break up the large expanse of concrete are dividing it with rows of pavers or stone, or the use of alternate materials. (b) Paving a driveway is a good alternative to concrete and is more appealing in color and texture, but more expensive. *(Photo (a) courtesy of Visual Impact Imaging; photo (b) courtesy of Blue Ribbon LLC, Maryland.* www.blueribbonllc.com*)*

(b)

Figure 8–26 Contraction Lines
(a) Grooves in the concrete visually help break up the large driveway. (b) On this large concrete sidewalk at an elementary school, contraction lines are used to add visual interest by breaking up space and repeating the angle of the brick structure.

Surface Finishing

There are several finishes to the surface of concrete that can add interest. Consult a concrete contractor for specialty finishes.

Contraction Jointing   Concrete often cracks as it dries. **Contraction joints** are 3/8″ deep grooves that help control cracking. Jointing creates a weak line in the concrete where the cracking will occur, rather than running randomly across the slab.

Jointing lines are often seen as grooves running perpendicular across sidewalks, but they can also be used to create patterns over large slabs of concrete to be more visually interesting (Fig. 8–26).

Exposed Aggregate   **Exposed aggregate** is one of the more attractive surfaces and has a natural appeal. It has pea gravel embedded in the surface of the concrete (Fig. 8–27). The pea gravel adds a textural element that is visual and physical.

Colored Concrete   **Colored concrete** has a color additive that can be added to concrete before it is poured (Fig. 8–27). Warming the concrete with a slight tan color adds an attractive earth-tone appeal that complements the natural colors of the surrounding mulch and soil. This can also be used in conjunction with the exposed aggregate technique.

(a)

(b)

***Figure 8–27* Exposed Aggregate and Colored Concrete**
Exposed aggregate concrete has pea gravel embedded into the surface. (a) This concrete is warmed with an addition of tan coloring. Deep contraction lines that help control cracking also help break up the large slab. (b) Close-up of exposed aggregate.

(a)

(b)

(c)

***Figure 8–28* Stamped Concrete**
(a) Concrete can be colored and stamped into patterns, such as this herringbone paver pattern.
(b) Driveway stamped into basketweave pattern;
(c) Entrance stamped into flagstone pattern. *(Photos (b) and (c) courtesy of King's Materials, Cedar Rapids, IA.* http://www.kingsmaterial.com)

Stamped Concrete **Stamped concrete** uses numerous approaches to create specialty effects on the concrete surface (Fig. 8–28). It can be used in conjunction with colored concrete to create a brick paving effect, cobblestone, or any number of patterned effects.

Stone and Pavers

Paved areas are more expensive to install than concrete but are more decorative and just as functional (Fig. 8–29). There are many types and sizes of bricks and stones.

Stone

Stone is often used in the form of flagstone, which is a sheet-like stone that comes in various colors, shapes, and sizes (Fig. 8–30). It's often used as an informal walkway because the stones are of the irregular variety. **Cut stone** is shaped, or cut, into various rectangular shapes that are more consistent in shape and size. Cut stone has a more formal appeal than flagstone.

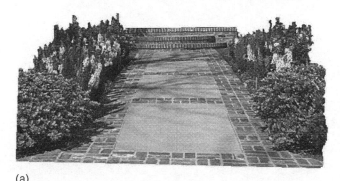
(a)

(b)

Figure 8–29 **Stone and Pavers**
(a) Pavers, or bricks, used in conjunction with concrete in this example are an effective way to create a visually interesting walk. (b) Stone is large and flat and can be irregular or square shaped. *(Photos courtesy of Visual Impact Imaging)*

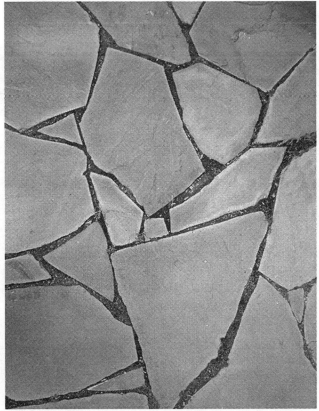
(a)

(b)

Figure 8–30 **Stone**
(a) Irregular-shaped stone, often referred to as flagstone. (b) Square stone is often referred to as cut stone, or bluestone (a common type of stone that is cut). *(Photos courtesy of Visual Impact Imaging.)*

Stone Tiles   Stone tiles are concrete paving modules that are colored and textured to simulate a natural appearance. Much like cut stone, seams fit tightly and there are numerous textures, colors, and patterns to choose from (Fig. 8–31a).

Pavers

Pavers are like bricks made from concrete or clay and come in various shapes and colors (Fig. 8–31b). They can be used in patios, sidewalks, and driveways (Fig. 8–31c). Shapes can be rectangular, square, or interlocking. There are numerous patterns that can be created with pavers. A few of the commonly used patterns are

- Running bond
- Herringbone
- Basket weave
- Interlocking
- Fan

Stone and Paver Construction

Stone and pavers are commonly constructed free-laid with sand or wet-laid with mortar (Fig. 8–32).

Dry-Laid   **Dry-laid** construction utilizes a foundation of crushed granite or limestone (or similar material) and a setting bed of sand on which the pavers are laid (Fig. 8–33). Once all the pavers are laid, sand is swept into the cracks between the pavers. Some techniques mix dry mortar with sand to sweep in the cracks to set up a weak cement bond. Dry-laid installation is a quick means of installation, but very reliable when done properly. Since it uses porous materials such as sand, water will infiltrate through the hardscape and reduce runoff. **Flagstone** is more susceptible to weeds since the cracks are often wider than pavers or cut stone.

Wet-Laid   **Wet-laid** construction sets pavers or stone in **mortar,** a concrete mixture that bonds units together (Fig. 8–34). This uses a concrete foundation with a setting bed of mortar in which the pavers or stone are laid. Space between the pavers and stone are then filled and leveled with mortar for a smooth, durable surface. This is much more stable for stone and there is no potential for weeds to grow in cracks.

Figure 8–31a **Stone Tiles**
Paving modules that come in a variety of shapes, colors, and textures. *(Photo courtesy of King's Materials, Cedar Rapids, IA.* http://www. kingsmaterial.com.*)*

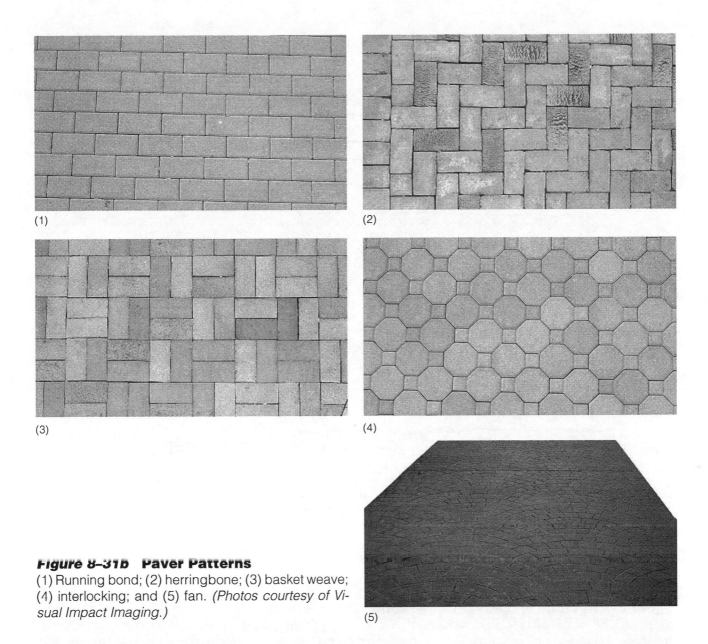

Figure 8–31b Paver Patterns
(1) Running bond; (2) herringbone; (3) basket weave;
(4) interlocking; and (5) fan. *(Photos courtesy of Visual Impact Imaging.)*

Figure 8–31c Patio
Patio constructed with (1) pavers and (2) stone.
*(Photos courtesy of Robert J. Kleinman Landscaping,
East Lansdowne, PA. www.kleinberg.com)*

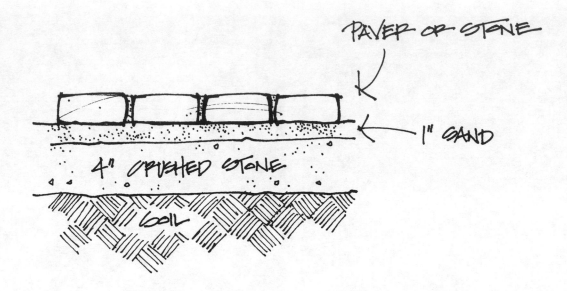

(a)

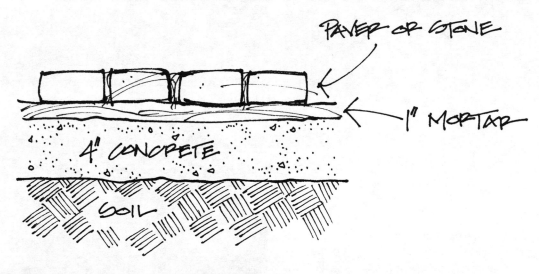

(b)

Figure 8–32 **Stone and Paver Construction**
(a) Dry-laid construction lays pavers or stone in a thin layer of sand over a compacted layer of crushed lime-stone. Sand is swept into the cracks. (b) Mortar construction lays pavers or stone in a layer of wet mortar over a base of concrete. Mortar is pressed into the cracks of pavers or stone.

Wood

Wood has numerous uses in the landscape, in outdoor furniture, edging, and storage sheds, as well as decks and fences, which will be covered in this section.

Decks

Some designers will be asked to design the layout of the deck that will be integral to the landscape. Designers often will provide a contractor with the layout who will then determine the substructure required to build it.

(a)

(b)   (c)

Figure 8–33 Dry-Laid Construction

(a) Pavers are laid on a compacted layer of sand. (b) Stone set in crushed aggregate. (c) Stone set in soil for informal path that allows ground cover and moss to grow between stones. *(Photo (c) only courtesy of Big Sky Landscaping, Inc., Clackamas, OR.)*

Figure 8–34 **Wet-Laid Construction**
Stone is set in wet mortar.

Figure 8–35 **Single-Level Deck**
This single level provides a dry, level area for a small gathering and to cook out.

Single Level versus Multilevel **Single level** is the simplest construction that works fine for small gatherings and outdoor cooking (Fig. 8–35). **Multilevel** decks are effective in creating different rooms on the deck (Fig. 8–36). Smaller areas can be developed for cooking, eating, a hot tub, or intimate relaxation, while main areas can be developed for entertaining larger groups.

Circulation Be aware of the flow of traffic as it goes into the house and out into the yard (Fig. 8–37). Access points should allow for convenient access to the deck and house. Try to direct traffic around gathering areas and not through them.

Seating Make considerations for seating space, whether it's going to be built-in seating along the perimeter of the deck or deck furniture (Fig. 8–38).

(a)

(b)

Figure 8–36 **Multilevel Decks**
(a) Deck has multiple levels for entertaining large parties. (b) This single deck (upper deck) had a lower deck added to create another outdoor room for entertainment. (c) The vine on the railing provides some separation between the upper and lower deck, while the vine growing up the arbor will provide overhead enclosure. *(Photo (a) courtesy of JRW Decks in Seattle.* www.jrwdecks.com*)*

(c)

Figure 8–37 **Entertainment Circulation**
Lay out the entertainment area to account for circulation through the area.

Figure 8–38 Deck Seating
These benches are built into the deck to provide seating as well as a railing. *(Photo courtesy of JRW Decks in Seattle.* www.jrwdecks.com*)*

(a)

(b)

Figure 8–39 Steps
(a) Steps should be placed at convenient access points to circulate into the surrounding landscape. (b) Combining deck and patio materials for interest. *(Photos courtesy of JRW Decks in Seattle.* www.jrwdecks.com*)*

Steps   Steps will be the access points connecting the deck to the yard. They should make access convenient from the house to deck to yard (Fig. 8–39a).

Combining Materials   Wood decking and paver/stone patios can be combined for visual interest and to develop outdoor rooms (Fig. 8–39b).

Fences

Fences are typically used to enclose the backyard for children and pets as well as provide entertainment privacy (Fig. 8–40). Many regional codes prevent privacy fences in the front yard. Fencing in the front yard is often limited to 3-feet-high picket fences (Fig. 8–41).

There are many different patterns of fences. Some of the more common ones are mentioned here (Fig. 8–42).

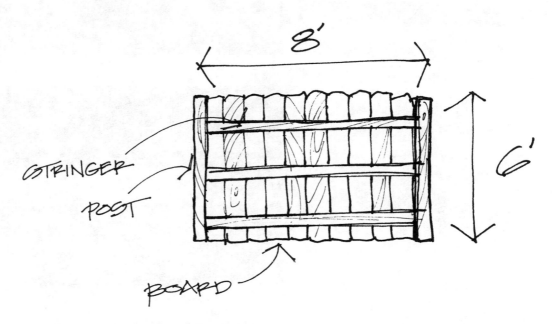

Figure 8–40   Fencing Dimensions

Privacy fences are typically limited to 6 foot tall in the backyard. Construction with fence panels that are 6 feet high and 8 feet wide is a common approach where posts are set on 8-foot centers to attach the panel.

Figure 8–41   Front Yard Fence

Regional codes restrict fences in the front yard to 3 feet high or none at all.

Figure 8–42 Fence Styles
(a) Solid board; (b) board-on-board;
(c) basket weave; (d) lattice-top; and
(e) picket.

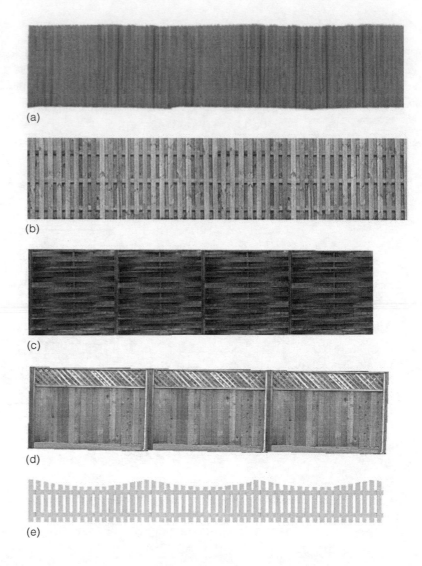

(a)

(b)

(c)

(d)

(e)

Solid Board Privacy (Dog-Ear)   One of the most common patterns is the **solid board privacy fence,** sometimes referred to as **dog-ear** (Fig. 8–43). This pattern has all the fence boards on one side. This offers complete privacy, but the downside is that the fence has a "bad side" showing the **stringers** where the fence boards attach. The fence board side is considered the "good side." Most codes require that the good side must face out toward the public.

Board-on-Board (Shadowbox or Alternate Board)   Another common fence pattern is **board-on-board,** sometimes referred to as **shadowbox** or **alternate board.** This pattern alternates the fence boards on each side of the stringer. This creates a semiprivate barrier since you can see through the fence at an angle (Fig. 8–44). The advantage is there is no bad side.

Basket Weave   **Basket weave** has a strong horizontal effect since the fence boards are installed horizontally to the posts. The horizontal pattern is considered to have a calming effect on the area. Like board-on-board, it has no bad side since there are no stringers.

Lattice-Top   With **lattice-top fencing,** the bottom portion of the fence is solid board or board-on-board. There is a decorative effect with a panel of lattice across the top of the fence.

Picket   Decorative picket fencing is often used in the front yard to contain and define the property, but offers no privacy.

Figure 8–43 **Bad Side of Fence**
Solid board fence has a good side (boards) and bad side showing where the stringers are to support the fence boards. Some
codes stipulate that the bad side needs to be constructed facing
the property and the good side facing outward to the public.

(a)   (b)

Figure 8–44 **Semiprivate Board-on-Board**
(a) A view through the board-on-board fence; (b) at an angle.

Retaining Walls

Retaining walls have numerous functional properties as well as design value (Fig. 8–45).

Reduce the slope of the ground: Retaining walls create a level surface on a sloped area. For large slopes, terracing the area with more than one wall will level it out in sections.

Lower maintenance: Steep slopes can be difficult to maintain. Turfgrass is hard to mow and trees and shrubs are difficult to water. Ground covers work well, but getting them established can be difficult. Any bare ground on a slope is prone to erosion.

Raised planting bed: Raised beds can utilize trailing vines and ground cover to grow over the edge.

Elevations: Retaining walls create a stepping effect. The change in elevation adds another dimension to the landscape.

Most residential retaining walls are generally kept less than 3 feet high. Higher walls will require more expertise to offset the higher degree of failure.

(a)

***Figure 8–45* Retaining Walls**
(a) Retaining walls can be used to reduce the slope of the ground, lower maintenance, and create visual interest; (b) multilevel retaining wall. *(Photo courtesy of King's Materials, Cedar Rapids, IA,* http://www.kingsmaterial.com.*)*

(b)

Retaining Wall Materials

Retaining walls can be constructed with landscape timbers, railroad ties, concrete blocks, or free stone. Regardless of the material, retaining walls have to be built on a solid foundation and have sufficient drainage to avoid wall failure.

Landscape Timbers and Railroad Ties   **Landscape timbers** are wooden timbers that are often 6″ × 6″ in dimension or greater (Fig. 8–46). Use timbers that are treated for ground contact to avoid decay. **Railroad ties** are similar to timbers but are treated with creosote, a preservative to reduce wood decay. Railroad ties should be weathered with age to reduce detrimental effects of the creosote on plants.

Horizontal construction stacks timbers and can either stagger the seams or stack the seams in a line (Fig. 8–47). Wall support is achieved by deadman installation and/or vertical posts. Deadman support is a timber installed perpendicular in the backfill that acts like an anchor. Walls that don't utilize support posts or a deadman are built with **batter,** which is the leaning back or stepping back of the wall toward the hill.

Vertical construction installs the timbers and ties on end into the ground. To achieve stability, the timbers/ties are installed as deep as the wall is high above the ground in addition to attaching a 2″ × 6″ along the back side.

(a)

(b)

(c)

***Figure 8–46* Timber Walls**
(a) Timbers used to reduce slope by terracing.
(b) Landscape timbers, such as 6″ × 6″ or 8″ × 8″ lumber, are commonly used. (c) Vertical construction is a unique approach.

Figure 8–47 Timber Wall Construction
(a) Horizontal construction (top) installs a course below grade for stability. Vertical construction (below) installs each timber at a depth below grade equal to how high it is above grade. (b) Batter, the leaning of the wall, or vertical posts are used to stabilize the wall.

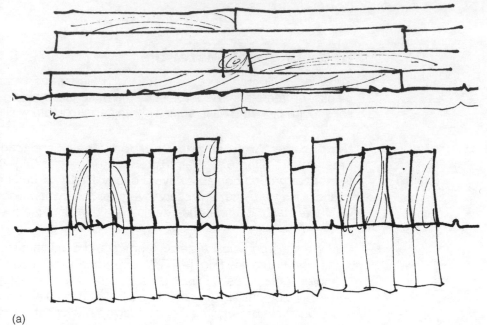

(a)

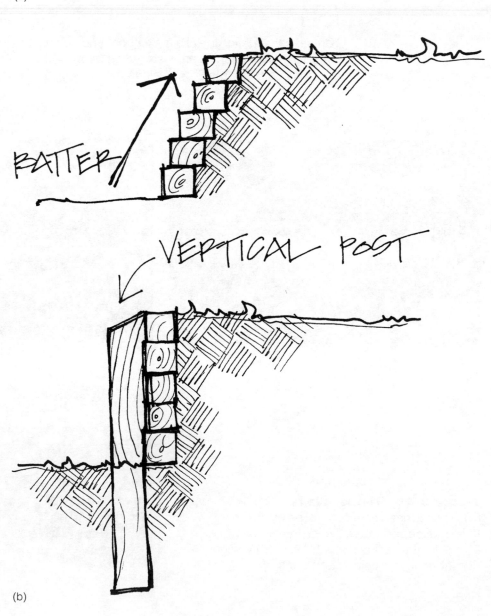

BATTER

VERTICAL POST

(b)

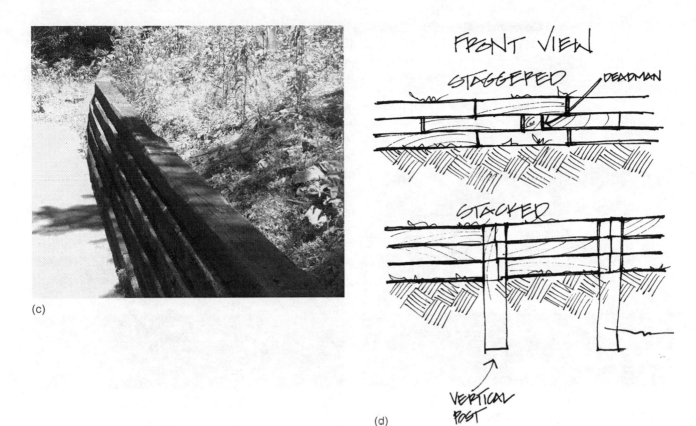

FRONT VIEW

STAGGERED — DEADMAN

STACKED

VERTICAL POST

(c)

(d)

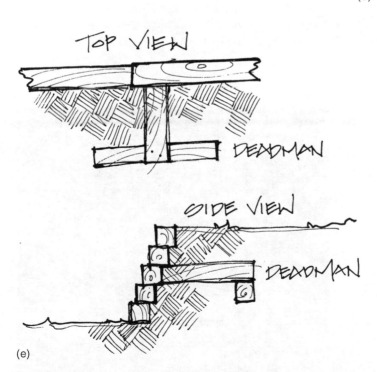

TOP VIEW

DEADMAN

SIDE VIEW

DEADMAN

(e)

Figure 8–47 Timber Wall Construction—continued
(c) example of batter; (d) stacked vs. staggered horizontal construction; (e) deadman installed like an anchor
for stability.

Concrete Blocks   **Concrete blocks** for the retaining wall construction come in a variety of sizes and colors (Fig. 8–48). Choosing an appropriate color may depend on the color of surrounding material, such as the house. There are variations of block types, but two commonly used blocks are lipped and pinned.

Lipped Blocks   **Lipped blocks** have an extended edge, or lip, on the bottom rear portion (Fig. 8–49). This lip hangs over the top of the block below it, creating a built-in stepping-back effect with additional support to prevent slippage.

(a)

(b)

***Figure 8–48* Block Retaining Walls**
(a) Retaining walls built with segmental, concrete blocks providing a raised foundation bed with variations in height. (b) This wall provides visual interest where the ground cover will grow and trail over the wall. *(Photo (a) courtesy of King's Materials, Cedar Rapids, IA.* http://www.kingsmaterial.com.*)*

***Figure 8–49* Lipped Blocks**
One of the easier to come by blocks has a lip on the bottom back portion for wall stability and creates a step-back effect of the wall to offset backfill pressure.

Pinned Blocks   **Pinned blocks** utilize fiberglass rods, or pins, that slide through internal holes that attach them to the block above (Fig. 8–50). **Geogrid** is laid between courses for additional support. These are typically used for larger wall construction.

Stone   Stone is an effective material with a natural appeal that can be either free-laid or mortared (Fig. 8–51).

***Figure 8–50* Pinned Blocks**
These types of blocks utilize pins that interlock the top course (row) to the bottom one. *(Photo courtesy of King's Materials, Cedar Rapids, IA. http://www.kingsmaterial.com)*

***Figure 8–51* Stone Walls**
Stone used to create retaining walls. *(Photo (b) courtesy of Big Sky Landscaping, Inc., Clackamas, OR.)*

(a)

(b)

(c)

***Figure 8–52* Edging**
Edging is valuable to keep mulch and beds separate and to maintain a sharp bed line. Without edging, the turf will encroach into the mulched bed and create a weak bed line that is higher maintenance.

Edging

The edge that separates the planting bed from the turf needs to be defined and reinforced (Fig. 8–52). It's important that the edge be sharply maintained. A sharp edge dramatically improves the definition of the beds and the flow of the line throughout the design. It also helps to keep turf from encroaching into the bed.

Edging material can be decorative or relatively unseen. Regardless, it should perform two functions:

Easy to maintain: Avoid edging materials that require a lot of trimming.

Reduce turf encroachment: It should be set deep enough (3″ to 40″) to keep turf from growing under.

Strip Edging

Strip edging is a solid, thin strip of material made of steel, aluminum, or plastic (Fig. 8–53). This type of edging is best installed so it is unseen and only draws attention to the sharp edge of the bed and not the edging itself. Therefore, the edging is best installed with the top as high as the turf grows and no higher. Strip edging works best to establish curving bed lines because it is very flexible. Anchoring with spikes will reduce edging from frost heaving in northern climates.

Steel and Aluminum   Steel and aluminum are the most durable and create one of the sharpest lines, but are more expensive than plastic.

Plastic   There are some favorable plastic edgings that are rigid enough to create a crisp bed line, however, most brands of inexpensive plastic edging are not durable and often create a weak line (Fig. 8–54).

Wood

Straight bed lines are created with 2″ × 4″, 2″ × 6″, or 4″ × 4″ wood (Fig. 8–55). Curved bed lines can be created with 1″ × 6″ wood because 1″ dimension is much more flexible. Anchor wood edging with spikes to prevent frost heaving.

Concrete, Brick, and Stone

Unlike strip edging, concrete, brick, and stone define the bed with a decorative appeal (Fig. 8–56). In these cases, the edging is meant to be seen as the defining edge. This type of edging is effective in keeping out turfgrass encroachment because of the width and is also very easy to maintain.

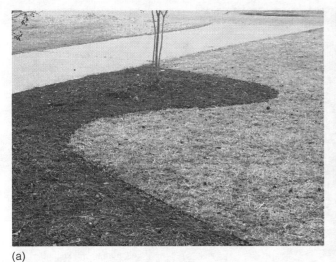

(a)

(b)

(c)

Figure 8–53 **Strip Edging**
(a) The edging maintains a sharp bed line and the integrity of the design with minimal maintenance. (b) Strip edging and weed barriers shortly after installation. (c) After 3 years, this bed line has maintained its integrity with minimal maintenance.

Figure 8–54 **Plastic Edging**
A popular strip edging used by homeowners is black, plastic edging. Often it creates a weak line and has poor longevity. Another common shortcoming is that the edging is installed too high, increasing maintenance and susceptibility to damage from equipment.

***Figure 8–55* Wood Edging**
Wood that is 1 inch thick and can be bent to create curves. Two-inch or 4-inch-thick wood is most likely used for straight lines.

***Figure 8–56* Brick Edging**
Bricks and pavers used as an edging material.

Mulch

Mulch is used to cover planting beds and around the base of trees (Fig. 8–57). The advantages are numerous:

- Reduces weed competition
- Reduces mowing
- Adds organic matter to the soil
- Conserves moisture
- Reduces temperature fluctuation and extremes

***Figure 8–57* Mulch**
Mulching material is used to cover beds, conserve moisture, moderate temperature, and control weeds.

The demands for mulch will be high at the installation of the design, since plants will be small and more space will be exposed. The demand for mulch will reduce as shrubs and ground cover become established.

Mulching Materials

Organic   **Organic mulch** is decomposable (Fig. 8–58). The advantage is it helps condition the soil. However, the disadvantage is it has to be replenished annually.

There's a great selection of organic mulches, most of which are wood products.

Bark   These are chunks of **bark,** often from pine (Fig. 8–58a). This type of organic mulch is often described as **nuggets.** They can be small to very large. Nuggets break down slowly because of lesser surface area and have to be replenished less often.

Wood   This material is usually shredded (Fig. 8–58b). The degree of shred varies from very fine to coarse. Shredded mulch works well on slopes and will resist washing down. Wood mulch can also be chipped more like mini-nuggets.

> **Cedar:** Has a reddish color and is aromatic, but these effects will fade. It is relatively expensive.
>
> **Cypress:** A blonde color that is relatively expensive.
>
> **Pine** and **hardwood:** These are inexpensive mulches.

(a)

(b)

***Figure 8–58* Organic Mulch**
Organic mulch decomposes and can be used to amend the soil. It needs to be occasionally replenished. (a) Bark nuggets; (b) shredded mulch.

> *Tip Box*
>
> Shredded mulch works well in annual flower beds because it can be tilled at the end of the season to condition the soil. **Double-hammered mulch** is shred extremely fine for this reason.

Recycled Wood   **Recycled wood mulch** comes from wood products such as disposed pallets and is shredded and often dyed. Colors range from bright red to tan to black. Beware that recycled wood can serve as a food source to termites and should be used with caution around the foundation of the house.

Non-Wood   **Pine straw** is one of the most popular mulches in the South (Fig. 8–59). It's relatively inexpensive, and effectively holds to slopes. The disadvantage is that it breaks down rapidly and has to be replenished more than once a year. Other non-wood materials include **shells of cocoa bean, pecan,** and **peanuts.** Some of these materials will release as much as 3 percent nitrogen as they decompose. Cocoa shells can be poisonous to dogs because they are derived from the bean to make chocolate.

Figure 8–59   Non-Wood Mulch
A non-wood organic mulch popular in the Southeast is pine straw.

> *Tip Box*
>
> On slopes or berms, use shredded mulch or pine straw that will knit together and resist washing out during heavy rain. Do not use nuggets because they are prone to washing out (Fig. 8–60).

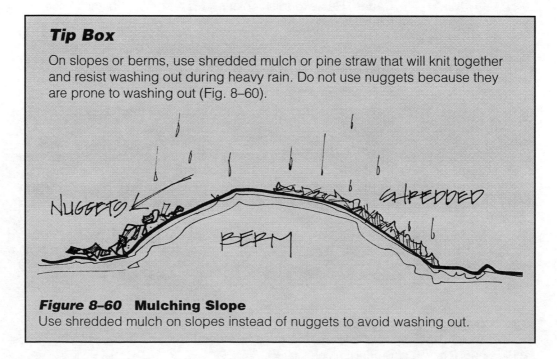

Figure 8–60   Mulching Slope
Use shredded mulch on slopes instead of nuggets to avoid washing out.

Figure 8–61 **Inorganic Mulch**
Inorganic mulch, such as stone, does not need to be replenished, although it can elevate temperatures in planting beds.

Figure 8–62 **Rubber Mulch**
Another inorganic mulch is recycled rubber that can appear like bark or shredded mulch.

Inorganic   **Inorganic mulch** will not decompose, and thus does not have to be replenished like organic mulch. The disadvantages can be higher temperatures around plants and the fact that it does not condition the soil.

Gravel and Stone   The most common form of inorganic mulch is **gravel,** or stone (Fig. 8–61). There are numerous sizes, shapes, and colors available. It is commonly used in dry regions to reduce turf areas.

Recycled Rubber   Another inorganic mulch that is popular in some regions is **recycled rubber** (Fig. 8–62). Old tires are shredded or ground up and look very much like organic mulch.

Weed Barrier

One big concern with mulched beds is weed competition (Fig. 8–63). Weedy beds can weaken a design because it looks poorly done. In addition, weeds will compete with the plantings and slow their establishment.

Figure 8–63 **Weed Barrier**
Weed barrier under mulch creates a physical barrier to prevent weeds from growing.

One good approach to controlling weeds is using a high-quality grade weed barrier underneath the mulch. **Weed barrier** is a mat of material, often a woven fabric or similar material, which creates a physical barrier preventing weeds from emerging in planting beds. If done correctly, beds can appear virtually weed-free for years. The cost up front will reduce the need to spray herbicides and pull weeds.

Tip Box

Avoid using plastic as a weed barrier. It can create a moisture lock and have a suffocating effect on the roots.

Drainage

The degree of drainage required depends on the region. In some areas, the design will have to implement drainage, either subsurface tile or surface grading (Fig. 8–64). The designer should have some knowledge of common approaches to drainage.

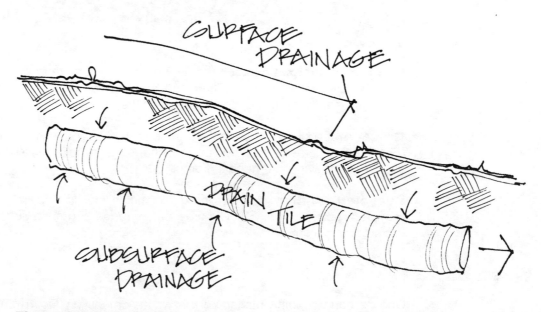

Figure 8–64 **Drainage**
Water needs to drain in the correct direction on the surface. Drain tile can be used to collect subsurface water and direct it to an acceptable outlet.

Surface Drainage

Surface drainage is directing water flow over the surface of the ground. Any changes to the surface should allow water to drain toward a catch basin or storm sewer in the road. At the very least, do not create drainage problems by grading surface water toward traffic areas, house, or creating water problems in the neighbor's yard.

Tip Box

Grade is the term used to describe the slope of the surface (Fig. 8–65). Typically 2 to 3 percent is sufficient to move water, but it may be as high as 10 percent around the foundation. The percent of the grade can be measured by dividing the **rise** (vertical difference between two points) by the **run** (horizontal difference between two points) and multiplying by 100.

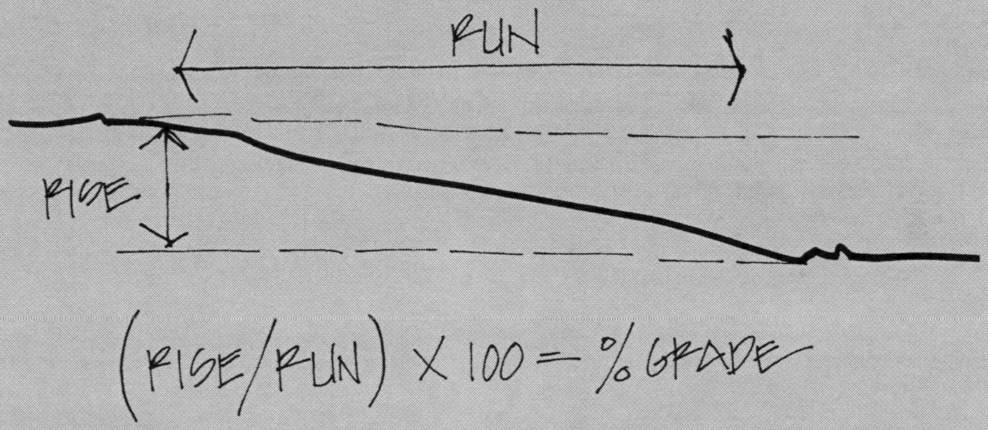

$$(RISE/RUN) \times 100 = \% \ GRADE$$

Figure 8–65 Surface Drainage
Properly grade the surface so that water flows toward the street or drain. Grade is typically 2 or 3%, but may be as high as 10% near the foundation.

Subsurface Drainage

Where soil moisture is a problem, the construction of **subsurface drainage** will facilitate the removal of excess soil moisture (Fig. 8–66).

French drains are trenches that are filled with drainage gravel to increase pore space to the ground. The main purpose of the French drain is to allow water to drain off the soil surface and into the ground. The French drain does not have an outlet since it acts mostly like a holding tank that facilitates water percolation off the surface. They are relatively short-lived, being effective for 5 to 10 years.

Tile drainage utilizes a 4-inch perforated drain pipe installed in a trench and surrounded by drainage gravel (Fig. 8–67). Its main purpose is to take subsurface water and direct it to an outlet. It is much more efficient at removing water from an area than a French drain.

House

One of the most important areas of drainage is to get water away from the house (Fig. 8–68). This is especially true for houses built over a basement or crawl space. When water drains back toward the house, moisture causes mildew problems, promotes wood decay, and can create termite problems.

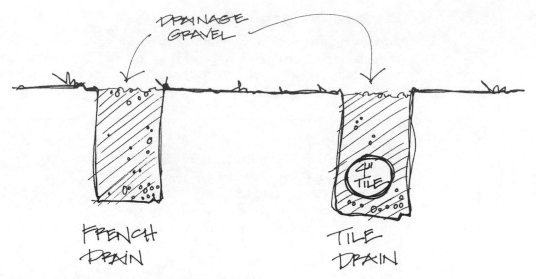

Figure 8–66 French and Tile Drains
A French drain is a ditch filled with pea gravel that allows a high degree of pore space to get water below the surface. A tile drain utilizes a perforated pipe that will collect water and carry it to an outlet.

(a)

(b)

Figure 8–67 Black Plastic Drain Tile
(a) Drain tile is sold in rolls (100′) or lengths (10′).
(b) Perforated tile has slots around the entire perimeter to allow water to seep in. Drain tile can also be nonperforated to simply carry water to an outlet.

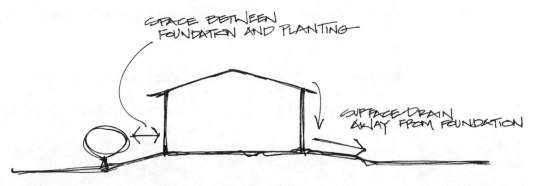

Figure 8–68 **Drain Away from the Foundation**
Be sure that water drains away from the foundation to reduce moisture problems. Shrubs should keep enough space from the foundation to allow ventilation.

(a)

(b)

Figure 8–69 **Planting at the Foundation**
(a) Shrubs should be far enough away from the foundation to allow adequate ventilation. (b) These shrubs are planted right against the foundation, limiting their growing space and possibly causing moisture problems around the house.

Homebuilders should grade the soil so that surface drainage runs away from the house. Do not disturb this surface drainage by building up beds or berms around the house.

Foundation Planting Avoid planting up against the house (Fig. 8–69). This will create a high-humidity microclimate that can cause wood decay. This is often evident by the molding around windows rotting because the wood is not treated.

Plant shrubs so that their mature diameter leaves a couple feet of space from the house to allow enough air movement to keep things dry. Some recommendations suggest keeping as much as 5 feet of space.

Gutters   If the house has gutters, subsurface tile systems can take water from the downspouts and direct it to an outlet away from the house (Fig. 8–70). This can be done with nonperforated drain tile that will dump all water at an outlet. Oftentimes, a pop-up

(a)   (b)

(c)   (d)

Figure 8–70   **Downspouts**
(a) Downspouts from gutters should drain away from the foundation or into a nonperforated drain tile that carries water (b) to a pop-up outlet. (c) This is a pop-up outlet installed. (d) This downspout gets water away from the house but interferes with the sidewalk.

outlet can be installed at the curb and disperse water when it rains. The advantage to this setup is that water is directed away from the house without any downspout extensions lying on the ground that often get damaged or create wet areas around plantings.

Lighting

The aspect of low-voltage lighting adds an entirely new dimension to the design at night in addition to improved security and safely lit paths.

Lighting Effects

Silhouetting is highlighting the form of an object, such as tree trunks, by lighting an object behind it, such as a wall (Fig. 8–71). The lit wall will contrast with the dark tree trunks for an interesting effect (Fig. 8–72). A floodlight will effectively spread light and fully illuminate the wall.

SILHOUETTE

Figure 8–71 **Silhouette**
Lighting a wall behind an object creates a silhouetting effect.

Figure 8–72 **Silhouette**
The bench and potted plants are highlighted by lighting the wall. (Photo courtesy of Ken Griess, Texas Natural Concepts, LLC, Houston, TX.)

***Figure 8–73* Shadow**
Lighting an object to cast a shadow for an interesting effect.

SHADOW

***Figure 8–74* Uplight**
Lighting objects from below.

UP LIGHT

***Figure 8–75* Uplight**
The trees are up-lit, popping them out of the dark and casting a reflection on the water. (Photo courtesy of Ken Griess, Texas Natural Concepts, LLC, Houston, TX.)

Shadowing is lighting an object to cast a shadow across a wall (Fig. 8–73). This not only illuminates the object but creates an interesting form on the wall. This can be used to cast shadows of trees, palms, fences, and gates.

Uplighting is placing a light source at the base of an object to cast light up (Fig. 8–74). For trees, this illuminates the trunk and canopy (Fig. 8–75). This is very effective on palms, casting shadows from the short boots (Fig. 8–76). It is commonly used to light trees because the fixture can be easily installed at the ground. **Grazing** is uplighting a surface to enhance texture by casting shadows up. This is effective on stone surfaces or vine-covered walls.

***Figure 8–76* Uplight**
Uplighting will cast shadows up the object; very effective on palms.

***Figure 8–77* Downlight**
Lighting objects from above.

DOWN LIGHT

Downlighting is placing the light source above an object (Fig. 8–77). For trees, the light can be attached within the canopy and cast shadows on the ground below. For large trees, more than one light source can be used, in conjunction with a pale blue or green lens, to simulate a **moonlighting effect** (Fig. 8–78). Fixtures should be mounted to branches with stainless steel anchors or rubber straps.

Tip Box
Colored Lenses

Colored lenses can alter the quality of light. Blue or green lenses can enhance the moonlighting effect of downlights.

Figure 8–78 Moonlight

A soft downlight mimics moonlight. To enhance the effect, a blue or green lens can color the light. (Photo courtesy of Ken Griess, Texas Natural Concepts, LLC, Houston, TX.)

Path lighting utilizes short light fixtures to illuminate a small area of a sidewalk or path. These fixtures are often in the shape of lanterns or flowers (Fig. 8–79). **Spread lighting** accomplishes the same goal but disperses a broader and softer light (Fig. 8–80).

Figure 8–79 Path

Path lights cast a spot of light on the ground to light a path.

PATH

Figure 8–80 Spread

Spread lights cast a wider, softer light than path lights.

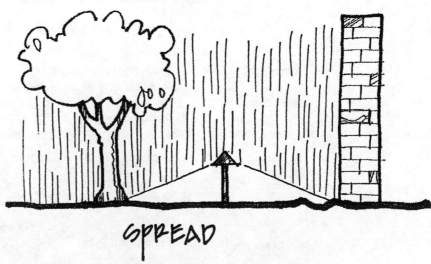

SPREAD

***Figure 8–81* Downlights Illuminate Path**
An interesting technique to illuminating paths is via downlights. Not only is the tree lit, but the light source casts interesting shadows on the ground while lighting it. (Photo
courtesy of Ken Griess, Texas Natural Concepts, LLC,
Houston, TX.)

Lighting Design

There are a few rules for effective lighting design.

Placement

Identify accent points in the landscape, such as sculpture or specimen trees. These
should be points that need attention, such as near the house and entrance but not the
neighbor's house. Lights can also be used to frame the residence.

Effective lighting should not only look pleasing but also illuminate paths. Obviously path
lights do this, but consider downlighting to not only light a tree from above but the path
below (Fig. 8–81).

Tip Box
Don't Overlight

Resist the temptation to add so many lights that the effect is diminished (Fig. 8–82). Many
homeowners buy lighting kits that contain 10 or so path lights and line the driveway. The effect
ends up looking more like an airport than an accent point. Ideally, path lights should be a minimum
of 10 feet apart and staggered on each side of the path for interest.

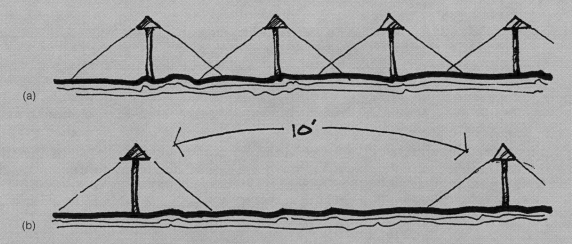

***Figure 8–82* Avoid Overlighting**
(a) Using too many fixtures will lessen the lighting effect. (b) Path lights should be spaced a minimum of 10′ apart.

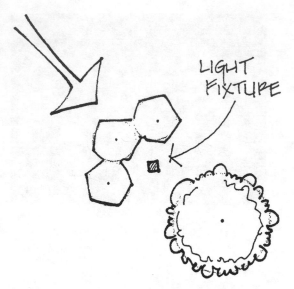

Figure 8–83 **Conceal Light Source**
When possible, conceal the light fixture to keep attention on the effect.

Figure 8–84 **Lighting Maintenance**
Lights will need maintenance. As plants grow, light effects will change. In some cases, the lights can damage plants.

Conceal Light Source

When possible, hide the fixture to avoid the brightness of the light source (Fig. 8–83). This can distract from the lighting effect. Consider locations behind shrubs or fences. However, watch that shrubs don't grow into the fixture and obscure the illumination (Fig. 8–84).

Summary

Plant selection is vital to the success of the landscape design. Incorrect selection will result in plants with poor health that may eventually die. Many factors need to be considered when selecting plants besides the design attributes such as plant size, thorns, attractive bark, fragrant flowers, and appealing fruit. This includes things like hardiness, availability, and cultural factors (exposure, moisture, and soil). Many resources are available that aid the beginning designer with plant selection, including books, software, and Web sites.

In addition to plants, hardscapes are an important component of the landscape. This includes concrete, pavers, and stone used to establish surfaces for sidewalks, patios, and driveways. Fences are important to establish boundaries and decks create a comfortable entertainment area. Retaining walls can be functional by reducing slopes while creating planting areas. Edging is important to maintain a sharp boundary between planting bed and turf. Mulch will cover the planting beds for visual appeal as well as reduce weeds, while a weed barrier can be used in addition to mulch to reduce weed growth. Drainage is important to manage excess water and runoff for healthy plants and sound house maintenance. Lighting can be added to create another dimension to the landscape at night.

Key Terms

Alternate board fence: see board-on-board fence

American Standard for Nursery Stock: standardization of plant terminology established by the American Association of Nurserymen

ANSI Standards: see American Standard for Nursery Stock

Balled-in-burlap: field-grown plants dug and wrapped in burlap to contain the root-ball

Bare root: small plants sold without soil around the roots

Bark: chunks of organic mulch; referred to as nuggets

Basket weave fence: fence boards installed horizontally to the posts; strong horizontal effect; no bad side

Batter: the leaning back or stepping back of the wall toward the hill

Board-on-board fence: alternates the fence boards on each side of the stringer; semiprivate barrier since you can see through the fence at an angle; no bad side

Caliper: the diameter of the tree trunk measured at 6 inches from the ground for trunks up to 4 inches in diameter and 12 inches from the ground for larger trees

Cedar: organic mulch; reddish color and aromatic; relatively expensive

Cocoa bean shells: organic mulch

Colored concrete: a color additive added to concrete

Concrete blocks: used for retaining wall construction; come in a variety of sizes and colors

Concrete: one of the most inexpensive forms of paving

Container grown: plants for sale grown in a plastic pot

Contorted branches: branches that are twisted and curled

Contraction joints: 3/8″ deep grooves that help control cracking in concrete

Corkscrew: see contorted branches

Cultural requirements: the growing conditions for optimal growth

Cut stone: shaped, or cut, into various rectangular shapes that are more consistent in shape and size

Cypress: organic mulch; blonde color; relatively expensive

Dog-ear: see solid board privacy fence

Double-hammered mulch: organic mulch shred extremely fine

Downlighting: light is secured within a tree or to an outside structure and shines down through the canopy of a tree, shrub, or object

Dry-laid: construction that utilizes a foundation of crushed granite (or similar material) and a setting bed of sand

Exfoliating: peeling characteristics of trunks and branches

Exposed aggregate: attractive concrete surface that has pea gravel embedded in the surface

Exposure: location of the plant with respect to light, wind, salt, city conditions, and durability

Flagstone: see stone

French drains: trenches filled with drainage gravel to increase pore space to the ground

Geogrid: laid between courses of pinned blocks for additional support of retaining walls

Grade: the term used to describe the slope of the surface

Gravel: common inorganic mulch

Grazing: uplighting a surface to enhance textured by casting shadows up

Hardiness zones: areas of average annual minimum temperature assigned throughout the United States

Hardwood: organic mulch; inexpensive

Heat zones: areas based on the average number of days over 86 degrees Fahrenheit, considered the threshold beyond which plants begin to suffer physiologically

Inorganic mulch: stone or gravel that will not decompose; creates higher temperatures around plants; does not condition the soil

Landscape timbers: wooden timbers that are often 6″ × 6″ in dimension or greater

Lattice-top fence: bottom portion of the fence is solid board or board-on-board; decorative effect with a panel of lattice across the top of the fence

Lipped blocks: used for retaining wall construction; have an extended edge, or lip, on the bottom rear portion

Microclimates: areas warmer or cooler than predominate growing conditions in the area

Mortar: concrete mixture that bonds units together

Moonlighting effect: using more than one light source in conjunction with a pale blue or green lens to simulate moonlight

Mulch: covers planting beds and around the base of trees

Multilevel decks: effective in creating different rooms on the deck

Nuggets: see bark

Organic mulch: mulch that is decomposable and helps condition the soil

Path lighting: short lights that illuminate a walking area

Pavers: bricks made from concrete or clay and come in various shapes and colors

Peanut shells: organic mulch

Pecan shells: organic mulch

Pine straw: popular organic mulch in the South

Pine: organic mulch; inexpensive

Pinned block: used for retaining wall construction; utilizes fiberglass rods, or pins, that slide through internal holes that attach them to the block above

Plant palette: compilation of plants and their uses and cultural requirements

Railroad ties: similar to timbers but treated with creosote

Recycled rubber: inorganic mulch; old tires are shredded or ground up and look very much like organic mulch

Recycled wood mulch: wood products such as disposed pallets are shredded and often dyed

Retaining walls: create a level surface on a sloped area

Rise: vertical difference between two points

Run: horizontal difference between two points

Shadowbox fence: see board-on-board fence

Shadowing: lighting an object to cast a shadow across a wall

Single-level deck: simplest construction that works fine for small gatherings and outdoor cooking

Silhouetting: highlighting the form of an object, such as tree trunks, by lighting an object behind it, such as a wall

Solid board privacy fence: the fence boards are on one side; offers complete privacy; has a "bad side" showing the stringers

Spines: sharp points that can grow on the margins or at the tips of foliage, technically are modified leaves

Spread lighting: diffuses the light out over a larger area that may light up a bed or path

Stamped concrete: specialty effects on the concrete surface; creates a brick paving effect, cobblestone, or any number of patterned effects

Standard: see American Standard for Nursery Stock

Stone: sheet-like stone that comes in various colors, shapes, and sizes

Stringers: boards that support fence boards

Strip edging: solid thin strip of material made of steel, aluminum, or plastic

Subsurface drainage: the removal of excess soil moisture with an underground drainage system

Surface drainage: directing water flow over the surface of the ground

Thorns: sharp, woody extensions that are a modified branch

Tile drainage: Four-inch perforated drain pipe installed in a trench and surrounded by drainage gravel

Uplighting: light source that shines up into the canopy of a tree or shrub from below

Weed barrier: a mat of material, often a woven fabric or similar material, which creates a physical barrier preventing weeds from emerging in planting beds

Weeping branches: flimsy branches with little structural support

Wet-laid: construction that sets pavers or stone in mortar

9 The Master Plan

Objectives

- Understand the components and role of the master plan
- Know how to label symbols
- Be familiar with a plant list and its application

In the final step of designing, the master plan refines the preliminary plan with detail.

Analysis → Concept Plan → Preliminary Design → Master Plan

The **master plan** is the final document that, based on changes at the preliminary phase, will illustrate all materials, amounts, and specifications (Fig. 9–1). Materials include all plants and hardscapes as well as their location, and may also include construction details. Plant and hardscape materials covered in the previous chapter will be used to fully detail the master plan. The master plan may be drawn with presentation graphics, es-

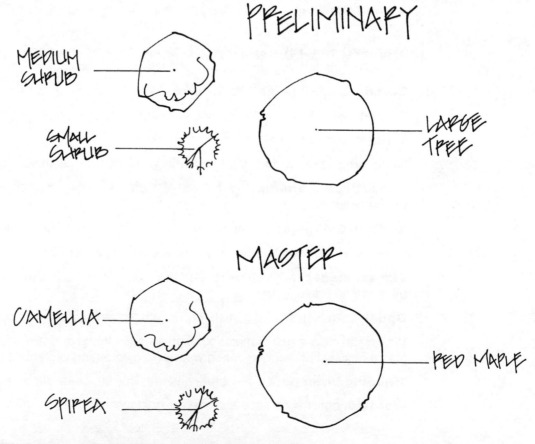

Figure 9–1 Preliminary versus Master Plan
While the preliminary plan uses general plant material to convey the overall design concept, the master plan specifies plant name and number.

pecially when presented to the client. It will maintain all the preliminary design criteria, such as client information, scale, north arrow, and so on.

Implementation Plans

The master plan may be the final document presenting all the information including installation. Many small landscape design companies use the master plan for presentation and implementation, while many large landscape design firms use the master plan primarily for presentation while other plans are drawn and bundled together for installation and construction (Fig. 9–2).

A project may include all or some of the following (Fig. 9–3):

- **Planting plan** is used to specify planting specifications: name, number, and size.

- **Layout plan** shows the location of all plants and dimensions of ground plane areas.

- **Construction drawings** show three-dimensional drawings of planting methods, paver construction, edging installation, or other construction.

- **Grading plan** illustrates the proposed changes in slope.

- **Irrigation plan** shows the irrigation system.

Drawing the Master Plan

As with the preliminary plan, the order of these steps is not necessarily the only approach to completing the master plan but seems logical and easy for many beginning students.

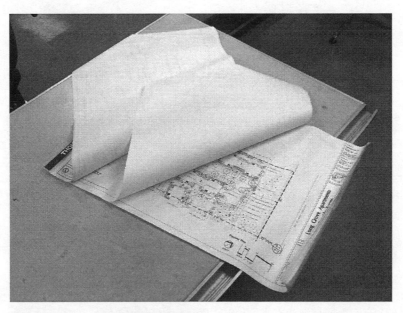

Figure 9–2 **Bundled Plans**
Large design projects may have several plans that are bundled together.

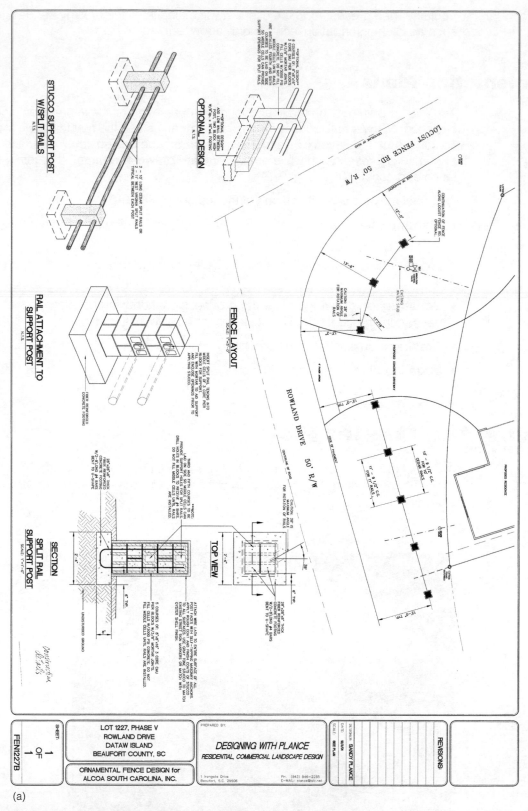

Figure 9–3   Implementation Plans

Other plans may be drawn and included with the master plan, especially from larger projects. (a) Construction details. *(Plans courtesy of Sandy Plance.)*

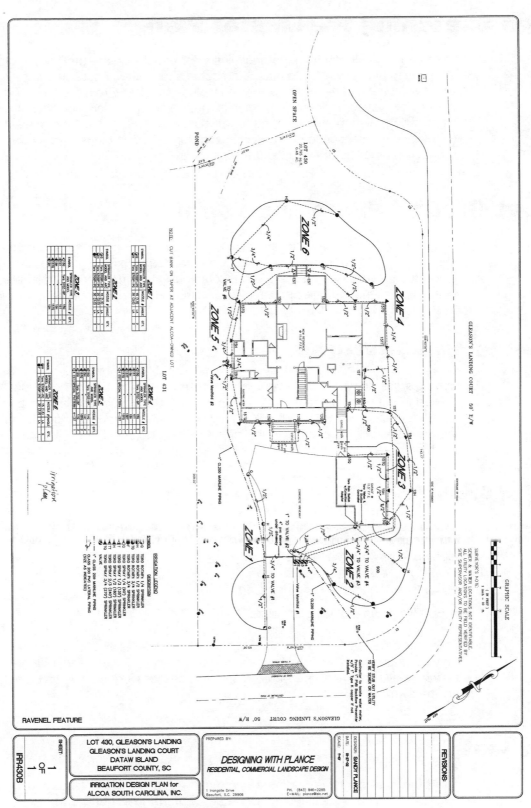

Figure 9–3   Implementation Plans—continued
(b) Irrigation plan.

Rough Sketching the Master Plan

Doing a rough sketch from the preliminary (or directly on the preliminary plan) allows students to place symbols to accurately scale and label without concern for detail. This will often combine preliminary plans and include feedback from the client. This can also be a quick way to work out final, specific details such as plant selection, before the final drawing. Sketch on tracing paper and once complete, draw the master on vellum (or Mylar). As mentioned in a previous chapter, vellum is higher-quality paper that reproduces good line drawings and avoids tearing easily.

Layout Ground Plane and Label

When drawing the final plan on vellum, start by drawing the ground plane with any changes worked out in the sketch. Once the ground plane is completed, clearly label areas of turf, driveway, mulch, and so on. Some designers may choose to label the ground plane after all the symbols are completed so that a label doesn't appear misplaced.

Symbols and Textures

Symbols are drawn as they were in the preliminary plan. They should be accurately placed in the plan with a center dot illustrating the exact spot where the trunk is to be located. Each symbol will be labeled with the name and amount of plants in the grouping. Textures will be applied to the ground plane to identify the illustrated materials. Each of these areas should be clearly labeled as well.

Labeling Symbols

All symbols, objects, and areas need to be accurately labeled (Fig. 9–4). While objects other than plants and ground plane areas need to be simply labeled, plants should be labeled to provide the following:

- Number of plants in each grouping
- Botanical name of the plant or key

There are several ways that designers label information. The botanical name of the plant may be written out in its entirety on each label or a key may be used, referring to a plant list where all information is organized. In some cases, a legend may be created to identify the symbols.

Plant List

The **plant list** contains pertinent information pertaining to plants and hardscapes (Fig. 9–5). This is sometimes referred to as a **planting schedule.**

Plant lists should contain columns of the following information:

Key: includes all the keys from the plan drawing

Botanical name: Genus, species, and cultivar (if necessary)

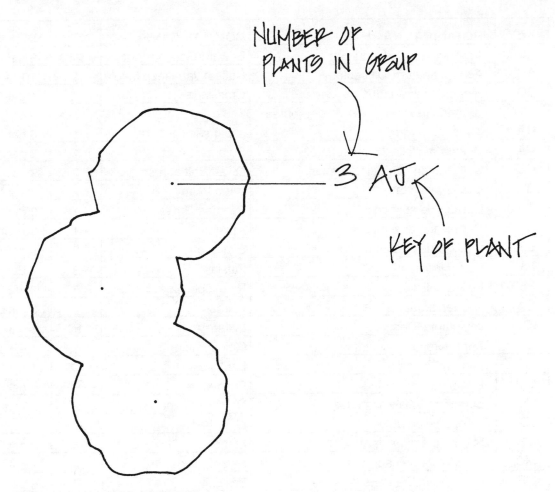

Figure 9–4 **Labeling Symbols**
Plant symbols need to be clearly labeled. Each label includes the plant name or plant key that refers back to a plant list and the number of plants in the group.

Common name: common name of plant (some designers omit this column)

Quantity: total number of each plant in the design

Size: specifies the planting container, caliper, or height and width of plant

Spacing: refers to distance on center of plants in mass. Some designers omit this column and include spacing notations in the "Notes" column. **"On center"** may be abbreviated as O.C.

Notes: additional comments, if necessary. This might include flower color, growth habit (such as multi-trunk), or plant spacing (if "Spacing" column is not used).

The plant list may be drawn directly on the plan or created on a separate document. If created on a separate document, the plant list can be copied and attached to the plan drawing for reproduction. If changes to the plant list are required at a later time, the document can be reprinted to replace the preceding plant list. This is much easier to edit than redrawing the plant list on the plan.

KEY	BOTANICAL NAME	COMMON NAME	QTY	SIZE	NOTES
AEG	Abelia x 'Edward Goucher'	Edward Goucher Abelia	21	3 gal	
AP	Acer palmatum 'Dissectum'	Cutleaf Japanese Maple	1	10 gal	
BC	Bignonia capreolata	Crossvine	7	1 gal	
BT	Berberis thunbergii var. Atropurpurea 'Crimson Pygmy'	Japanese Barberry	1	3 gal	
CA	Clethra alnifolia 'Compacta'	Summersweet	7	3 gal	
CC	Callistemon citrinus 'Compacta'	Dwarf Bottlebrush	3	3 gal	
CR	Cycas revoluta	Sago Palm	2	30 gal	
CS	Cortaderia selloana	Pampas Grass	1	3 gal	
CAR	Cupressus arizonica	Arizona Cypress	1	30 gal	
EP	Elaeagnus pungens	Elaeagnus	5	5 gal	
FJ	Fatsia japonica	Fatsia	3	3 gal	
FS	Feijoa sellowiana	Pineapple Guava	5	3 gal	
GA	Gardenia agusta	Gardenia	1	3 gal	
IG	Ilex glabra 'Densa'	Inkberry	15	1 gal	
KP	Koelreuteria paniculata	Goldenraintree	1	1.5" cal	
LC	Lantana camara	Lantana	17	1 gal	
LCH	Loropetalum chinese	Fringetree	9	5 gal	
LN	Lagerstroemia x 'Natchez'	Natchez Crape Myrtle	3	30 gal	
LS	Liriope spicata	Liriope	300	4"	12" O.C.
MB	Mahonia bealei	Mahonia	3	3 gal	
MC	Muhlenbergia capillaris	Sweetgrass	54	1 gal	
OF	Osmanthus fragrans	Tea Olive	3	5 gal	
OP	Ophiopogon planiscapus 'Nigrescens'	Black Mondograss	50	4"	6" O.C.
QV	Quercus virginiana	Live Oak	1	1.5 cal	
WF	Weigela florida	Weigela	1	3 gal	

(a)

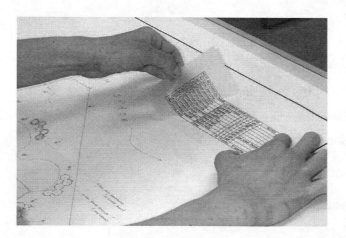

(b)

Figure 9–5 **Plant List**
(a) The plant list includes information on plant material, and occasionally other material, in the master plan. Columns include key (if symbols are labeled with key instead of entire plant name), botanical and common name, total quantity of each item, size of each plant to be installed, and a column for miscellaneous notes such as substitutions or plant spacing. (b) Placing a plant list on the master plan.

KEY	BOTANICAL	COMMON	QTY	SIZE	NOTES	COST	TOTAL	INSTALL
AG	Abelia grandiflora	Abelia	3	3 gal		$10.00	$30.00	$90.00
AGR	Abelia x grandiflora 'Rose Creek'	Rose creek abelia	5	3 gal		$10.25	$51.25	$153.75
AP	Acer palmatum	Japanese maple	1	15 gal		$110.00	$110.00	$330.00
APD	Acer palmatum 'Dissectum'	Japanese maple	1	5 gal		$45.00	$45.00	$135.00
AG	Agapanthus 'Mood Indigo'	Agapanthus	5	1 gal		$3.00	$15.00	$45.00
AD	Agave desmettiana	Smooth agave	2	1 gal		$5.25	$10.50	$31.50
AHB	Alocasia 'Hilo Beauty'	Elephant ear	5	1 gal		$6.70	$33.50	$100.50
AS	Aloe saponaria	Soap aloe	10	1 gal		$6.00	$60.00	$180.00
AE	Aspidistra elatior	Cast iron	15	1 gal		$5.25	$78.75	$236.25
AJ	Aucuba japonica 'Gold Dust'	Aucuba	3	3 gal		$11.00	$33.00	$99.00
AZ	Azalea 'Gumpo pink'	Gumpo azalea	7	3 gal		$11.00	$77.00	$231.00
BM	Bambusa multiplex 'Alphonse Karr'	Bamboo	1	5 gal		$20.60	$20.60	$61.80
BN	Betula nigra	River birch	1	15 gal		$66.30	$66.30	$198.90
BC	Bignonia capreolata	Crossvine	2	1 gal		$13.00	$26.00	$78.00
BP	Brugmansia 'Pink'	Angel's trumpet	1	5 gal		$15.00	$15.00	$45.00
BDB	Buddleia davidii 'Black Knight'	Butterfly bush	1	3 gal		$10.00	$10.00	$30.00
BDP	Buddleia davidii 'Purple Emperor'	Butterfly bush	1	3 gal		$10.00	$10.00	$30.00
BDR	Buddleia davidii 'Royal Red'	Butterfly bush	1	3 gal		$10.00	$10.00	$30.00
BCA	Butia capitata	Pindo palm	3	15 gal		$110.00	$330.00	$990.00
BMA	Buxus macrophylla	Boxwood	9	3 gal		$10.00	$90.00	$270.00
CA	Callicarpa americana	American beautyberry	3	3 gal		$9.80	$29.40	$88.20
CD	Callicarpa dicondra 'Issia'	Beautyberry	5	3 gal		$12.00	$60.00	$180.00
CS	Callistemon species	Bottlebrush	1	5 gal		$15.00	$15.00	$45.00

Figure 9–6 Master Plant List
Use a spreadsheet program to create a plant list for easy editing. A master list can be maintained so new projects can be copy and pasted from the master file to avoid misspellings and retyping. Price columns can also be added to quickly estimate installation costs.

Spreadsheet Master

Many design software products automatically build a plant list with a touch of the button. No more looking up botanical names to make sure they're spelled correctly. Revisions are automatically updated.

For designers who do not use design software, spreadsheet programs, such as Microsoft Excel, can be used to build a plant list instead of hand-drawing lists. A spreadsheet can be easily alphabetized for organization and editing is quick. New columns and rows can be inserted and information changed during revisions. An even easier approach is to avoid retyping the entire plant list for every project by compiling a master plant list file (Fig. 9–6). Add new plants and material to the file with each project. As the list grows, you will reduce the need to retype by simply copying and pasting from the master file to the new project file. This is especially helpful in keeping things spelled correctly, such as botanical names.

Include a column for prices, also. Some companies have standard prices of installation for container sizes. For instance, some contractors double or triple the cost of material for installation to cover overhead, labor, material, and profit. This is a simple calculation function that can help make proposals effortless.

Print

Once the master plan is completed, a copy should be obtained to give to the client and/or contractor (Fig. 9–7). The original drawing should remain with the designer. If implementation plans are included in the project, they will be bound together at the top.

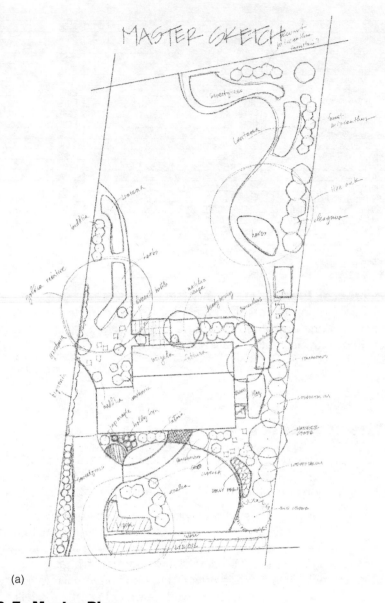

(a)

Figure 9–7 **Master Plan**
The master plan, based on the preliminary plans, has been labeled and drawn to completion. (a) Sketch.

Storage

The originals should be stored in a safe, dry area. Ideal storage is lying flat in shelf storage, but they can be rolled for storage as well. If it is rolled, have the design facing out so that it lies flat when it is unrolled.

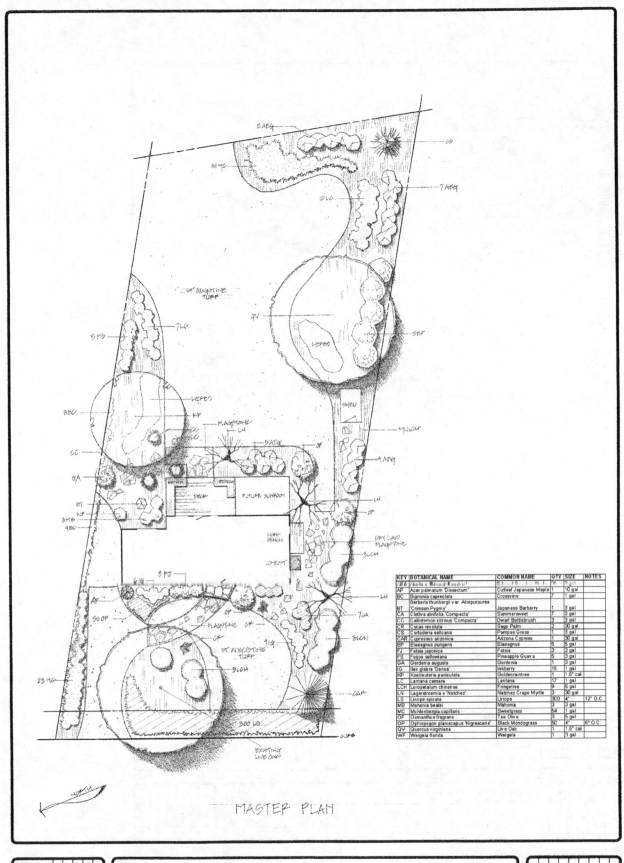

KEY	BOTANICAL NAME	COMMON NAME	QTY	SIZE	NOTES
			31	3 gal	
AP	Acer palmatum 'Dissectum'	Cutleaf Japanese Maple	1	10 gal	
BC	Bignonia capreolata	Crossvine	7	1 gal	
BT	Berberis thunbergii var. Atropurpurea 'Crimson Pygmy'	Japanese Barberry	1	3 gal	
CA	Clethra alnifolia 'Compacta'	Summersweet	7	3 gal	
CC	Callistemon citrinus 'Compacta'	Dwarf Bottlebrush	3	3 gal	
CR	Cycas revoluta	Sago Palm	2	30 gal	
CS	Cortaderia selloana	Pampas Grass	1	3 gal	
CAR	Cupressus arizonica	Arizona Cypress	1	30 gal	
EP	Elaeagnus pungens	Elaeagnus	5	5 gal	
FJ	Fatsia japonica	Fatsia	3	3 gal	
FS	Feijoa sellowiana	Pineapple Guava	5	3 gal	
GA	Gardenia augusta	Gardenia	1	3 gal	
IG	Ilex glabra 'Densa'	Inkberry	15	1 gal	
KP	Koelreuteria paniculata	Goldenraintree	1	1.5" cal	
LC	Lantana camara	Lantana	17	1 gal	
LCH	Loropetalum chinense	Fringetree	9	5 gal	
LN	Lagerstroemia x 'Natchez'	Natchez Crape Myrtle	3	30 gal	
LS	Liriope spicata	Liriope	300	4"	12" O.C.
MB	Mahonia bealei	Mahonia	3	3 gal	
MC	Muhlenbergia capillaris	Sweetgrass	54	1 gal	
OF	Osmanthus fragrans	Tea Olive	3	5 gal	
OP	Ophiopogon planiscapus 'Nigrescens'	Black Mondograss	50	4"	6" O.C.
QV	Quercus virginiana	Live Oak	1	1.5" cal	
WF	Weigela florida	Weigela	1	3 gal	

MASTER PLAN

GRANT RESIDENCE
724 WEST MARKET ST
ANYTOWN, USA

PELICAN DESIGNS

(b)

Figure 9–7 **Master Plan—continued**
(b) Hand-drafted master plan.

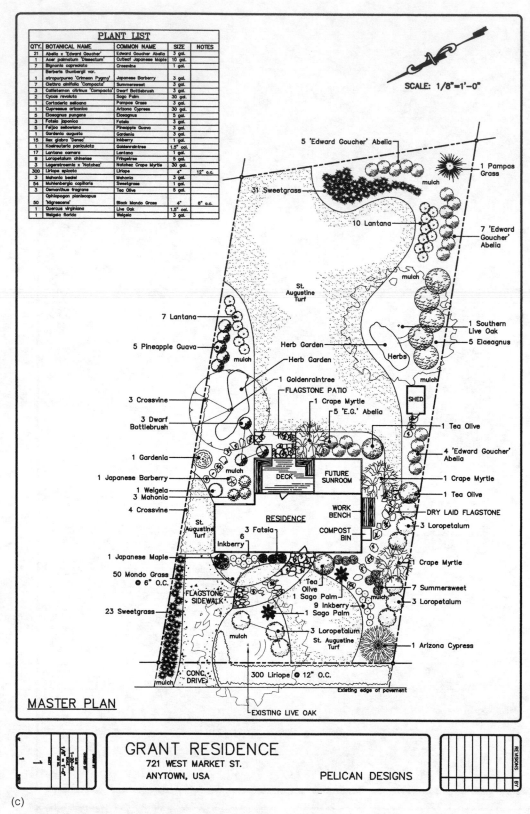

PLANT LIST

QTY.	BOTANICAL NAME	COMMON NAME	SIZE	NOTES
21	Abelia x 'Edward Goucher'	Edward Goucher Abelia	3 gal.	
1	Acer palmatum 'Dissectum'	Cutleaf Japanese Maple	10 gal.	
7	Bignonia capreolata	Crossvine	1 gal.	
1	Berberis thunbergii var. atropurpurea 'Crimson Pygmy'	Japanese Barberry	3 gal.	
7	Clethra alnifolia 'Compacta'	Summersweet	3 gal.	
3	Callistemon citrinus 'Compacta'	Dwarf Bottlebrush	3 gal.	
2	Cycas revoluta	Sago Palm	30 gal.	
1	Cortaderia selloana	Pampas Grass	3 gal.	
1	Cupressus arizonica	Arizona Cypress	30 gal.	
5	Elaeagnus pungens	Elaeagnus	5 gal.	
3	Fatsia japonica	Fatsia	3 gal.	
5	Feijoa sellowiana	Pineapple Guava	3 gal.	
3	Gardenia augusta	Gardenia	3 gal.	
15	Ilex glabra 'Dense'	Inkberry	1 gal.	
1	Koelreuteria paniculata	Goldenraintree	1.5" cal.	
17	Lantana camara	Lantana	1 gal.	
9	Loropetalum chinense	Fringetree	5 gal.	
3	Lagerstroemia x 'Natchez'	Natchez Crape Myrtle	30 gal.	
300	Liriope spicata	Liriope	4"	12" o.c.
3	Mahonia bealei	Mahonia	3 gal.	
54	Muhlenbergia capillaris	Sweetgrass	3 gal.	
3	Osmanthus fragrans	Tea Olive	5 gal.	
50	Ophiopogon planiscapus 'Nigrescens'	Black Mondo Grass	4"	6" o.c.
1	Quercus virginiana	Live Oak	1.5" cal.	
1	Weigela florida	Weigela	3 gal.	

SCALE: 1/8"=1'-0"

MASTER PLAN

GRANT RESIDENCE
721 WEST MARKET ST.
ANYTOWN, USA

PELICAN DESIGNS

REVISIONS BY

(c)

Figure 9–7 Master Plan—continued
(c) CAD master plan. *(Photo (c) courtesy of Sandy Plance.)*

312

Summary

The master plan is the final plan in the landscape design process. It includes all specifications and details in the design illustrated on the plan with plant symbols and ground plane textures that are all clearly labeled. A plant list concisely organizes all the names, quantities, and sizes of material included in the design. A copy of the design (print) is presented and given to the client and/or contractor; the original is kept by the designer and stored in a cool, dry place, either rolled or flat, to preserve the longevity of the design. Sketching the master plan to combine preliminary plans and make changes from feedback allows the designer to work out the final plan before drawing it on vellum.

Key Terms

Botanical name: scientific name of plant

Common name: name plant is commonly referred to

Construction plan: shows three-dimensional drawings of planting methods, paver construction, edging installation, or other construction

Grading plan: illustrates the proposed changes in slope

Irrigation plan: shows the design of the irrigation system

Key: an abbreviated code used to label symbols; appears in the plant list with plant information

Layout plan: shows the location of all plants and dimensions of ground plane areas

Master plan: final document that, based on changes at the preliminary phase, will illustrate all materials, amounts, and specifications

On center: space between plantings; abbreviated O.C.

Plant list: includes plant material names, quantities, sizes, and other information; located on the master plan

Plant list schedule: see plant list

Planting plan: specifies planting specifications: name, number, and size

10 The Presentation

Objectives

- Understand how to present the design
- Learn how to assist in the client's understanding of the design
- Learn an orderly approach to selling the design

The presentation of the design is as important as the drawing itself. It is essentially *selling the design.* This is a product that needs explanation and guidance for most clients to fully understand and appreciate. Without the explanation of the layout, design concepts, and plants, the client may not understand or recognize the potential of the design. Instead it may appear only as a pretty picture.

Tip Box

There are instances where an average drawing can appear as a brilliant design purely on the enthusiasm and clarity of the presentation.

What to Bring to the Presentation

A Copy of the Design

Present a **copy** (or **print**) of the design rolled out on a table or attach the design to **foam** or **posterboard** to prop up or even to walk around the property and discuss each part of the design, giving the client better ability to visualize it (Fig. 10–1).

(a)

(b)

Figure 10–1 Copy of Design
(a) A copy of the design will be used to present; (b) attaching it to foam or posterboard makes it easier to prop up on a wall or carry around the yard.

Pictures

If not walking around the residence, bring along pictures and refer to them with each point of the design. Help the client visualize the design by flipping through the pictures while discussing each area.

What the Presentation Is NOT

So how does a designer present a design? Every designer has his or her own style and procedure, but let's take a look at what makes it less effective.

NOT Reading the Plant List

The presentation is NOT just reading the plant list to the client. This can take the form of pointing to each symbol and telling the client the name of the plant without describing anything about it. This may continue until every single symbol has been identified and named before the presentation ends abruptly.

In the classroom, students are often dealing with the stress of public speaking as well as presenting their ideas. In addition to having the clients' attention (or the entire classroom!), offering their own ideas is stressful for fear of being criticized, especially in the beginning of the design process when they may not have a lot of confidence in the first few attempts.

NOT Speaking to the Design

Speaking to the design refers to the designer looking at the plan drawing, sometimes with his or her back to the client, for the entire presentation. This, again, is often due to nervousness about making eye contact, but results in a cold, less engaging approach with the client.

NOT Overly Critical of Design

There will be many times that right in the middle of a class presentation a student will suddenly realize an oversight or mistake. Avoid criticizing or apologizing for your design. Some beginning students lack confidence in their ideas and feel more comfortable talking about their indecision or lack of talent. (Some students even introduce their design as "this is not a good design.") And, in some cases, this may be a subconscious effort to lower expectations and avoid criticism from others. In other words, "I know my design stinks, so you don't have to tell me."

NOT Unprepared

Avoid giving presentations without preparation. This may be more applicable to a classroom or formal presentations to a group of clients (such as a board of directors) rather than the informal presentation with a couple at their residence. Even though the designer has spent many hours with the design, without prior thought and preparation, the presentation will often lack confidence and clarity.

What the Presentation IS

The presentation needs to consist of more than what appears on the drawing. As with the interview, be warm and personable with the client while presenting the design. It is important to continue to be engaging and enthusiastic. Guide the client through the design with excitement and explain the site potentials, the types of plants and materials in the plan, and how the design will improve the quality of living and value of the property.

Answer the Question "Why?"

Give a brief explanation with each plant symbol and ground plane texture. As mentioned earlier, the client can look at the symbols and read the plant list without the aid of the designer. What the clients need is the designer to explain to them WHY those plants are there.

> What ideas and knowledge is the client buying?
>
> What is it about the plants and the layout that makes them a good selection?
>
> In general, what makes it a good design?

It does *not* have to be a major explanation of every plant and material; just a simple reason may sometimes be enough.

For instance, "In this shady area under the tree there is a group of Fatsia, which has a striking leaf shape and is very shade tolerant." This is a simple explanation of why the Fatsia is used, as opposed to pointing to the symbol and saying, "That's Fatsia."

Tip Box

In a nutshell, *every point mentioned should answer the question "Why?"*

The following is another way of how it may, but should not be, presented:

> *"This is a Gardenia, that is a Pyracantha, and that is a Bloodtwig Dogwood."*

Instead, present it this way:

> *"This Gardenia provides a* nice scent in the spring, *this Pyracantha has* brilliant orange fruit during the late summer and early winter when few things are flowering, and the *Bloodtwig Dogwood has* bright red twigs in the winter that add color to a gray landscape."

Speak to the Client

Make eye contact and engage the client with a discussion of the design (Fig. 10–2). Be excited about the project the clients are receiving—enthusiasm is contagious! *Smile,* be open and animated during the presentation so the clients feel the same energy. Flat, monotonic presentations are boring; they lack the luster and shine that a warm personality can add to the design. The clients will believe the design is good if the designer tells them it is, verbally and nonverbally.

(a)

(b)

***Figure 10–2* Make Eye Contact**
A presentation to a group or committee (or classroom). (a) Speak to the client about the design. (b) Do not speak to the design with your back to the client.

Be Confident

Resist any temptation to bring undue attention to oversights or mistakes, particularly minor ones. Most people don't notice small mistakes unless they are pointed out. This is not to suggest lying about an inaccuracy. If needed, discuss it honestly and straightforwardly while asking for feedback.

A poor approach to this example may be

> *"There is a barberry over there that has thorns and would scratch you when walking by … that probably was not a good idea. I should have put something else there."*

Instead, put a positive spin on the decision and, if needed, recommend a possible alternative.

> *"That's a barberry that will add color with deep red foliage throughout the summer. However, it does have thorns and if that looks like it would be a problem, there are other plants that would work."*

Be Prepared

Practice, practice, practice. This is especially true for a formal presentation to a group of people, such as a classroom or board of directors (Fig. 10–3). This is the key to good public speaking. The more it is practiced, the more familiar it becomes. For many people it is hard to think clearly when addressing a group, which makes it easy to forget topics and details, often resulting in a person "freezing" because the train of thought is too disrupted. Being familiar with the information makes it much easier to know the

***Figure 10–3*   Practice the Presentation**
Going over note cards to remind the student about the order and key points of the presentation is helpful to keep it smooth and organized.

order of presentation. Make **note cards** of all the points that you want to cover and go through the presentation alone a few times. This helps you become familiar with the flow of the presentation and what direction it may go.

Starting the Presentation

Some designers like to begin by briefly discussing the analysis before pulling out the design. This explains how the design addresses the landscape potentials and solves problems. This may be a discussion with pictures or even include some rough sketches of the analysis.

Start with the Positives

Clients may feel good about their property if they hear about the upside first. This may just be references to the potential of particular areas and how they can be developed.

Don't Be Overly Critical of the Site

The existing landscape may be unimaginative and poorly installed, but some people may take criticism of their property personally, especially if they have been working on it. Opening a presentation by blatantly criticizing the residence may be offensive and cause the clients to be less receptive to new ideas.

Display a Copy of the Design

Once initial discussions have concluded, roll out a copy of the design. This will be the copy the clients will keep.

Orient the Client to the Plan Drawing

To many people, a plan drawing can be confusing. They may not recognize the house on the plan. In this case, quickly orient them to what they are looking at. Briefly mention, "This is the front door of the house, the front yard is here, and of course this would be the backyard." It can be as quick as that and would avoid the look of confusion on their faces and prevent them from feeling embarrassed to ask a simple question like "Where's the garage?"

Explain the Plan Details

It's a good idea to briefly explain a few other concepts that you may take for granted, such as scale. Briefly state, "This plan is drawn so that every 1/8 inch is equal to 1 foot." Then refer to the graphical scale to show them what a 5- or 10-foot line looks like.

Other things might include which way is north, property lines, right-of-way, and easements.

Present in an Orderly Fashion

Have some order in the way the design is presented. For example, start in the front yard and cover all the points before moving to the side yard then to the backyard. The one thing to avoid is jumping all over the design, from front to back to front to side … in no apparent order. It's easier to follow along when presented in an organized, sequential manner.

Introduce the Design Goals

Ease into the presentation with an overview of the goals that the design achieves. Give the "big picture" of the design first, what they can expect to see in the design. This may repeat some of the requests from the interview organized into a checklist. Some examples are

"Approached your residence with low maintenance in mind … "

"Since you don't care for mowing, this design reduces the amount of turf … "

"Created comfortable areas for entertaining and relaxation … "

"Developed some interesting views from the back of the house … "

"This design will improve the curb appeal of your residence … "

Know the Plant Material

The designer is the expert; therefore, he or she should know the contents of the design with minimal referencing. Know what every symbol represents. Many beginning students, as a result of being unprepared or extremely nervous, rely on looking up all the symbols in the plant list. This can give the impression of unfamiliarity with the design.

The designer should be intimately familiar with the plant material to answer any additional questions a client may have about it. This will include discussing outstanding qualities or the reasons it was selected, such as

When does it bloom?

What color does it bloom?

Does it handle dry conditions?

How fast does it grow?

Repeat the Clients' Requests

Instill competence in the design by repeating the clients' requests (from the interview) and show them how it has been incorporated in the design. This helps the client recognize how the design addresses their wants and needs. Statements may include

"You mentioned you liked palms ... "

"During the interview, you said you liked scented plants ... "

"You were interested in creating an entertainment area and deck ... "

"Because you don't like the neighbor's view into your backyard ... "

"You spend a lot of time looking out the office window ... "

"Since you don't like backing out of the driveway ... "

Explain the Design Concepts

You may need to explain the design concepts because many people will not understand the significance of repeating plant material to create a sense of connection, or how placing certain plants of unique character creates interesting views, or the effect of sweeping lines in the beds. For instance, briefly explain how, "I've used Indian Hawthorne in these three areas to create a sense of connection, by means of visual recall, between the front and side yard." Another example is, "This is a sharply variegated plant that will draw your attention to this part of the yard as you enter the back and will help provide a sense of direction."

Address the Analysis

The analysis was discussed briefly in the beginning of the presentation, but be sure to repeat these points during the presentation. This helps explain how the design will improve the functional aspect of the property.

Widen the sidewalk for better access?

Accommodate two people?

Interesting approach?

Screen the air-conditioning unit?

Accent an interesting view or plant?

Visually Support Your Design

Verbal descriptions may be very good, but nothing works like actually seeing the product (Fig. 10–4).

Books and Catalogs

Use books or catalogs to give the client a visual idea of certain aspects of the design (Fig. 10–5). This is helpful when discussing outstanding characteristics of specimen plants or the look of hardscape materials. It can be useful to show someone what bluestone looks like, or a particular paving pattern like herringbone. Other examples can be water features, fountains, flowers, fruit, retaining walls, arbors, and fence construction.

Figure 10–4 **Visual Support**
This student, presenting to a church group, has ample visual support—pictures, digital imagery, and samples.

Figure 10–5 **Books and Catalogs**
Pictures from books and catalogs can help clients visualize plants and materials used in the design.

Some designers include pictures of plants and material in their portfolio to always have a reference available.

Personalize the Visual Support

One way to personalize the visual aids is to use plant software (see Appendix B) to print pictures of each plant and material in the design. These images can be loosely bound together and given along with the design for reference, or can be recorded on a compact disc.

In addition to photos, a brief explanation of each plant's characteristics and its management provides the client with comprehensive information about the design they can refer back to at a later time. These little blurbs can be saved in a document and each time the plant is used in different projects it can be simply cut and pasted to the client's plant list.

PowerPoint Slides

If you don't have plant database software, most images can be found on the Internet. Go to Google (*http://www.google.com*) or Yahoo! (*http://www.yahoo.com*) and search through the image database. Once you find your plant, right-click on the image and print.

Microsoft PowerPoint is useful to organize your images (Fig. 10–6). When you have images of your plants and material, use PowerPoint to create a master file. Each slide contains an individual plant, structure, or material with a title. For each project, copy and paste the desired slides. The more projects you complete, the larger your library will grow, with less searching to do for commonly used plants and material.

***Figure 10–6* PowerPoint Slides**
PowerPoint software can be used to organize a library of images. For each project, copy and paste selected slides to a new file and print slides individually to be organized in a binder and presented to client.

When you have copied and pasted all the slides from the master file to a new project file, the slides can be individually printed and organized in a binder. The file can also be shown on a loop from a laptop for presentations or saved on a CD and given to the client.

Elevation Illustrations

Many people will have difficulty imagining three-dimensional aspects from the bird's-eye view of the plan drawing (Fig. 10–7). To help them visualize the idea, it is helpful to provide an **elevated drawing,** even if it is a rough sketch.

Digital Imaging

With the aid of computer design, a client can see what the proposed design looks like on their house (Fig. 10–8). This sidesteps the artistic interpretation of the planting and uses an actual picture of the house while images of plants and other materials are blended into the photo. Car dealers rely on buyers seeing, touching, driving, and even smelling (new car smell!) the car to get them to visualize themselves owning it. The automobile is a very tangible product that can hook the buyer. The landscape design is a product that relies on descriptions, sketches, and imagination that is ultimately *intangible.* **Digital imaging** makes the design more real because it appears as an actual photo of the project.

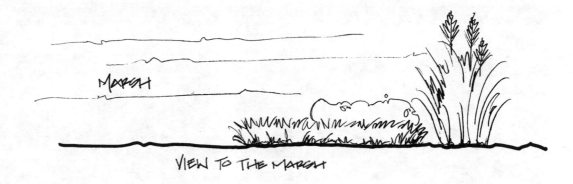

VIEW TO THE MARSH

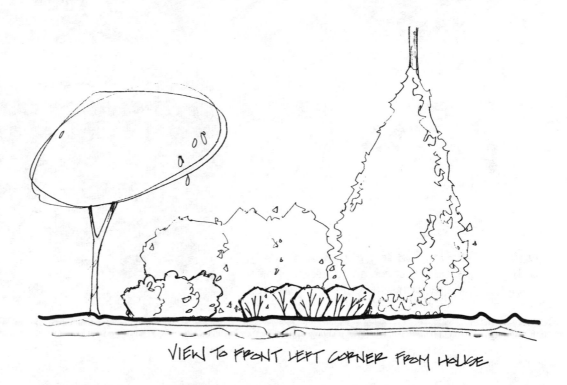

VIEW TO FRONT LEFT CORNER FROM HOUSE

***Figure 10–7* Section Elevations**
Elevated drawings can help the client visualize the design concept and spatial relationships.

Plant and Hardscape Samples

When appropriate, have samples of some of the material in the landscape design. This would be limited to materials that are a highlight of the design, such as stone tile on the patio or exceptional foliage or flower. In these cases, bring in a sample of the stone tile or a cutting of the foliage or flower (if available). Clients are more excited with the design when they can see and feel elements of it.

Word of caution, don't overdue samples. Limit them to the special elements, such as accents and specimens. Too many samples can be overwhelming.

(a)

(b)

(c)

Figure 10–8 **Digital Imaging Software**
(a) The designer is presenting computer-generated
renditions of the design. Computer graphics can
be used to build a picture of the design. (b) Before
and (c) after.

Concluding the Presentation

Quite often the client will have questions that come up that you will answer during the course of the presentation. Once you have covered all the points of the design, ask if there are any final questions or input that the clients would like to add.

Set a Date for the Next Meeting or Conclude the Contract

If presenting a preliminary design, be sure to agree on the next meeting to give the clients the **master plan** and collect the rest of your fees. If this is the presentation of the master plan, then collect the remainder of the contract due and conclude the transaction.

Summary

The presentation is as important as the design itself. It should be informative so that the client better understands the functional and design aspects as well as the plant material. It should not be simply reading the plant list to the client without explanation. The presentation should explain why plants were selected and their value to the design. It should address the analysis to explain the functionality of the design. And the presentation should visually support the design with pictures from catalogs and software or digital imaging.

Key Terms

Copy: a reproduction of original drawing presented to client

Digital imaging: software used to create the design from a picture of the site

Elevated drawing: sketch that illustrates width and height of design

Foam board: used to mount design for presentation

Master plan: the final design that includes all detail, specifications, and names

Note cards: used to prepare key points for presentation

Posterboard: see foam board

Print: see copy

A   The Design Process

This appendix is an in-depth look at the landscape design project (Ann and Jeff Grant) illustrated in this text. It contains a lengthy interview with the clients and an inventory and analysis of the site. The third section is an example of presenting the design to the Grants. The fourth section contains all the drawings illustrated throughout the text, sequentially arranged, ending with the final master plan.

Grant Interview

Family

How many family members?

- Ann, 52, works as a full-time nurse
- Jeff, 55, teaches English at a local college
- Children are grown up
- Grandchildren, ages 2 to 11, frequently come to visit

Are there any allergies to consider, such as bees or to specific plants?

None.

Are there any pets to consider?

Ann has a toy poodle that is mostly an indoor pet.

Design Goals

Ann and Jeff had several items they wanted to address:

- Widen the driveway to develop a turnabout.
- Develop perennial and herb beds, as well as her gardening nook.
- Reduce the maintenance of the front drainage ditch.
- Screen some of the views coming into their yard.
- Develop a wildlife habitat to attract birds and butterflies to the backyard.
- Create an informal, low-maintenance landscape in their front yard.

Lifestyle

What kind of things do you do in the . . .

Front yard?

They spend little time in the front, other than going from the driveway to the front door or from the front door to around the corner of the house.

Side yard?

The left side of the house has the driveway so it's mainly just to get from the front to the back. The right side of the house is where Ann would like to develop a gardening work area.

Backyard?

They spend most of their time here, either relaxing on the patio, gardening, or playing with the grandchildren.

Hobby

Do you have any outdoor hobbies?

Ann loves to work in the garden and would like to develop areas for herbs, perennials, and vegetables. Jeff is mainly an indoor person.

They're interested in developing a playground for the grandchildren.

Entertaining

Do you spend time entertaining guests?

Besides family, they usually only have a few friends over on occasion. For the most part it's just the two of them relaxing with a great view to the marsh.

They would like to improve their sitting area but not really expand it.

Do you need to develop an area for outdoor cooking and eating?

No. They rarely cook outside.

Views

Are there views you would like to keep?

They purchased the house because of the exceptional view over the marsh.

Are there views you would like to block?

They spend a lot of time in the office, which has a large bay window looking over the front and another looking out to the backyard. They want to keep the view open to the backyard but would like to create a screening from the road into the front window.

Are there any unpleasant items to be screened?

They don't care for the view of the neighbor's privacy fence, which appears barren, or the telephone pole and fire hydrant in the front yard.

What about from inside the house?

Ann also spends a lot of time looking out a small kitchen window and would like to develop something pleasant to look at.

They also have a grand view from the living room to the marsh, which they want to keep.

Is there any need for more privacy from neighbors' views?

They'd like to have a bit more privacy in the backyard from the neighbors on each side, not anything enclosing, just something partial.

Taste

Do you prefer informal, natural areas, or formal, well-defined areas?

They insist on something natural looking.

Their living habits reflect a stylish, unkempt appearance; large bookcases, scuffed wooden floors, antique chairs.

What level of maintenance would you care to have?

They want very little lawn and would prefer a low-maintenance approach. Although Ann will spend lots of time tending to gardens and flowers, she doesn't want to maintain trees, shrubs, and turf.

What are your favorite plants?

Anything that is fragrant. Gardenia, Tea Olive, Jasmine . . . things like that. Also, plants that attract birds and butterflies.

Things that are unique; more specifically, things that aren't commonly found in most landscapes.

What are your least favorite plants?

Anything that is thorny.

Ask if there's a yard they've seen that they really like.

No. But Ann would like to replicate some of the garden styles she's seen at local botanical gardens.

Ask about other parts of a design they may be interested in looking at.

They're not really interested in developing any other amenities in great detail.

Grant Residence Inventory and Analysis

Let's take an example of a residence to analyze the inventory (Fig. A–1). The Grant residence will be illustrated with pictures taken on-site (Fig. A–2). From the initial interview, the following information was gathered:

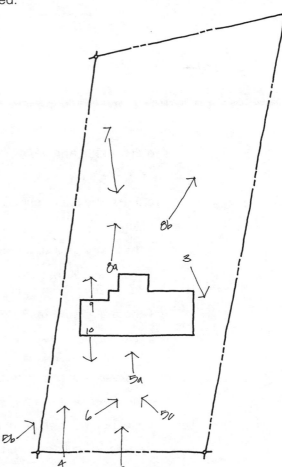

***Figure A–1* Grant Residence Camera Angles**

These are camera angles that correspond to the following figures.

***Figure A–2* Grant Residence**
Front of house from road.

***Figure A–3* Grant Residence**
The gardening area on side of house. Keep access
available to front and backyard.

How many family members are there?

Two. Ann and her husband, Jeff.

Are there kids and what ages are they?

None in the house. All grown up and moved away.

Are there any allergies to be aware of?

None.

Are there any pets to consider?

Yes. A small toy poodle. He spends limited time outdoors and is too small to
cause any problems in the yard.

Are there any hobbies?

Yes. Gardening. Ann would like to develop an area with a compost bin and bench
for gardening (Fig. A–3).

Analysis: Develop area for gardening that has privacy and is accessible.

Do the clients entertain guests?

Very few. Most of their time is spent amongst themselves.

Analysis: Limit the entertainment area to a few people and include more privacy.

House

Color of the house and materials

Tan siding with light blue shutters.

Locate doors and windows

Doors and windows were located. The kitchen window is left of the front door and about 5 feet off the ground. The office, which is a converted garage, has large bay windows that are only a few feet off the ground.

Analysis: Avoid tall plantings in front of the office windows.

Circulation

Parking

How many cars does the client want to accommodate?

Two. Currently there is not enough room for both cars. They have difficulty getting cars out because they are parked single file (Fig. A–4). They have also expressed concern about having to back out onto the road that is often busy with traffic, and their view is partially obstructed. They would like to look at ideas of parking side-by-side and also being able to turn the car around before pulling out onto the road.

Analysis: Widen the driveway and develop a turnabout so that the cars are not blocked in and can get to the road without backing out.

Where are the major paths of foot traffic?

Major foot traffic is from the driveway to the house (Fig. A–5). Currently there is no path or sidewalk established. The only sidewalk leads from the front door straight out to the road, which Ann and Jeff say is never used.

Analysis: Develop a hardscape path from the driveway to the front of the house to accommodate traffic from the house and road.

How would guests approach the house?

Up the driveway.

Figure A–4 **Grant Residence**
The driveway is not large enough to accommodate two cars. The residents would also like to develop a turnabout.

(a)

(b)

Figure A–5 **Grant Residence**

(a) The entrance lacks a warm, accommodating approach. The entry walk will be rerouted. (b) The most common path of primary circulation to the front door.

Figure A–6 **Grant Residence**

The right side of the front yard needs better definition from the neighbor. Keep secondary circulation open to the side yard.

Is the traffic around both sides of the house or just one?

In order to get to the backyard, people walk up the driveway and around the house. Ann also walks from the front door around the right side of the house when she is gardening (Fig. A–6).

Analysis: Keep the access available to the right side of the house from the front.

What about movement from the side and back doors?

There are no side doors. There is a back door that opens into the living room and out onto the back patio.

Is there adequate space for each one?

No. The back patio is too small to sit comfortably and funnels up a narrow set of stairs (Fig. A–7).

Analysis: Improve the circulation over the back patio and create a more usable space.

***Figure A-7* Grant Residence**
Entertainment area is small, lacks interest
and enclosure, and is crowded.

Pavement

Are the materials suitable for each path?

There are no materials for paths. The driveway contains gravel that lacks edging
and scatters out into the yard.

Analysis: Develop a warm path to the front door. Also improve the gravel drive
containment and consider a warmer material.

Is the material in good condition?

The loose gravel is appropriate for the informal style of Ann and Jeff's yard. There
could be a better material that is warmer.

Does it look visually appealing?

No. Primarily due to the lack of edging.

Is it functional?

No. It is too small for the cars and does not facilitate foot traffic.

Secondary Paths

Is the turf suitable?

Yes. There's not enough traffic to require hard pavement.

What about inexpensive paths of mulch and gravel?

Leaving an opening around the right side of the front, possibly mulch, would be
suitable.

Utilities

Is there a septic tank?

No.

Are there overhead lines?

Yes. Along the road over the right-of-way and from the front corner of the yard to
the front right corner of the house.

Analysis: Avoid tall plantings that would interfere with the overhead lines.

Are there air-conditioning units and washer/dryer exhaust?

The air-conditioning unit is on the right side of the house.

Analysis: The air-conditioning unit does not appear to be a visual nuisance.

Are there other visual utilities that still need access such as gas meters?

Yes. Ann doesn't like the telephone pole that is in the front right corner of the yard.

Analysis: Screen the telephone pole from the house.

Additions

Are there any additions that don't appear on the site plan?

Yes. There is a storage shed in the backyard.

Analysis: Keep the access available to the shed. Consider moving the shed to allow adequate space for the addition.

Are there any future additions that will be accounted for?

Yes. They will build an enclosed sunroom onto the back of the house.

Views

Bad Views

Yes. They don't care for the view of the neighbor's privacy fence along side of the yard and would like to screen it. Also, they would like to screen the telephone pole in the front yard.

Analysis: Plant to break up the long empty space of the neighbor's privacy fence.

Good Views

There's an outstanding view to the marsh in the backyard that should not be obstructed (Fig. A–8).

Analysis: Avoid tall plantings in the backyard that would obstruct the view. Also, consider framing the view.

(a)

(b)

Figure A–8   Grant Residence
(a) Outstanding view to marshy area from the house across large backyard. Keep the view unobstructed.
(b) View to right part of the backyard can use some visual interest and definition.

(a)   (b)

***Figure A–9*   Grant Residence**
(a) View from office needs to remain unobstructed to marshy area. (b) View from office to front yard needs to remain open, but screen the view from the road into the office.

Important Views

Entertainment Area

> This will be the view to the marsh.

Inside Views

> The bay window in the office looks out through the backyard to the marsh (Fig. A–9). The bay window looks into the front yard and is open to passing traffic. They both have expressed a desire to screen the view from the road.

> *Analysis:* Screen the view of the traffic from the office window without obstructing the view of the front yard (Fig. A–9b).

Kitchen Window

> They would like to create a view from the kitchen window since they spend a moderate amount of time in front of it.

> *Analysis:* Create a view from the kitchen window into the front yard.

Exposure

Sun

Full Sun

> The backyard is mostly full sun (Fig. A–10).

> *Analysis:* The backyard plants need to be full-sun tolerant.

Full Shade

> The front yard is mostly shade to partial shade due to the northern exposure and overhead trees.

> *Analysis:* The front yard needs to be tolerant of partial shade.

Figure A–10   Grant Residence
Backyard of residence.

Time of Exposure

Back of the house will be in the shade in the mid to late afternoon, while the front of the house will get dappled sun at that time.

Wind

Is the prevailing wind a problem?

No.

Temperature

Is the southwest exposure a problem?

No.

Salt

Brackish water in marsh.

Analysis: Use salt-tolerant plants.

Existing Plants

Do the owners want to get rid of any particular plants? Keep any?

All plants are expendable except for the Live Oak and Pecan in the front yard.

Analysis: Avoid disturbing the existing Live Oak and Pecan.

Soil

Texture

Sandy soil. Beds should be amended with organic matter for moisture retention.

Analysis: Recommend amending planting beds with organic matter where possible.

Soil Test

pH is good at 6.9. No other deficiencies.

Drainage

Foundation

House is built on a slab.

Surface

No problems except for a low spot in the middle of the backyard. However, sandy soil drains rapidly.

Downspouts and Gutters

There are no gutters. Runoff from roof does not appear to be a problem; the house is built on a slab.

Traffic

Previously mentioned problem with view into office.

Are there any concerns with obstructed views of traffic when pulling out of the driveway?

Difficult pulling out of driveway due to large Live Oak.

Analysis: Minimize plantings at the entrance. Allow for cars to pull out forward.

Are there concerns with traffic and children?

No.

Other Observations

The ditch. Ann and Jeff expressed a dislike for the drainage ditch running along the road in the front because it was difficult to maintain.

Analysis: Consider ground cover in the drainage ditch to reduce mowing, or installing drain pipe.

Wildlife. They love to attract birds, butterflies, and other wildlife and expressed an interest in developing a small habitat outside the office window in the backyard.

Analysis: Develop a wildlife habitat outside of office window in the backyard.

No turf. Ann didn't care for turf and asked for solutions that would reduce the amount of lawn in the front yard.

Analysis: Expand the beds in front yard to reduce lawn.

Presenting the Master Plan

The following is an abbreviated approach to presenting the master plan to the clients. Take note of how it explains how and why the design is laid out and plants are selected. Also note that pictures or examples of materials are shown to the client during the presentation, either printed on paper or from a laptop. All pictures can be burned to a CD and given to the client at the end of the presentation. Keep in mind that this design is located in hardiness zone 8b/9a.

Before we get started, let me explain a few things about the design so you will get the most out of the presentation. This is a plan drawing that is like a bird's-eye view of your property, looking straight down on it from above. Here is your front door (pointing) and this is the back door (pointing). It is drawn to a 1/8″ scale, which means that every 1/8 of an inch is equivalent to 1 foot. You will also notice there is a plant list on the plan. Each one of the symbols is labeled with a key that can be found in the plant list that will identify it by the botanical and common name.

All right, if you have any questions about the design while I am presenting it, do not hesitate to ask. Let us start in the front yard and we will work our way toward the back.

Based on the interview, I have put together a plan that allows for plenty of planting space and working areas for gardening. It includes low-maintenance plants that provide a lot of variety and interest. These include plants of fragrance and attraction to birds and butterflies. You will find that this design not only provides you with a rich variety of sights, smells, and sounds but also creates a useful plan that addresses the activities of your home and property.

You had concerns about backing out of the driveway onto the busy road. As a result, the driveway has been expanded to allow room for a turnabout to pull out onto the road forward. The same crushed aggregate will remain in the drive, but the borders will be defined with edging materials to contain the aggregate and maintain a sharp edge. Off the end of the driveway, the neighbor's fence, which you didn't care to see, will be covered with Crossvine, which has vivid orange, tubular flowers in the spring and, in addition, attracts hummingbirds.

The entry walk that went directly out to the street and was seldom used has been removed from the middle of the yard and routed from the turnabout of the driveway. Guests from the road or parking will approach the house up the driveway. The walkway will be constructed with a beige flagstone (example of material shown to client), which is an irregular stone that is a few inches thick and will pick up the color of the siding. This stone will continue onto the step and porch.

The rest of the front yard has been designed to reduce the amount of turf and increase the bed space. The turf in the front yard, as well as the back, will be St. Augustine, which handles the shade and full sun.

I have kept fragrance in mind by placing a Tea olive near the entrance that will flower in the late winter and early spring with a potent essence that should drift into the house during warm weather. You will see the Tea olive, as well as other plants and materials, repeated throughout the property in order to provide some continuity.

There are a variety of colors that will develop throughout the growing season. In the early spring the Loropetulam will flower bright pink with a dark burgandy foliage throughout the rest of the year; Crape myrtle will flower white in late spring with an interesting mottled trunk during the winter; Clethra will flower white in profuse numbers in midsummer; in late summer–early fall, Sweetgrass, planted in mass along the driveway, will bloom a soft, pink color while the Inkberry will set an interesting black fruit.

Also, at the entrance you will find the Fatsia, an interesting large, coarse foliage that will contrast nicely with the Inkberry along with a uniquely black, low-growing Mondograss, which will pick up the black fruit of the Inkberry. In addition there will be a cutleaf Japanese maple, which grows slow and low with a graceful form and soft texture.

At the ditch near the road where you wanted to reduce the maintenance, we discussed the possibility of filling in the ditch with a drainpipe but came to the conclusion it was too expensive. Instead, the ditch can be planted with a ground cover, Liriope, which is a dark green, grassy plant that will spread effectively. It is a real tough plant that will cover the ground and require very little maintenance. This plant, as well as the Sweetgrass on the other side of the driveway, are low growing and will not hinder the view to the road when pulling out.

Here, where you were concerned with the view from the road into the office window, a Loropetulum will create a screen and the Sago palm will be a nice focal point to enhance the view from the office.

Over here is the telephone pole that you would like to screen from the house. This Arizona cypress, which is a bluish evergreen conifer, grows quickly and handles dry, hot conditions well.

Around the right side of the house there is an informal path that is paved in the planting bed with the same flagstone used on the front walk. It goes to the work area that is on the south side of the house where you will find plenty of space on a workbench to store pots and materials for gardening, in addition to the compost bin. The large oak trees in the neighbor's yard protect the southern exposure, so this will be a comfortable place to work. The area is framed by Crape myrtles for overhead enclosure during the summer; you will also have Tea olives to provide fragrance in late winter and early spring. From the work area there is direct access to the storage shed that is relocated to allow room for the sunroom addition.

In the backyard there are two large areas reserved for herbs, annuals, or perennials. The right side of the yard is defined with a bed that extends to the back property line and partially screens the view from the neighbor's yard. The bed includes Elaeagnus, which is a tough shrub with unique evergreen foliage that will grow 8 to 10 feet or taller; Abelia has attractive, shiny reddish foliage that flowers white in the spring; the Sweetgrass that is planted along the driveway is also planted in mass along the back; Pampasgrass grows 8 to 10 feet tall with outstanding plumes in the summer. The Lantana, which are low-growing perennials, flower yellow all summer long and attract butterflies.

The view to the marsh is preserved with an open area on the left and low plantings along the right. Right outside the office window there are several plantings that attract birds, hummingbirds, and butterflies. They are low growing and will not obstruct the view to the marsh. There is also a Gardenia planted near the office window that has extremely fragrant flowers in the summer and will fill the corner and office with a wonderful smell.

This large tree outside the office is called a Goldenrain tree. It is covered with yellow flowers in the spring and sets fruit in a cluster of dry capsules in the late summer, which rustles in the wind like rain is falling.

Further down the fence is a group of shrubs called Butterfly bushes that, as the name implies, are very attractive to butterflies. In front of the shrubs is Lantana, which also attacts butterflies.

Since the back deck was very cramped and provided little more than a walkway from the back door, I have expanded it to include bench seating for a couple of people and planters for annuals to provide color that can also be seen from inside the house. The Natchez crape myrtle is planted next to the deck in order to provide some overhead enclosure and color from the bark and flowers. The same flagstone used in the front yard and work area will create a wide landing area at the bottom of the steps and continue through the planting bed to the left side of the house.

That concludes the presentation of the landscape design, are there any questions that I can answer for you?

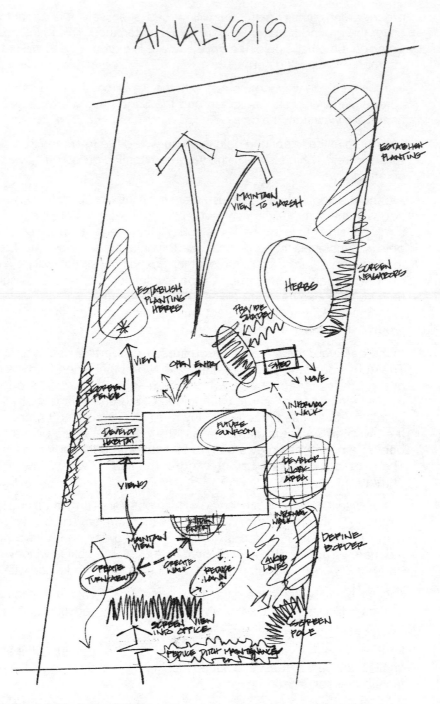

Graphical Analysis
The analysis of the inventory done graphically on the site plan.

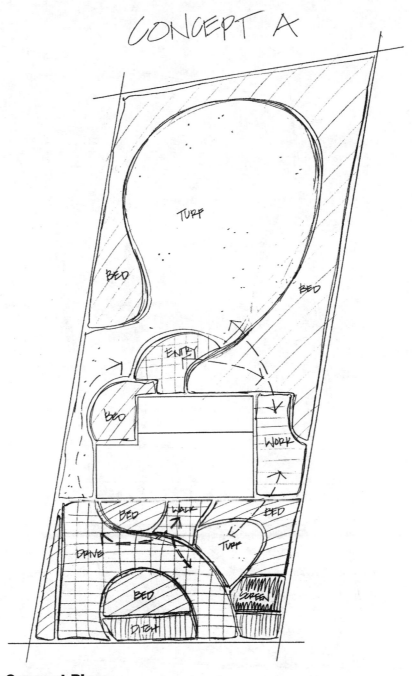

CONCEPT A

Concept Plans

Three concept plans organize the ground plane in a different arrangement, each one addressing the analysis.

(continues)

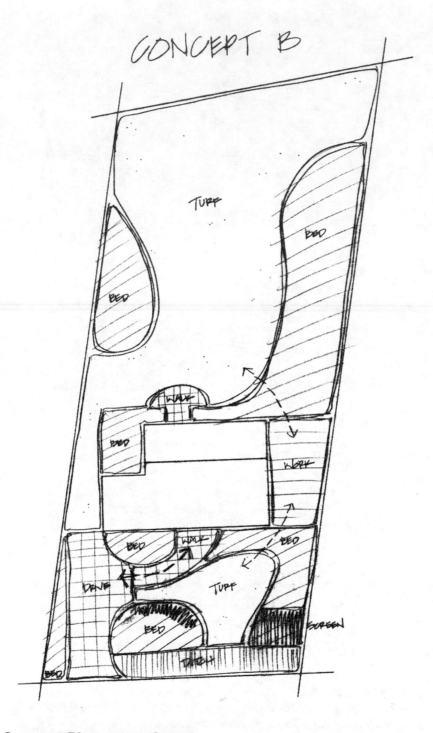

Concept Plans—continued

Three concept plans organize the ground plane in a different arrangement, each one addressing the analysis.

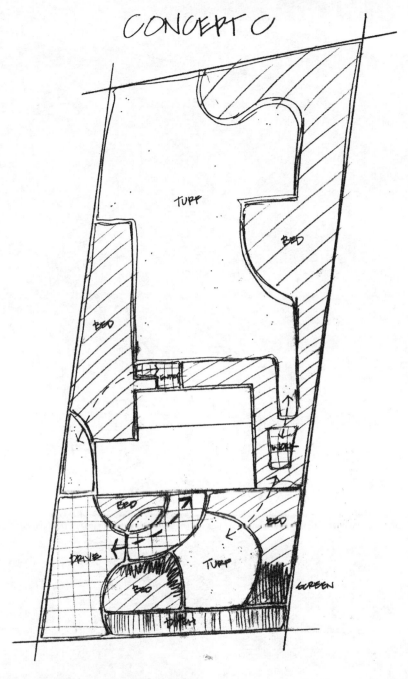

Concept Plans—continued
Three concept plans organize the ground plane in a different arrangement, each one addressing the analysis.

(continues)

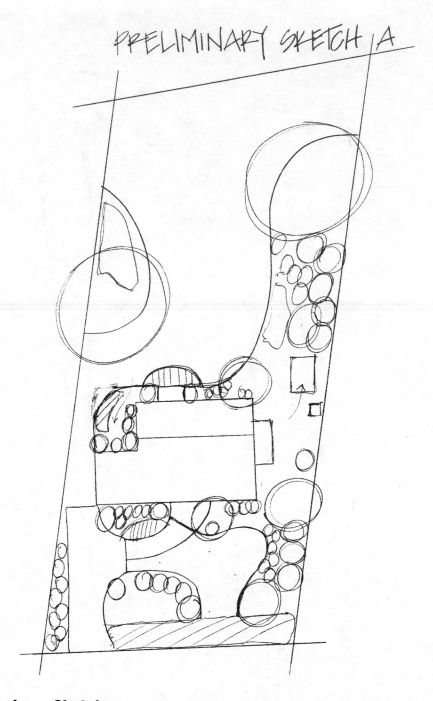

PRELIMINARY SKETCH A

Preliminary Sketches

Using a concept plan, or combinations of concept plans, a preliminary design takes shape. Sketches are useful in defining the ground plane and getting a rough idea of plant size and placement.

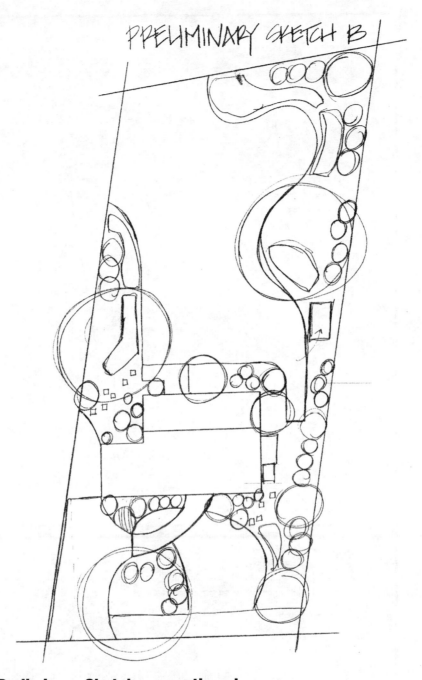

PRELIMINARY SKETCH B

Preliminary Sketches—continued

Using a concept plan, or combinations of concept plans, a preliminary design takes shape. Sketches are useful in defining the ground plane and getting a rough idea of plant size and placement.

(continues)

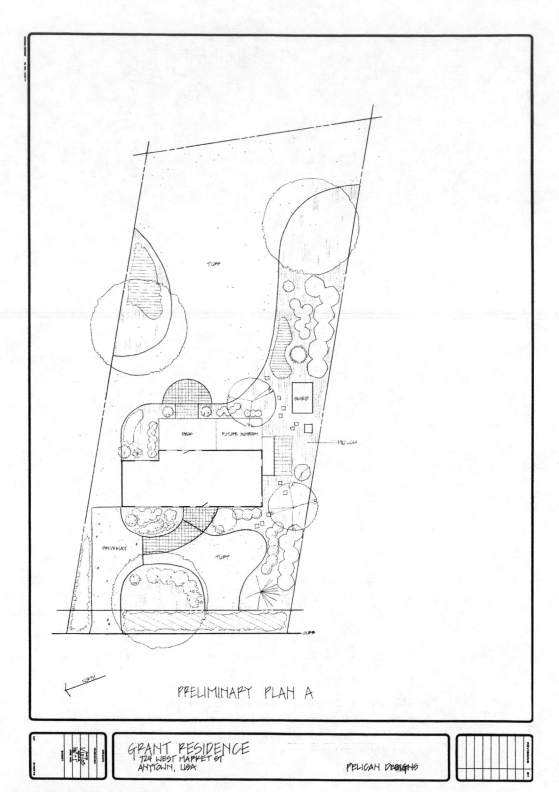

PRELIMINARY PLAN A

NORTH

GRANT RESIDENCE
724 WEST MARKET ST
ANYTOWN, USA

PELICAN DESIGNS

Preliminary Design

Two preliminary designs are developed with generic plant symbols and ground plane textures. They convey the arrangement, flow, and balance of the design concept without the details of specific plants and materials. They will be used to get feedback from the client.

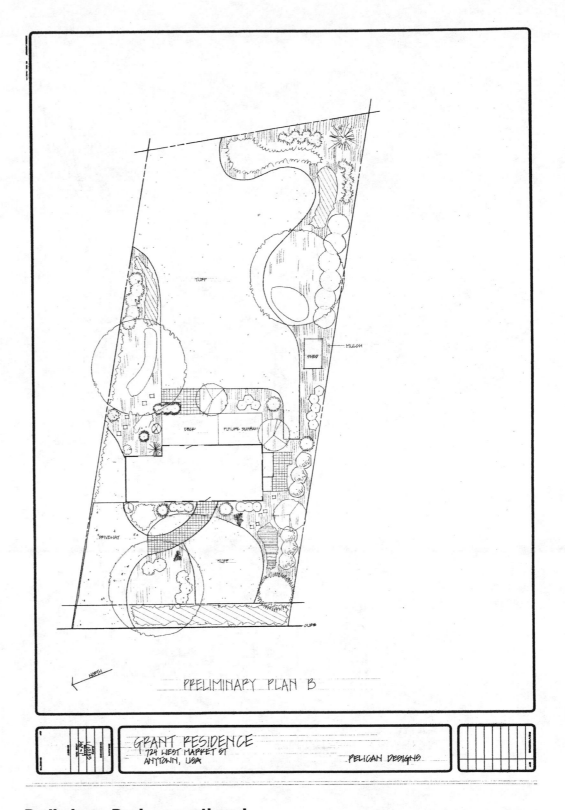

PRELIMINARY PLAN B

NORTH

GRANT RESIDENCE
724 WEST MARKET ST
ANYTOWN, USA

PELICAN DESIGNS

Preliminary Design—continued

Two preliminary designs are developed with generic plant symbols and ground plane textures. They convey the arrangement, flow, and balance of the design concept without the details of specific plants and materials. They will be used to get feedback from the client.

(continues)

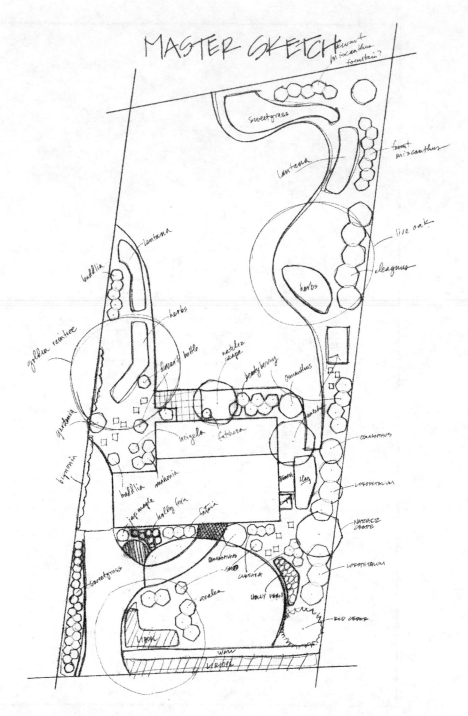

Master Sketch

A sketch of the master plan helps specify the ideas of the master plan.

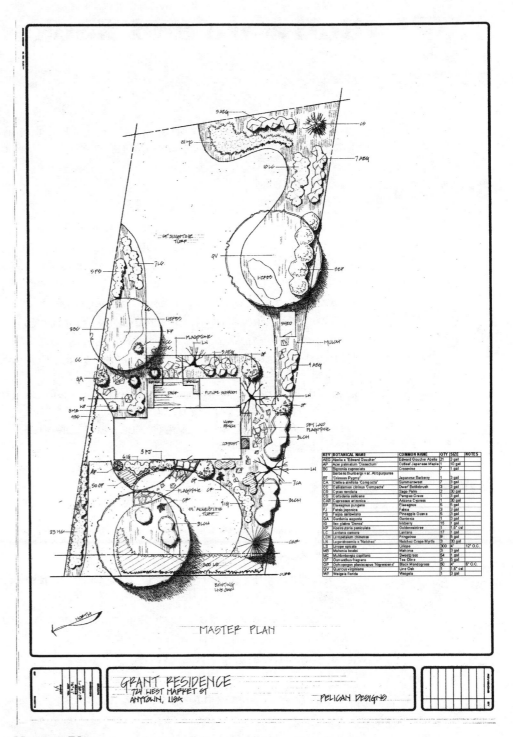

MASTER PLAN

KEY	BOTANICAL NAME	COMMON NAME	QTY	SIZE	NOTES
AEG	Abelia x 'Edward Goucher'	Edward Goucher Abelia	21	3 gal	
AP	Acer palmatum 'Dissectum'	Cutleaf Japanese Maple	1	10 gal	
BC	Bignonia capreolata	Crossvine		1 gal	
BT	Berberis thunbergii var. Atropurpurea 'Crimson Pygmy'	Japanese Barberry	1	3 gal	
CA	Clethra alnifolia 'Compacta'	Summersweet	7	3 gal	
CC	Callistemon citrinus 'Compacta'	Dwarf Bottlebrush	3	3 gal	
CR	Cycas revoluta	Sago Palm	2	30 gal	
CS	Cortaderia selloana	Pampas Grass	1	3 gal	
CAR	Cupressus arizonica	Arizona Cypress	1	30 gal	
EP	Elaeagnus pungens	Elaeagnus	5	5 gal	
FJ	Fatsia japonica	Fatsia	3	3 gal	
FS	Feijoa sellowiana	Pineapple Guava	5	3 gal	
GA	Gardenia augusta	Gardenia	1	3 gal	
IG	Ilex glabra 'Densa'	Inkberry	15	1 gal	
KP	Koelreuteria paniculata	Goldenraintree	1	1.5" cal	
LC	Lantana camara	Lantana	17	1 gal	
LCH	Loropetalum chinense	Fringetree	9	5 gal	
LN	Lagerstroemia x 'Natchez'	Natchez Crape Myrtle	3	30 gal	
LS	Liriope spicata	Liriope	300	4"	12" O.C.
MB	Mahonia bealii	Mahonia	3	3 gal	
MC	Muhlenbergia capillaris	Sweetgrass	54	1 gal	
OF	Osmanthus fragrans	Tea Olive	3	5 gal	
OP	Ophiopogon planiscapus 'Nigrescens'	Black Mondograss	50	4"	8" O.C.
QV	Quercus virginiana	Live Oak	1	1.5" cal	
WF	Weigela florida	Weigela	1	3 gal	

GRANT RESIDENCE
724 WEST MARKET ST
ANYTOWN, USA

PELICAN DESIGNS

Master Plan

The master plan is the final plan in the design process; it specifies all plants and other materials.

B Software and Books

Most of the following books and software are sold by the American Nurseryman Publishing Company (*http://www.amerinursery.com*), or at other book retailers.

Software

Betrock's Guide to Landscape Palms CD, Alan W. Meerow, Ph.D.

The Color Encyclopedia of Ornamental Grasses on CD-ROM, Rick Darke

Field Notes CD-ROM, American Nurseryman Publishing Company

Horticopia Titles

The Interactive Guide for Herbaceous Perennial Plants, Allan M. Armitage

The Interactive Manual of Woody Landscape Plants on CD-ROM, Michael A. Dirr

Landscaping Plants and Trees, Delmar Publishers

Michael A. Dirr's Photo-Library of Woody Landscape Plants on CD-ROM, Michael A. Dirr

Ornamental Plants Plus 3.5, Michigan Landscape and Nursery Association and Michigan State University Extension

This is Gardening, Allan Armitage (annuals and perennials)

Water Gardening CD-ROM

Internet Links

Google
http://www.google.com

> When in doubt, go to Google and click the "Images" tab, then search for the plant.

> Your search will yield all the photos of that plant on the Internet found by Google.

Salisbury University Arboretum
http://www.salisbury.edu/arboretum/

> Salisbury University in Maryland; great photos!

Landscape Plants of the Upper Midwest
http://www.midwestlandscapeplants.org

> University of Wisconsin; great photos and plant selector, also an audio file to pronounce names

Oregon State University, Landscape Plants, Volume 1
http://oregonstate.edu/dept/ldplants/

> Oregon State University; excellent photos from large database

Connecticut College Arboretum
http://arboretum.conncoll.edu/

> Connecticut College; adequate photos arranged by family

Ornamental Plants plus Version 3.0
http://www.msue.msu.edu/msue/imp/modzz/masterzz.html

> Michigan State University; no photos on Web site, can purchase photos on CD

Missouri Botanical Gardens
http://www.mobot.org/MOBOT/otherwww.html

> Missouri Botanical Gardens; comprehensive list of links

Horticulture on the Internet
http://www.ces.ncsu.edu/depts/hort/consumer/hortinternet/

> NC State University; great comprehensive list of photos, links, and horticulture information

The University of Delaware Botanical Gardens
http://ag.udel.edu/udbg/

> University of Delaware Botanical Gardens; good collection of plant descriptions and photos

University of Connecticut Plant Database
http://www.hort.uconn.edu/plants/

> University of Connecticut; excellent database of photos and plant selector, also an audio file to pronounce names

US National Arboretum Plant Photo Gallery
http://www.usna.usda.gov/

> United States National Arboretum; photos of daylilies, Crape myrtles, and azaleas

PLANTS National Database
http://plants.usda.gov/

> United States Dept. of Agriculture; source of plant photos and information

Floridata
http://www.floridata.com/

> Floridata Marketplace; good source of photos, descriptions, and other horticulture-related items, organized into plant categories including flowers, herbs, trees, palms, etc.

Palm and Cycad Societies of Florida
http://www.plantapalm.com/

> Source of palm photos and information

Evergreen Nursery

http://www.evergreennursery.com

> Evergreen Nursery, Inc; great source of ground cover photos

Monrovia Nursery

http://www.monrovia.com

> Monrovia Nurseries; great source of photos and criteria filter

HortiPlex Plant Database

http://hortiplex.gardenweb.com/plants/

> Very extensive database of plant information and pictures

Plants Database

http://plantsdatabase.com/

> Locate plant information and pictures by name

Plantfacts

http://plantfacts.osu.edu/

> Lots of plant photos! Easy to navigate through the site.

Books

Trees and Shrubs

The American Horticultural Society A–Z Encyclopedia of Garden Plants, C. Brickell and J. Zuk

The American Horticultural Society Encyclopedia of Garden

The American Horticultural Society Gardening Manual, Gillian Roberts

Botanica's Trees and Shrubs

The Botanical Garden, R. Phillips and M. Rix

Broad-Leaved Evergreens, Stephen G. Haw

Choosing Plant Combinations, Cathy Wilkinson Barash

The Complete Plant Selection Guide for Landscape Design, Marc C. Stoecklein

Conifers, D. M. Van Gelderen and J. R. P. Van Hoey Smith

Dirr's Hardy Trees and Shrubs, Michael A. Dirr

Dirr's Trees and Shrubs for Warm Climates, Michael A. Dirr

The Encyclopedia of North American Trees, Sam Benvie

The Encyclopedia of Planting Combinations, Tony Lord

Garden Plants, C. Brickell and J. Zuk

Gardening with Conifers, Adrian Bloom

Great Plant Guide, The American Horticultural Society

The Illustrated Book of Trees, W. C. Grimm

Landscape Plants, Ferrell M. Bridwell

Manual of Woody Landscape Plants, Michael A. Dirr

Native Trees, Shrubs, and Vines, William Cullina

Native Trees, Shrubs, and Vines for Urban and Rural America, Gary L. Hightshoe
Pictorial Library of Landscape Plants, Vol. 1, Dr. Jane Coleman Helmer; *Vol. 2*, Dr. Ruth Fortune Woods
Plants, Christopher Brickell and John Elsley
Plants for American Landscape, N. G. Odenwald, ASLA, C. F. Fryling, Jr., ASLA, and T. E. Pope
The Random House Book of Shrubs, Roger Phillips and Martyn Rix
The Random House Book of Trees of North America and Europe, Roger Phillips
Right Plant, Right Place, Nicola Ferguson
Trees and Shrubs for Flowers, Glyn Church
Trees and Shrubs for Foliage, Glyn Church
Trees and Shrubs for Fragrance, Glyn Church
Trees for Urban and Suburban Landscapes, Edward F. Gilman
Xeriscape Plant Guide, David Winger

Herbaceous Plants (Flowers, Ground Covers, Herbs, etc.)

Annuals and Biennials, R. Phillips and M. Rix
Annuals with Style, M. A. Ruggiero and T. Christopher
Armitage's Garden Perennials, Allan M. Armitage
Armitage's Manual of Annuals, Biennials, and Half-Hardy Perennials, Allan M. Armitage
Bamboo for Gardens, Ted Jordan Meredith
Botanica's Annuals and Perennials,
Continuous Bloom, Pam Duthie
Designing with Perennials, Pamela J. Harper
An Encyclopedia of Shade Perennials, W. George Schmid
Hardy Herbaceous Perennials, Leo Jelitto and Wilhelm Schacht
Herbaceous Perennial Plants, Allan M. Armitage
Landscaping with Herbs, James Adams
Manual of Herbaceous Ornamental Plants, Steven M. Still
Perennial Combinations, C. Colston Burrell
Perennial Ground Covers, David S. MacKenzie
Perennials, R. Phillips and M. Rix
Taylor's Guide to Ground Covers, N. Sinton and D. C. Michener
The Well-Tended Perennial Garden, Tracy DiSabato-Aust

Ornamental Grasses

Color Encyclopedia of Ornamental Grasses, Rick Darke
The Encyclopedia of Ornamental Grasses, John Greenlee
Gardening with Grasses, M. King and P. Oudolf
Taylor's Guide to Ornamental Grasses, Edited by R. Holmes and F. Tenenbaum

Palms

Betrock's Guide to Landscape Palms, Alan W. Meerow
Cultivated Palms of the World, D. Ellison and A. Ellison
Ornamental Palm Horticulture, Tim Broschat and Alan Meerow
Tropical Ornamentals, W. Arthur Whistler

Estimation

Estimating for Landscape and Irrigation Contractors, James Huston
Grounds Maintenance Estimating Guidelines, Professional Grounds Management Society
Landscape Designer and Estimator's Guide, National Landscape Association
Landscape Estimating and Contract Administration, S. Angley, E. Horsey and D. Roberts
Landscape Estimating Methods, Sylvia Hollman Chattin
Means Site Work and Landscape Cost Data
Time-Saver Standards for Landscape Architecture, C. Harris and N. Dines

Water Gardening

The American Horticultural Socitey Complete Guide to Water Gardening, Peter Robinson
Gardening, Peter Robinson
The Master Book of the Water Garden, Philip Swindells
Rock and Water Gardening, Peter Robinson
The Ultimate Water Garden Book, Jean-Claude Arnoux
The Water Garden Design Book, Y. Rees and P. May

Hardscaping

Brick in the Landscape, Rob W. Sovinski
Complete Construction, Christine Beall
A Guide to Dry Stone Walling, Andy Radford
Landscape Specification Guidelines, Landscape Contractor Association
Stonework, Charles McRaven

C Estimating the Materials

Some designers continue on beyond the design and prepare a materials list and bid for installation. A freelance designer may prepare a formal bid and give it to several companies for installation. There are some basic calculations that can be made to get an accurate estimate of the materials in the design.

Square Footage

Materials like sod and hardscaping will require the amount of square footage to estimate amounts (Fig. C–1). There are four basic geometric shapes that can be used to estimate square footage:

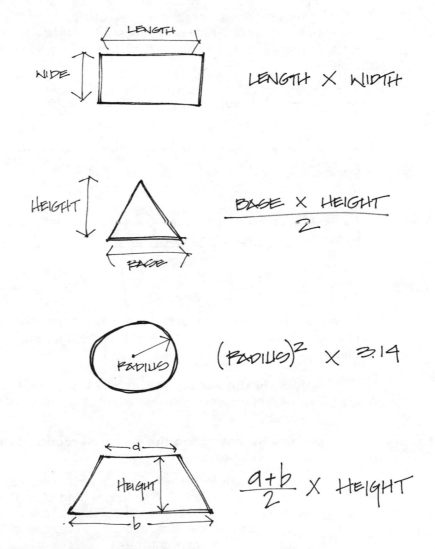

Figure C–1 Square Footage
Square footage of basic geometric areas include rectangle, triangle, circle, and trapezoid.

Figure C–2 **Estimating Area on the Plan**
With a piece of tracing paper over the master plan, square footage can be estimated with a scale by dividing large areas into smaller geometric areas to calculate total amount of material requirements.

These simple formulas can be easily applied to shapes that conform to a rectangle, triangle, circle, or trapezoid. Unfortunately most often the areas are irregular and don't fit to a single shape. Irregular areas are estimated by breaking them up into smaller components of rectangles, circles, triangles, and trapezoids until all of the space is accounted for, and then the smaller parts can be summed up to equal the total square footage.

These estimates can be calculated by placing tracing paper over the master plan and using a scale to sketch out square footage (Fig. C–2).

Tip Box

Many items are estimated by the number of **palettes** to complete the job, such as sod or stone. Palettes can be estimated by dividing the total square footage of area by the square footage a palette will cover.

Volume

Materials like mulch, sand, and gravel will require estimates of volume (Fig. C–3). Mulch, for instance, can be supplied in bulk in cubic yards or bags in cubic feet. To calculate volume,

1. **Calculate the square footage of the area.** To estimate mulching requirements of a bed, estimate the square footage of the bed. For example, 200 square feet.

2. **Determine how deep the material required needs to be.** For example, 4 inches deep.

3. **Convert depth into feet.** If the depth is in inches, divide by 12 to convert to depth in feet. (For example, four inches divided by 12 = 0.33 feet deep.) This is to keep all the measurements in the same units, square feet and depth in feet, in order to correctly calculate cubic feet. They cannot be calculated if measurements are feet and inches.

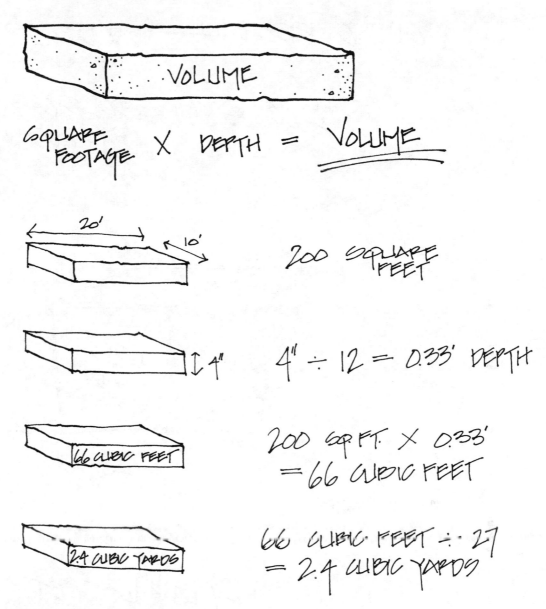

Figure C–3a Volume
Volume can be calculated with the use of square footage and depth.

4. **Calculate cubic feet.** Multiply square footage and depth. For example, 200 square feet × 0.33 feet deep = 66 cubic feet.

5. **Calculate cubic yards.** Divide cubic feet by 27. For example, 66 cubic feet divided by 27 = 2.4 cubic yards.

CUBIC FEET ⟶ CUBIC YARDS

CUBIC FEET ÷ 27 = CUBIC YARDS

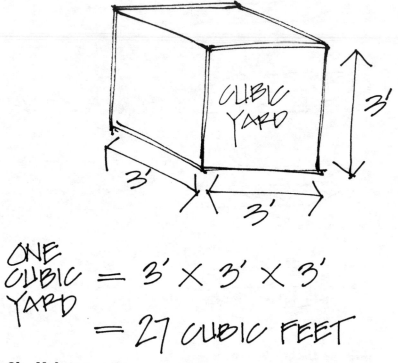

CUBIC YARD

3'

3'

3'

ONE CUBIC YARD = 3' X 3' X 3'

= 27 CUBIC FEET

Figure C–3b   Volume
Volume can be calculated with the use of square footage and depth.

Materials

The following are common materials in the design that will have to be estimated by square footage, palettes, cubic feet, or yards.

Sod

Sod will require square footage for an estimate and most often palettes of sod will be required. Sod is sold in rolls or square pieces but is often delivered in bulk on palettes for large jobs (Fig. C–4). In many cases, depending on the type of turf, one palette of sod will cover approximately 500 square feet (check with supplier).

To estimate the number of palettes required, divide the total square footage by 500 square feet (Fig. C–5).

Figure C–4 Palette of Sod
Sod is usually ordered and delivered on palettes that normally cover about 500 square feet (check with the supplier).

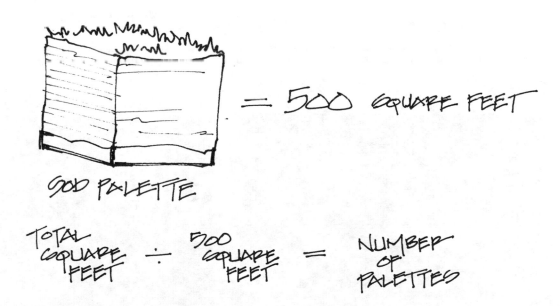

= 500 SQUARE FEET

SOD PALETTE

TOTAL SQUARE FEET ÷ 500 SQUARE FEET = NUMBER OF PALETTES

Figure C–5 Estimating Palettes
Divide total square by the number of square feet a palette will cover.

Concrete

Concrete will require square footage for an estimate. In most cases, a 4-inch-deep slab is suitable and will be subcontracted by a concrete company. They will use the square footage to give an estimate.

Pavers

Pavers require square footage for an estimate. In order to estimate the number of pavers required, it will take some additional math.

1. **Get square inches of the paver.** For instance, a brick paver may measure 8 inches by 4 inches (Fig. C–6). Calculate square inches of the paver by multiplying length times width.

$$8 \times 4 = 32 \text{ square inches}$$

2. **Convert square inches to square footage.** Every paver occupies 32 square inches of space. The area of the brick will be divided into the total square footage of the paving. But first it must be converted into square feet, the same units of the total area. One square foot = 144 square inches. To convert square inches into square feet, divide by 144 (Fig. C–7).

$$32 \text{ square inches} \div 144 \text{ square inches} = 0.22 \text{ square feet}$$

3. **Divide the total area by the square footage of the paver.** This will get the total number of pavers.

$$\text{Total area} \div 0.22 = \text{Number of pavers}$$

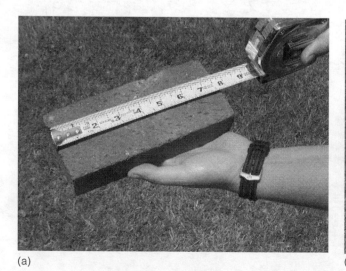
(a)

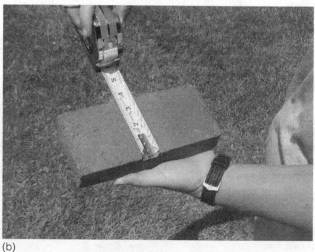
(b)

Figure C–6 Estimating Pavers
To estimate paver requirements, measure the (a) length and (b) width of the paver.

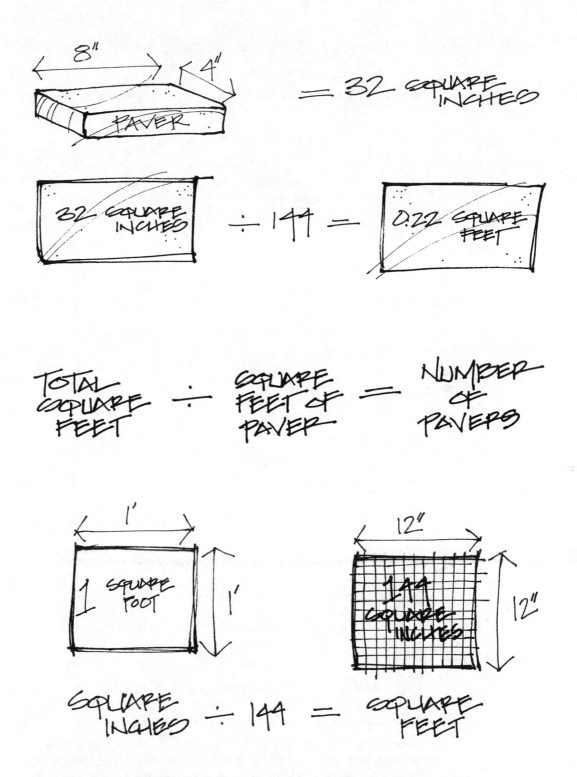

Figure C–7 Converting Square Inches into Square Feet
To convert square inches into square feet, divide by 144.

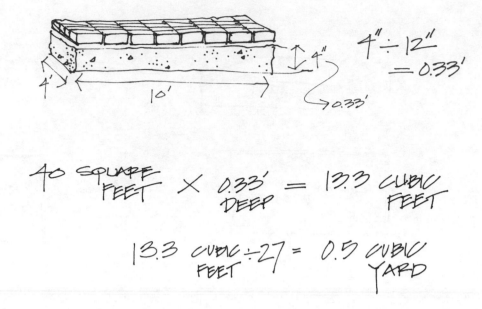

40 SQUARE FEET × 0.33' DEEP = 13.3 CUBIC FEET

13.3 CUBIC FEET ÷ 27 = 0.5 CUBIC YARD

1 CUBIC YARD SAND ≈ 1.5 TON

0.5 CUBIC YARD × 1.5 = 0.75 TON SAND

Figure C–8 Estimating Foundation Material
Estimate the volume of materials, such as sand, to lay the foundation of a paved area. Aggregate material such as sand is often sold in tons.

Base Material

Depending on how the pavers or stone are to be constructed, the base materials can also be estimated. For dry-laid, there is typically a 4-inch layer of crushed limestone or other suitable material (Fig. C–8). Over this is a 1-inch layer of setting sand.

Estimate the volume in cubic feet or yards. Sand and other aggregate material is often ordered in tons. For instance, 1 cubic yard of sand is approximately equal to 1.5 tons. Be sure to check with supplier before ordering

1 cubic yard of sand = Approximately 1.5 tons

Flagstone

Estimating flagstone requires the total square footage of the flagstone area. Since flagstone comes in various sizes, the number of stones is difficult to estimate. Instead, the number of palettes required can be estimated (Fig. C–9). The number of square feet that a palette will cover depends on the type of stone used. Typically a palette

Figure C–9 **Stone Palettes**

Stone is sold on palettes. The area of one palette varies depending on the type of stone, but is often 120 to 200 square feet. Check with the supplier. To estimate number of palettes, calculate the same as sod: the total square feet divided by the square footage of a palette.

Tip Box

Estimate the square footage a palette of stone will cover on-site by first getting the square footage of the palette and then multiply by the number of rows of stone stacked on the palette (Fig. C–10).

Figure C–10 **Estimating Stone Palettes**

Get square footage of palette and multiply by the number of stacked rows.

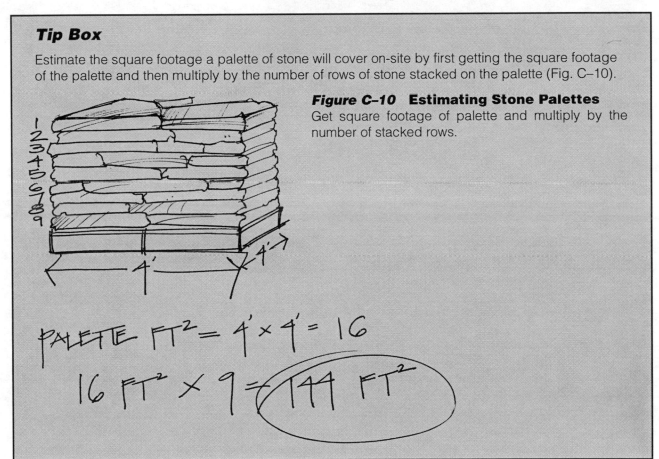

will cover 120 to 200 square feet, but check with a supplier on the type of stone to be estimated.

Estimate the number of palettes by dividing the total square footage of the area by the square footage of the palette.

Total square footage / 120 square feet = Number of palettes

Edging

The amount of edging is estimated by linear feet. Edging will be installed primarily between turf and planting beds. To get an estimate of the linear requirements of edging, use a flex curve to follow the bed lines and anywhere else edging will be installed. Know the length of the flex curve to scale and calculate the edging by using it as a flexible scale or digital scale (Fig. C–11).

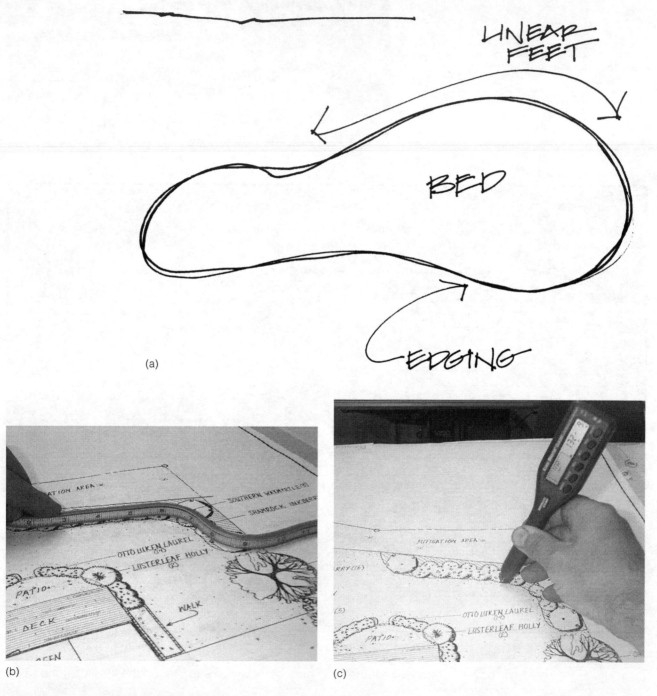

(a)

(b)

(c)

Figure C–11 **Estimating Edging**
(a) Edging is estimated in linear feet. To estimate the total length of edging required, use a (b) flex curve or (c) digital wheel that tabulates much like a measuring wheel; the scale can be changed according to plan.

Once the total number of linear feet is known, calculate the number of edging units required to complete the work (Fig. C–12). Divide the total linear feet by the unit feet of the length of edging. For instance, a piece of steel edging is 8 feet long.

Total number of linear feet ÷ 8 feet = Number of edging pieces

Mulch

Estimate the mulch requirements in cubic feet or cubic yards (Fig. C–13). Most bulk mulch is sold in cubic yards, while bagged mulch is sold in cubic feet. First, calculate the number of cubic feet that the mulched areas will require at a given depth.

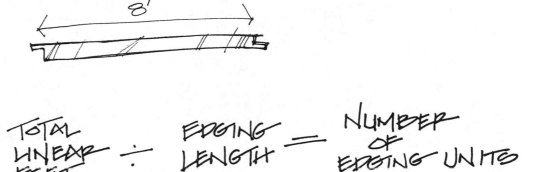

Figure C–12   Units of Edging
Edging is sold in lengths. Steel edging, for instance, is sold in 8-foot lengths. Divide the total length of edging by the length of one edging unit.

(a)   (b)

Figure C–13   Mulch
Mulch can be acquired in (a) bags, measured in cubic feet, or (b) bulk, measured in cubic yards.

For instance, the mulch will be applied 3 inches deep (Fig. C–14). Convert depth of inches to depth of feet and multiply by the square footage to get the cubic feet. If estimating for bulk mulch supply, then the cubic feet can be converted to cubic yards by dividing by 27.

If estimating for the number of bags required, then divide the total number of cubic feet by the number of cubic feet in a bag. If a bag contains 3 cubic feet,

Total cubic feet ÷ 3 cubic feet = Number of bags

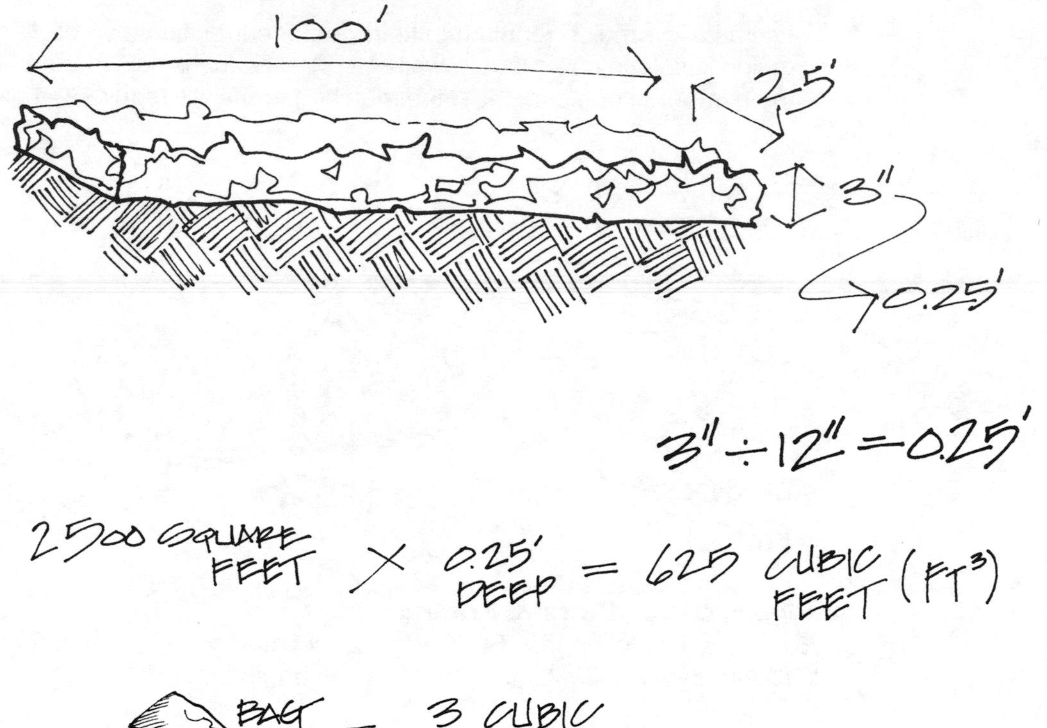

$$3'' \div 12'' = 0.25'$$

$$2500 \text{ SQUARE FEET} \times 0.25' \text{ DEEP} = 625 \text{ CUBIC FEET (FT}^3\text{)}$$

$$\text{BAG} = 3 \text{ CUBIC FEET}$$

$$625 \text{ CUBIC FEET} \div 3 \text{ CUBIC FEET (ONE BAG)} = 208 \text{ BAGS}$$

$$\text{CUBIC YARD} = 27 \text{ CUBIC FEET}$$

$$625 \text{ CUBIC FEET} \div 27 \text{ CUBIC YARDS} = 23 \text{ CUBIC YARD (YD}^3\text{)}$$

Figure C–14 **Estimating Mulch Requirements**
Estimate the volume of mulch requirements. Then an estimate of bags, based on cubic feet, or bulk, based on cubic yards, can be calculated.

The number of palettes of bagged mulched can be estimated by dividing the total number of bags by the number of bags on a palette.

Total bags ÷ Bags on a palette = Number of palettes required

Weed Barrier

The amount of weed barrier can be estimated by the square footage of the beds that will be covered (Fig. C–15). To estimate the number of rolls required to do the job, determine the square footage of the weed barrier roll. For instance, a roll that is 3 feet × 100 feet would cover 300 square feet of ground. Once the square footage of a roll is determined, calculate the number of rolls by dividing the total square footage of beds by the square footage of the roll (Fig. C–16).

Total square footage ÷ 300 square feet (roll) = Number of rolls

Ground Cover

To estimate the quantity of plants to fill an area of ground cover, first the spacing between the plants must be determined (Fig. C–17). For instance, plants may be planted on 4-, 6-, 8-, 10-, or 12-inch centers (or larger). This is usually specified as "on center."

Second, determine how many square inches each plant would occupy.

Figure C–15 Weed Barrier
Weed barrier is sold in rolls of various widths and lengths.

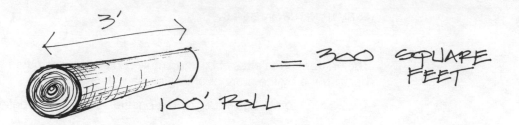

3′

100′ ROLL

= 300 SQUARE FEET

$$\text{TOTAL SQUARE FEET} \div \text{SQUARE FEET PER ROLL} = \text{NUMBER OF ROLLS}$$

Figure C–16 Estimate Weed Barrier
Estimate the weed barrier requirements by dividing total area of beds by the square foot one roll will cover.

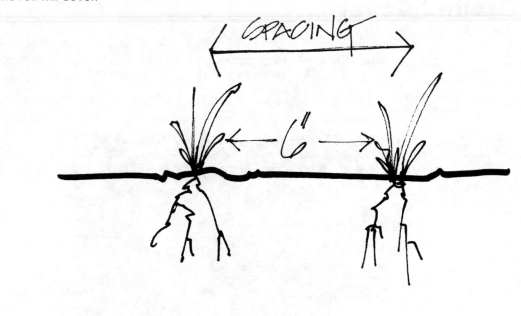

SPACING

6″

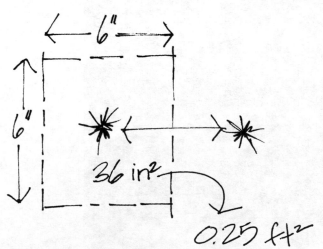

6″

6″

36 in² → 0.25 ft²

Figure C–17 Ground Cover Estimate
Once the spacing is determined, calculate the square footage a plant will occupy and then divide into the entire ground cover area.

Example

If a ground cover is to be planted 6 inches on center, then each individual plant will occupy a square space that is 6 inches by 6 inches. This would equal 36 square inches.

Third, calculate how many square feet each plant will occupy by dividing the square inches by 144.

Example

If the ground cover occupies 36 square inches, then the square footage is 0.25.

Fourth, determine the total square footage of the area to be planted.

Example

The total area is 10 feet by 20 feet, equal to 200 square feet.

Fifth, estimate the total number of plants required to fill the determined area. Take the total area divided by the square footage of each plant.

Example

In this case, 200 square feet is divided by 0.25 square feet to equal 800 ground cover plants.

Cost Estimate

The bid for the installation will cover the company's cost and profit and is based on several factors: materials, driving distance, estimated man-hours, soil conditions, and so forth. The bids will vary from company to company. To get an approximate estimate of what range of bids to expect, some designers look at the cost of the materials and figure the installation will be between two to three times the cost of materials.

$$\text{Cost of materials} \times 2 \text{ or } 3 = \text{Approximate cost of installation}$$

Estimate Example

The following is a materials estimate of the master plan. The area calculations are located at Figure C–18.

Turfgrass

Amount of sod required for lawn

Square footage

Front yard = 787.5 square feet

Side yard = 208 square feet

Backyard = 5875 square feet

Total square footage = 6870.5 square feet

An estimate of the amount of sod required

Palette of sod = 500 square feet

6870.5 total square footage / 500 square feet of palette = **13.7 or 14 palettes**

Mulch

Amount of mulch required for planting beds

Square footage of planting beds

Front = 1983.5 square feet

Back and side yard = 4862 square feet

Total square footage of beds = 6845.5 square feet

Volume of mulch required if 3 inches deep

Cubic feet = 6845.5 square feet × 0.25′ (3 inches deep) = **1711 cubic feet**

Cubic yards = 1711 cubic feet / 27 cubic feet = **63.4 cubic yards**

Weed Barrier

The amount of weed barrier required to cover all planting beds

Total square footage of beds = 6845.5 square feet

Roll of weed barrier = 6′ wide and 500′ long = **3000 square foot of coverage per roll**

Number of rolls required to cover all planting beds

Total square footage of beds = 6845.5 / 3000 square feet = **2.3 or 3 rolls**

Edging

The amount of edging required to separate planting beds from turf

Total linear feet = 486 linear feet

Number of steel edge pieces required

One piece of steel edging = 8′

486 total linear feet / 8′ per piece = **60.75 or 61 pieces of steel edging**

Driveway

A stone aggregate will be used for the driveway

Driveway = 676 square feet

Tons of stone aggregate required to fill driveway 4 inches deep

Cubic feet = 676 square feet of driveway × 0.33′ (4 inches deep) = **225.3 cubic feet**

Cubic yards = 225.3 cubic feet / 27 cubic feet = **8.3 cubic yards**

Tons = 8.3 cubic yards × 1.5 tons = **12.5 tons**

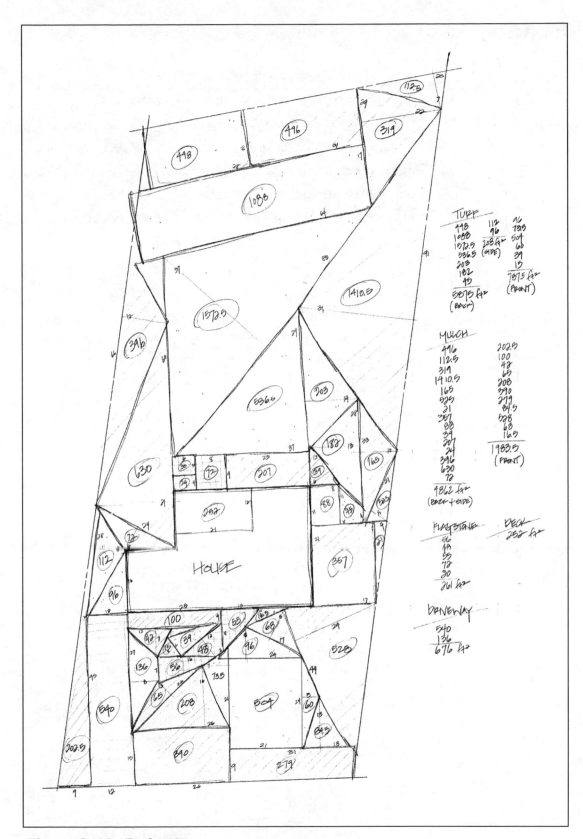

Figure C–18 Estimate
Example of estimating material for master plan.

Stone

The amount of stone required for front and back walk

Total square footage of flagstone = 261 square feet

Number of palettes required for flagstone construction

261 square feet / 120 square feet of palette = 2.2 palettes

Amount of crushed granite required for base material 4 inches deep

Cubic feet = 261 square feet of stone $\times$ 0.33' (4 inches deep) = **86.1 cubic feet**

Cubic yards = 86.1 cubic feet / 27 cubic feet = **3.2 cubic yards**

Tons = 3.2 cubic yards $\times$ 1.5 tons = **4.8 tons**

D Computer Graphics

Computer-aided drafting systems are referred to as CAD. AutoCAD is a software program that allows the user to draw lines, arcs, and circles in addition to many other functions. For the landscape designer, however, it lacked a symbol library early in its development. LANDCADD, released in 1984, evolved from AutoCAD to include numerous symbols and applications that relate to landscape design, irrigation, estimating, and construction details, among others. Larger companies, such as landscape architecture, engineering, or commercial landscaping, commonly use AutoCAD or LANDCADD. But for many landscape designers, it is very expensive, difficult to learn, and more software than needed.

The advantages to software design are numerous. Site surveys can be readily scanned to file and designing can begin without having to draw the site. Symbols can be sized and instantly duplicated throughout the plan. Revisions are easily done without redrawing; symbols can be moved, deleted, or added as needed. All materials can be tagged with specifications and exported to develop a complete materials list and estimation. Files can easily be printed at various sizes or e-mailed.

Software Products

Since the mid-1980s, design software other than AUTOCAD and LANDCADD have developed to include imaging, plan drawing, and estimators. Many of these products are easier to learn, relatively inexpensive, and more applicable for many landscape designers.

If considering design software other than AUTOCAD and LANDCADD, be sure to purchase high-quality design software. They are much different than the programs that are on the shelf at a local store and selling for less than $50. Although inexpensive, they are limited in their applications, quality, and database of images. As a landscape designer, the professional grade software offers a wide range of applications, high-quality prints, and program and database upgrades.

This appendix is not intended to promote any of the products that are listed at the end of the section. They all have some outstanding qualities. But regardless of which product is learned by the user, there are several common techniques used by each program. This appendix is not intended to teach you how to use each program since the actual execution of the commands will vary between products. Its intention is, however, to give you an idea of what design software can do and what kind of finished products they create. If you decide to pursue design software, most products have very good tutorials that will walk you through the design process step by step.

Also, this appendix is not complete in the extent of what each program can do. In fact, most the programs that I have experienced can do much more than the basic commands. However, what is described in the following is the basic approach to using design software.

In considering purchasing a product, shop around at the various retailers listed at the end of this appendix. Some can send you the fully operational product that will run for a 30-day trial before requiring the user to purchase a password to unlock it for further use.

Plan Drawing and Estimator Software

Once a site survey is scanned to file, the operating scale is set. One of the most basic functions of the plan drawing software is the ability to draw lines (Fig. D–1). These lines can be straight, curves, arcs, or any number of options, depending on the software. Beds, patios, walks, driveways, and other areas can be drawn on the ground plane. Many programs have the capability to estimate the square footage of the area as well as calculate volume, which can then be used to estimate materials such as mulch or pavers (Fig. D–2). With the drawing in scale, a dimension tool can be used to automatically specify distances for layout (Fig. D–3).

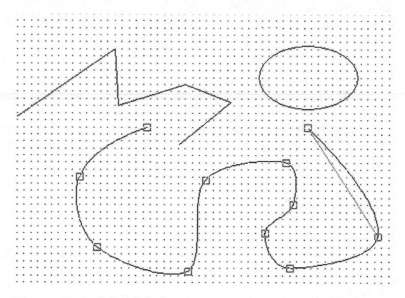

Figure D–1 **Line Tool**
The most basic function of design software is to draw lines, arcs, and shapes.

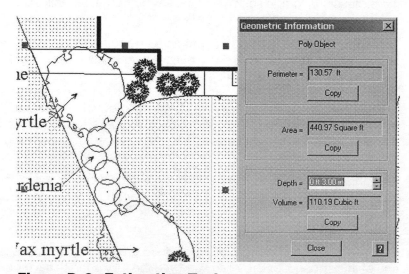

Figure D–2 **Estimating Tool**
Area and volume is automatically calculated to estimate materials.

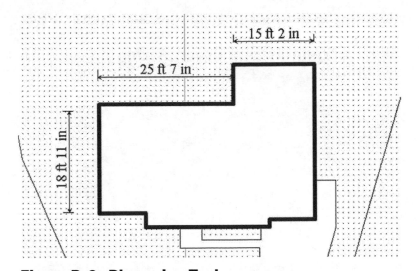

Figure D–3 **Dimension Tool**
Lines and areas can have dimensions added for layout.

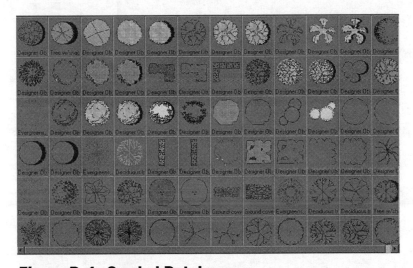

Figure D–4 **Symbol Database**
Symbols can be added to the design from a database.

The image database contains a collection of plant symbols that can be dropped onto the design (Fig. D–4). These symbols can then be sized and transformed to the correct scale. Properties can also be assigned to the symbol. These can include, but are not limited to, the plant name, planting size, price, and inventory number. The symbols can be duplicated quickly with a copy command that places the same exact symbol with every click. When all the symbols are placed, the design can be quickly labeled (Fig. D–5). Most programs have an automatic labeling command that will place the name of the symbol on the label without having to type it again. All it takes is selecting a symbol and then placing the label. Since the properties of the symbol contain the name, the command can automatically assign the name to the label. This makes labeling a snap that is completed in seconds.

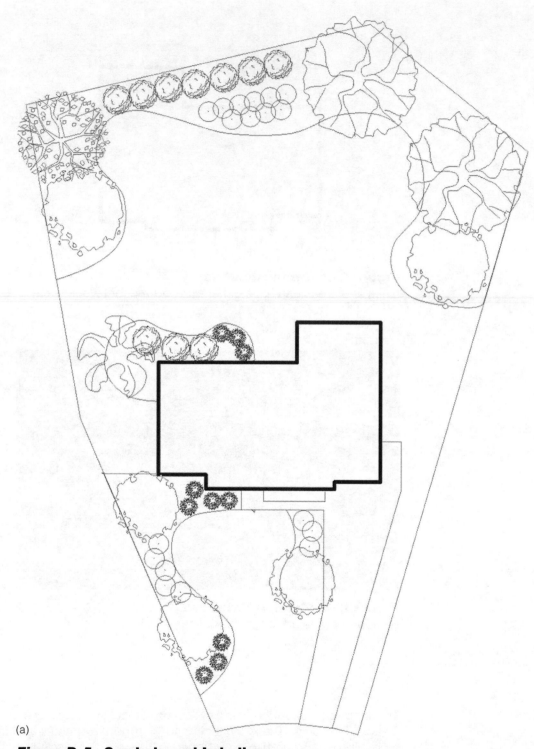

(a)

Figure D–5 Symbols and Labeling
(a) Once symbols are sized and placed,

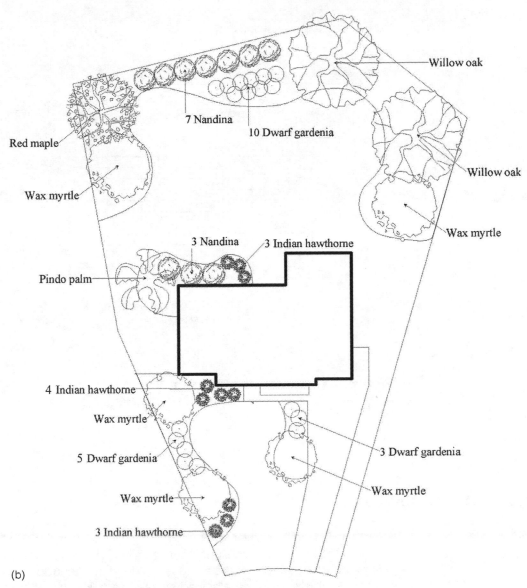

***Figure D-5* Symbols and Labeling—continued**
(b) labels can be quickly added.

Some programs have the capability to color the plans for presentation. The plan can then be printed on high-quality paper for presentation or e-mailed to the client.

When the plan drawing is complete, all the plants and other materials can be exported to an estimator program. The estimator can organize all the material and assigned properties, as well as square footage and volume of ground plane areas, into a proposal format that can add up the cost of materials for an estimate (Fig. D–6). This software can be customized for your company as a proposal template that can be printed and presented to the client.

Pepperdam Nursery and Landscaping

John Doe	Tel: (843) 555-1143	Date 8/15/2001
111 Carolina Lane	Fax: (843) 555-1433	Estimate # 00000153
Charleston, SC 29111		

Name	Qty.	Size	Price	Tax	Total
CLEYERA	3	5 gallon	20.00	3.75	63.75
DOGWOOD	1	5 gallon	25.00	1.56	26.56
JUNIPER	6	3 gallon	12.00	4.50	76.50
RIVER BIRCH	1	15 gallon	55.00	3.44	58.44
SPIREA	8	3 gallon	12.00	6.00	102.00
Tax Total				19.25	
Grand Total					327.25

Signature   Date

Figure D–6   Estimator Program
All materials can be exported and formatted for a proposal.

Imaging Software

Landscape design imaging has been used to simulate landscape designs on an actual photo of the site. Older versions oftentimes had the result of a photo with pictures of plants, like refrigerator magnets, stuck on top of it. Although this was helpful, it wasn't believable. Imaging software has advanced to a point that realistic photos of proposed designs, where objects and textures could be blended into a photo of the site, can be easily created. As a result, a much more tangible product is created where clients see a picture of what they are purchasing instead of an artist's drawing. Rather than relying on descriptions and vague imagery to "paint" a picture of the design, a client sees what actual plants and hardscape material look like.

First, a picture of the site is acquired, either digitally or from scanning a photo. The picture is opened in the software program to design. The picture can be cropped and sharpened to improve the quality. Existing objects can often be erased from the picture, if needed, using a cloning tool (Fig. D–7). A database of images, similar to the symbols database, is opened that contains trees, shrubs, grass, sidewalks, driveways, and more (Fig. D–8). The objects, such as trees, can be loaded onto the picture, just as symbols were loaded onto the plan drawing, and adjusted for size and color, then duplicated as needed (Fig. D–9). As more objects are loaded onto the picture, they "stack" like objects on a table and can be moved forward and backward. Shadows can also be added to the objects for additional depth (Fig. D–10).

Once the image is finalized, it can be printed on high-quality paper and presented along with the plan to the clients (Fig. D–11). It can also be e-mailed.

(a)

(b)

(c)

Figure D–7 Cloning Tool

(a) Erasing an existing object on the photo, (b) a cloning tool borrows texture from the photo, such as turf in this case, to paint over the object (c) making it appear as if it were never there.

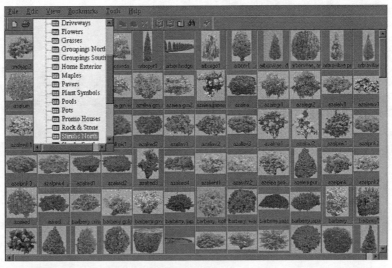

Figure D–8 Object Database

Objects such as trees, shrubs, pavers, and turf are added to the photo.

Figure D–9 **Duplicating**

Objects from the database can be added to the photo, transformed, and duplicated with a few clicks of the mouse.

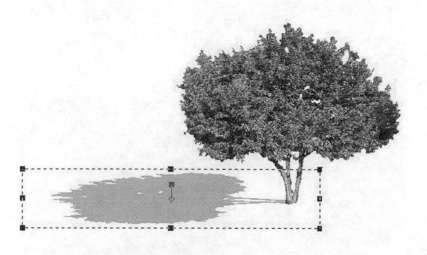

Figure D–10 **Shadows**

To create more realism and perspective, shadows can be added to objects.

(a)

(b)

(c)

(d)

Figure D–11   **Imaging Examples**
Before and after pictures. *(Photos courtesy of Visual Impact Imaging.)*

Software Products

Design Imaging Group
http://designimaginggroup.com

Drafix Software, Inc.
http://www.drafix.com/

Visual Imapact Imaging
http://www.visualimpactimaging.com/

Eagle Point Software
http://www.eaglepoint.com/

LSI Software Inc.
http://www.lsisoft.com/

Dynascape
http://www.gardengraphics.com

Software Republic
http://www.softwarerepublic.com

LANDMARK
http://www.nemetschek.net

Visual Nature Studio
http://3dnature.com

Land F/X
http://www.landfx.com

Realtime Landscaping
http://www.ideaspectrum.com

E   Butterfly Gardening

Plants offer constantly changing colors throughout the year with flowers, foliage, fruit, and stems, but they can also attract interesting colors in the form of butterflies. Butterflies are naturally seen in any landscape, but there are several design approaches to increase butterfly diversity and presence by developing a butterfly garden.

Puddling

Groups of butterflies can often be found sitting on a wet, muddy area. This is referred to as **puddling**. Butterflies will feed on minerals and salts from the wet ground to get nutrients. Preparing a low area that remains wet naturally or connected to a low-flow water source can be a way to attract butterflies. This can be enhanced by burying a shallow container, like a bird bath, to hold moisture for a longer period of time.

Basking

Butterflies require warm weather to fly, ideally when temperatures are between 85 and 100 degrees Fahrenheit. They will warm their bodies by spreading their wings to absorb the sun's heat, often on a rock or concrete. Flagstones and rocks may provide space for butterflies to **bask.**

Protection

Plan a butterfly garden in an area protected from the wind. Butterflies are more likely to spend time in a garden that does not require fighting the wind. Planting a dense shrub protection around the area will create a more calm, quiet microclimate.

Hibernation

Most species of butterflies overwinter in the same region. The monarch is the only butterfly that migrates to another area to overwinter, and in that case all the way to Mexico. They will hibernate, depending on the species, as larva, pupa, or adults in protected areas such as loose bark, debris, buildings, or logs.

Hibernation Boxes

Hibernation boxes are decorative houses with narrow slots on one side. It is intended to attract butterflies to shelter over the winter. However, most butterflies do not overwinter as adults. Many experts believe that the value of hibernation boxes is mainly as a garden decoration. While they might attract insects and spiders, rarely do butterflies utilize them.

Reduce Pesticides

Pesticide usage will kill caterpillars and butterflies just as it does the pests. Many insecticides are **contacts,** meaning that the butterfly or insect only has to come in contact with a treated surface to kill it.

Food Source

Butterflies have two growth stages: caterpillar (larval) and butterfly (adult). Attract both stages by planting the appropriate food source.

Host Plants

Host plants provide food for caterpillars. Butterflies will search out a particular plant to lay eggs, so that upon hatching the caterpillar will immediately have an appropriate food source. Host plants will be consumed like an insect pest, sometimes completely defoliated, so these plants are often considered expendable because the caterpillar will pupate into a butterfly. Host plants are often located in low-visibility areas.

Nectar Plants

Nectar is produced by flowers and consumed by butterflies. Butterflies uncoil a long tubular mouthpart, called a proboscis, to siphon nectar from flowers. They are often attracted to bright, warm colors such as pink, red, yellow, and orange. Butterflies will seek out nectar all season long when temperatures are above 60 degrees Fahrenheit through frost.

Abbreviated List of Host Plants for Butterflies

Butterfly—Host Plant

Poplar Admiral—Poplar, aspen

Red Admiral—Nettle

Apollo—Stonecrops, houseleeks

Silvery Blue—Lupine

Yellow Brimstone—Senna

Buckeye—Platain, gerardia

Comma—Nettle, hops, elm

Meadow Fritillary—Violets

Pearl-Bordered Fritillary—Violets

Shepherd's Fritillary—Violets

Silver-washed Fritillary—Violets

Purple Emperor—Willow, poplars, aspen

Colorado Hairstreak—Oak

Purple Hairstreak—Oak

Monarch—Milkweed

Mourning Cloak—Willow, birch, elm

Mylitta Crescentspot—Thistles

Orange Tip—Cuckoo-flower

Sara Orange Tip—Wild mustard

Two-tailed Pasha—Strawberry tree

Painted Lady—Thistles, nettles, yarrow

The Peacock—Nettles

Swallowtail—Fennel, milk parsley, queen Anne's lace

Black Swallowtail—Carrot, celery, parsley, fennel

Giant Swallowtail—Hop Tree, Citrus

Tiger Swallowtail—Black cherry

Cloudless Sulphur—Senna

Orange-barred Sulphur—Peas

Small Tortoiseshell—Nettle

The Queen—Milkweed

Nectar plants

Botanical Common Name

Arabis alpina Alpine rockcress

Aster species Aster

Rudbeckia hirta Black-Eyed Susan

Ajuga species Bugleweed

Buddleja davidii Butterfly Bush

Silene campion Catchfly

Nepeta x *faassenii* Catnip

Allium schoenoprasum Chives

Origanum vulgare Common marjoram

Bellis perennis Daisy

Daphne species Daphne

Hemerocallis species Daylily

Eryngium species Field eryngo

Tagetes patula French marigold

Solidago canadensis Golden rod

Heliopsis helianthoides Heliopsis

Eupatorium purpureum Hemp agrimony

Lonicera species Honeysuckle

Hyssopus officinalis Hyssop

Vernonia species Ironweed

Centaurea species Knapweed

Lavandula angustifolia Lavendar

Doronicum species Leopards-bane

Syringa species Lilacs

Cerastrium species Mouse-ear

Caragana aurantiaca Pea tree

Phlox species Phlox

Dianthus species Pink

Scabiosa species Pincushion flower

Primula species Primrose

Echinacea purpurea Purple coneflower

Lythrum salicaria Purple loosestrife

Salvia species Sage

Scilla sibiria Siberian squill

Liatris spicata Snakeroot

Veronica species Speedwell

Stokesia laevis Stoke's Aster

Sedum species Stonecrops

Asclepias incarnata Swamp milkweed

Lathyrus species Sweet pea

Armeria species Thrift rose

Cirsium species Thistle

Coreopsis species Tickseed

Verbena species Vervain

Vicia species Vetch

Anthemis tinctoria Yellow chamomile

Viburnum species Viburnum

Zinnia elegans Zinnia

F Deer

Much like insects cause problems by consuming plants for food, deer, also in much the same way, are pests. It is often a problem at the edge of woods where deer will graze in the evening and then return to the safety of the wooded area to sleep during the day. They will rip the foliage from trees and shrubs, trim all the flowers from an annual bed, and even feed on turf in the summer. Deer problems are more pronounced during droughty summers when nutritious, green food is scarce; deer are more likely to wander further from the woods in search of food. The winter following a hard drought is especially tough on deer that have less fat stored, which perhaps sets the stage for more severe deer problems. In search of green food, they will eat plants in the winter that they will ordinarily leave untouched in the summer.

In the fall, other problems can occur when deer are mating. They will damage the trunks of trees by rubbing their antlers on them to remove the fuzz from the new antlers. Tree trunks may need protection from gouging.

Deer-Resistant Plants

The most effective way to reduce damage from deer is using deer-resistant plants. For one reason or another, deer will not feed on certain plants unless near starvation, and for some plants not even then. Some plants develop physiological defenses to ward off deer, such as thorns, spines, or prickles. Others defend themselves by tasting foul or even poisonous (to deer, not necessarily humans). Deer typically do not care for bitter-tasting plants.

In regions where deer are a serious problem, deer-resistant plants are the best means of deterrence. Research or check with local plant nurseries for plants that are deer resistant. If plants are not deer resistant, there are a few other approaches to protecting plants from being eaten.

Deer Deterrents

Deer will stay away from plants and areas that taste or smell offensive to deer, not necessarily us. Taste repellence will sustain some feeding damage before deer stop. If plants that are not deer resistant are used, an area or plant that is regularly sprayed or planted with an offensive taste or smell can steer deer away. If the plants are edible to humans, the repellent needs to be able to wash off easily, thus effective for longer periods of time. Be aware the repellent is only protective on what is sprayed. New growth will not be protected so reapplication is required. Rotate repellents to prevent deer from becoming used to one product. Some products claim to remain active for two to three months; check the product for application.

Odor Repellents

Odor repellents work better in warm weather because the colder weather reduces the effectiveness of scent. One of the more popular odor deterrents is **egg solids.** They are very safe and last one to three months. **Garlic** and **soaps** are recommended for edible plants because they wash off easily and become ineffective after rain. **Meal meat** is placed in sachets and hung around the plants for protection, and it requires no spraying. It's effective for several months and rain makes it even more effective. **Predator urine** signals to the deer that danger is in the area, making them leave to feed in safer pastures. It is not applied to the plants but placed in dispensers near plants or applied around them.

Taste Repellents

Taste repellents are preferred in colder weather. When applied, the foliage and flowers need to remain dry for approximately 10 hours. **Hot pepper,** much like garlic, is good for edible plants. **Denatonium Benzoate** is a bittering agent that is absorbed by the plant and creates a bitter taste that is said to last for years. Some products like **Thiram,** the fungicide, and **blood-type ingredients** are effective as a taste and odor repellent.

Deer Barriers

Deer fence or **netting** is typically a six-and-a-half-feet-tall barrier to keep deer away from an area. It is effective for large areas, but unsightly and often unacceptable in residential and many commercial areas. **Baited electric fences** attract deer to touch the wires and deliver a harmless shock that chases them from the area. **Wireless baited electric fencing** has also been developed (*www.wirelessdeerfence.com*).

Abbreviated List of Deer-Resistant Plants

Perennials

Achillea filipendulina Yarrow

Aconitum napellus Monkshood

Agastache species Hyssop

Ajuga reptans Bugleweed

Anemone nemorosa Windflower

Aquilegia species Columbine

Artemisia schmidtiana Wormwood

Asarum canadense Wild ginger

Asarum europaeum European wild ginger

Asclepias species Butterfly weed

Aster species Aster

Astilbe arendsii False spiraea

Belamcanda chinensis Blackberry lily

Boltonia asteroides Boltonia

Carex species Sedge

Caryopteris clandonensis Bluebeard

Chrysanthemum superbum Shasta daisy

Convallaria majalis Lily-of-the-valley

Coreopsis lanceolata Coreopsis

Coronilla species Crown vetch

Delphinium species Larkspur

Dicentra eximia Fringed bleeding heart

Dicentra spectabilis Bleeding heart

Digitalis species Foxglove

Echinacea purpurea Purple coneflower

Eschscholzia californica California poppy

Euphorbia species Spurge

Gaillardia grandiflora Blanket flower

Galium odoratum Sweet woodruff

Gaura lindheimeri Whirling butterflies

Helleborus species Hellebore

Heuchera species Coralbells

Hibiscus moscheutos Rose mallow

Kniphofia uvaria Red-hot-poker

Lamiastrum galeobdolon Yellow archangel

Lamium maculatum Dead nettle

Lavandula angustifolia English lavender

Liatris spicata Gayfeather

Ligularia dentata Bigleaf ligularia

Matteuccia struthiopteris Ostrich fern

Monarda didyma Beebalm

Myosotis scorpioides True forget-me-not

Nepeta species Catmint

Opuntia compressa Prickly pear cactus

Osmunda cinnamomea Cinnamon fern

Paeonia species Peony

Papaver orientale Oriental poppy

Perovskia atriplicifolia Russian sage

Polygonatum species Solomon's seal

Polystichum acrostichoides Christmas fern

Pulmonaria saccharata Bethlehem sage

Salvia nemorosa Perennial sage

Santolina chamaecyparissus Lavender-cotton

Sedum species Stonecrop

Sempervirens tectorum Hens and chicks

Solidago species Goldenrod

Stachys byzantina Lamb's ears

Thymus species Thyme

Yucca filamentosa Adam's needle

Ground Cover

Ajuga reptans Bugleweed

Asarum canadense Wild ginger

Asarum europaeum European wild ginger

Brunnera macrophylla Siberian bugloss

Convallaria majalis Lily-of-the-valley

Coronilla species Crown vetch

Cyrtomium falcatum Holly fern

Galium odoratum Sweet woodruff

Juniperus procumbens Japanese garden juniper

Lamiastrum galeobdolon Yellow archangel

Lamium maculatum Dead nettle

Lantana camara Lantana

Leymus arenarius Lyme grass

Liriope species Lilyturf

Myosotis scorpioides True forget-me-not

Nepeta species Catmint

Pachysandra procumbens Allegheny spurge

Pachysandra species Pachysandra

Perovskia atriplicifolia Russian sage

Phalaris arundinacea Ribbon grass

Polygonatum species Great Solomon's seal

Sedum species Stonecrop

Stachys byzantina Lamb's ears

Shrubs

Abelia X grandiflora Glossy abelia

Berberis thunbergii Japanese barberry

Buxus species Boxwood

Callicarpa species Beautyberry

Camellia japonica Camellia

Cephalotaxus harringtoniana Japanese plum yew

Cephalotaxus species False yew

Cornus alba Red twigged dogwood

Cornus mas Cornelian cherry dogwood

Cycas revoluta Sago palm

Cytisus species Broom

Daphne species Mezereon

Elaeagnus pungens Elaeagnus

Feijoa sellowiana Pineapple guava

Gardenia augusta Gardenia

Hamamelis species Witch hazel

Hypericum species St. John's wort

Ilex species Holly

Illicium species Anise

Juniperus chinensis Hollywood juniper

Juniperus procumbcns Japanese garden juniper

Kalmia latifolia Mountain laurel

Leucothoe species Leucothoe

Ligustrum species Privet

Lonicera species Honeysuckle

Loropetalum chinense Chinese fringe

Mahonia aquifolium Oregon grape holly

Mahonia species Mahonia

Nandina domestica Heavenly bamboo

Nerium oleander Oleander

Osmanthus fragrans Tea olive

Picea pungens Spruce

Pieris floribunda Mountain Pieris

Pieris japonica Lily-of-the-valley shrub

Pieris species Pieris

Podocarpus species Podocarpus

Potentilla fruticosa Shrubby cinquefoil

Prunus laurocerasus Cherry laurel

Rosa rugosa Rose

Rosmarinus officinalis Creeping rosemary

Spiraea bumalda Spiraea

Viburnum rhytidophyllum Leatherleaf viburnum

Viburnum suspensum Viburnum

Trees

Acer griseum Paperbark maple

Acer japonicum Japanese maple

Acer palmatum Coralbark maple

Acer palmatum Japanese maple

Acer saccharum Sugar maple

Betula nigra River birch

Butia capitata Pindo palm

Cedrus atlantica Blue atlas cedar

Cercidiphyllum japonicum Katsura

Cornus florida Flowering dogwood

Cornus kousa Kousa dogwood

Fagus sylvatica European beech

Magnolia virginiana Sweetbay magnolia

Myrica cerifera Wax myrtle

Picea pungens Colorado spruce

Prunus subhirtella Higan cherry

Stewartia pseudocamellia Japanese stewartia

Styrax japonicus Japanese snowbell

G Xeriscaping

Xeriscaping is a practice that utilizes native plants and proper planning to conserve water and maintenance costs in the landscape. "Xeros" is Greek for *dry* and "scape" means *view* or *scene,* which equates to drought-tolerant plants in the landscape. This approach to landscape design is critical in arid regions, such as the Southwest, where restrictions on water use limit irrigation. Elements of xeriscaping include proper design, limited turf areas, mulching, efficient irrigation practices, and proper landscape management.

Proper Design

As this book has stressed, thoughtful planning and design will make the landscape useful as well as practical for the homeowner. Identifying microclimates and selecting appropriate plants will limit problems and maintenance requirements. In particular, using plants adapted to dry conditions will require less water.

Turf Areas

In arid regions where xeriscaping is much more common, it is easy to notice limited, if any, turf areas. They are often smaller turf panels surrounded by large planting beds often mulched with rock that does not need to be replenished. This reduces irrigation since turf often requires more water than many trees and shrubs that have deeper root systems.

Mulch

Mulch is an integral component of the landscape around trees, shrubs, and ground cover. As discussed in the "Plants and Hardscapes" chapter, it conserves water by reducing the amount of evaporation from the soil surface. It keeps the soil cooler by protecting it from the direct sunlight. It also reduces weeds that would otherwise grow on exposed soil and compete with landscape plants.

Irrigation

Good irrigation design is more efficient at delivering water to the plants and reducing waste. Poor irrigation design often applies water to sidewalks, parking lots, and other areas outside of the target plants. As a result, more water is used to get the proper amount to the plants.

Whenever possible, *drip irrigation* is very efficient at delivering water to the root systems of plants in beds. There is little water loss to evaporation since it is dripped through emitters at the base of each plant. Also, no water is applied outside the root zone between plants where weeds would grow.

Proper Management

Although landscape design may have less of an impact on maintenance, analyzing and recommending proper preparation of the soil should preclude design recommendations. Improve the soil by first having a soil test to study the pH and nutrients and then adding organic matter to improve the structure and adding other amendments as recommended by the soil test.

Other management practices, such as fertilization, pruning, and pest control, will be minimized if proper planning and design are done. Good plant selection and placement will reduce the need for pruning, allowing the plants to fill in the area. There should also be few pest problems if the plants are adapted to the region as well as the microclimate.

With fewer clippings from mowing and pruning there is less waste that will end up in the landfill. Proper design will also reduce the number of inputs used to maintain the landscape.

H Design Projects

Tobias Preliminaries

Tobias Master Plan

Depatie Preliminaries

Depatie Master Plan

Kerwin Preliminaries

Kerwin Master Plan

Garrison Preliminaries

Garrison Master Plan

Blunt Preliminaries

Blunt Master Plan

Biedler Preliminaries

Biedler Master Plan

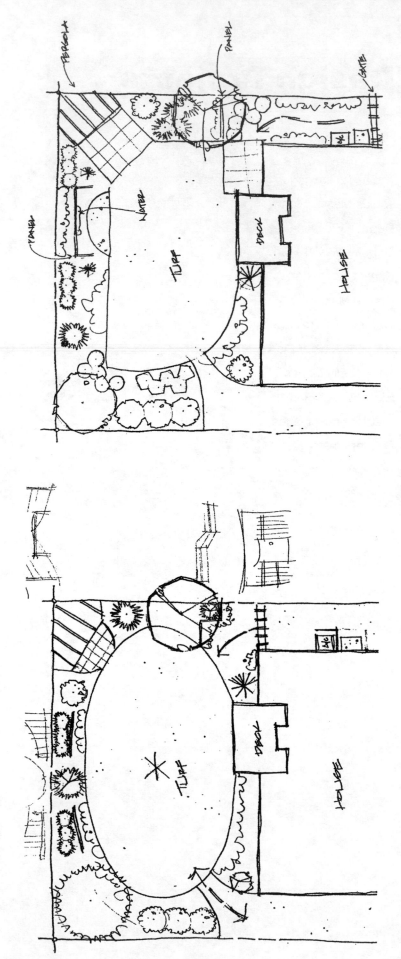

Tobias Preliminaries

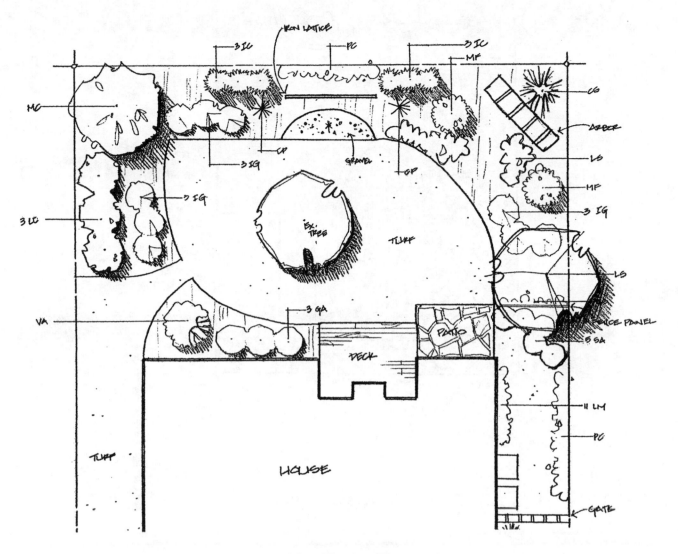

Tobias Master Plan

397

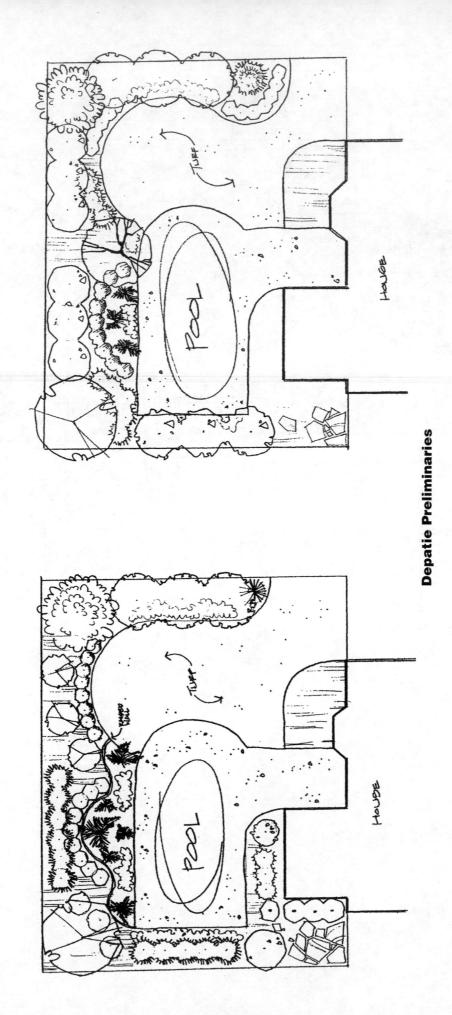

Depatie Preliminaries

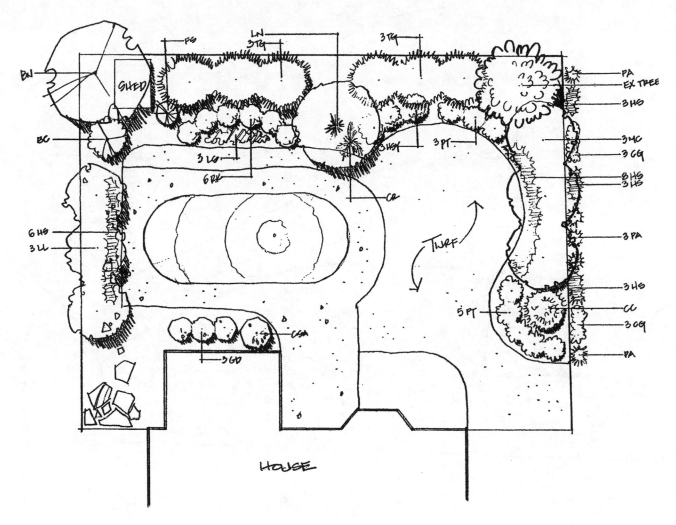

Depatie Master Plan

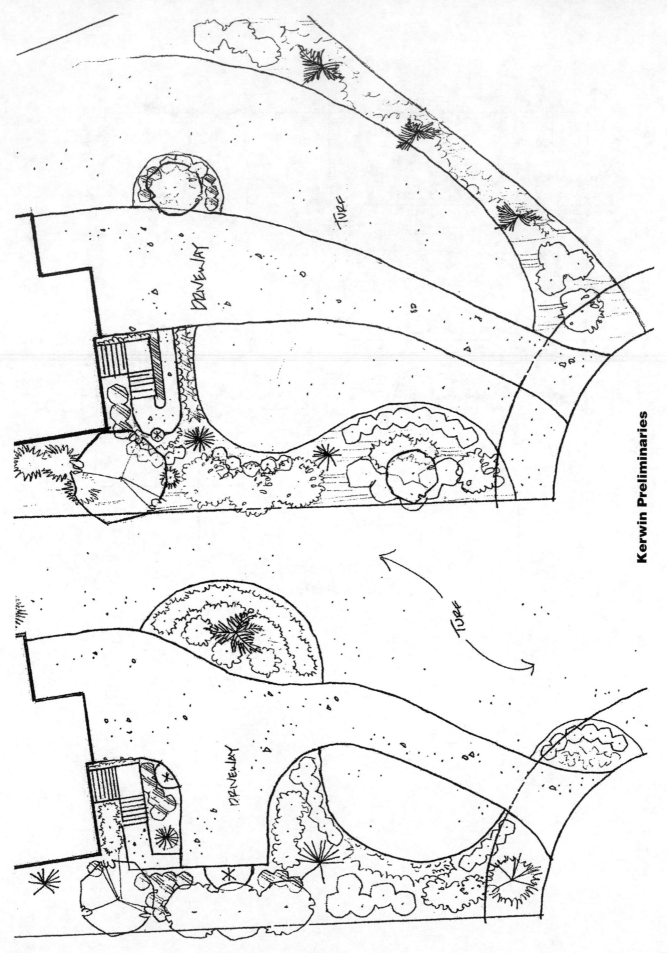

TURF

DRIVEWAY

TURF

DRIVEWAY

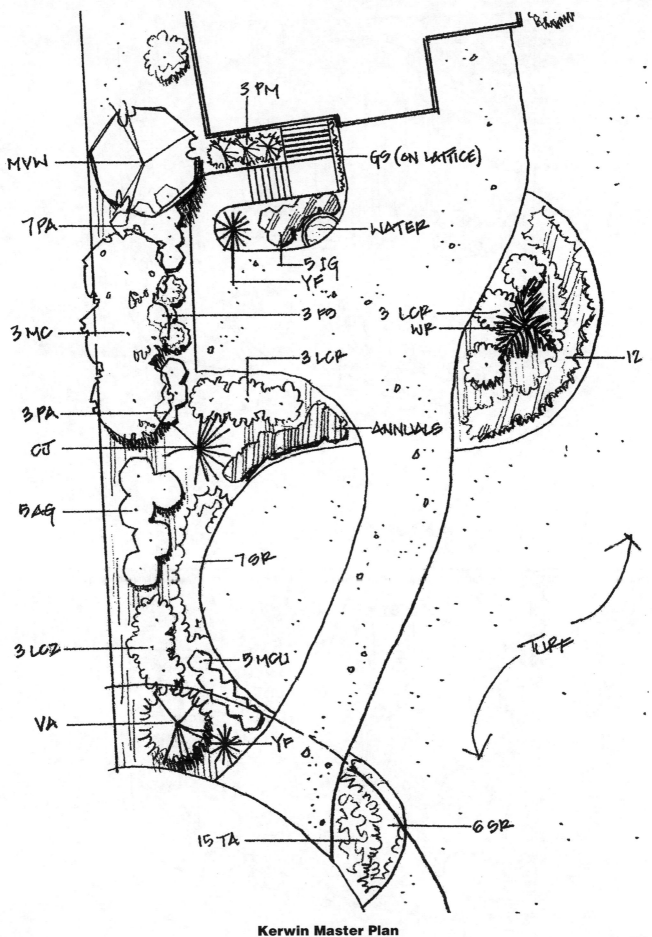

Kerwin Master Plan

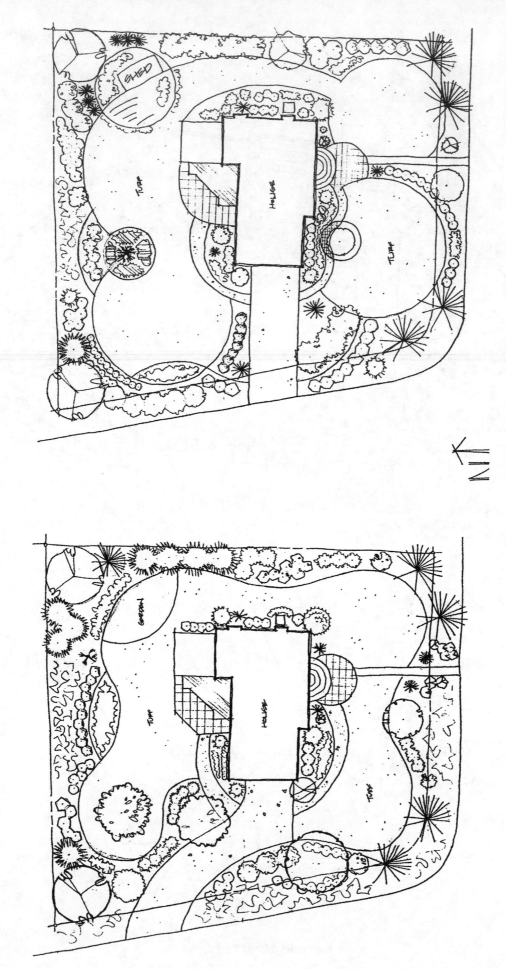

Garrison Preliminaries

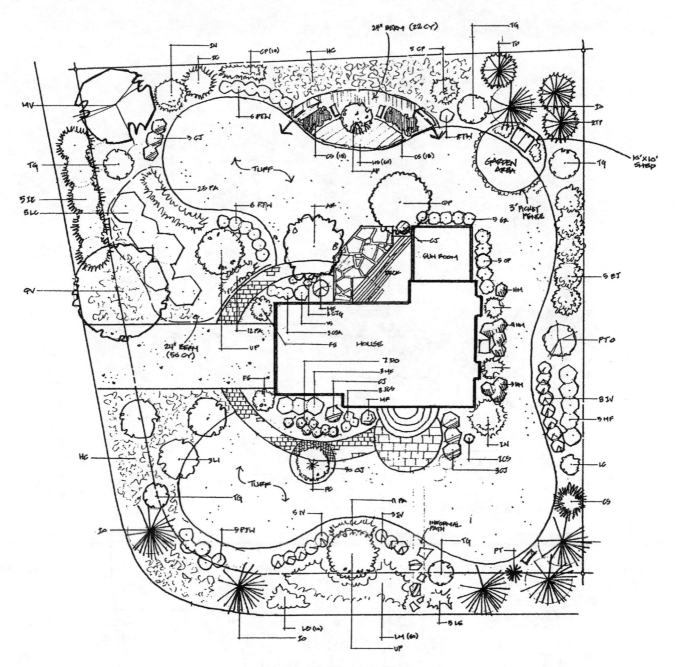

Garrison Master Plan

Blunt Preliminaries

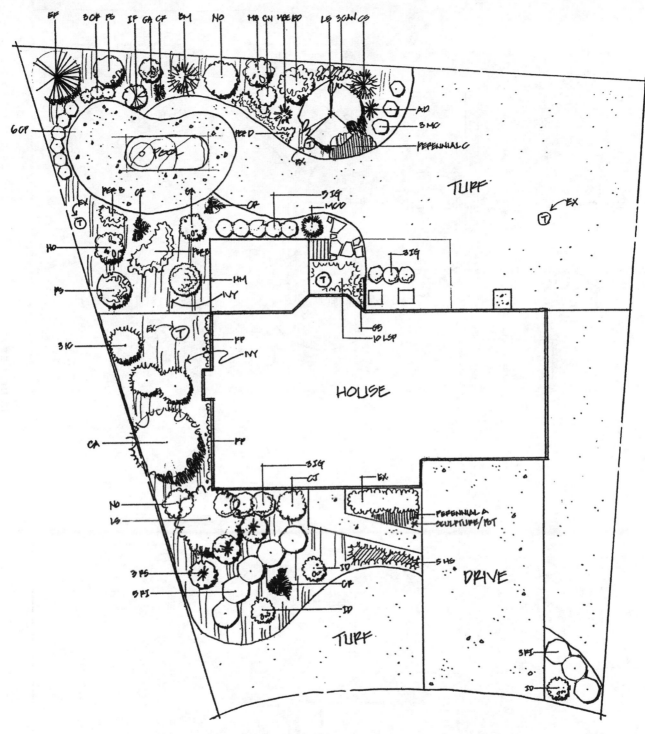

Blunt Master Plan

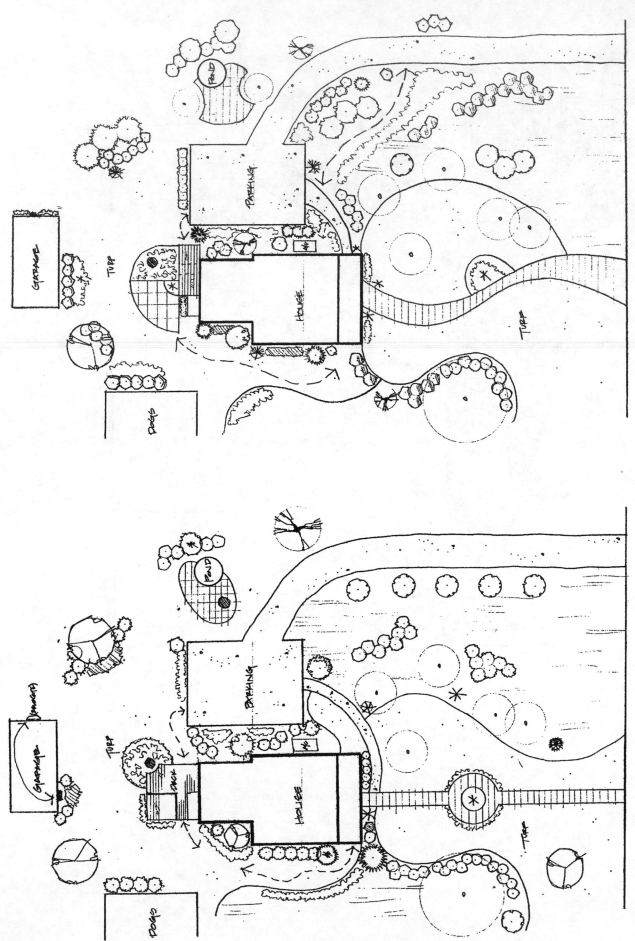

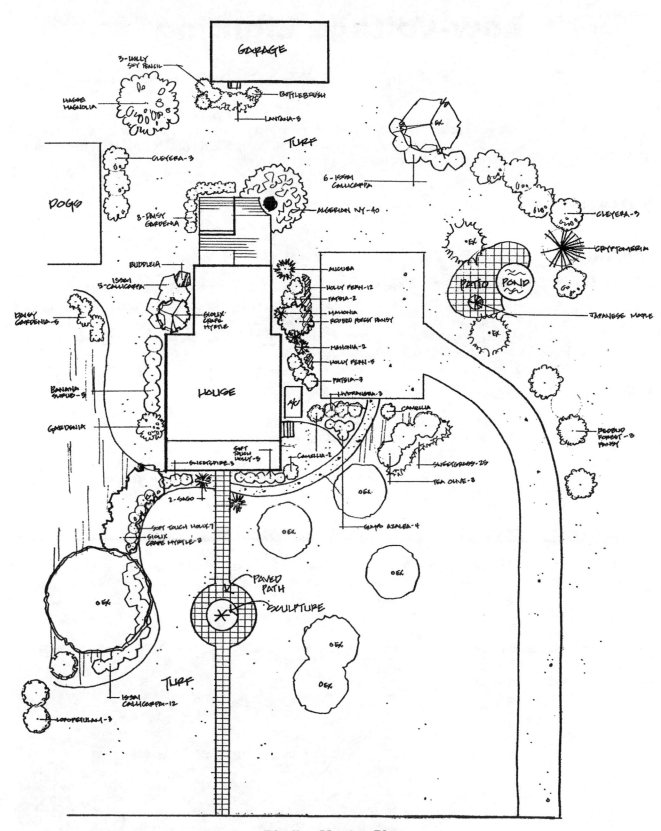

Biedler Master Plan

I | Low-Voltage Lighting

Low-voltage lighting is safe and simple to install. A contractor does not need to be a licensed electrician to handle 12 volts. The components of the lighting system include power, fixtures, and cable.

Power

Voltage

Voltage is the force that "pushes" electrons through an electrical conductor. It is measured in **volts.** Depending on where you live in the United States, outlet voltage in your home is 110 V to 120 V. Licensed electricians are trained to handle this dangerous voltage level. Landscape lighting, often referred to as low-voltage lighting, powers lights with 12 V, a very safe voltage level.

Current

Current is a measure of the intensity (number of electrons) being pushed through an electrical conductor. It is referred to as **current flow** and measured in units called **amps**.

The severity of electrical shock is dependant on the amount of current flowing. In the case of a household appliance, when too much current flows too quickly (too many amps) the appliance could be fried or, worse, start an electrical fire.

In the house, circuit overloading is prevented by a **circuit breaker** (Fig. I–1). A typical **circuit** has a certain number of outlets. If too many electrical devices are connected to these outlets, too many amps will be drawn. To prevent this overload, a circuit breaker "trips" and shuts the electrical current off to prevent damage and danger. In some circuits, **fuses** are used instead of circuit breakers. Fuses open (burn out) when a set amount of amps are exceeded.

Figure I–1 Circuit Breakers
Homes are protected by circuit breakers that interrupt circuits to prevent electrical overloading.

Power

The combination of voltage and current in an electrical circuit determines the amount of power that is consumed. **Power** is measured in units called **watts** and results in heat being generated.

A typical household lamp uses a 60-watt bulb (Fig. I–2). Landscape lighting fixtures utilize bulbs in the range of (but not limited to) 10 watts to 50 watts. **Wattage** is a measure of the heat that is produced, not light. Light output is measured in units called **lumens**.

Ambient light refers to the light from other sources, such as street lamps (Fig. I–3). In a backyard with no ambient light, a 10-watt bulb will provide plenty of light to illuminate a small tree. However, in the front yard with street lights, 20-, 30-, or 50-watt bulbs might be needed to get the same effect.

***Figure I–2* Incandescent Bulbs**
Typical bulbs used in the household are incandescent bulbs.

***Figure I–3* Ambient Light**
Because of the high amount of ambient light from the street light, the uplights around the tree have high-wattage bulbs to get a lighting effect.

Resistance

As current flows through a conductive material, such as copper wire, it meets **resistance** (opposition to current flow) which causes power to be consumed in the form of heat, due to this power loss. Wires can feel warm, even hot, due to resistance. If the circuit breaker is working, the wires will not heat up enough to cause a fire.

Resistance is measured in units called **ohms.** As resistance increases, voltage is used. This is referred to as **voltage drop.** For instance, the available voltage may be 12 V, but the voltage dropped by the resistance of the wire may cause only 10 V to reach the light. Two volts were used by the resistance of the wire. Heat buildup in a wire depends on the amount of current flowing through the wire and the resistance of the wire. Resistance of the wire is determined by its size. The bigger the wire, the less resistance and the smaller the wire, the more resistance.

The Water Analogy

For some people, imagining the flow of electrons is difficult. Water functions in a similar way to electricity, so here's an analogy to help understand electricity.

The car needs to be washed. A garden hose is attached to the water spigot. The nozzle attached to the end of the hose is shut off. The spigot is turned on. Water pressure (voltage) is present in the hose, but water (electrons) does not move through the end of the hose (current) because the nozzle is shut off (maximum resistance). No work (power) is done while the nozzle is shut off.

When the nozzle is opened, water (electrons) is pushed through the hose by water pressure (voltage). The amount of water flowing (current) through the hose is limited by the internal diameter of the hose (cross-sectional area of a wire), kinks in the hose (resistance), and how much the nozzle is opened (also resistance). To increase the water flow (current), a bigger hose could be used (larger wire), the kinks removed, or the nozzle opened more. The amount of soapy suds rinsed from the car (power, or work accomplished) is proportional to all these factors.

Lamps

Incandescent Lights

An **incandescent bulb** is the common light found in most households. Electricity flows through a filament, creating heat and light. In fact, approximately 90 percent of the energy flowing through the filament is converted to heat and only 10 percent is light. However, incandescent bulbs are rapidly giving way to energy-efficient fluorescent bulbs that are more expensive but longer lasting.

Most low-voltage systems utilize **halogen bulbs** (Fig. I–4). Incandescent bulbs are threaded into the fixture while halogen bulbs have two pegs at the base. Halogen bulbs are more energy efficient than incandescent bulbs. Incandescent bulbs tend to cast a yellowish light, whereas halogen lights illuminate truer colors. Both bulbs contain a filament that glows when electricity flows through it, creating heat and light. Halogen bulbs contain halogen that prevents the bulb from dimming and maintains good light quality.

Figure I–4 **Halogen and Incandescent Bulbs**

Halogen bulbs (left) have two prongs that plug into a fixture; incandescent bulbs (right) screw into a fixture.

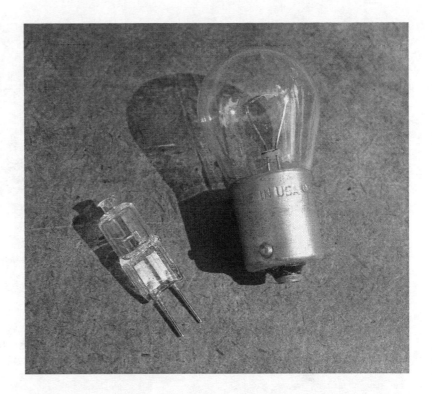

Tip Box

Do Not Touch Halogen Bulbs

When replacing halogen bulbs, do not touch them with your bare fingers. Use a clean rag. The oil from your skin can shorten the life of the bulb.

Fluorescent Lights

Some systems utilize **fluorescent light bulbs.** These are extremely efficient light sources that provide light when an electrical arc crosses the bulb and excites gases to emit light. Fluorescent bulbs require a **ballast** to boost the electrical arc across the bulb. Compact fluorescent bulbs are available for landscape lighting, but, currently, are not as common as halogen. Fluorescent bulbs can be temperamental in operation and are not generally recommended in areas where the temperature drops below 0 degrees Fahrenheit.

Solar Lights

Solar-powered lights capture the sun's energy with solar panels and store the power to light the bulbs at night (Fig. I–5). Miniature solar panels may be on the light fixture or separately connected to the fixtures via wire.

Although these fixtures cost nothing to power, many of the inexpensive solar landscape lights available to the homeowner are often little more than a bluish glow that provides little in the way of illumination. As solar technology improves, quality solar lights will become more common in the landscape.

Figure I–5 Solar Lights
Solar panels, built into the fixture or separate from fixtures (as shown), capture light and convert it to energy to power lights.

LED Lights

Solar lights utilize **LEDs** (light-emitting diodes). LEDs will become more commonplace in the lighting industry, and not just as solar light but electrical as well. Unlike incandescent and fluorescent bulbs, LEDs emit light without heat. LEDs are extremely efficient, converting approximately 90 percent energy to light. In comparison to incandescent bulbs that convert only 10 percent to light, that's a significant difference. LEDs can be expected to light for 50,000 hours before replacing. That's approximately 20 times more than incandescent bulbs.

Fixtures

The shape, design, and placement of fixtures determine how the light bulb distributes light. Choosing a fixture depends on the desired lighting effect.

Directional Fixtures

Directional fixtures, or **spotlight fixtures,** direct light as a beam (Fig. I–6). They are typically used in uplighting, downlighting, and silhouetting. Uplighting fixtures are staked into the ground, whereas downlighting fixtures are anchored with stainless steel fasteners or strapped to a tree limb or structure.

Tip Box
Hide the Light Source

Good lighting design hides the light fixture so that the light source cannot be seen. This way, only the lighting effect is seen and not the bright source. Fixtures can be hidden behind shrubs, posts, or walls.

(a)

(b)

(c)

***Figure I–6* Directional Fixtures**

(a) Uplights are typically staked in the ground to direct a beam of light upward. (b) Downlights will be used to illuminate this sitting area. (c) This downlight is attached to the pergola and blends into the vines.

***Figure I–7* Flood Fixture**

Illuminates a large area.

Flood Fixtures

Floodlights disperse light over a wide area (Fig. I–7). In landscape lighting, this is commonly used to silhouette a tree by flooding a wall behind it. Floodlights are mostly seen as security lights, illuminating the yard.

Figure I–8 **Path Fixture**
Typically a decorative fixture not meant to be hidden, path fixtures direct a spot of light on the ground.

Figure I–9 **Spread Fixture**
Like path fixtures, spread fixtures are often decorative. They disperse light over a larger area than path fixtures.

Path and Area Fixtures

Whereas the source of a directional fixture is hidden from sight, **path** (Fig. I–8) and **area** (Fig. I–9) fixtures are intended to be seen. The inexpensive homeowner varieties are plastic lanterns, but commercial variations are metal or copper. Commercial fixtures range in cost but are much sturdier.

Tip Box

Colored or Diffused Lens

To change the mood, a colored lens can be fit into the fixture. Pale blue or green is effective when downlighting to simulate moonlight. Also, in some cases a directional fixture spotlights too harshly. A diffusing lens can be used to soften the light. A dremel tool can be used to scuff the lens to soften the light quality.

Step and Deck Fixtures

Step and **deck fixtures** are small and built into steps or railings. They accommodate low-wattage bulbs and are meant to safely illuminate the steps or accent parts of the deck.

Figure I–10 **Well-light**
This fixture is installed on the ground for uplighting.

In-ground Fixtures

Fixtures installed at ground level, such as **well-lights** (Fig. I–10), create a unique up-lighting effect but can be high maintenance. Be sure drainage is adequate so that the fixture does not fill with water. In the South, fire ants love a heat source in the winter and will quickly cover the fixture with a mound.

Underwater Fixtures

Be sure to use high-quality **underwater fixtures** that have dependable seals. Once water leaks into the fixture, it will fail.

Power Console

A **transformer** is the power source (Fig. I–11). Low-voltage lighting operates on 12 V. If you plugged low-voltage lights directly into an outlet (110/120 V), it would be too much voltage. Therefore, a transformer steps the voltage down from 110/120 V to 12 V.

The transformer is often a black box plugged into an alternating current (AC) outlet. This outlet must be a ground fault circuit interrupter (GFCI) when installed outside. Cable (discussed in the next section) is connected to the transformer and carries the 12 volts to the lights.

In order for lights to work, current needs to flow through them (Fig. I–12). Think in terms of a waterwheel. The flow of water turns the wheel. Therefore, in order to power the lights, the first wire (called the **hot wire** or **power wire**) carries the current to the lights and a second wire (called the **common wire**) returns the current to the transformer. Together, these two wires and the lights are referred to as a **single circuit.**

Figure I–11 **Transformer**

The black box is a transformer plugged into a GFCI outlet (with protective outdoor cover removed). The 120 V coming from the outlet will be stepped down to 12 V and distributed to light fixtures.

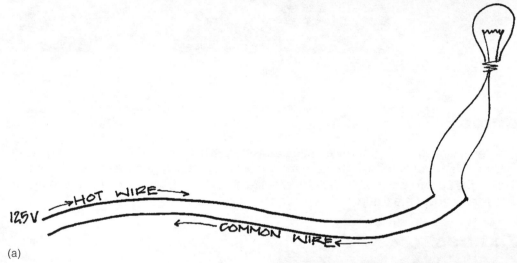

(a)

Figure I–12 **Single Circuit**

(a) An electrical circuit has two wires. The hot wire carries current from the transformer and the common wire returns it so that a continuous flow lights the bulbs. (b) One wire sends 12.5 V (hot) through the lightbulb and back down the other wire (common).

(b)

Small transformers will have two terminals to attach cable to a single circuit. One terminal is hot and the other is the common wire. The 12 volts push the current out the hot terminal, which then travels through the light bulb and returns through the common wire to the transformer.

> ### *Tip Box*
> ### Outdoor Outlet
>
> An outdoor outlet is required to be a **ground fault circuit interrupter (GFCI).** Additionally, it must be installed in a weatherproof box with a cover to prevent rain from tripping the circuit. The transformer should be installed at least 1 foot above the ground. Also, avoid placement near irrigation.

Size

Transformers are sized based on their total wattage capacity. The greater the transformer's wattage capacity, the more expensive it is. It behooves the designer to size the transformer correctly to save money and run the lights effectively.

> ### *Tip Box*
> ### Transformer Wattage Capacity
>
> Transformers are typically used with wattage capacities of 300 W, 600 W, 900 W, or 1200 W.

To properly size the transformer, add the wattage of all the lights to be connected to the transformer. The transformer capacity needs to exceed the total wattage of the light system. Ideally, the total wattage demand should be approximately 60 to 80 percent of the transformer capacity to allow for future expansion and allow the transformer to run cooler and more efficiently. For instance, if the total wattage of all the lights is 240 watts, a 300-watt transformer should be used.

> ### *Tip Box*
> ### Transformer Selection
>
> Add the wattage of all the lights in the system. This total should not exceed 60 to 80 percent of the transformer capacity.

Multitap Transformers

Larger capacity transformers have more than one circuit to connect wires (Fig. I–13). Often, there is one common terminal and multiple hot terminals. All the cables will share the same common terminal. For instance, a 300-watt transformer may have two hot terminals, each with a capacity of 150 watts.

***Figure I-13* Transformer Size and Terminals**
This transformer has a capacity of 300 watts. The 300 watts are divided among two circuits: two hot terminals of 150 watts each. No matter how many hot terminals, only one common terminal is needed to return the current from all hot wires.

Multivoltage Transformers

Some transformers have higher voltage terminals to account for voltage drop caused by wire resistance (Fig. I–14). Low-voltage lights should ideally run between 10.5 V to 12 V. Long cable runs can have significant voltage drop. Multivoltage terminals may provide more than 12 V at the source, such as 13 V, 14 V, or more. This allows voltage drop to be taken into account so that 12 V is delivered to the lights.

***Figure I-14* Multivoltage Transformer**
Some transformers have multiple terminals with higher voltage output to allow for voltage drop on long cables. In this example, there are 6 terminals, an 11-volt, two 12-volt, one 13-volt, one 14-volt, and one 15-volt along with two common terminals.

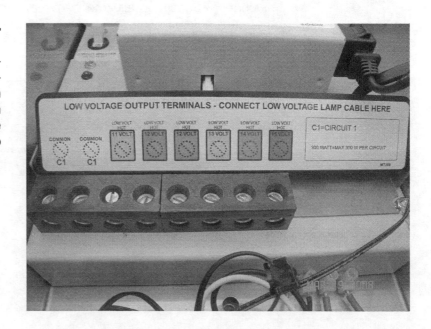

Timer

Most transformers have a **timer** to turn lights on and off (Fig. I–15). Basic transformers utilize a simple gear clock and pins to set the on and off times. The disadvantage is that the starting times have to be adjusted during the year to account for day length.

Light Sensor

Some transformers are equipped with a **light sensor** to turn lights on at dusk and off at dawn (Fig. I–16). The starting time self-adjusts and saves energy. However, unless the light sensor can be overridden, sensor failure will require replacement.

Figure I–15 **Timers**
Transformers have timers to turn lights on and off.

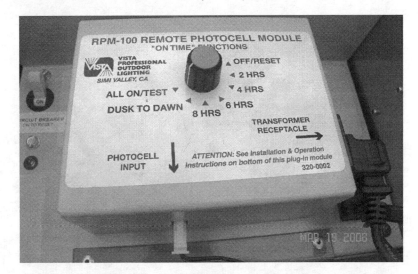

Figure I–16 **Light Sensor**
A sensor can be used to turn the lights on and off instead of a timer.

Cable

Lighting **cable** consists of two multistrand copper wires insulated inside black, sunlight-resistant PVC plastic (Fig. I–17). Most lighting contractors use single-circuit cable: two separate insulated conductors attached together into one cable. Installation is easier with one cable instead of two separate conductors.

Tip Box

Hiding Cable

Low-voltage cable can be covered with mulch. Slit-trenching lawns with a spade, wedging open a trench, can be done to get cable at least 6 inches deep (Fig. I–18). If cable can be installed deeper, it will reduce the risk of it being cut.

Figure I–17 Landscape Cable
Two separate wires are bound together for a single circuit.

Figure I–18 Slit-trenching Wire
Using a spade or shovel, a V-shaped trench can be cut into the turf to get cable below ground.

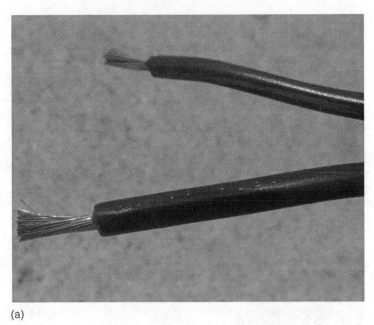

(a)

Figure I-19 American Wire Gauge (AWG)
(a) Wire cross-sectional area is measured by gauge. Multistrand copper is encased by UV-resistant insulation; (b) the larger the AWG, the smaller the wire.

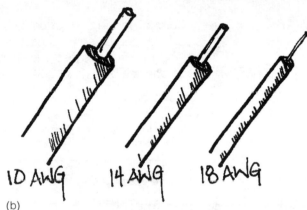

(b)

Size

Cable cross-sectional area is measured by gauge, or **AWG (American Wire Gauge)** (Fig. I-19). The smaller the number, the larger the wire. Using correct wire size is important to save money and to properly run the lights. Larger wire is more expensive, so it's important to use wire as small as possible without causing excessive voltage drop.

Tip Box

Typical Residential Wire Size

Many residential landscape lighting systems will use 12 AWG or 14 AWG wire.

When cable is too small, voltage drop increases due to increased resistance (Fig. I-20). The amount of voltage loss depends on the length and cross-sectional area of the wire.

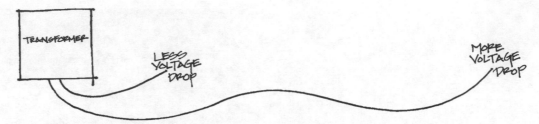

***Figure I–20* Voltage Drop**
Long cables have more resistance and drop more voltage by the end.

Wire length The longer the wire, the higher the resistance, which increases voltage drop.

Wire gauge The smaller the wire (cross-sectional area), the higher the resistance, which increases voltage drop.

Voltage Drop

To choose the correct cable size, or AWG, calculate how many volts each cable size would drop given the length and gauge of the wire and the total watts. Because smaller gauge wire costs less, it is often desirable to specify the smallest cable that allows lights to operate between 10.5 V to 12 V.

On a basic transformer, which has an output of 12 V, the maximum allowable voltage drop would be 1.5 V so that at least 10.5 V are available at the lights. Specify the smallest wire that loses no more than 1.5 V.

Tip Box
Wire Sizing

Low-voltage lights should operate between 10.5 V and 12 V. Use the smallest size cable that delivers at least 10.5 V to save money on wire.

Some contractors run larger wire out to the lights to minimize voltage drop in order to use a smaller wire to run up a post or tree.

Another approach to minimize cable size is to use a high-voltage tap (see multivoltage taps on page 392). If the transformer tap puts out 14 V instead of 12 V, then a voltage drop of 3.5 V still delivers 10.5 V to the lights.

There are various methods that estimate voltage drop in landscape lighting (Fig. I–21). An accurate way is to calculate each section of cable between light fixtures and add the losses for total voltage drop.

Calculating Voltage Drop

1. Measure the length of the section of wire.
2. Add the watts of all the bulbs beyond that section of wire.
3. Calculate the voltage drop using the formula in Fig. I–22.
4. Subtract the voltage drop from the voltage at the beginning of the section of wire.

14-GAUGE WIRE

Calculate voltage drop of each section of wire

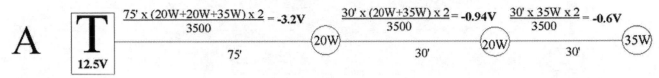

A [T 12.5V] $\dfrac{75' \times (20W+20W+35W) \times 2}{3500} = -3.2V$ 20W $\dfrac{30' \times (20W+35W) \times 2}{3500} = -0.94V$ 20W $\dfrac{30' \times 35W \times 2}{3500} = -0.6V$ 35W

75'   30'   30'

Subtract voltage losses starting at the transformer (12.5V)

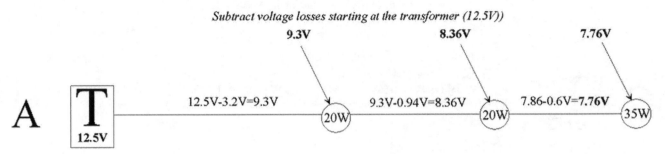

9.3V   **8.36V**   **7.76V**

A [T 12.5V]   12.5V-3.2V=9.3V   20W   9.3V-0.94V=8.36V   20W   7.86-0.6V=7.76V   35W

The last light is receiving 7.76V

(a)

12-GAUGE WIRE

Calculate voltage drop of each section of wire

B [T 12.5V] $\dfrac{75' \times (20W+20W+35W) \times 2}{7500} = -1.5V$ 20W $\dfrac{30' \times (20W+35W) \times 2}{7500} = -0.44V$ 20W $\dfrac{30' \times 35W \times 2}{7500} = -0.28V$ 35W

75'   30'   30'

Subtract voltage losses starting at the transformer (12.5V)

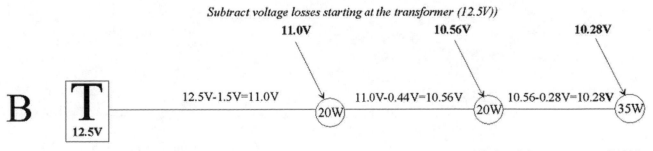

11.0V   **10.56V**   **10.28V**

B [T 12.5V]   12.5V-1.5V=11.0V   20W   11.0V-0.44V=10.56V   20W   10.56-0.28V=10.28V   35W

The last light is receiving 10.28V

(b)

Figure I–21 **Voltage Drop Examples**

(continues)

10-GAUGE WIRE

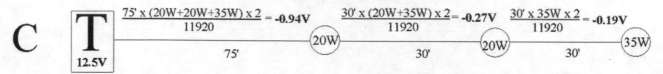

Calculate voltage drop of each section of wire

C   T
12.5V

$$\frac{75' \times (20W+20W+35W) \times 2}{11920} = -0.94V$$ 20W $$\frac{30' \times (20W+35W) \times 2}{11920} = -0.27V$$ 20W $$\frac{30' \times 35W \times 2}{11920} = -0.19V$$ 35W

75'   30'   30'

Subtract voltage losses starting at the transformer (12.5V)

11.56V   **11.29V**   **11.1V**

C   T
12.5V

12.5V-0.94V=11.56V   20W   11.29V-0.27V=11.29V   20W   10.79-0.19V=11.1V   35W

The last light is receiving 11.1V

(c)

12-GAUGE WIRE

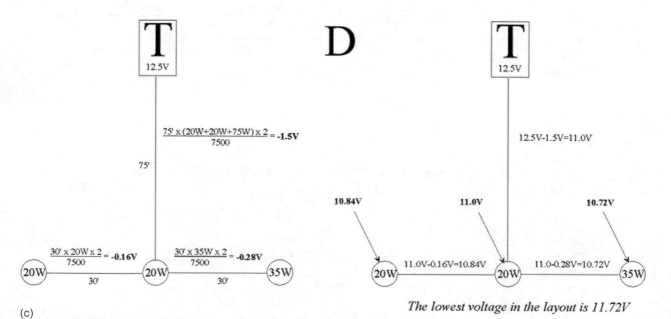

Calculate voltage drop of each section of wire   *Subtract voltage losses starting at the transformer (12.5V)*

T
12.5V

D   T
12.5V

$$\frac{75' \times (20W+20W+75W) \times 2}{7500} = -1.5V$$

75'

12.5V-1.5V=11.0V

10.84V   11.0V   10.72V

$$\frac{30' \times 20W \times 2}{7500} = -0.16V$$ $$\frac{30' \times 35W \times 2}{7500} = -0.28V$$

20W   20W   35W

30'   30'

20W   11.0V-0.16V=10.84V   20W   11.0-0.28V=10.72V   35W

(c)

The lowest voltage in the layout is 11.72V

Figure I–21 **Voltage Drop Examples—continued**

```
VOLTAGE DROP FORMULA AND CONSTANTS

              Wattage X Length X 2
              ─────────────────────
                 Cable constant

Wattage: total watts of all light bulbs beyond section of wire
Length: length of wire in section (between light fixures)
2: accounts for two wires in a single circuit
Cable constants: accounts for various wire sizes
```

Wire Size	Cable constants
#18	1380
#16	2200
#14	3500
#12	7500
#10	11920
#8	18960

Figure I–22 **Voltage Drop Formula and Constants**

Example A

Example A has a transformer with an output of 12.5 volts. It has three lights using a 14-gauge cable (14/2).

First section

The first section is 75′ long. The first section will carry voltage to two 20-watt bulbs and one 35-watt bulb. Therefore, the first section will be servicing a total of 75 watts (the sum of the three bulbs).

1. 75′ long
2. 75 watts (20 W + 20 W + 35 W)
3. 75′ × 75 watts × 2/3500 (cable constant of 14 AWG) = 3.2 volts
4. 12.5 volts (transformer) − 3.2 volts = 9.3 volts

Second section

The second section is 30′ long to a 20-watt bulb and a 35-watt bulb.

1. 30′ long
2. 55 watts (20 W + 35 W)
3. 30′ × 55 watts × 2/3500 = 0.94 volts
4. 9.3 volts (after first section) − 0.94 volts = 8.36 volts

Third section

The third section is 30′ long to a 35-watt light bulb.

1. 30′ long
2. 35 watts
3. 30′ × 35 watts × 2/3500 = 0.60 volts
4. 8.36 volts (after second section) − 0.60 volts = 7.76 volts

In this example, all three lights are running below the minimum 10.5 volts. There are many methods that reduce voltage drop, but let's examine the impact of wire size. Take a look at example B where 12-gauge wire is used.

Example B

First section

1. 75' long
2. 75 watts (20 W + 20 W + 35 W)
3. 75' × 75 watts × 2/7500 (cable constant of 12 AWG) = 1.5 volts
4. 12.5 volts (transformer) − 1.5 volts = 11.0 volts

Second section

1. 30' long
2. 55 watts (20 W + 35 W)
3. 30' × 55 watts × 2/7500 = 0.44 volts
4. 11.0 volts (after first section) − 0.44 volts = 10.56 volts

Third section

The third section is 30' long to a 35-watt light bulb.

1. 30' long
2. 35 watts
3. 30' × 35 watts × 2/7500 = 0.28 volts
4. 10.56 volts (after second section) − 0.28 volts = 10.28 volts

In this example, 12-gauge wire reduces the voltage drop so that the first two lights run above the minimum 10.5 V, but the last light is only receiving 10.28 V. Go to example C to see how a larger wire (10 AWG) will affect voltage drop.

Example C

First section

1. 75' long
2. 75 watts (20 W + 20 W + 35 W)
3. 75' × 75 watts × 2/11,920 (cable constant of 10 AWG) = 0.94 volts
4. 12.5 volts (transformer) − 0.94 volts = 11.56 volts

Second section

1. 30' long
2. 55 watts (20 W + 35 W)
3. 30' × 55 watts × 2/11,920 = 0.27 volts
4. 11.56 volts (after first section) − 0.27 volts = 11.29 volts

Third section

1. 30' long
2. 35 watts
3. 30' × 35 watts × 2/11,920 = 0.19 volts
4. 11.29 volts (after second section) − 0.19 volts = 11.1 volts

In this example, 10-gauge wire minimized the voltage drop so that all three lights are running above 10.5 V. This is one example of a successful lighting design by correctly sizing the wire. However, larger wire is more expensive. There are other methods to minimize the voltage drop (as you'll see in the next section), but go to example D to see how 12 AWG wire could be used if the layout is changed from a straight line to a T-shaped configuration.

Example D

First section

The first section does not change because it is the same length and still carries enough voltage to run all three lights.

1. 75′ long
2. 75 watts (20 W + 20 W + 35 W)
3. 75′ × 75 watts × 2/7500 (cable constant of 12 AWG) = 1.5 volts
4. 12.5 volts (transformer) − 1.5 volts = 11.0 volts

Second section

However, after the first section, the circuit splits in two directions. This minimizes the total load on the second section. Since there is only a 20-watt demand on the second section (instead of 55 watts), we can expect less voltage drop.

1. 30′ long
2. 20 watts
3. 30′ × 20 watts × 2/7500 = 0.16 volts
4. 11.0 volts (after first section) − 0.16 volts = 10.84 volts

Third section

The voltage drop in the third section will remain the same as the straight layout because the length and wattage do not change. However, notice that voltage drop is not compounded by the second section, which is no longer between the first and third section.

1. 30′ long
2. 35 watts
3. 30′ × 35 watts × 2/7500 = 0.28 volts
4. 11.0 volts (after second section) − 0.28 volts = 10.72 volts

All three lights are now running above the minimum 10.5 V. The cost of the system is reduced by using 12 AWG instead of 10 AWG without compromising the lighting.

Minimizing Voltage Drop

There are several design techniques to reduce voltage drop.

Center Transformer

Centrally locating the transformer will shorten the length of cable. Consider a smaller transformer in the front yard and another one in the backyard rather than one large transformer for both. Smaller transformers will run more efficiently and you'll save money using smaller wire.

Reduce Wattage

Consider using lower wattage bulbs when possible to reduce the load demand placed on the transformer.

Shorten Wire Length

Using several shorter circuits rather than one long circuit will allow you to use smaller wire (save money) and reduce voltage drop.

Multivoltage Taps

Specifying higher voltage transformers allows for more wire voltage drop. For instance, if the transformer terminal has an output of 14 V, 3.5 V could be dropped by the cable.

Connecting Cable

The cable acts like a main line of power (Fig. I–23). The lights can be set in the ground and connected to the cable. Two cables are required for a complete circuit. One cable carries the voltage from the transformer (hot) and the other will return it (common). The light has two short wires attached, often referred to as a **pigtail.** One wire in the pigtail can be connected to the hot wire coming from the transformer and the other to the common wire. It doesn't matter which wire from the light is connected to the hot wire. The voltage will travel through the bulb and back to the common wire.

There are two basic approaches to connecting cable to lights: quick connectors and splicing. With either approach, this connection needs to be waterproof. When copper wire is exposed to moisture, corrosion will reduce the electrical conductivity and could also allow the circuit to be ground-faulted, which will cause the circuit breaker and/or the GFCI outlet to trip.

Quick Connectors

Quick connectors cross-connect the main cable to the pigtail with copper prongs that pierce the insulation and penetrate the copper wire (Fig. I–24). Quick connectors are fast and easy to install and typically come with the fixture. However, many lighting contractors will not use quick connectors outdoors because they are not waterproof and can be faulty if the prongs don't squarely penetrate the copper wire.

Tip Box

Quick Connections Faulty

Quick connections are not as waterproof as grease/silicone-filled wire nuts and DBYs. Thus, they are prone to corrosion when exposed to moisture.

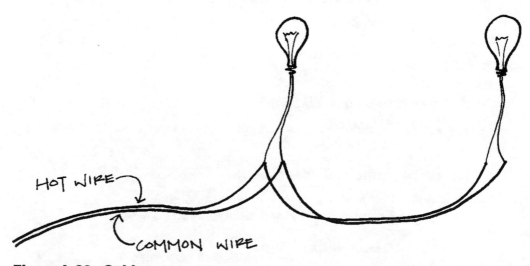

HOT WIRE

COMMON WIRE

Figure I–23 Cable
Each wire in the circuit, the hot and common, is cut and attached to a pigtail on the light.

(a)

(b)

***Figure I–24* Quick Connector**
One way to attach a light to cable is with a quick connector. (a) The copper spikes pierce and (b) cross-connect the light fixture to the power cable.

Splicing

Splicing cable is a more reliable and waterproof way of connecting lights to cable. To splice cable, about 1/4″ of insulation is stripped from the end of each cable to expose the copper wire. The bare copper wires of the transformer cable and light fixture cable are twisted in a clockwise direction with a wire nut until tight to ensure that they do not disconnect (Fig. I–25).

To waterproof this connection, the wire nut needs to be filled with silicone or submerged in a tube of grease. There are several products available. The simplest product is a silicone-filled **wire nut** (Fig. I–26). A popular product is a **Direct Burial tube,** commonly referred to as **DBY.** The *Y* refers to yellow, the color of the wire nut that is used to fit 12 and 14 AWG.

(a)

(b)

Figure I–25 **Splicing Cable**
(a) Strip black insulation from the end of each cable to expose the copper cable and twist in a clockwise direction. (b) Twist a wire nut over the splice until tight.

Figure I–26 **Wire Nuts**
For outdoor splices, the wire nut is filled with silicone to make it watertight.

***Figure I–27* Direct Burier Yellow (DBY)**
Another water-resistant splice is a DBY. Wires are connected with a wire nut (not silicone filled) and submerged into a tube of grease.

Troubleshooting

A **digital multimeter** or **analog volt-ohm-milliammeter** can measure voltage, resistance (ohms), and current (amps). Two simple tests to troubleshoot a low-voltage lighting system are a voltage test and a continuity (ohms) test.

Voltage Test

Voltmeters measure two types of current: direct current (DC) and alternating current (AC) (Fig. I–28). **Direct current** utilizes a positive and negative connection. A battery is the best example. **Alternating current** is found in the household. Low-voltage transformers use alternating current.

Set a voltmeter to measure the amount of AC volts. Be sure the voltmeter is set on AC and not DC. To measure voltage at the transformer, touch one probe to the common terminal and the other to the hot. This can be used to confirm the transformer is not only working but the correct amount of voltage is being produced.

To measure voltage in the cable, touch one probe to the hot wire and the other to the common. If the splice cannot be accessed, use the probes to pierce the insulation and contact the copper wire. This test can be used to verify power in the cable to indicate a break in the wire. It can also be used to measure the amount of voltage drop. If the wire is undersized, too much voltage will be dropped and bulbs will burn dim.

Continuity Test

A **continuous circuit** is a **closed circuit** that allows current to flow down the hot wire and return on the common wire. A continuity test verifies whether the circuit is closed or open.

Turn the multimeter to measure ohms (resistance). An inexpensive multimeter contains a battery that sends a small current through one of the probes and returns it to the multimeter down the other probe, thus measuring how much voltage was dropped due to resistance. Touch the probes together and the reading will be virtually zero because the current only travels to the end of one probe and back down the other probe. No significant drop of voltage is measured.

Figure I–28a **Digital Multimeter**
A digital multimeter is used to measure voltage, current, and resistance. The one in the illustration is set to measure alternating current.

Figure I–28b **Analog Multimeter**
An analog multimeter is used to measure voltage, current, and resistance. The one in the illustration is set to measure ohms (resistance).

As an example, squeeze each probe with each hand and see the needle barely move. A tremendous amount of resistance drops most of the voltage as it goes from one hand, through the body, to the other hand. Now wet your fingers and see if the needle moves differently. There should be slightly less resistance since moisture on the fingers reduces your overall body resistance.

A continuity test can be used to check for breaks in the wire and the filament of a bulb. At the transformer, touch a probe to the hot wire and the other to the common. There should be a small amount of resistance, if the cable is the correct size. More importantly, this tells you there is a continuous circuit; current is going out and returning.

Testing an incandescent bulb can tell you if the bulb(s) is defective and not the cable. On a halogen bulb, touch a probe to each prong. If the bulb's filament is intact, the current will go through the intact filament and back out the other prong to the voltmeter and read very little resistance. When a bulb burns out, the filament breaks and current cannot flow. Therefore, there will be no reading on the multimeter.

Key Terms

Alternating current: is found in the household. Low-voltage transformers use alternating current

Ambient light: refers to the light from other sources, such as street lamps

Amps: is the unit of measure of electrical current flow

Area fixtures: are low to the ground and disperse light much wider than path lights

AWG (American Wire Gauge): is the measure of the cross-sectional area of a wire

Ballast: boosts the electrical arc across the gas in a fluorescent bulb

Circuit: includes the components of a lighting system, circuit breaker, transformer, wire, outlets, and lights

Circuit breaker: prevents electrical wires from overheating due to current overloads

Closed circuit: is a continuous circuit when current flows through wire from the transformer out to the light fixture and back to the transformer

Common wire: returns the electricity from the light fixture to the transformer to complete the circuit

Current: is the flow of an electrical charge

Deck fixtures: used to illuminate steps or railings

Direct Burial tube (DBY): a tube filled with waterproof grease. The wire nut splice is sunk into the DBY to protect it from corrosion.

Direct current: utilizes a positive and negative connection. A battery is the best example.

Directional fixtures: direct light as a beam for uplighting, downlighting, and silhouetting (see spotlight fixtures)

Floodlights: disperse light over a wide area

Fluorescent bulbs: extremely efficient light sources that provide light when an electrical arc crosses the bulb and excites gases to emit light

Fuses: burn out when currents are exceeded to prevent damage to the wire and fixtures

Ground fault circuit interrupter (GFCI): is an outlet that protects people

Halogen bulbs: contain halogen that prevents the bulb from dimming and maintains good light quality

Hot wire (or power wire): carries the current to the light and a second wire (called the common wire) returns the current to the transformer. These two wires together are referred to as a **single circuit.**

Incandescent bulb: is a common light found in most households; electricity flows through a filament, creating heat and light

LED (light-emitting diode) light: emits light without heat

Light sensor: turns lights on instead of a timer

Lighting cable: consists of two multistrand copper wires insulated inside black, sunlight-resistant PVC plastic

Lumen: is the unit of measure of light output

Multimeter: measures voltage, resistance (ohms), and current (amps)

Multitap transformers: have more than one hot terminal

Multivoltage transformers: have terminals greater than 12 V to account for voltage drop

Ohm: is a unit of measurement for resistance

Path fixtures: illuminate paths and areas for walking

Pigtail: has two short wires attached to the light fixture

Quick connectors: cross-connect the main cable to the pigtail with copper prongs that pierce the insulation and penetrate the copper wire

Resistance: is opposition to current flow

Solar-powered lights: capture the sun's energy with solar panels and store the power to light the bulbs at night

Splicing: is cutting cable and connecting with wire nuts

Spotlight fixtures: are used for directional effects (see directional fixtures)

Step lights: are small fixtures used to illuminate steps

Timer: included on transformers to turn lights on and off

Transformer: is the power source that steps 120 V down to 12 V

Underwater fixtures: are used in ponds or pools below water

Volt: is the unit of measure of electrical force

Voltage: is the force of an electrical charge

Voltage drop: the voltage lost to resistance

Watt: is the unit of measure of power

Wattage: is referred to as power, the combination of voltage and current

Well-light fixtures: sit at ground level for uplighting

Wire nut: is a cap that twists wires together. Wire nuts filled with silicone are used outdoors to protect from corrosion.

Index

Accents, 198–201, 216
Access, 158, 159. *See also* Entry walk
Acid, 89–90, 100
Acid-loving plants, 90, 100
Activities, in concept plan, 152, 155
Additions, 334
Aggregate. *See* Exposed aggregate
Air-conditioning units, 70, 100, 137, 138
Alkaline, 89–90, 100
Alternate board fence. *See* Board-on-board fence
Alternate concepts, 163, 164–166
Alternating current (AC), 431, 433
Aluminum, for strip edging, 282
Ambient light, 409, 433
American Association of Nurserymen, 261
American Standard for Nursery Stock (ANSI Standards), 261, 299
American Wire Gauge (AWG), 421, 433
Amps, 408, 433
Analog volt-ohm-milliammeter, 431, 432
Analysis, 21, 62, 63
  circulation, 65–68
  clipboards, 62
  concept plan, 152, 154
  definition, 100
  design process example, 320–337
  drainage, 93, 95–96
  drawing, 97–99
  exposure, 75–78, 79
  house, 65, 66
  key terms, 100–101
  landform, 90–93, 94
  landscapes, existing, 82–83
  pets, hobbies, and other notables, 96–97
  presentation of, 320
  seasonal impact on light and temperature, 78, 80
  site survey, 62, 64
  soil, 84–90
  summary, 99
  utilities, 68–71
  views, 72–75
  wind, 81–82
Analysis graphics, 97–99
Appearance, professional, 2
Appointments, scheduling, 21
Architect scale, 29, 30, 60

Arc lines, 207, 208, 216
Area fixtures, 414, 433
Arrival, at interviews, 10
Asymmetrical balance, 184–185, 186, 216
Attributes. *See* Design attributes
AutoCAD, 224, 373

Back yard, 139
  entertainment, 139–145, 146
  recreation, 145, 147–148
Baited electric fences, 388
Balance, 180–181
  asymmetrical, 184–185, 186
  symmetrical, 181–184
Ballast, 411, 433
Balled-in-burlap, 259–260, 261, 299
Bare root plants, 260, 299
Bark, of specimen plants, 200
Bark mulch, 285, 299
Baseline measurement, 43–44, 60
Base maps, 23
  creating, 51–59
  definition, 60
  drafting tools, 23, 25–30
  key terms, 60–61
  lot, 32–39
  measurements, 40–50
  on-site items, 50
  plan drawing, 23, 24
  site survey, 31, 39
  summary, 59–60
Base material, measurement/estimation of, 362
Base sheet, 59, 60
Basic. *See* Alkaline
Basic functional principles, 109–110
Basket weave fence, 274, 299
Basking, 383
Batter, 277, 278, 279, 299
Beam compass, 46, 47, 60
Bearings, 32–35, 60
Bed lines, 196, 197, 205
Beds, 152, 157, 206, 276
Berms, 90, 91, 100, 208, 216, 286
Birds, 252
B leads, 26, 27, 60
Blending, 115
Blocks, 280–281

Blood-type ingredients, 388
Blooms, 172, 173, 174
Board-on-board fence, 274, 275, 299
Books, 242–243, 320–322, 352–354
Borders
    drafting, 225, 226, 240
    front yard, 115–117
Botanical name, 306, 308, 309, 313
Boulders, 230, 240
Branching, 254–256
    color of, 175
    symbols, 232, 233, 240
    texture of, 176–178
Brick edging, 282, 284
Bricks, 227–228, 240
Broadleaf symbols, 232, 233, 240
Brochures, 6, 7, 22
Bubble diagram. See Concept plan
Bubbles, 12–13, 152, 153, 163, 223
Bumwad, paper. See Tracing paper
Bundled plans, 303
Business cards, 6, 7, 22
Butterflies, 252
Butterfly gardening, 383–386

Cables, 420
    connecting, 428–431
    hiding, 420
    size, 421–422
    voltage drop, 422–427
Caliper, 260, 261, 299
Cameras, 5, 22, 55
Catalogs, 8, 9, 22, 320–322
Cedar mulch, 285, 299
Ceilings, in outdoor rooms, 108–109
Characteristic repetition, 190, 192
Circuit, 408, 433
Circuit breakers, 408, 433
Circulation
    concept plan, 158, 160
    decks, 270, 271, 272
    design process example, 331
    entry walks, 126, 127, 149
    inventory and analysis, 65–68
    side yard, 134, 135, 149
City conditions, 249
Clay soil, 84, 100
Cleanliness, during interviews, 3
Client information, 3, 13–18
Client preferences, 15
Client presentation. See Presentation
Client requests, presentation and, 320
Clients
    budgets of, 12–13
    listening to, 12

meeting, 1–2
    See also Interviews
Client screening, 1
Clipboards, 3, 62, 64
Cloning tool (imaging software), 379
Closed circuit, 431, 433
Closing survey. See Site survey
Clothing, for interviews, 3
Coarse texture, 177, 178
Cocoa bean shells, for mulching, 286, 299
Cohesiveness, 167
Color
    contrast and, 200, 201
    definition of, 216
    design attributes, 171–175
    house and materials, 65
Colored concrete, 263, 264, 299
Colored lenses, 295, 414
Color repetition, 190
Combining materials, 272
Commitment, 10
Common name, 307, 308, 309, 313
Common wire, 415, 433
Compact discs (CDs), 8, 22
Company catalogs, 8, 9
Compass, 4, 22, 28, 29, 60
Computer-aided drawing (CAD), 224, 240, 312, 373
Computer graphics. See Graphics
Computers. See Laptop computers
Concept drawings, 151, 154, 164–166
Concept plan, 151–152
    activities and materials, 152, 155
    alternate, 163, 164–166
    analysis, 152, 154
    circulation, 158, 160
    concepts, 154–157, 158
    definition of, 163
    design process example, 341–343
    drawings, 164–166
    exposure, 162
    key terms, 163
    location, 157–158, 159
    preliminary design, 219, 220
    space, 152, 153
    summary, 163
    views, 160–161
Concepts, 154–157, 158, 320
Conclusion, of presentation, 324
Concrete, 227, 262–264, 299, 360
Concrete blocks, 280, 299
Concrete edging, 282
Confidence, during presentation, 317
Connection, 185
    definition of, 216
    ground plane, 221, 222

repetition, 185–192
   space, 192–197
Construction plan, 303, 304, 313
Consultation fees, 2
Contact information, 3
Contacts, 384
Container grown plants, 259, 260, 299
Continuity circuit, 431
Continuity test, 431, 433
Contorted branches, 254, 256, 299
Contour lines, 91, 94, 100
Contract conclusion, 324
Contraction joints, 263, 299
Contraction lines, 263
Contracts, 5, 10, 18, 19, 20, 22
Contrast, 200–201, 216
Cooking areas, in back-yard entertainment areas,
      141, 143
Cool colors, 171, 216
Copy (print)
   definition of, 325
   master plan, 309–312
   presentation, 314, 318–319
Corkscrew branches. *See* Contorted branches
Corners
   curiosity of, 203, 204
   ground lines and, 197
   ground plane, 226–227
Cost estimates, 369
Covenants, 38, 39, 60
Criticism, during presentation, 315, 318
Cultural requirements, for plants, 244–251, 299
Curb appeal
   definition of, 149
   front yard, 111–115
   side yard, 138–139
Curiosity, 201–203, 204, 216
Current flow, 408
Current, 408, 433
Curved lines, 205–206, 216
Curves, triangulating, 46, 47
Curving beds, 206
Cut stone, 265, 299
Cypress mulch, 285, 299

DBY (Direct Burial tube), 429, 431, 433
Deciduous, 179–180, 216
Decimal conversions, 42
Deck fixtures, 414, 433
Decks, 268, 270–272
Deer, 253, 387–392
Deer barriers, 388–392
Deer deterrents, 387–388
Deer fence, 388
Deer-resistant plants, 387, 388–392

Defined borders, in front yard, 115–117
Denatonium Benzoate, 388
Design attributes, 168
   color, 171–175
   form, 168–171
   maintenance concerns, 179–180
   texture, 176–179
Design concepts, 154–157, 158, 320
Design copy. *See* Copy
Design criticism, during presentation, 315
Design fees, 18–19
Design goals, 14, 319, 327
Design philosophy, 11
Design presentation. *See* Presentation
Design principles, 167
   balance, 180–185, 186
   cohesiveness, 167
   connection, 185–197
   design attributes, 168–180
   flow, 203, 205–209
   interest, 198–203, 204
   key terms, 216–217
   mass planting, 210–215
   summary, 215
Design process example, 327
   concept plans, 341–343
   graphical analysis, 340
   interview, 327–329
   inventory and analysis, 329–337
   master plan, 349
   master sketches, 348
   preliminary design, 346–347
   preliminary sketches, 344–345
   presentation, 337–339
Design projects, 395–407
Design questionnaires, 15–18
Design theft, 218
DesignWare (software), 381
Design work, interview discussion about, 11–13
Diffused lenses, 414
Digital cameras, 5, 55
Digital imaging, 322, 324, 325
Digital multimeter, 431, 432
Dimension tool (software), 375
Dioecious, 175, 216
Direct current (DC), 431, 433
Directional fixtures, 412–413, 433
Direct measurement, 42, 60
Discussions, of design, 11–13
Dog-ear fence. *See* Solid board privacy fence
Dogs. *See* Pets
Door hangers, 8, 22
Doors, 65, 113–114
Double-hammered mulch, 286, 299
Downlighting, 295, 297, 299

Downspouts, 95, 96, 100, 292–293, 337
Drafting, 224–226, 232, 234–239, 311
Drafting tools, 23, 25–30, 225
Drainage, 93, 95, 96, 288–293, 337
Drawing
    analysis, 97–99
    base maps, 55–59
    concept, 151, 154, 164–166
    construction, 303, 304, 313
    design process examples, 344–349
    elevated, 322, 323, 325
    master plan, 303, 304–305
    preliminary design, 219–224, 232, 234–239
    See also Computer-aided drawing; Drafting;
        Plan drawing; Sketching
Drawing pencils, 27, 60
Drawing software, 374–378
Dress, for interviews, 3
Drip irrigation, 394
Driveways
    design process example, 337
    functional principles, 118–121, 122, 123
    hardscape materials and, 262
    measurement/estimation of, 370
    views, 121, 122
Dry-laid construction, 266, 268, 269, 299
Duplicating tool (imaging software), 380
Durability, of plants, 250
Dynascape (software), 382

Eagle Point Software, 382
Earthscapes (software), 382
Easement, 37, 60
Eastern exposure, 78, 100
Eating areas, in back-yard entertainment areas,
    144
Edging, 282–284, 301, 364–365, 370
Egg solids, 387
Electric fences, 388
Elevated drawing, 322, 323, 325
Elevations, 276
Enclosures
    back-yard entertainment areas, 141,
        142, 143
    concept plans, 162
    definition of, 149
    greeting areas, 132, 133
    outdoor rooms, 107
Engineer scale, 29, 30, 60
Entertainment areas, 149
    back yard, 139–145, 146
    concept plans, 155, 156
    decks, 271
    design process example, 328

greeting areas, 132, 133
    interviews and, 14
Entertainment interest, 145, 146
Entertainment slab, 140
Entry walk, 121, 123, 124–130, 131, 149, 157, 158
Espalier, 170, 216
Estimating tool (software), 374
Estimation. *See* Measurement
Estimator software, 374–378
Evergreen, 179–180, 216
Exfoliation, 254–255, 299
Explanations, during presentation, 316, 319
Exposed aggregate, 227, 263, 264, 299
Exposure
    concept plan, 162
    design process example, 335–336
    gardens, 147
    inventory and analysis, 75–78, 79, 80
    plant material and selection, 248, 300
Extender bar, 46, 47, 60
Extension points, 221
Eye contact, 316, 317

Fall colors, 172
Family information, 14, 327
Feedback, 218, 219
Fees, 18–19, 22
Fences, 107, 108
Filler plants. *See* Primary plants
Film, 23, 60
Film cameras, 5
Fine texture, 177, 178
Fixtures, for lighting, 412–415
Flagstone, 264, 265, 266, 300, 362–363
Flood fixtures, 413
Floodlights, 413, 433
Floorplan. *See* Footprint
Floors, of outdoor rooms, 104–106, 149
Flow, 203, 205–209, 216
Flower books, 353
Flowering, of specimen plants, 200
Flowers, 172–173, 174. *See also* Plant material and
    selection
Fluorescent lights, 411, 433
Foam board, 314, 325
Focal points, 152
Focalized accents, 198–200, 216
Foliage
    color of, 171, 172
    specimen plants, 200
    texture of, 176
    See also Plant material and selection
Follow-up calls, 10, 21
Food sources, in butterfly gardens, 384

Footprint, 35, 55, 57, 58, 60
Form
    contrast and, 200, 201
    definition of, 216
    design attributes, 168–171
    flow and, 209
    specimen plants, 199, 200
Formal balance, 181, 183
Form repetition, 190, 192
Formulaic balance, 182, 183
Foundation, 95
Foundation drainage, 291, 337
Foundation material, estimating, 362. *See also*
    specific materials
Foundation planting, 291–292
Foundation plants, 189, 190, 216
Fragrance, 257
Framing, 113
French drains, 289, 290, 300
Front door, drawing attention to, 113–114
Front yard, 110
    borders, defined, 115–117
    curb appeal, 111–115
    driveway, 118–121, 122, 123
    entry walk, 121, 123, 124–130, 131
    fences, 273
    greeting area, 130, 131, 132–134
Fruit, 174–175, 258
Full sheet, 25, 26, 60
Functional diagram. *See* Concept plan
Functional principles, 102
    back yard, 139–148
    basic, 109–110
    front yard, 110–134
    key terms, 149–150
    outdoor room concept, 104–109
    people spaces, 102–103
    side yard, 134–139
    summary, 149
Functional, 102, 149
Funneling effect, 113, 149
Fuses, 408, 433

Gardens, 147, 148
Gardenworks (software), 382
Garlic, 387–388
Generic symbols, 232, 233, 240
Geogrid, 281, 300
Goals. *See* Design goals
Goldfish, 203
Good views, 73–74, 100, 160, 334
Grade, 289, 300
Grading plan, 303, 313
Graphical analysis, 97–99, 340

Graphics, 373
    imaging software, 378–381
    plan drawing and estimator software, 374–378
    preliminary design, 219
    software products, 381–382
Grasses, books for, 353. *See also* Plant material
    and selection
Gravel mulch, 287, 300
Grazing, 294, 300
Greeting area, in front yard, 130, 131, 132–134
Greeting interest, 134
Grid, 48–50, 60
Grid paper, 23, 25, 60
Ground angles, 226–227
Groundcover
    books, 353
    deer-resistant, 390
    measurement/estimation of, 367, 368, 369
    outdoor rooms, 105, 106
    preliminary design, 227
Ground fault circuit interrupter (GFCI), 415, 417,
    433
Ground labels, 227–230
Ground lines, 195, 196, 197
Ground plane, 220, 221, 226–230, 306. *See also*
    Floors
Gutters, 95, 96, 292–293, 337

Hair care, for interviews, 3
Half sheet, 25, 26, 61
Halogen bulbs, 410, 411, 433
Hardiness, 244, 245, 246
Hardiness zones, 244, 245, 300
Hardscapes, 241, 261
    books for, 354
    concept plan, 152
    concrete, 262–264
    drainage, 288–293
    edging, 282–284
    functional principles, 104–105
    key terms, 299–301
    lighting design, 297–298
    lighting effects, 293–296
    mulch, 284–287
    retaining walls, 276–281
    samples, 323
    stone and pavers, 265–268, 269, 270
    summary, 298
    weed barrier, 287–288
    wood, 268, 270–275
Hardwood mulch, 285, 300
Heat zones, 244, 246, 300
Herb books, 353
Herbaceous perennials, 179, 216, 353, 388–390

Hibernation boxes, 383
H leads, 25, 26, 27, 60
Hobbies
    backyard recreation and, 147, 148, 149
    design process example, 328
    interviews and, 14
    inventory and analysis, 96–97
Horizontal construction, 277, 278, 279
Host plants, for butterflies, 384–385
Hot pepper, 388
Hot wire, 415, 433
House
    blending, 115
    design process example, 331
    drainage from, 289, 291
    framing, 113
    inventory and analysis of, 65, 66
    symmetrical, 184
    views from, 74, 75
House color, 65

Imaging software, 378–381
Implementation plans, 303, 304–305
Implied screens, 107, 149
Incandescent lights, 409, 410–411, 433
Indoor living space, extension of, 103
Indoor views, 102
Informal balance, 183, 185
In-ground fixtures, 415
Ink, 26, 28, 61
Inorganic mulch, 287, 300
Insecticides, 384
Interest
    back-yard entertainment areas, 145
    design principles, 198–203, 204
    greeting areas, 134
Internet sites. See Web sites
Interviews, 1
    appearance, 2
    appointments, scheduling, 21
    arrival, 10
    client information, 13–18
    commitment, 10
    contract, 18, 19, 20
    definition, 22
    design fees, 18–19
    design process example, 327–329
    design work discussion, 11–13
    dress, 3
    follow-up calls, 21
    inventory and analysis, 21
    key terms, 22
    meetings, scheduling, 10
    payment schedule, 19
    photos, 10
    professionalism, 3

    setting up, 1–2
    site survey, 10
    summary, 21
    supplies and materials, 3–6, 7, 8–9
    thank-you cards, 21
    trust, 6
Interview tools, 3–6
Inventory, 21, 62, 63
    circulation, 65–68
    clipboards, 62
    definition, 100
    design process example, 329–337
    drainage, 93, 95–96
    exposure, 75–78, 79
    house, 65, 66
    key terms, 100–101
    landform, 90–93, 94
    landscapes, existing, 82–83
    pets, hobbies, and other notables, 96–97
    seasonal impact on light and temperature, 78, 80
    site survey, 62, 64
    soil, 84–90
    summary, 99
    utilities, 68–71
    views, 72–75
    wind, 81–82
Irrigation, 303, 305, 393

Jar test, 87, 88, 100

Key, 306, 308, 309, 313
Koi, 203

Labeling, 306, 307, 376–377. See also Symbols
Lamps, 410–412
LANDCADD, 373
Landform, 90–93, 94
Landmark (software), 382
Landscapes, existing, 82–83
Landscape timbers, 277–279, 300
Laptop computers, 5, 6, 22
Lattice, 107
Lattice-top fence, 274, 300
Lawn, 152, 157
Layout ground plane and label, 306
Layout plan, 303, 313
Lead, 25, 26, 27, 61
Lead-holders, 27, 61
LED lights, 412, 433
Length, of property lines, 32–35
Lenses, colored and diffused, 295, 414
Lifestyle information, 14, 327–328
Light
    exposure and, 75, 76
    plant material and selection, 248
    seasonal impact on, 78, 80

Lighting (low-voltage), 293, 408
    cable, 420–427
    connecting cable, 428–431
    fixtures, 412–415
    key terms, 433–434
    lamps, 410–412
    lighting design, 297–298
    lighting effects, 293–296
    power console, 415–419
    power, 408–410
    troubleshooting, 431–433
Lighting cable, 434
Lighting design, 297–298
Lighting effects, 293–296
Lighting maintenance, 298
Light sensors, 419, 434
Light sources, concealing, 298, 412
Lime, 89, 100
Lines
    bed, 196, 197, 205
    contraction, 263
    definition of, 216
    flow and, 203, 205–208
    ground, 195, 196, 197
    overhead, 70, 100
    triangulation, 46
    See also Contour lines
Line tool (software), 374
Lipped blocks, 280, 300
Listening, 12
Loamy soil, 87, 100
Location, concept plan and, 157–158, 159
Lot, 32–39, 61
Low-voltage lighting. *See* Lighting
Lumens, 409, 434

Maintenance
    bed lines, 197
    lighting, 298
    retaining walls and, 276
    texture and, 179–180
Management practices, for xeriscaping, 394
Markers, 28, 61
Mass planting, 210–215, 216
Master plan, 302–303
    definition of, 313, 325
    design process example, 349
    drawing, 303
    implementation plans, 303, 304–305
    key terms, 313
    layout ground plane and label, 306
    measurements/estimations, 371
    plant list, 306–309
    preliminary plan versus, 302
    presentation and, 324
    printed copy, 309–312
    rough sketching, 306
    spreadsheet, 309
    summary, 313
    symbols and textures, 306, 307
Master plan presentation. *See* Presentation
Master sketches, 348
Material measurement. *See* Measurement
Material repetition of, 190, 191
Materials
    concept plan, 152, 155
    connecting, 192–194
    entertainment areas, 141
    interviews, 3–6, 7, 8–9
    mulching, 285–287
    retaining walls, 277–281
    See also Specific materials
Meal meat, 388
Measurement (estimation), 355
    base maps, 40–50
    base material, 362
    books for, 354
    concrete, 360
    cost estimate, 369
    driveway, 370
    edging, 364–365, 370
    flagstone, 362–363
    groundcover, 367, 368, 369
    master plan and, 371
    mulch, 365–367, 370
    pavers, 360–361
    sod, 358–359
    square footage, 355–356
    stone, 372
    turfgrass, 369
    volume, 356–358
    weed barrier, 367, 368, 370
Measuring tape, 4, 40, 41
Measuring wheel, 4, 40
Mechanical pencils, 27, 61
Meetings, scheduling, 10, 324
Microclimates, 247, 300
Moisture, 251
Monoecious, 175, 216
Moonlighting effect, 295, 296, 300
Mortar, 266, 268, 270, 300
Mortgage plat. *See* Site survey
Mounds
    inventory and analysis, 90, 100
    outdoor rooms, 108
Mulch, 284–287
    definition of, 240, 300
    measurement/estimation of, 365–367, 370
    outdoor room concept, 105–106
    preliminary design, 227
    xeriscaping and, 393
Mulching materials, 285–287

Multilevel decks, 270, 271, 300
Multimeter, 431, 432, 434
Multitap transformers, 417, 418, 434
Multivoltage taps, 427
Multivoltage transformers, 418, 434
Mylar, 23, 25, 61

Natural balance, 185
Nectar plants, for butterflies, 384, 385–386
Needle symbols, 232, 233, 240
Needs assessment. *See* Analysis; Inventory
Netting, 388
Neutral, 89, 100
Non-wood mulch, 286
Northern exposure, 77, 100
Northwest exposure, 81
Notebooks, 3
Note cards, 318, 325
Nuggets. *See* Bark mulch
Nuisance fruit, 258
Nurseries, 243

Object database (imaging software), 379
Observations, 62, 64
Odd numbers, in mass plantings, 212, 213, 214
Odor repellents, 387–388
Ohms, 410, 431, 432, 434
On center, 307, 313
One-hour interview, 2
Onionskin. *See* Tracing paper
On-site items, 50
Open areas, in back yards, 145, 147
Opening, of presentation, 318–319
Order, in presentation, 319–320
Organic mulch, 285, 300
Orientation, 32–35
Ornamental grasses, books for, 353. *See also*
    Plant material and selection
Outdoor living, 102
Outdoor outlets, 417
Outdoor room concept, 104–109
Overaccenting, 200
Overhead enclosures, for back-yard entertainment
    areas, 141, 142
Overhead lines, 70, 100
Overlighting, 297
Overplanting, 179

Pacing, 42, 61
Palettes, estimating, 358, 359, 363
Palms, books for, 353. *See also* Plant material and
    selection
Paper, 23, 25, 26
Paper dimensions, 25, 26
Parking, 65, 66, 331–332. *See also* Driveways

Partial screens, 106–107, 149
Path fixtures, 414, 434
Path lighting, 296, 300
Paths
    concept plan, 157, 158
    narrow, 203, 204
    primary, 65, 67
    secondary, 67, 68, 333
    See also Entry walk
Patio materials, 141
Patios, 267
Pavement, 67, 68, 333
Pavers, 265–268, 269, 270, 300, 360–361. *See
    also* Bricks
Paver edging, 282, 284
Paving material, color of, 65
Payment schedule, 19, 22
Peanut shells, for mulching, 286, 300
Pecan shells, for mulching, 286, 300
People spaces, functional principles for, 102–103
Perennials. *See* Herbaceous perennials
Pergolas, 109
Pesticides, 384
Pets, 96–97
pH, 89–90, 100
Phasing-in, 13, 22
pH meter, 90, 100
Photos, for interviews, 10
Photoscape (software), 382
Picket fence, 274
Pictures, for presentation, 315
Pigment liners, 28, 61
Pigtail, 428, 434
Pine, 285, 300
Pine straw, 286, 300
Pinned blocks, 281, 300
Plan drawing, 23, 24, 61, 319
Plan drawing software, 374–378
Planscape (software), 381
Plant characteristics, 253–258
Plant choices, 179
Planting
    mass, 210–215
    overplanting, 179
    shade and, 248
Planting plan, 303, 313
Planting schedule. *See* Plant list
Plant list, 306–309, 313, 315
Plant material and selection, 241
    availability, 243–244
    books and software, 242–243, 350, 352–353
    butterfly gardens, 384–386
    characteristics, 253–258
    cultural requirements, 244, 248–251
    deer-resistant plants, 387, 388–392

hardiness, 244, 245, 246
Internet links, 350–352
key terms, 299–301
microclimate, 247
preliminary design, 230–232, 233
presentation, 319
size and quality, 258–261
soil, 251
summary, 298
wildlife, 251–253
Plant palette, 244, 300
Plant production, 259–261
Plant repetition, 189–190
Plants
acid-loving, 90
existing, 82, 83, 336
See also Design attributes; Design principles;
Plant material and selection
Plant samples, 323
Plant size and quality, 258–261
Plant symbols, 222, 223
Plan view drawing. *See* Plan drawing
Plastic edging, 282, 283
Plat, 31, 61
Playgrounds, 147, 148
Points of extension, 221
Pollinator, 175, 216
Poor views, 72–73, 100, 161, 334
Portfolios, 5, 22
Positive opening, of presentation, 318
Posterboard. *See* Foam board
Potential views, 74–75, 100, 161, 335
Power, for lighting, 408–410
Power console, for lighting, 415–419
PowerPoint presentation, 5, 321–322
Power wire, 415, 433
Predator urine, 388
Preliminary design, 218
concept plan, 219, 220
design process example, 346–347
drafting, 224–226
examples, 232, 234–239
ground plane, 226–230
key terms, 240
master plan versus, 302
plant material, 230–232, 233
presentation, 218–219
sketching, 219–224
summary, 240
Preliminary sketches, 344–345
Preparation, for presentation, 315, 317–318
Presentation, 218–219, 314
conclusion of, 324
confidence, 317
design copy, 314

design criticism during, 315
design process example, 337–339
explanations, 316
key terms, 325
opening of, 318–319
order and organization, 319–320
pictures, 315
plant list, reading of, 315
preparation, 315, 317–318
speech tips, 315, 316, 317
summary, 325
visual support, 320–324
warning about, 315
Prevailing wind, 81, 100
Primary circulation, 158, 160
Primary paths, 65, 67
Primary plants, 190, 216
Print. *See* Copy
Printing, site surveys, 51
Private areas, 110, 149
Professionalism, 3
Project cost, 12–13
PRO Landscape (software), 382
Proofreading, site surveys, 39
Property lines
bearings and length of, 32–35
definition, 61
drawing, 55, 57
Property stakes, 32, 33, 57, 61
Proposals, 19, 22
Protection
butterfly gardens, 383
greeting areas, 132
See also Enclosures
Public areas, 109, 150
Puddling, 383

Quarter sheet, 25, 26, 61
Questionnaires, 15–18
Quick connectors, 428–429, 434
Quietness, at interviews, 11

Rag vellum. *See* Vellum paper
Railroad ties, 277, 301
RainCAD (software), 382
Reading, during presentation, 315
Recreation, in back yard, 145, 147–148
Recycled rubber mulch, 287, 301
Recycled wood mulch, 286, 301
Referrals, 1, 22
Regional plants, 243
Repetition, 185–192
Residence, interviews at, 1
Resistance, 410, 434
Restrictive covenant. *See* Covenants

Retainer fee, 19, 22
Retaining walls, 276–281, 301
Ribbon test, 86, 100
Right-of-Way (R/W), 35–36, 61
Rise, 289, 301
Roads, entry walk from, 130, 131
Roofs, of outdoor rooms, 108
Room identification, 65, 66
Rough sketching, 306
Roundabout, 121, 123
Rubber mulch, 287
Run, 289, 301

Salt, 250, 336
Sandy soil, 84, 100
Scale
    asymmetrical, 186
    site survey, 51, 52, 53–55
    symmetrical, 182
Scale (ruler), 28–30, 61
Scanning, site surveys, 51, 53
Screening
    back-yard entertainment areas, 145
    clients, 1, 22
    concept plans, 152
    curiosity and, 201, 202
    definition of, 150
    driveway view, 121, 122
    northwest wind, 82
    outdoor rooms, 106
    side yard, 136–138
    southwest exposure, 78, 79
    summer breezes, 81–82
Seasonal impact, on light and temperature, 78, 80
Seating, on decks, 270, 272
Secondary circulation, 160
Secondary paths, 67, 68, 333
Semi-evergreen, 179, 217
Septic tanks, 68, 69, 100
Sequence. *See* Flow
Service areas. *See* Utility areas
Setback, 38
Shade, 162, 248, 249
Shadowbox fence. *See* Board-on-board fence
Shadowing, 294, 301
Shadows, 78, 80, 380
Shear, 170, 217
Shells, for mulching, 286
Shrubs
    books for, 352–353
    deer-resistant, 390–392
    walls, 108
    See also Design attributes; Design principles;
        Plant material and selection

Side enclosures, for back-yard entertainment areas, 141, 143
Sidewalk, driveway serving as, 118–121. *See also*
        Entry walk; Paths
Side yard, 134
    circulation, 134, 135
    curb appeal, 138–139
    screening, 136–138
    storage area, 136
Silhouetting, 293, 301
Silt, 87, 101
Single circuit, 415, 416
Single-level decks, 270, 301
Site plan, 51, 58, 61
Site survey
    base map, 31, 39, 51–53
    definition of, 61
    interview and, 10
    inventory and analysis, 62, 64
Sitting areas, in greeting areas, 132, 133
Sketching
    design process examples, 344–349
    master plan, 306, 310
    preliminary design, 219–224, 232, 234–239
    See also Drawing
Slabs, for entertainment, 140
Slit-trenching wire, 420
Slopes, 91, 92, 101, 276, 286
Small talk, 10
Smiling, 316
Soaps, 387–388
Sod, measurement/estimation of, 358–359
Software, 350
    imaging, 378–381
    plan drawing and estimator, 374–378
    plant selection, 242–243, 350
    products, 381–382
Soil, 84–90, 251, 336
Soil amendments, 87
Soil fertility, 90
Soil pH, 89–90
Soil probe, 84, 85, 101
Soil structure, 87, 89
Soil test, 84, 101, 336
Soil texture, 84–87, 101, 336
Solar-powered lights, 411–412, 434
Solid board privacy fence, 274, 275, 301
Sound, curiosity of, 201
Southern exposure, 77, 101
Southwest exposure, 78, 79, 81, 101, 248
Space/spacing
    concept plan, 152, 153
    connecting, 192–197
    curiosity of, 202

mass planting, 210–211
people, 102–103
plant list, 307
texture and, 178
Specimen plants, 198, 199, 200, 217
Speech tips, for presentation, 315, 316, 317
Spines, 253, 301
Splicing, 429–430, 434
Spotlight fixtures. *See* Directional fixtures
Spread fixtures, 414
Spread lighting, 296, 301
Spreadsheet, of master plan, 309
Spring flowering, 173, 174
Square corners, 226–227
Square footage, estimation of, 355–356
Stacked horizontal construction, 279
Staggered horizontal construction, 279
Staggered placement, 212, 215
Stamped concrete, 264, 301
Steel, for strip edging, 282
Step fixtures, 414, 434
Steps, on decks, 272
Stippling, 227, 240
Stone, 227–228, 240
    definition of, 301
    measurement/estimation of, 362–363, 372
    selection of, 265–268, 269, 270
Stone edging, 282
Stone mulch, 287
Stone tiles, 266
Stone walls, 281
Stoops, 130, 131, 150
Storage, of master plan, 310
Storage areas
    side yard, 136, 150
    inventory and analysis, 71, 101
Straight lines, 207, 217
Stringers, 274, 275, 301
Strip edging, 282, 283, 301
Subsurface drainage, 289, 290, 301
Sulfur, 89, 101
Summer breezes, 81
Summer flowering, 173, 174
Summer shadows, 78, 80
Sun exposure. *See* Exposure
Supplies, for interviews, 3–6, 7, 8–9
Surface drainage, 289
    definition of, 101, 301
    design process example, 337
    inventory and analysis, 91, 93, 95, 96
Surface finishing, 263–264
Symbol character, 232, 233
Symbol database (software), 375
Symbol placement, 230, 232

Symbols
    ground plane and textures, 227–230
    master plan, 306, 307
    plant material, 230–232, 233
    sketching, 222, 223
    software, 376–377
Symbol size, 230, 231
Symmetrical balance, 181–184, 217

Tangent lines, 207, 208, 216
Tape measure, 4, 40, 41
Taste, 328–329
Taste repellents, 388
Technical pens, 28, 61
Temperature, 75, 76, 78, 81, 336
Texture
    contrast and, 200, 201
    definition of, 217
    ground plane, 227–230
    master plan, 306, 307
    plants, 176–179
    soil, 84, 85, 86–87, 101, 336
    specimen plants, 200
Texture accents, 177
Texture repetition, 190, 192
Thank-you cards, 21
Theft, design, 218
Thiram, 388
Thorns, 253, 301
Tile drainage, 289, 290, 301
Timbers. *See* Landscape timbers
Timers, 419, 434
Title block, 225, 226, 240
Topiary, 170, 217
Topographic maps, 94
Topography, alterations to, 91, 94
Total screens, 106, 150
Tracing paper, 23, 25, 61
Traditional landscaping, 111, 112, 150
Traffic, 337
Transformers, 415–419, 427, 434
Transition. *See* Flow
Trash cans, 71, 101
Trash paper. *See* Tracing paper
Tree canopy, 108, 109
Trees
    books for, 352–353
    deer-resistant, 392
    See Design attributes; Design principles; Plant
        material and selection
Triangulation lines, 46
Triangulation, 44–47, 61
Troubleshooting, 431–433
Trunk color, 175

Trust, 6
Turf, 104, 105, 227
Turf areas, 393
Turfgrass, 369
Twig color, 175

Underwater fixtures, 415, 434
Units of measurement, 42
Unity. *See* Connection
Uplighting, 294, 295, 301
Urban impact, 249
Utilities, 68–71, 333–334
Utility areas, 110, 150

Variegation, 172, 217
Vellum paper, 23, 25, 61
Vertical construction, 277, 278
Views, 14–15
    back-yard entertainment areas, 144–145, 146
    concept plan, 160–161
    design process example, 328, 334–335
    driveway, 121, 122
    entry walks, 126, 129–130
    inventory and analysis, 72–75
    screening, 138
Visibility, concept plans and, 158, 159. *See also*
    Screening
Visual support, for presentation, 320–324
Volt, 408, 434
Voltage, 408, 434
Voltage drop, 410, 422–427, 434
Voltage test, 431, 432
Volume, estimation of, 356–358

Walls
    outdoor rooms, 106–108, 150
    retaining, 276–281, 301

Warm colors, 171, 217
Water, 228
Water analogy, 410
Water gardening, books for, 354
Water sources, for gardens, 147
Watt, 409, 434
Wattage, 409, 417, 427, 434
Web sites, 8, 22, 242, 243, 350–352
Weed barrier, 287–288
    definition of, 150, 301
    measurement/estimation of, 367, 368, 370
    outdoor room concept and, 106
Weeping branches, 254, 256, 301
Well-lights, 415, 434
Western exposure, 78, 101
Wet areas, 95. *See also* Drainage
Wet-laid construction, 266, 268, 270, 301
Wildlife, 251–253
Wind, 81–82, 162, 249, 336
Windows, 65, 74, 75
Winter shadows, 78, 80
Winter wind, 81
Wire gauge, 422
Wire length, 422, 427
Wireless baited electric fencing, 388
Wire nut, 429, 430, 434
Wire sizing, 422
Wood, 228, 268, 270–275
Wood edging, 282, 284
Wood mulch, 285

Xeriscaping, 393–394

Yard. *See* Back yard; Front yard; Side yard